TRANSOCEANIC STUDIES
Ileana Rodríguez, Series Editor

Prophetic Visions of the Past
Pan-Caribbean Representations of the
Haitian Revolution

Víctor Figueroa

THE OHIO STATE UNIVERSITY PRESS
COLUMBUS

Copyright © 2015 by The Ohio State University.
All rights reserved.

Library of Congress Cataloging-in-Publication Data
Figueroa, Víctor, 1969–
 Prophetic visions of the past : pan-Caribbean representations of the Haitian revolution / Víctor Figueroa.
  pages cm. — (Transoceanic studies)
 Includes bibliographical references and index.
 ISBN 978-0-8142-1277-6 (hardback) — ISBN 978-0-8142-9382-9 (cd-rom)
 1. Caribbean literature—History and criticism. 2. Literature and revolutions—Caribbean area. 3. Haiti—History—Revolution, 1843. 4. Haiti—In literature. I. Title.
 PN849.C3F55 2015
 809'.89729—dc23
                    2014039542

Cover design by Janna Thompson-Chordas
Text design by Juliet Williams
Type set in Adobe Caslon

♾ The paper used in this publication meets the minimum requirements of the American National Standard for Information Sciences—Permanence of Paper for Printed Library Materials. ANSI Z39.48–1992.

9 8 7 6 5 4 3 2 1

*To Anne,
with deep love*

Contents

Acknowledgments ix

Introduction 1

Chapter 1 The Kingdom of Black Jacobins: C. L. R. James and
Alejo Carpentier on the Haitian Revolution 32

Chapter 2 Between Mackandal and Tembandumba: Luis Palés
Matos's Haitian Poems 64

Chapter 3 Between Louverture and Christophe: Aimé Césaire on the
Haitian Revolution 94

Chapter 4 A Tragedy of Success: Derek Walcott's Haitian Heroes 126

Chapter 5 Maroons in the Tout-Monde: Edouard Glissant's
Monsieur Toussaint 166

Chapter 6 An Afrocentric Theodicy of Liberation: Manuel Zapata
Olivella's *Changó el gran putas* 196

Conclusion The Spirit of the Haitian Revolution in the Caribbean 237

Notes 249

Works Cited 275

Index 291

Acknowledgments

I thank my colleagues, friends, and students at Wayne State University for their help and support in the completion of this project. Special gratitude goes to Walter Edwards and Wayne State University's Humanities Center, for their research fellowships and strong support for the Liberal Arts, and to the Office of the Provost at Wayne State, for the Career Development Chair grant—their financial support and the time for writing provided by their grants were tremendously helpful in my work on this manuscript. Many thanks also to Ileana Rodríguez, Malcolm Litchfield, Lindsay Martin, and the readers and staff at the Ohio State University Press, for their faith in this book. My family and friends in Puerto Rico and across the United States constitute the best web of support anyone could ask for. And my dear Anne, Frankie, and Phoebe made the long days of research and writing more than endurable: they actually made them fun.

Chapter 1 of this book includes a revised version of my article "A Kingdom of Black Jacobins: Alejo Carpentier and C. L. R. James on the Haitian Revolution," which was published in *Afro-Hispanic Review* (Vol. 25, No. 2: Fall 2006); it is reprinted here with permission. Chapter 2 includes a revised version of my article "Between Africa and Puerto Rico: Haiti and Lyric Self-Fashioning in the Poetry of Luis Palés Matos," published in *Latin American Literary Review* (Vol. 35, No. 70: July-December 2007); it is reprinted here with permission. Chapter 3 includes a revised version of my article "Between Louverture and Christophe: Aimé Césaire on the Haitian Revolution," published in *The French Review* (Vol. 82, No. 5: April 2009); it is reprinted with permission from *The French Review;* permission conveyed through Copyright Clearance Center, Inc. I thank the three journals for the permissions to reprint that material.

Introduction

Haitian Revolutions

Toward the end of his classic historical study, *The Black Jacobins*, the Trinidadian writer C. L. R. James boldly suggests that "West Indians first became aware of themselves as a people in the Haitian Revolution" (391). There is probably much truth in those words, for there are few other events about which the three largest linguistic regions of the Caribbean (Anglophone, Francophone, and Hispanophone) have produced acknowledged literary masterpieces. Perhaps only the "discovery" by Columbus, in 1492, has given rise to a similar number or works of comparable quality and breadth in all three languages. Not surprisingly, one of the two events represents the official beginning, and the other one of the most significant and dramatic challenges, to the colonial system and logic that came to dominate the history of the Caribbean.

However, if James's words are true, then West Indian (Caribbean) self-awareness is a very perplexing and fragmented phenomenon indeed, since the Haitian Revolution has been a site of conflicting readings throughout the centuries. One might describe the revolution as a floating signifier within the Caribbean region, one that writers and artists appropriate and fill with their own preoccupations and obsessions, until the event is unavoidably clouded by the very approaches that also articulate it for readers.

It is to the analysis of several of those multiple representations that this book will devote itself, focusing on how the Haitian Revolution has been approached and depicted in literary works from the Caribbean region in the twentieth century, and how intellectuals from the region have translated that important event into sometimes broader, sometimes narrower social and cultural preoccupations arising from the writers' specific contexts. The writers that I will explore in the following chapters are among the Caribbean's most fundamental, sometimes foundational literary voices. In fact, most of them have already acquired that (admittedly somewhat arbitrary) status of modern classics: Aimé Césaire (Martinique), C. L. R. James (Trinidad), Luis Palés Matos (Puerto Rico), Alejo Carpentier (Cuba), Derek Walcott (Saint Lucia), Edouard Glissant (Martinique), and Manuel Zapata Olivella (Colombia).

It is to be expected that an event of such radical significance and symbolic import—the only successful slave revolt in world history—should have made such a deep impact in the Caribbean imaginary. Beyond the foundation of an independent Haiti and the clear demonstration that a determined group of slaves could challenge and defeat an imperial power, the Haitian Revolution had multiple concrete, material repercussions throughout the region. Those include but are not limited to: the occupation of the neighboring Dominican Republic by Haitian armies (first briefly in 1801, then from 1822 to 1844, with repeated attempts later on), which would greatly affect the tense relations between the two countries; the diaspora of French colonists and their sugar production technology, which was transplanted to neighboring territories, particularly Cuba, the island that would take Haiti's place as the main Caribbean sugar producer throughout the rest of the nineteenth century; slave revolts in the other French Caribbean colonies, followed by renewed repressive measures on the part of the metropolis, which after abolishing slavery in 1794 would reinstate it again from 1802 until 1848; and the U.S. purchase of Louisiana as part of Jefferson's agreement of noninterference with Napoleon. Thus, the reader of the diverse pan-Caribbean accounts of the revolution encounters a complex web of recurrent problems and questions intertwined with a multifarious diversity of views on the cultural, social, and political implications of the event.[1]

Beyond its material and symbolic implications, the revolution itself is a fascinating, epic, moving story, whose fundamental episodes I will attempt to outline here. The revolution was preceded by centuries of slave resistance, in which one must highlight the heroic figures of the maroon slaves, who would escape to the mountains and create isolated communities that survived and thrived in spite of the attacks of colonial authorities. One of those maroons, Mackandal (died 1758), designed one of the first organized conspiracies against the slave-owners; for months the food and supplies of plantations were poisoned, until the authorities captured Mackandal and burned him alive. It is speculated that Mackandal was an *houngan*, a Vodou priest, and it is undeniable that the syncretistic religion played an important philosophical and tactical role in the development of slave resistance. Another possible houngan, Boukman (died ca. 1791), is known for organizing in 1791 a ceremony in Bois Cayman that sparked the beginning of the Haitian Revolution. There were several important chiefs in the early period, such as Jean François, Biassou, and Jeannot, but eventually the indisputable leader was François-Dominique Toussaint, better known as Toussaint Louverture (1743–1803). Toussaint was a former slave who had acquired an education, and was steeped in the revolutionary ideals of the French Enlightenment. He quickly developed a reputation for military genius, political astuteness, rectitude, and fairness in his treatment of friends and foes. A radical opponent of slavery, he joined forces with the Spanish in order to defeat the French; when the French abolished slavery, he switched back to their side, all the while consolidating his power over the colony. At the same time, he made secret treaties with the British. By 1801, he was able to draft a constitution appointing himself governor-for-life of the colony.

Always trying to avoid excessive spilling of blood, Toussaint attempted to restrain some of the brave men fighting under him, like generals Jean Jacques Dessalines (1758–1806) and Henri Christophe (1767–1820). This was not easy, since the former slaves were engaged in a struggle not only against the power of white French colonists but also against the interests of many of the free people of color, who were engaged in their own conflict with colonial authorities but did not always show solidarity with the former slaves. As long as he was in charge of the island, Toussaint tried to defend the hard-won freedoms of the former slaves while also insisting that he did not want to sever links with France, links that he deemed essential to the colony's prosperity. In order to retain good relations with the French government, Toussaint felt forced to make decisions like the execution of his nephew, the general Moyse, who, frustrated with Toussaint's concessions to the former slave-owners, had led an uprising against Toussaint. This was a tactical error, for Moyse was much loved among the newly free slaves. As Toussaint kept trying to demonstrate his loyalty to the French government, his men became increasingly impatient with their leader: they could not understand what his objectives were or why he needed to be so subservient to the French. In the meantime,

Napoleon had risen to power in France and sent an enormous expedition to recapture the colony and reinstate slavery. Toussaint still tried to negotiate with Napoleon's general, Leclerc, but he was betrayed by his men and taken prisoner by Leclerc. He was sent to a prison in the Jura Mountains, where he died in 1803.

Dessalines, a fiercer leader than Toussaint, took over the leadership. He transformed the struggle into one for national independence, which was finally declared in 1804. There were presumed massacres of whites, and Dessalines declared Haiti a black country, crowning himself emperor shortly thereafter. After Dessalines was murdered in 1806, his fellow revolutionary leader, Henri Christophe, was waiting in the shadows to take power and declare himself king. At that point the country was divided in two, with Christophe as king in the north and another fellow revolutionary, Alexandre Pétion (1770–1818), as president (eventually president-for-life) in the south. Not surprisingly, neither France nor the other slaveholding European powers of the period (nor the United States) officially acknowledged Haiti's independence, so the new nation's first steps in the world were full of internal and external violence fueled by imperial interests.[2]

As suggested above, the diversity of readings and representations of the revolution arises from the writers' attempts to place the event in broader regional and global contexts, with the slave revolt in Haiti functioning as a conjunctural moment in the development of those larger processes, questions, or debates. Or, to use a spatial figure rather than a temporal one, the Haitian Revolution is often synechdochally regarded as *part* of a larger *whole*, in which the whole determines or unveils the "true" meaning or significance of its constituent part. What determines the difference between the diverse approaches to the revolution is, naturally, of which whole is the revolution regarded to be an emblematic part.

C. L. R. James provides an excellent example of that synechdochal approach. Fundamentally, in his *Black Jacobins*, James addresses the revolution in terms of a Marxist dialectical reading of history. He regards the Haitian events as an emblematic situation in which the masses and their leaders took advantage of the contradictions inherent in the imperialist expansion of capitalism, and rose up against the established order. In James's optimistic reading, it was a process that could eventually lead to World Revolution. Thus, Haiti's revolution both symbolizes the emancipating process as a whole and constitutes a significant, concrete step in that process. As Anna Grimshaw points out, the Haitian Revolution also allowed James to make the important point that such a revolution need not have its origin in an advanced European capitalist country, as Marxist orthodoxy would have it ("Introduction," 7). Moreover, James's emphasis on Haiti and Africa reflects his resolve, clearly shown in the public transcripts of his conversations with Leon Trotsky in the late 1930s, not to let the race problem be subsumed under the category of class but rather to open a space within Marxist revolutionary agenda for the particular plights of the Black peoples of all continents.[3]

However, an attentive reading reveals that *that* synechdocal reading of the revolution (as part of a larger process of World Revolution) does not fully coincide with the passage by James that I quote at the beginning of this chapter, in which West Indians "first became aware of themselves as a people" in the Haitian Revolution. This second position that James takes suggests still another whole of which the Haitian Revolution would be a part: in this case an acknowledged West Indian identity, a fully acquired "national" (in a broad regional sense) self-awareness. It is worth noticing that James highlights the second regional/nationalist reading of the revolution in his 1963 appendix to the second edition of *The Black Jacobins*; in fact, the body of the book itself, as published in 1938, is not mainly concerned with nationalist politics but with an internationalist Marxist revolution.[4] Indeed the whole 1963 appendix fluctuates between divergent "wholes" on which to anchor the synecdochal reading of Haiti, such as nationalist endeavors ("the West Indian struggle for national independence" [*Black Jacobins*, 395]); pan-Africanism and black pride ("Negritude is what one race brings to the common rendez-vous" [ibid., 401]); and Marxist dialectics ("The sugar plantation . . . required that the slaves live together in a social relation far closer than any proletariat of the time" [ibid., 392]). Although these "wholes" do not necessarily exclude each other, they are not always fully compatible with each other either. That is to say, they may be in tension or may exclude each other as ultimate explanations or keys to Haitian and Caribbean history rather than fitting neatly together as part of a larger whole. However, James skillfully weaves them together by highlighting each at a different moment in his narrative.

Just as James does in his appendix, the authors who constitute the object of this study juggle divergent contexts in which to inscribe the Haitian Revolution. It will certainly not be my intention to simply reduce these multiple visions to a set of common denominators. On the contrary, the multiplicity of readings is the best reflection of the multiplicity of cultural, political, and social questions raised by the often violent encounters of peoples and cultures in the Caribbean, all of them under the signs of empire and colonialism, and all of them informing key conjunctural events such as the revolution in Haiti. However, I would also like to suggest at this point that what I am calling the "synechdochal approach" has significant implications in the Caribbean that go beyond the obvious fact that everything, naturally, could be regarded as part of a larger whole. In the Caribbean, the matter of wholeness and of being part of, not part of, marginal to, or close to the center of a "whole" is unavoidably linked to the region's colonial history. In Caribbean history we find the pervasive imposed presence of a colonial *negative whole*. By this I mean that its positive content (which we may identify with Europe's grand narrative of progress and civilization) has defined local inhabitants and cultures through exclusion. From the perspective of those who have been defined as marginal to that whole, as excluded from it, or as partial but never full participants in it, what matters is that they are *not it:* this sense of incompleteness and inaccessibility permeates most of the accounts of the revolution that I will examine in the following chapters.

In order to better appreciate what I mean by the relation between synecdoche and Caribbean colonial history, I want to turn to a revealing passage of Aimé Césaire's *Toussaint Louverture,* which I will examine in more detail in chapter 3. In setting the stage for his account of the Haitian Revolution, which he regards as closely linked to the events and development of the French Revolution, Césaire indicates: "Telle était la société coloniale: mieux qu'une hiérarchie, une ontologie: en haut, le blanc—*l'être* au sens plein du terme—, en bas, le nègre, sans personalité juridique, un meuble; la chose, autant dire *le rien;* mais entre ce tout et ce rien, un redoutable entre-deux: le mulâtre, l'homme de couleur libre" (33) ["Such was the colonial society: it was, more than hierarchy, an ontology: at the top, the white man—*Being* in the fullest sense of the term—, at the bottom, the black man (the slave), with no juridical individuality, movable property; a thing, which amounts to saying: *Nothing;* but between this All and this Nothing, a formidable intermediary: the mulatto, the free man of color" (my translation)].

Césaire's words point to the heart of what I call synechdochal ontocolonialism. The phrase may seem initially obscure, but the Césaire quote explains it quite succinctly. Under colonialism, the colonizer claims for himself more than a superior position in a political or military balance or structure of power. The colonizer's advantage is not only *quantitative* (better arms and better trained soldiers under classic colonialism, with the emphasis shifting to more capital and economic control under neocolonial relations) but also *qualitative.* Following a logic that had its earliest manifestations in the debates on whether the indigenous populations of the Americas were "natural slaves" or not, during the period of the early Spanish conquest, the colonizer claims to *be* in a full and self-contained manner: he is *fully* human (a status that is always somewhat suspect in the case of the colonized, who must constantly prove his own worth as a human being), and he has access to *universal* truths, as opposed to the cultural practices of colonized peoples, which are always local and of limited value.[5] Thus, the colonized is not only in an ontologically synechdochal relation to the colonizer but also in an epistemologically synechdochal relation too. Colonized peoples can aspire, in the best of cases, to participate in (to be *part of*) that fullness of Being that is European civilization, but they cannot aspire to be *it*.[6] The colonizer, on the other hand, is *it:* each European is fully Europe, each colonized is at best partially *Europeanized.* This difference is what critic Walter Mignolo has called the *colonial difference* (*Local Histories*), and as Peruvian sociologist Aníbal Quijano has eloquently expressed, this colonial difference has most often been articulated through the trope of race and the attendant racism that became the dominant logic of modern colonialism ("Coloniality of Power, Eurocentrism and Social Classification").

In that essentialist, Eurocentric logic, members of other *races* have been, at best, *part of* the fullness of being fully incarnated by white, European males. Inasmuch as the Haitian Revolution constituted a radical attempt to dismantle many of those colonial structures (from the actual military defeat of the French army to Jean Jacques Dessalines' proud proclamation that the newly independent Haiti would be a *black* country), Césaire's insightful words capture what many of the works studied in the following chapters share: the exploration and critique of this colonial ontology, and the imaginative formulation of alternative, ever more inclusive "wholes" on which to locate Caribbean history. "Imaginative" does not mean here "untrue," but rather the creative attempt to transform and transcend the dead-ends of the region's colonial history, thus achieving what Edouard Glissant calls in his *Monsieur Toussaint* a "prophetic vision of the past" (15).

Coloniality and the Myth of Modernity

Since I understand the different accounts of the Haitian Revolution to be engaged with an examination and critique of diverse aspects of the "colonial condition" of the Caribbean region, in this section I clarify a number of concepts that will recur in all the chapters of the book, even as each focuses on a unique approach to the events in Haiti.

As indicated above, my understanding of the "colonial condition" draws upon ideas that the Argentinean critic Walter Mignolo has developed, particularly his concept of "colonial difference," itself indebted to notion of "coloniality of power" exposed in the work of Peruvian sociologist Aníbal Quijano. By "colonial difference" Mignolo refers to the results of a Eurocentric view of the world that constitutes the basis for the "modern/colonial world system," colonialism itself being nothing less than the "underside" of modernity, as Argentinean philosopher Enrique Dussel has aptly suggested.[7] In that view, colonial "others" are inherently inferior and destined to occupy a subordinate (subaltern) position with regards to the European colonizer, while also perpetually aspiring to "catch up" and achieve an equality with the European man that remains by definition impossible, thus eternally pursued and out of reach. Using the terms I introduced in the previous section, one could argue that Eurocentric colonialism was quite adept at defining itself as a "whole" differently at different times, a "whole" to which, each time, colonial peoples or territories remained subordinated, but also a "whole" from which each time they remained excluded. The colonial condition perpetuates and is sustained by the myth of a "lack" in the colonized that does not exist in the colonizer. That lack—of a soul, of intelligence, of civilization, of a stable and unified self with access to transcendental and universal principles that are not restricted or defined by the specificities of history and location—condemns the colonized to be partly human, part of a whole that always remains out of reach. As Césaire eloquently puts it, within the colonial ontology, the colonizer is being, whereas the colonized is nothingness.[8]

In an essay that discusses the "colonial difference" with regards to Latin American philosophy, Mignolo aptly describes this process by quoting philosopher Robert Bernasconi, who writes in an essay on African philosophy: "Western philosophy traps African philosophy in a double bind: either African philosophy is so similar to Western philosophy that it makes no distinctive contribution and effectively disappears; or it is so different that its credentials to be genuine philosophy will always be in doubt" ("Philosophy," 82).[9] The "double bind" that Bernasconi refers to corresponds to the synechdochal onto-colonialism that I referred to above: colonial attempts at "catching up" or achieving full identity with the "whole" will always be incomplete, because there will always be a different or larger "whole" that the subaltern subject cannot be a part of; where the whole is, the part is not. As we will see in the following chapters, Caribbean intellectuals have occasionally recurred to positing an "alternative whole" (Latin America, Negritude, etc.) as a challenge to the colonial framework. However, that other "whole" is often acknowledged by the colonial metropolis as insufficient, as simply a limited fragment of the larger, truer "whole" that really matters, the "whole" that always remains out of reach for the colonized.[10] To be black, or Latin

American, or a proletarian, is always a parcel of, and qualitatively less than, being "human," and that full, undivided, and unstained humanity is always a privilege of the European man.

Paradoxically, it is the colonial relation itself, the cultural and political exchanges that it necessarily entails, that constantly and ultimately puts into question the colonizer's fictional claim to that stable and unified self. There is no self or culture (either that of the colonizer or of the colonized) that was not always already the result of difference, encounter, exchange, and conflict. That "self," and that supposedly unassailable wholeness, were always a myth, always articulated and fractured by difference. However, one must not minimize the pull and power of that mythical frame. Always "overdetermined from without" as Fanon has aptly phrased it (*Black Skin*, 116), the colonial subject (and often the colonial intellectual), frequently finds him/herself torn between challenging the myth of wholeness and a homogeneous self, and trying to appropriate it. While the basis of that superior wholeness may be mythical, the privileges it legitimizes and gives access to are not.[11]

As indicated above, Mignolo's concept of "colonial difference" is indebted to Aníbal Quijano's concept of "the coloniality of power." In the following chapters I will refer repeatedly to Quijano's concept, sometimes using the terms "colonial logic" or "the logic of coloniality." The point here is relatively simple but enormously important: modern colonialism, as the direct physical occupation of foreign territories that are militarily and politically dominated, economically exploited, and culturally and socially restructured, operates on the basis of certain ideological assumptions. It follows a certain cultural and philosophical logic, and that logic and those assumptions do not end with the end of formal colonialism, that is to say, when colonies acquire their national independence from the colonial metropolis. The persistence of that colonial logic—the Eurocentric ordering of global power structures—manifests itself not only in the phenomenon of neocolonialism (endemic in most postcolonial nations) and the subordinate, subaltern role most former colonies play in contemporary neoliberal globalization but also in the internal structures, institutions, attitudes, and beliefs that dominate and organize the newly independent states.

For Quijano, a principal structuring axis of the coloniality of power (though not the only one) is the category of race, with its concomitant racial/racist distinctions. Race, described by Quijano as "a mental category of modernity" ("Coloniality of Power, Eurocentrism, and Latin America" 534), becomes "a way of granting legitimacy to the relations of domination imposed by the conquest" (ibid.). Thus, "the conquered and dominated peoples were situated in a natural position of inferiority and, as a result, their phenotypic traits as well as their cultural features were considered inferior" (ibid., 535). This essentialist distinction marks the colonized with what Mignolo calls "the colonial difference," which the colonized is invited to overcome but is persistently barred from escaping. As Quijano emphasizes, even after the end of formal colonialism the structuring matrix of coloniality remains in place, both in global relations and internally in "postcolonial" nations.[12] Haiti, as we will see in the following chapters, has often been a tragic example of that reality.

Another theorist whose work informs this study is the Argentinean Enrique Dussel, whose articulation of a "Liberation Philosophy" beginning in the 1970s has been vastly influential in Latin American philosophical thought and within the broad movement of Liberation Theology in the continent. Dussel's engagements with philosophy, theology, history, and other disciplines are too vast to summarize here, so I will focus on a single concept that clearly links him to Quijano's and Mignolo's concerns—that of "the myth of modernity." Using this expression, Dussel refers to another way in which the West has justified its hegemonic global colonial domination, namely, the notion that such domination is the natural result of Europe's technical and philosophical superiority over the rest of the world—in other words, Europe's modernity. By contrast, the rest of the colonized world is regarded, at best, as irretrievably lagging behind Europe in development: as premodern. Thus, history has moved in teleological fashion toward its summit, which is European modernity. In Dussel's analysis,

> One defines one's culture as superior and more developed and the other as inferior, crude, barbaric, and culpably *immature*. While one culture may be superior to another in many respects, the critical observer realizes that the criteria are always qualitative, and so uncertain in their application. Even the violence inflicted on the Other is said to serve the emancipation, utility, and well-being of the barbarian who is civilized, developed, or modernized. (Dussel, *The Invention*, 64)

For Dussel there are at least two aspects of Europe's self-proclaimed modernity that make it a "myth." First, there is the claim to universality, the idea that Europe's modern notions of truth, beauty, and ethics are self-evidently superior to others from around the world, and that in fact they justify Europe's domination of the rest of the world, that is to say, colonialism. Second, there is the notion that "modernity" (whichever content we ascribe to the concept) is an exclusively *intra-European* affair—that it is a single and simple development from the institutions and ideas of classical Greece, through the development of Christianity (for the most part emptied of its Semitic roots), to the gradual unfolding of European capitalism since the Renaissance, to the secularism and scientific breakthroughs of the early modern period. The long history of centuries of intellectual and commercial contacts and influences in the multicentered world before European global hegemony is not considered. Moreover and even more important, what is not acknowledged is that the development of European "modernity"—presumably rational, ethical, progressive—is inseparable from Europe's brutal colonial domination on a global scale, which starts with the "discovery" of the Americas in 1492. Although those dominated regions of the world are systematically excluded from accounts of European modernity, the fact is that they were always part of European modernity, as Dussel indicates, as its *underside*, as an exterior (excluded) margin that allows for Europe's internal "coherence." Colonies—first Spain's, then England's, France's, Holland's, etc.—also provided enormous wealth, resources, products, labor (in the form of slavery for several centuries), and cultural and intellectual riches (from conquered cultures) which were instrumental in the material and conceptual developments that Europe associates with its modernity (Dussel "Europe, Modernity").

For Dussel, it is certainly not a matter of a priori rejecting any values or institutions associated to Western modernity but rather an issue of acknowledging a complex history in which no group can claim inherent superiority and universal value above all others, and in which the West has in fact acquired its questionable superiority by conquering and exploiting other regions of the world. Dussel proposes the notion of *transmodernity* as an alternative to the myth of modernity. By this he means a multivocal world, a pluralistic coming together of multiple ontologies and perspectives in which none is a priori rejected, although, naturally, some may prove more adequate than others depending on circumstances. Dussel's term clearly suggests that his purpose is not a rejection of modernity (he retains the word) but a historicization of the concept that acknowledges the claims to justice of those who were always part of its developments but from its oppressed underside. Such a multiperspectival approach (a "pluriversality" in Dussel's formulation ["Transmodernity," 50]) is also linked to Mignolo's notions of "pluritopic hermeneutics" (*The Darker Side of Renaissance*, 15–18; *Local Histories*, 16) and "border thinking"—both of which point to ways of thinking that acknowledge their always concrete locations and attempt to open a space for Other excluded perspectives, while remaining vigilant and critical of any attempt of fundamentalist or hegemonic thinking to appropriate that epistemological unleashing. The goal is to release "knowledges that have been subalternized" (*Local Histories*, 67).

Another name that I must briefly add to those of Dussel, Quijano, and Mignolo is that of the Portuguese sociologist Boaventura de Sousa Santos. Although his ideas are only highlighted explicitly in chapter 1, they certainly underlie many of my arguments throughout the book. My main interest lies in the link Sousa Santos establishes between global social justice and what he terms "cognitive justice" (*Another Knowledge*, xix). In other words, Sousa Santos refers to the epistemological dimension of the coloniality of power, or what we may call the coloniality of knowledge—how non-European forms of knowledge and traditions have been marginalized, when not totally crushed, in the name of Europe's universal claims to truth. Thus decolonization must occur not only at the levels of territorial sovereignty and economic development but also in the defense of multiple *other* ways of knowing, and relating to, the world.

Lastly I should mention the important contributions of the Puerto Rican philosopher Nelson Maldonado-Torres, who has developed the ideas of Quijano, Mignolo, and Dussel by establishing a dialogue between them and the thought of Frantz Fanon. Maldonado-Torres has elaborated the notion of the "coloniality of being," a concept initially used by Mignolo and by Sylvia Wynter, in order to demonstrate how the political, economic, and epistemological dimensions of what Quijano terms the coloniality of power in fact constitute the very ontology (in an existential sense) of modern colonial subjects. In his exploration of Quijano's ideas, Maldonado-Torres recurs to Dussel, who, in his discussion of Emmanuel Levinas's challenge to Heidegger's ontology, has compellingly argued how the Cartesian "ego cogito," the supposed foundation of the Western European modern self (which neatly divided reality between *res cogitans* and *res extensa*, consciousness and matter), was in fact preceded by, and cannot be fully disengaged from, Europe's "ego conquiro," which displays another kind of foundational modern skepticism: doubt "regarding the humanity of the enslaved and colonized sub-others" ("On the Coloniality," 245). Maldonado-Torres aptly locates an exemplary phenomenological description of this ontological exclusion in Fanon's well-known passage in *Black Skin, White Masks*, in which his whole being is put into question by the encounter with the racist other who exclaims: "Look, a Negro!" As Maldonado-Torres indicates, "If Dussel spells out the historical dimension of the coloniality of Being, Fanon deploys the existential expressions of coloniality in relation to the colonial experience in its racial and, to some extent as well, its gendered dimensions" ("On the Coloniality," 242–43). It should be clear that this notion of the "coloniality of being" provides a frame for the understanding of what I have called "synechdocal onto-colonialism" in the previous section, as it appears not only in the Césaire example that I used but also in manyfold ways in all the works that I examine in the following chapters. Moreover, the element of existential angst that results from that imperial questioning of the very being, the very humanness, of colonized subjects is a dimension that may be easily lost in broader sociological and political discussions, and yet it is not only fundamental, but also recurrent in these representations of the Haitian Revolution. Throughout the text, I will freely move between the coloniality of power, of knowledge, and of being, sometimes simply referring to the logic of coloniality, or colonial logic, which encompasses them all.

All of the above mentioned concerns, questions and proposals that Dussel, Quijano, Mignolo, Sousa Santos, and Maldonado-Torres elucidate arise at different moments in the discussions of the diverse works in the chapters that follow. As already indicated, I want to allow and even highlight how these works and writers tell their own stories, their own versions of the events in Haiti. However, since its colonial inception the Caribbean has been what the Dominican writer Juan Bosch calls an "imperial frontier," that is to say, a space where empires have crashed with each other and with local populations. Given the recurrent and common threads that have dominated the historical development of the region, similar preoccupations and even literary strategies inevitably recur in many of these works.

Haiti's history, for example, certainly displays colonial exploitation at its most virulently violent. It also shows the racist logic of the coloniality of power, even after Haiti's independence, when European nations refused to acknowledge the existence of a nation created by former slaves, and when despotic local leaders tried to preserve and adopt the exploitative structures and assumptions of the colonial system in the newly independent Haiti. Thus, colonial racial hierarchies, in different manifestations, remain in place to this day in Haiti, and in their attempt to incorporate the new nation to already existing (colonial) global markets, many early Haitian leaders attempted to preserve oppressive labor systems that the former slaves stubbornly resisted. For instance, Henri Christophe virtually re-enslaved his people before they rebelled. In its international relations, Haiti has clearly exemplified the double bind of the colonial difference.

In another example, the revolution itself has sometimes been reduced (even by admirers) to an appendix of the French Revolution, as if the slaves needed to hear about "liberty, fraternity and equality" from their French masters before they could truly aspire to them.[13] Such an approach shows the need for what Sousa Santos calls "cognitive justice," in order to open a space to a deeper appreciation of how the Haitian slaves themselves understood and conceptualized their revolution, which clearly included elements from the French Enlightenment but was not limited to them.[14]

In spite of the dire realities presented in all of their works, the writers examined in the next chapters also look at the Haitian Revolution as a source of inspiration, as a moment when, in spite of the violence of the process, an oppressed population was able to come together in solidarity and a claim for justice and liberation. Thus, without idealizing the events in Haiti, one may also catch in these works a glimpse of the possibility, however distant and obscured, of Dussel's transmodern project—the irruption of other voices and agencies which, although well acquainted with the Western world of which they are part through exclusion and exploitation, bring to the table an Other perspective that aspires to reassembling that corrupt, exploitative world. That in fact such aspirations have often failed in the case of Haiti; that the logic of coloniality, both locally and beyond, seems to conspire even with natural events like the 2010 earthquake so that the Haitian people's ordeals are persistently and tragically renewed—all of these realities point to the urgency and fundamental importance that Haitian history has for its Caribbean neighbors. For Haiti is not only a sibling in pain but also a powerful mirror whose reality is never all that distant from that of the other members of its watchful family.

Regarding the theoretical parameters and problems that this book explores, one final significant issue should be briefly addressed here, since its shadow pervades not only the events and historical accounts of the Haitian Revolution but also the literary representations explored in the following chapters. I am referring to the problem of gender. Accounts of the Haitian Revolution mostly rely on a masculinist rhetoric that echoes that of many of the revolution's leaders—most of whom aspired to create paternalistic regimes modeled on those of European states. But it should be clear that if, as indicated above, the logic of coloniality attempts to define the human in exclusively Eurocentric terms, then it is also the case that the Eurocentric human is almost invariably the heterosexual male. Although issues of gender are not the main focus of my analysis of these writers, their fundamental importance must be acknowledged, and in the case of the problems that occupy us here, they point in at least three slightly different directions or possibilities of further exploration.

First, there is the issue of the actual role of women in the Haitian Revolution, both as agents of revolutionary change and as victims of both colonial and revolutionary violence. Although the participation and place of women has been mostly erased in most accounts, efforts are rapidly progressing toward at least some partial recovery of their interventions. As Jana Evans Braziel points out, "when and where women are evoked in the revolutionary historiographies, the historians often do so to reify their bodies, minds, and creative contributions within patriarchal notions of history, nation, and historical embodiment" (Braziel, "Re-membering Defilée," 60). Joan Dayan has also attempted to explore the paradoxical role of some women like Dédée Bazile (Défilée-la-folle), who were paradoxically "mythologized by men, metaphorized out of life into legend" (*Haiti*, 48).[15]

Second, there is the important question of the limits or further necessary refinements of the decolonial frame that guides many of my arguments, as expressed by writers like Quijano, Dussel, and Mignolo. If the category of race has been instrumental in the organization of coloniality's global ontology of power, it is also true that other essentialist taxonomies have played fundamental roles in that organization (something that the three thinkers explicitly acknowledge), and that the emphasis on one category may at times minimize or even erase the crucial impact of others. Gender has certainly been one of those dimensions of coloniality that is often neglected in theoretical formulations, and critics like María Lugones have done breakthrough work in applying decolonial thought and concepts to the problem of systematic (and systemic) violence against women, particularly women of color. Lugones has created the category of "the modern/colonial gender system" in order to expand Quijano's frame to an exploration of essentialist gender categories that ultimately further "the cognitive needs of capitalism and the naturalizing of the identities and relations of coloniality" ("Heterosexualism," 192). Among those, Lugones mentions the imposition of "sexual dimorphism" (masculine/feminine) as the only frame to understand human sexuality, and the naturalizing of patriarchal and normative heterosexualism in cultures that might have had more fluid understandings of the sexual dimensions of human experience.[16]

Third, there is the fact that most of the Caribbean writers studied in the following chapters, in spite of their often progressive, even radical positions with regards to the political problems that their works explore, mainly remain within the confines of restrictive (and, Lugones might argue, ultimately colonial) views of gender. The issue here is not how much those writers could or should have known or done about issues of gender inequality in their contexts but the need to make sure that we, their contemporary readers, do not simply dismiss those limitations as unimportant or, even worse, value them as positive. Thus, we must face the fact that throughout his career Césaire, the poet who would be "the mouth of those who have no mouth," remained locked within a strongly masculinist view of revolutionary politics. Both Walcott and Palés Matos, writers separated by language and time, share a propensity to display female characters mostly as symbols of landscapes that men must save or agonize about. In *The Kingdom of This World*, Carpentier nonchalantly narrates Ti Noel's rape of his white master's wife, barely stopping short of presenting it as understandable, if not justifiable payback (this, after criticizing in his famous prologue to the novel those writers who, inspired by Lautréamont, fantasize about raping dead maidens, when the marvelous act, writes Carpentier, would be to rape them alive). To be sure, Zapata Olivella culminates his pan-African epic novel (which includes important allusions to Sojourner Truth and Harriet Tubman) with the figure of Agne Brown, inspired by Angela Davis and opening an important way for the confluence of colonial, racial, and gender resistances. Although these writers are not monolithic in their positions and may be productively read even through and beyond many of their conceptual dead-ends, that complexity must certainly include the acknowledgment and criticism of those limitations, which, regardless of how we understand them in their original context, are intolerable in ours. One can hardly do otherwise if one gives serious attention to works that clearly aspired, when they were produced, to address future readers committed to liberation practices.

Two Hundred Years and Counting

Although the revolution in Haiti has never ceased to attract the attention of some scholars, over the last twenty years, as the 200th anniversary of Haiti's independence approached and was commemorated (in 2004), there has been a veritable revival of interest and writing on the significance and impact of the Haitian Revolution. In the following chapters I will show my grateful indebtedness to many of those works, from historical accounts by writers such as Carolyn Fick, Laurent M. Dubois, David P. Geggus, Robin Blackburn, and Jeremy D. Popkin, among many others, to literary and cultural approaches by critics such as Nick Nesbitt, Chris Bongie, and Deborah Jenson, among many others. Susan Buck-Morss's compelling account of the impact of the Haitian Revolution on Hegel, ultimately a powerful meditation on the advantages and disadvantages of universal history for decolonial thought and action, has indelibly marked me as well as a whole generation of thinkers on these matters. In the next few paragraphs, I want to highlight three texts that have in many ways redefined the terms in which we discuss the Haitian Revolution, and a very recent one that responds to similar imperatives as those that guide my own study.

Michel Rolph Trouillot's *Silencing the Past: Power and the Production of History* develops its author's claim that the Haitian Revolution has been, in fact, silenced in most academic accounts of the "age of revolutions," as Eric Hobsbawn has termed it. That point is argued in a broader and insightful discussion of how historical narratives both reveal and silence voices and perspectives that do not fit the powerful interests or prejudices that often underlie historiographical production (a perspective that is itself indebted to Hayden White's important reflections on the writing of history).

Trouillot's claim is particularly significant if we appreciate its full implications. It is not simply a matter of information on the revolution being suppressed. In fact, one might plausibly argue that much information on the Haitian Revolution circulated in both Europe and the United States; after all, by 1803 Wordsworth had written a poem on Toussaint Louverture, and by 1826 Victor Hugo had published *Bug Jargal* (written several years earlier). Susan Buck-Morss has compellingly shown the impact of the revolution in Europe. However, the point that Trouillot makes is that the revolution's meaning, its break with what had come before it, was so radical, that the information that circulated about the event, the way the event was framed, actually made it a nonevent. Most of those representations foreclosed the revolutionary import of the event by fitting it into premade colonial narratives and models about black savagery and primitivism. The "fact" that black slaves were behaving violently against their white civilized masters did circulate, and as such was paradoxically both horrifying and unsurprising. The full implications of the event (the fact that it was, indeed, a revolution led by former black slaves) did not spread; they were, as Trouillot presents it, "unthinkable" (*Silencing the Past*, 27, 70).

Trouillot's claim has affinities with Gayatri Spivak's well-known dictum that "the subaltern cannot speak;" a claim that is best understood not as meaning that the subaltern cannot speak at all, which is patently absurd, but rather as pointing to the threat that anything that the subaltern does speak is rendered ineffective, foreclosed, thus "silenced" a priori by colonial power structures that have a firm grip on the communication process that makes "speaking" possible and meaningful at all to begin with. In that regard, the literary representations studied in the following chapters have played a tremendously significant role in actually articulating the Haitian Revolution as a historical event that can in fact "speak" in the twentieth century.

Sibylle Fischer, in her important *Modernity Disavowed: Haiti and the Cultures of Slavery in the Age of Revolution* has complicated Trouillot's picture by compellingly showing that the revolution was indeed thinkable but mostly articulated through utopias, fears and paranoia, and fantasies (291–92), all forms of disavowal that attempt to push the slave revolt to the margins of the formation of "modernity" just as, paradoxically, the revolution pushed so-called modern values like political liberty and progress to their most radical, yet logical manifestations. Fischer explores the ideological and symbolic impact of the revolution on neighboring Caribbean territories (such as nineteenth-century Cuba, where it fed the anxieties of both slavists and abolitionists; or the persistent anti-Haitian sentiment in the Dominican Republic), and on European thinkers such as Hegel. Thus, revolutionary antislavery and its disavowal must be regarded as constitutive elements in the formation of modernity, which cannot be read simply and linearly as the development and incarnation of enlightened principles in the West but rather as the clash between conflicting emancipating projects and concepts, with some of its most radical developments happening in places like Haiti, and being received with tremendous anxiety by Eurocentric thinkers. It is precisely that "struggle over what it means to be modern" (Fischer, *Modernity Disavowed*, 24) that gives Haiti a central place in a view of modernity that acknowledges it as a "heterogeneous, internally diverse, even contradictory phenomenon" (ibid.).

Fischer's reading of the Haitian Revolution has clear points of contact with the vision of thinkers I draw upon throughout this study, such as Enrique Dussel and Walter Mignolo, who try to make "visible" modernity's contradictions by attaching the concept to other qualifiers. By talking about "the underside of modernity," Dussel highlights the colonial exploitation of territories and populations regarded as "other," which was persistently linked to modernity's development; Mignolo's insistence on writing about "modernity/coloniality," emphasizes the same point. This does not mean that these thinkers simply "reject" modernity (itself a tremendously complex and heterogeneous term, as Fischer states), even if such a thing were possible. Dussel's view of a "trans-modern" future retains an engagement with the term in question, and Mignolo draws upon ideas such as "border thinking," "border gnosis," and "border epistemology," in which one of the borders in operation is definitely that of modernity in its multifarious forms.

However, it is also important to insist that given the brutal history of modernity's exclusions (its coloniality), a rhetoric of simply revising modernity's script in order to acknowledge its incompleteness and fill its gaps (in Habermasian fashion) is not sufficient. Fischer is certainly concerned about that possibility, which she brings up with emphasis in the conclusion of her book (*Modernity Disavowed*, 273), although she still frames the problem as one about "conflicts over the shape and meaning of modernity" (ibid.). In many of the writers discussed in the next chapters I see a slightly different formulation of the problem, one that Mignolo clearly expresses in the following way in a discussion of Dussel's ethics of liberation:

> The project of ethics of discourse (Apel, Habermas) means inclusion and reform . . . Ethics of liberation is transformation grounded in a philosophical discourse that questions the fact that in the politics of inclusion and recognition what is left unquestioned is the very place in and from which inclusion is proposed. Those who propose inclusion do not reflect critically on the fact that those who are welcomed to be included may not necessarily want to play the game generously offered by those who open their arms to the inclusion of the difference. (*The Darker Side of Western*, 249–50)

What possibilities remain open for those who want to play another game in a world already carefully sliced up by colonial powers is certainly a difficult question, and one can see some of those difficulties in Fischer's masterful analysis of the constitutions created by Toussaint, Dessalines, and Christophe. All the writers that I examine in the following chapters are engaged with the exploration of such difficulties.

In *Conscripts of Modernity: The Tragedy of Colonial Enlightenment*, David Scott importantly highlights the fact, which might seem evident but deserves repetition, that modern engagements with the events in Haiti (Scott focuses on James's *Black Jacobins*) are ultimately about the present of the writers that produce them; more precisely, about discerning how the political circumstances of that present emerge from the past, in order to more clearly articulate what kind of future one might aspire to. As I have indicated, that is certainly the case for all of the writers that I examine in the chapters that follow. Scott has been taken to task for the seeming bleakness of his outlook (Bongie *Friends;* Kaisary *The Haitian Revolution*), since he is not shy about expressing his opposition to what he regards as an exhausted anticolonial rhetoric that is anchored in the "heroism of the sovereign revolutionary subject and the renewal of humanity it promises to initiate" (Scott, *Conscripts*,

190), an "emplotment" of history that Scott associates to Romance, following Hayden White's categorization. Instead, Scott praises the genre of Tragedy (again, as initially conceptualized by White, and then by philosophers such as Martha Nussbaum) as more receptive to "the paradoxical reversals that can unmake and corrupt our most cherished ideals" (ibid.). In Scott's view, the harsh realities of the present have laid bare the collapse and ultimate inadequacy of the revolutionary ideals and discourses that might have made sense during the first half of the twentieth century; that approach is based on questions—can we resist colonial domination? how and in what ways?—"whose moment has passed, or better, whose moment over the past decade and a half has been steadily dismantled" (ibid., 119).

I fundamentally agree with the main points of Bongie's and Kaisary's critique of Scott's position, particularly Bongie's nuanced examination of Scott's "ventriloquial relation to James" (*Friends*, 264), which produces a problematic "we" that includes Scott, James (in the second edition of *Black Jacobins*), Toussaint as intellectual leader, and presumably most intellectuals from the contemporary postcolonial world. As Bongie indicates, that position "marginalizes and excludes a whole range of other identities and other worlds of value" (ibid., 265), thus reproducing precisely the kind of tendentious geography of reason that Mignolo eloquently criticizes in *The Darker Side of Western Modernity*. Having said that, I appreciate the main impact of Scott's book (in addition to its powerful close readings of certain aspects of James's work) in its descriptive, rather than prescriptive, power. For it is hard to deny, while studying the texts with which I work in this book, that disappointment with the results of revolutionary anticolonial practices, particularly with the way they often reproduce the unfair structures of exploitation and exclusion that they were fighting in the first place, has been pervasive among colonial writers and intellectuals. Moreover, that disappointment and sheer exhaustion are not recent, but rather have been parcel of all revolutions, from France to the United States and Russia, and beyond. We can see awareness of those realities, and an attempt to struggle with them, in writers ranging from Césaire and Walcott to Glissant and Carpentier.

However, my suggestion throughout the following chapters, one that in my view recurs in different forms in most of these writers, is that when we expand our focus from traditional colonialism to the coloniality of being and power that dominates the current globalized capitalist order (therefore making the adjective postcolonial not quite adequate to describe the present), it is simply not the case that anticolonial aspirations arise, as Scott suggests, from the desire for a naive recovery of a pristine precolonial free self (no serious anticolonial writer that I know of, from those examined in this book to Fanon and contemporary decolonial thinkers, proposes that), or from "nostalgia and clinging resentment" (*Conscripts of Modernity*, 207). The aspiration is to liberation (which, as Dussel emphasizes, is an openended process, not a goal achieved once and for all) from the persistence, *in the present,* of colonial domination. In other words, exploitation, exclusion and racism provoke the aspiration to justice, inclusion and equality: this is not a "normative expectation of resistance or overcoming" (ibid., 114) but rather more simply a concrete response to a situation. That in the history of modern colonialism some of those responses have led to dead-ends is most definitely true (some of the writers analyzed in this book point to that reality in the case of the Haitian Revolution); that new responses and conceptual frames of understanding are needed, is always the case; that oppression will provoke the aspiration to overcoming oppression not only by those who suffer it but also by those capable of empathy, remains a fact to be celebrated, in spite of the imperfections of the results.

Finally, I should also mention Philip Kaisary's *The Haitian Revolution in the Literary Imagination,* which was published in 2014 and thus becomes the first book, to my knowledge, that studies literary representations of the Haitian Revolution from a truly pan-Caribbean perspective. Kaisary studies many of the writers that I also examine in the following chapters and offers a useful overview of their main preoccupations; additionally, he includes other important ones such as René Depestre, Langston Hughes, and Madison Smartt Bell, plus an examination of some visual representations of the revolution. In his analysis, Kaisary divides the works of his writers and artists into two clearly distinguished groups: radical recuperations of the Haitian Revolution (James, Césaire, Hughes, Depestre), and conservative visions (Carpentier, Glissant, Smartt Bell, Walcott). In his analysis, he makes clear what he celebrates in the first group, namely that those writers focus on the revolution's radical character as a continuing inspiration for emancipation struggles; and what he objects to in the second, namely that their approaches obscure or otherwise minimize that revolutionary impulse. It should be evident from the following chapters that I do not concur with that neat categorization, although Kaisary makes a forceful case for it. From my perspective, all of these writers partake, to different degrees, in the same paradoxical *situation* (using that term in its existentialist meaning) of being the result of colonial societies which they feel compelled to criticize and confront, but whose structures and values they may often reflect and even share, whether consciously or unconsciously. That is the situation of most colonial (and more precisely here, Caribbean) intellectuals, one with which they often openly struggle in their works, and my emphasis has been on carefully exploring those complexities and paradoxes.

The Revolution Viewed from the Caribbean

The temporal and spatial limits of my corpus in this study are quite precise: the revolution as it has been represented in texts from the contemporary Caribbean. Spatially, this means I will not go beyond the Caribbean region, although fascinating accounts and reactions have been produced in other parts of the world since the very events of the revolution. These works include: William Wordsworth's poem "To Toussaint Louverture" (written in 1802, shortly before Toussaint's death in 1803); Alphonse de Lamartine's play *Toussaint Louverture* (1850); Wendell Phillips' famous lecture "Toussaint Louverture" (1861); Madison Smartt Bell's fascinating trilogy of novels on the revolution (*Master of the Crossroads* [1995], *All Souls' Rising* [2000], and *The Stone That The Builder Refused* [2006]); and Isabel Allende's *La isla bajo el mar* (2009). Needless to say, a fascinating study could be written on how those perspectives from around the globe have articulated the events in Haiti, and what purposes those representations have served. My present work will not venture into this territory, nor will it focus on how the revolution has been regarded and represented *within* Haiti itself, although there will be some references to that aspect of the subject at hand. To fully undertake such an endeavor would require a separate book, one that would necessarily be engaged with Haiti's often tragic national history after independence, and that should scrutinize the uses and misuses of the revolution and its figures in modern and contemporary Haitian politics.[17] Naturally the meaning of the revolution for Haiti and Haitians cannot be dissociated from its meaning to the wider Caribbean; however, I believe there is value in examining how these seminal events have taken shape in the literary imagination of Haiti's neighbors in the region, which although sharing in many of Haiti's historical problems, have nonetheless followed different paths.[18]

Contemporary problems that are differently experienced by different parts of the Caribbean, and not just questions of historical interest, are insistently raised by the Haitian Revolution. Those problems include: issues related to race and class (and gender, even if sometimes only by highlighting the strong heroic, masculinist tendency that dominates the region's self-representation); issues related to the application of abstract moral and political principles to concrete situations; the relation of the "universal" to the "local," and how those two poles have been articulated in the modern/colonial world system; and the problem of foreign colonial domination joined by local oppression once political emancipation is achieved. Writers addressing such problems have often used the Haitian Revolution as a symbolic place of encounter and make it a drama perpetually rehearsed in the imaginary of the region. In many ways, Haiti is the part that stands for the whole Caribbean, working as mirror, warning, and inspiration.

The Martinican Aimé Césaire articulated one dramatic example of Haiti's multifarious place in the Caribbean imaginary. In one of his last interviews, this champion of negritude exclaimed, when describing a visit to Haiti: "In Haiti I saw mainly what should not be done! A country that had supposedly conquered its liberty, which had conquered its independence, and which I saw more miserable than Martinique, which was a French colony! . . . It was tragic, and it was something that could well happen to us too in Martinique" (*Negre je suis* 56; my translation). This passage says as much if not more about Césaire than it does about Haiti, for it partly springs from Césaire's own attempts to justify his political decisions in Martinique: he was instrumental in transforming the island into a French "overseas department." But so is the case in different ways with all the writers examined in the following chapters. They write about Haiti, and what they write certainly sheds light on the Haitian Revolution, but they also, and mainly, write about what the revolution says about their own societies. Thus Césaire, who regards Haiti as the country "where negritude rose for the first time" (*Notebook*, 15), also looks at it as a cautionary tale, as an example of what to avoid, as a road better not taken. Haiti has become an illustration of all that can go wrong and that has gone wrong with the Caribbean, and a symbol of Caribbean pride, resistance, and the radical attempt to concretize an experiment of "universal emancipation," as Nick Nesbitt aptly describes it (*Universal Emancipation*). Haiti and its revolution stand at the crossroads of the region's deepest fears and loftiest possibilities.

It should be clear from what has been stated above that my analysis is double-edged. On the one hand, the revolution has been used, reinvented, or imagined throughout the Caribbean region to raise and explore many different contemporary issues: racial, political, and cultural. On the other hand, these issues are not simply imposed on the revolution: they are part of what that event was about, even if sometimes we can only see that retrospectively, as an unraveling of questions and concerns that were an integral part of the revolution but could not always be clearly articulated when it happened. This study is about how the Haitian Revolution has been used to talk about issues that go well beyond it, but it is also about how those multiple appropriations help us better understand what the revolution itself was all about, in its Caribbean context. That dual consideration will guide my analysis of the works of the seven major Caribbean writers in the chapters that follow.

Chapter 1 contrasts two classic narratives—one fictional, one historiographical—on the revolution: Alejo Carpentier's *El reino de este mundo* [*The Kingdom of This World*] (1949) and C. L. R. James's *The Black Jacobins* (1938; 2nd ed. 1963). My analysis will focus on the way the two works deal, on the one hand, with the figure of the revolutionary leader Toussaint Louverture (who is totally excluded from Carpentier's novel), and, on the other hand, with the role of Vodou beliefs in the revolution, which are mostly ignored in James's account precisely because of his privileging the principles that Toussaint Louverture emblematizes. Evidently, both strategies respond to each writer's objectives—of what "whole" each writer considers Haiti to be an exemplary part. Carpentier is engaged in a process of Pan-Latin Americanist cultural affirmation vis-à-vis Europe, highlighting Haiti as an example of the vital "marvelous real" character of the Americas, as opposed to Europe's decadent and in fact hypocritical rationalism. For his part, James uses Haiti as an illustrative instance of his Marxist perspective on "World Revolution," and as an exemplary representation of the always-fragile relations between the masses and the leaders of a revolutionary movement. Thus, each approach emphasizes what the other one minimizes (Toussaint and Jacobinism; Vodou's centrality for the masses of slaves), yet they do not simply come together as complementary halves, but rather remain in tension as alternative readings of the revolution's ultimate meaning for Caribbean history. I then expand my analysis to two subtler but equally powerful dimensions of each writer's work, namely, Carpentier's prescient incorporation of ecological preoccupations in his novel, and James's emphasis on the necessarily antiracist character of any truly anticolonial struggle in the Caribbean. Both of these themes are rooted in each writer's awareness that coloniality's objectification and exploitation of "the Other," whether nonhuman "natural resources" of colonized territories, or dehumanized human beings (slaves), in fact goes beyond mere economic and even military domination. It entails the symbolic production of irreducible ontological difference.

Chapter 2 focuses on the role that the Haitian Revolution plays in *Tuntún de pasa y grifería* ["Tom-toms of Black and Mulatto Things"] (1937; 2nd ed. 1950), the most important work of the Puerto Rican poet Luis Palés Matos, and one of the foundational literary texts of the Afro-Hispanic Caribbean.

At least two important poems in the book ("Elegía del duque de la Mermelada" ["Elegy of the Duke of Marmalade"] and "Lagarto Verde" ["Green Lizard"]) deal with the aftermath of the events in Haiti, while other poems make explicit references to important characters from the Revolution. In his Haitian poems, Palés mocks the monarchical aspirations of revolutionary leaders like Jean-Jacques Dessalines and Henri Christophe, criticizing how these generals and their aristocratic entourage "betray" their African roots by embracing the artificial imported values of the European aristocracy. Paradoxically, Palés then describes that betrayed "authentic Africanness" by recurring to European stereotypes of primitivism and exoticism. In order to explore Palés's paradox, I highlight the ambivalent position of blackness in Puerto Rico's cultural identity (an ambivalence that is itself a product of the logic of coloniality) and how Palés has become the best-known literary embodiment of that ambivalence. Against many Puerto Rican intellectuals of his period, Palés displays the African dimension of Puerto Rico's identity as an essential component of Puerto Rico's identity, one that links the island to the rest of the Caribbean and that works as an important source of inspiration in Puerto Rico's resistance to the United States—and Caribbean resistance to European—colonial interventions. This African dimension of the Caribbean is emblematized in several poems on Haiti and its revolution. Yet when it comes to the claims for justice that Puerto Rico's African dimension makes on local white elites, Palés hesitates and resists taking a definite stand, not unlike the dancing figures that populate his poems. In this regard, his ambivalent attitude mirrors that of the most progressive members of his intellectual generation. A strong position against colonialism has not always entailed an equally strong position against the racial axis of the coloniality of power.

Chapter 3 studies two of Aimé Césaire's works, the historical essay *Toussaint Louverture: La révolution française et le problème colonial* [*Toussaint Louverture: The French Revolution and the Colonial Problem*] (1961) and the play *La tragédie du roi Christophe* [*The Tragedy of King Christophe*] (1963). What interests me in these two works is the radically different ways in which Césaire approaches events from approximately the same historical period, and what the tension between these two approaches reveals about the imperatives that the Martinican poet and politician struggles with as a Caribbean intellectual. *Toussaint Louverture* attempts to explain the Revolution and the figure of Toussaint Louverture in terms of the enlightened, universalist ideals that shaped the French Revolution. Such an approach puts Toussaint in a difficult position, for, as Césaire suggests, Toussaint "deduces the right of his people to exist" from those seemingly abstract, "universal" principles that always have a very specific origin: Europe (*Toussaint*, 344). Thus, it is not evident from that supposedly "universal" perspective that Haitians (with their concrete, particular histories, belief systems and views of the world) should have a right to "exist." On the other hand, in the *Tragedy* that bears his name, Christophe consistently subordinates "universal" notions to the concrete aspiration of his specific, particular people to exist, which in itself requires no abstract "justification." Thus, in spite of his despotism, Henri Christophe—revolutionary leader and then self-proclaimed king of Haiti—can be celebrated or at least admired from a distance as a genuinely noble though tragic hero, because even when he acts against "universal" humanistic values, he does so in an attempt to affirm the rights of black populations in Haiti, and by extension, everywhere. Césaire himself vacillates between the two approaches, and anyone familiar with his literary and political career—with its radical rhetoric and its pragmatic compromises—may recognize how personal those questions were for the Martinican poet. An examination of how self-serving notions of "universalism" have sustained both European colonial practices and the logic of coloniality must play an important role in an analysis of Césaire's two works on Haiti, which furthermore illuminates the important place of those two works in the rest of his oeuvre and in his political thought.[19]

Chapter 4 focuses on Nobel Prize winning Saint Lucian author Derek Walcott's three plays on the Haitian Revolution: *Henri Christophe* (1948), *Drums and Colours* (1958), and *The Haitian Earth* (1984), which were collected in the volume *The Haitian Trilogy* (2002). This chapter will pay special attention to the last play of the trilogy. What is interesting about *The Haitian Earth* is the fact that the work highlights the figure of Jean-Jacques Dessalines. Dessalines has the historical honor of having actually led Haiti to its independence, but his legacy has been tarnished by a reputation of fierce cruelty and despotism. By crowning himself emperor of Haiti, Dessalines also arguably inaugurated Haiti's painful tradition of autocratic leaders (although, as we will see in chapter 5, some critics might argue that that tradition started with Toussaint Louverture himself, who declared himself governor-for-life of the colony in the constitution he made official in 1801). Thus, Dessalines has received relatively little attention in Caribbean literary accounts of the Haitian Revolution. From a stark perspective that differs significantly from the optimistic thrust of many of his earlier works, Walcott offers in *The Haitian Earth* his critique of a Caribbean ethics/aesthetics of individualistic heroism and "strongman" leadership that has pervaded many anticolonial and anti-imperialist works from the region. What this rhetoric forgets, for Walcott, is the importance and role of humble citizens in struggles of emancipation, and in the (re)construction of society after the violent phase of such struggles is over. Indeed, in the play the (former slave) peasant Pompey makes an explicit point of not distinguishing between the oppression his people have experienced under the French colonists and the new Haitian overlords (Dessalines and Christophe), thus clearly pointing to the pervasive coloniality of power that operates within, without, and beyond the formal traditional structures of colonialism. Moreover, through the figures of Dessalines and Christophe, Walcott explores questions that have concerned him throughout his career: the place of violence in anticolonial struggles; the status of Afrocentrism in Caribbean cultural and political self-affirmation; the blurry distinction between justice and revenge; and the fragile politics and ethics of forgiveness and reconciliation after long periods of oppression.

Chapter 5 studies *Monsieur Toussaint* (1961; revised version 1978), a play about revolutionary leader Toussaint Louverture by the Martinican poet, novelist, and theorist Edouard Glissant. The play makes complex use of different timeframes: its plot constantly switches between Toussaint's revolutionary struggles and the jail where he is imprisoned by Napoleon. Toussaint dies in that prison, visited—but also tormented—by Vodou spirits. Through such theatrical devices, the play performs what Glissant regards as a Caribbean inability to let go of historical legacies such as slavery, colonialism, and racism, which suffocate possibilities of progress. Thus, Glissant's Haitian Revolution embodies tensions and anxieties that are still very much alive in today's Caribbean: the perpetual return and re-enactment in the present of the wounds of a traumatic past, and the ever-renewed but ever-fleeting glimpse of new emancipating possibilities for the future. In its exploration of these issues, *Monsieur Toussaint* revolves around three main concerns: the political and economic fate of newly independent states, with the maroon slave Macaïa calling for a radical break with the past, and Toussaint aspiring to reinsert Saint Domingue into a (sugar) world economy that has up to that point exploited his people's labor; the persistence of the colonial logic in the institutions of the newly independent nation; and the struggle—so central during the age of negritude and decolonization movements in the 1950s and 1960s—between Eurocentrism and Afrocentrism in the articulation of a postcolonial Caribbean culture. I end the chapter with a discussion of how the play foreshadows important developments in Glissant's thought that would not come to full fruition until decades later.

After his 1990 *Poétique de la rélation* [*Poetics of Relation*], some critics, chiefly among them Peter Hallward, expressed concern (and disapproval) of Glissant's move from critiques grounded on seemingly more political, economic, and nationalist concerns to theoretical musings inspired by a more abstract, "postmodern" perspective that regards the world as a web of related, nonessentialist multiplicities that Glissant celebrated through increasingly multiplying neologisms like "tout-monde," "chaos-monde," and many others. Although it is true that one may identify a shift of emphasis in Glissant's works, I suggest that, politically, *Monsieur Toussaint* in fact works as a template of sorts for the rest of Glissant's oeuvre, since it focuses on questions and agonistic tensions that make any definite political pronouncements unavoidably difficult, even as they remain inevitably urgent. The play ultimately proves frustrating from a *programmatic* point of view because its focus is not on a prescription on how to move forward from colonialism (although the need to do so is certainly acknowledged) but rather on how difficult it is to determine what "forward" is, when one carefully explores the complexities and pervasiveness of the coloniality of power.

Chapter 6 deals with the Colombian writer Manuel Zapata Olivella's *Changó, el gran putas* [*Changó, the Biggest Badass*] (1983). Zapata Olivella's massive novel is an epic portrayal of the ordeals and vicissitudes of the black peoples throughout many centuries, focusing on the Middle Passage and the African Diaspora in the Americas. The novel highlights diverse moments, figures, and episodes in the centuries-long struggles for black emancipation, of which the Haitian Revolution is a central chapter. What makes Zapata Olivella's text quite radical is its attempt to create a fully Afrocentric account of the challenges and achievements of black populations throughout history. All the multiple narrators in his text are either black characters or divine beings from several African pantheons. This Afrocentric approach gives its black protagonists, including those in the Haitian Revolution, a sense of *agency* in the articulation of their own histories by challenging official versions of global history that are in fact deeply invested in what Dussel calls the Eurocentric "myth of modernity." *Changó* addresses these issues by highlighting three themes that remain fundamental throughout Zapata Olivella's oeuvre. First, the need to articulate a pan-African sense of solidarity and resistance throughout the Americas, one grounded on lucid awareness of, and willingness to denounce, the racial axis that dominates the coloniality of power on a global scale. Second, the importance of myth, religion, and other traditional cultural forms of knowledge in the expression of those links of solidarity; in other words, a call for epistemological decolonization, or what

Sousa Santos calls "epistemological justice." Third, the need to open black solidarity to other forms of oppression, such as those experienced by other ethnicities like Native Americans in the Americas and those based on economic exploitation, so that racial solidarity does not become a closed exclusive discourse but rather one that remains distinct yet linked to other claims for justice. I conclude the chapter in an attempt to read Zapata Olivella's mythical frame in the novel (in his Afrocentric approach, the ordeals of black peoples are regarded as the result of a "curse" by the Yoruba god Changó) as an allegorical attempt to articulate a call for the pursuit of a never fully achievable horizon of universal emancipation that must recur to religious language in order to better express the depth of human longing for liberation. In the novel, all of the above mentioned themes find expression in diverse episodes and figures of the Haitian Revolution.

In the light of the literary works examined in the following chapters, it could be argued that the Haitian Revolution is not one event, but rather a series of events. The distinction is not trivial: those events are then structured, given unity and significance, around certain organizing models, principles, ideas and even traditional literary forms. This certainly does not mean that these writers are not committed to revealing or unveiling the "truth" about the revolution as they understand it. In fact, that commitment to historical "reality" is symptomatic in most Caribbean writers: fanciful recreations of historical events or deviations from "historical fact" for purely aesthetic reasons are not regular features in the repertoire of writers who, for the most part, view their vocation as inseparable from their political commitments.[20] But inasmuch as these writers claim to be committed to that reality, one could (at least in a limited way) apply to them the logic that Hayden White applies to formal historical writing: the forms chosen by the historian—and even more those chosen by the novelist, even a novelist committed to unveiling historical truth—are not innocent or neutral. They carry ideological and anti-ideological consequences.

Regarding historical writing, White indicates in *Metahistory*: "First the elements in the historical field are organized into a chronicle by the arrangement of the events to be dealt with in the temporal order of their occurrence; then the chronicle is organized into a story by the further arrangement of the events into the components of a "spectacle" or process of happening, which is thought to possess a discernible beginning, middle, and end. This *transformation of chronicle into story* is effected by the characterization of some events in the chronicle in terms of inaugural motifs, of others in terms of terminating motifs, and of yet others in terms of transitional motifs" (5). White's observations inform the analyses in this study. Some accounts of the revolution choose to end with the death of Toussaint, while others that prefer to begin their account with a fictionalized rendering of Dessalines' life as a slave. Still others focalize all the events from the perspective of Christophe's postrevolutionary excesses. Each of these structuring choices construes a different symbolic meaning for the events in Haiti.

In *Tropics of Discourse,* White summarizes: "Histories gain part of their explanatory effect by their success in making stories out of *mere* chronicles; and stories in turn are made out of chronicles by an operation which I have elsewhere called 'emplotment.' And by emplotment I mean simply the encodation of the facts contained in the chronicle as components of specific *kinds* of plot structures" (83). It might seem inappropriate to invoke White's comments in a discussion of literary texts. What may still sound controversial in the historiographical field, with its commitment to "objective truth," should be hardly surprising when applied to literature, which has always recreated reality without being constrained by anything but aesthetic concerns. However, as I have indicated, all of the writers treated in this study make serious historical and political claims for their representations of the Haitian Revolution: they claim to be revealing fundamental aspects of its underlying meaning and significance. Perhaps even more importantly, they claim to be highlighting the revolution's pertinence and importance for the contemporary Caribbean. This they do, as a historian would in White's account, by "emploting" the revolution in specific ways.[21]

Moreover, in the next chapters I examine works belonging to very different literary genres: fiction, essay, historiography, drama, and poetry. Some of the writers worked primordially (although never exclusively) in one genre throughout their literary careers; thus, we know Palés Matos mainly as a poet, and Alejo Carpentier mainly as a novelist. The choice of genre is particularly pertinent in the case of others, such as Césaire, who switched from poetry to theater in the 1960s in order to reach wider audiences, and Zapata Olivella, who felt compelled to push the limits of the traditional novel in *Changó,* incorporating elements of poetry and mythology into the text. In other cases, like those of Glissant and Walcott, we see writers who moved between genres throughout their careers, and although Glissant, unlike Walcott, wrote only one play in his career, the fact that he wrote a second revised version and collaborated when the play was translated into English for a second time suggests that he gave it an important place in his oeuvre.

The diversity of genres certainly influences, without ever determining, the general thrust of many of these works. Thus, it is not surprising that the novels provide us with the most sweeping panoramic, even epic portrayals of the revolution. The plays, on the other hand, highlight the intersubjective conflicts and relations of the individual actors of the historical drama. The essays, understandably, embody attempts to analytically and philosophically isolate the principles and driving forces at play in the revolution. The poems, on the other hand, attempt to synthesize the meaning of the events in Haiti in images that, at their best, encapsulate and open up for interpretation multiple layers of historical information. Ultimately, none of the works examined in this book can be reduced to general considerations about their genre: Césaire writes an essay with poetic intensity; James, as several critics have pointed out, imbues his historical narrative with the pathos of a tragedy, and Palés Matos's poems often display as much satirical wit as lyric emotion. What brings all theses writers together, in spite of the different genres, is their commitment, as Caribbean intellectuals, to the examination of the historical realities of their region.

If even historiography, with its claim to objectivity, relies on forms provided by literature, then the study of these literary representations of the revolution should prove important for a better understanding of the events that shaped the revolution, of the revolution's lingering effects throughout the Caribbean, and last but not least, of the essential role played by literature, and the arts in general, in the development of that collective self-awareness that C. L. R. James refers to in the passage that opened this introduction. In spite of their different "emplotments," all of these literary works depict the structures, institutions and mind-frames that arise from, and sustain, the coloniality of power that pervades the modern/colonial world system. Even more importantly, they also represent the persistent resistance of those whom the "colonial difference" has chained to the exterior margins of that system, and who relentlessly provide and imagine alternative actions, knowledges, and relations that may heal and liberate the fractured map of coloniality. From that perspective, these works and the Haitian Revolution that they celebrate remain of vital importance not only for the Caribbean but also for the entire globe.

Chapter 1

The Kingdom of Black Jacobins
C. L. R. James and Alejo Carpentier on the
Haitian Revolution

In his magisterial study *Caliban's Reason: Introducing Afro-Caribbean Philosophy*, Paget Henry distinguishes between what he calls *historicist* and *poeticist* schools in Caribbean philosophy. Although such categories invite deconstructive efforts and should not be regarded as mutually exclusive in a rigid way, they remain useful as general pointers of tendencies and styles of intellectual engagement within the archipelago. The historicist tradition, as its name implies, regards history and active political engagement with it (particularly colonialism, slavery, and their legacies) as the necessary sources of human reflection and action in the world. For Henry, the Trinidadian C. L. R. James is exemplary of this position. The poeticist approach does not ignore history, but it focuses on the cultural and spiritual imaginaries of Caribbean peoples, and on the poet's (the artist's) mission to articulate a vision that will capture, or point to, a full embodiment (usually in symbolic form) of the possibilities, repressed contents, and aspirations of the Caribbean psyche. An exemplary figure in this position, for Henry, would be the Guyanese novelist Wilson Harris.

Needless to say, both positions have potentialities and limitations. Among those, Henry mentions the historicist tendency to operate from models of history that have been developed in the West, and which therefore may contain colonial biases. Historicist thinkers, for example, may have little use for traditional, non-Western, "premodern" forms of thought, such as those found in ancestral African cosmologies. Thus, they may inadvertently fall into Eurocentric prejudices. Poeticist thinkers, on the other hand, in their mythopoetic endeavors may pay insufficient attention to political, social, and economic forces that have severely conditioned (if not determined) the living conditions of many of the dispossessed masses in the Caribbean.

In this chapter, I will focus on two works that for a long time have enjoyed the status of Caribbean classics, written by two authors who in many regards emblematize Henry's two philosophical schools: *The Black Jacobins* (1938; 2nd ed. 1963), the well-known historical interpretation by C. L. R. James; and the novel *El reino de este mundo* (*The Kingdom of This World*) (1949), by the Cuban Alejo Carpentier.[1] As indicated above, Henry takes James as the model for historicist thinking in the Caribbean; Carpentier is included in the poeticist school (*Caliban's Reason*, 121). Again, the contrast is not meant to simplistically reduce either writer to a single position (for, as will see below, neither remains for long within boundaries his dominant tendency). However, the differences in their approaches to roughly the same historical period (although Carpentier's novel moves further into the first years of independent Haiti) are illuminating, and indeed exemplary of Henry's distinction. In fact, James and Carpentier present their historical material from such strikingly different points of view, that when one considers the philosophical implications and the symbolic import of each account, it is not a stretch to suggest that in many ways they are not writing about the same revolution. Taken together, they dramatically illustrate the way in which the revolution has become a space wherein Caribbean intellectuals can explore issues, problems and aspirations often quite distant from, yet perfectly incarnated in, the immediate events in the island of Saint Domingue.

Evidently, the exclusions and inclusions in each writer's account of the events in Haiti, particularly with regards to the important figure of Toussaint Louverture, can be best understood as the result of each writer's emphasis on a set of problems whose urgency arises from their own individual locations and contexts within the Caribbean continuum. Carpentier draws on the revolution to explore his concept of "lo real maravilloso" ("the marvelous real"), which is part of his attempt to pose a Latin American cultural specificity that remains vital and awake to magic and creativity, as opposed to Europe's decadent rationalist civilization. In James's case, the revolution is the forerunner, and a laboratory of sorts, for future revolutionary struggles that would necessarily combine the need for class and racial emancipation.

Although it is possible to categorize James's main approach as historicist and Carpentier's as poeticist, the interest of those categories lies in our understanding (an understanding that Henry also emphasizes) that they constitute divergent responses to a *shared* set of problems with common historical roots. James's study constitutes a historiographical critique of the development of institutions and production systems that concretized Europe's global colonial hegemony, and an examination of the evolution of subaltern (particularly black) resistance to such developments. Carpentier's novel attempts to redraw an imaginary map that reincorporates subaltern (particularly black) agency to the picture of Caribbean/Latin American identity, and which links that agency to a more holistic view of the universe that European instrumental reason has rejected. In both cases, there is a need to affirm a Caribbean specificity that will also make significant *material* and *symbolic* contributions to a wider, global scene of post/anticolonial efforts. That shared concern was succinctly expressed by C. L. R. James in a 1968 lecture in which he commented on the revolts that have taken place in the Caribbean: "West Indian people . . . have been the most rebellious people in history and that is the reason. It is because being a Black man, he was made a slave; and the White man, whatever his limitations, was a free subject, a man able to do what he could in the community. That is the history of the West Indies" (*You Don't Play,* 33–34). James's words point to the common ground he shares with Carpentier in the way they highlight what Aníbal Quijano calls the "coloniality of power" and what Maldonado-Torres has elaborated as the "coloniality of being"—the racist, Eurocentric matrix of social and political relations that constructs subaltern, colonized populations as inherently, ontologically inferior to Europeans. By historically examining the manifestations of that colonial perspective, and by poetically imagining alternative liberating perspectives, both writers address a concrete case of colonialism (Saint Domingue) and the broader problem of coloniality.

Any project against that colonial matrix must go through revolt against formal, material colonialism, but must continue well beyond it, towards the dismantling of a racist imaginary that has become normative. In spite of their dramatic differences (with their respective limitations), both the historicist James and the poeticist Carpentier share a commitment to confront both colonialism as a historical system and coloniality as a historical grammar that arranged the values and structures of the modern/colonial world, even in its supposedly postcolonial manifestations.

The Revolution Minus Toussaint

In his well-known prologue to *The Kingdom of This World*, Carpentier makes sure to clarify that "I narrate a series of extraordinary events which took place in the island of Santo Domingo . . . I allow the marvelous elements to flow freely from a reality that is strictly examined in all its details" (*El reino*, 8; my translation). He then goes on to warn us that the novel, "hides, beneath its apparent atemporality, a careful corroboration of dates and chronologies" (ibid.; my translation). In spite of this, he concludes, "everything ends up being marvelous," because, "what is the history of all of America if not the chronicle of the marvelous-real?" (ibid.; my translation). What we have here is Carpentier's well-known concept of "lo real maravilloso" ("the marvelous real"), which for him not simply a literary technique or perspective (as one could argue about "realismo mágico" ["magical realism"]), but rather a characteristic of Latin American reality that his novel merely depicts.[2]

We should notice Carpentier's emphasis: he is not merely saying that the story has marvelous elements, but that the story itself, just like the very history of Latin America, is marvelous, that the miraculous constitutes its very essence. Paradoxically, the miraculous emerges as the chronicler dutifully follows the empirical method of conscientious corroboration of "dates and chronologies." This already alerts us to the political dimensions of the "marvelous real" that Carpentier will develop later in the prologue: America—its "discovery," conquest and colonization—represents for the Cuban writer the irruption of something new into world history, something "marvelous" precisely to the degree that it challenges European epistemological and ontological normativity. It is not an accident that this encounter with the new coincides with European attempts to impose its self-servingly "universal" epistemology and ontology first on that new world and then *globally* (see Mignolo, *The Idea*). For Carpentier, that futile but destructive effort (which we might describe as the expansion of the modern/colonial order) leaves Europe exhausted by the twentieth century.

In his novel, Carpentier presents Latin America as a continent of living cosmologies, where the marvelous realm of the sacred remains alive through the faith of its inhabitants, as opposed to Europe, where the arid rationalism of colonial instrumental reason has extinguished all magic and wonder. That sacred, magical realm that escapes the dry attempts of "reason" but remains perceptible to the eye of faith and belief is the "marvelous real," or the "marvelous American reality." The marvelous should not be understood here in merely supernatural or fantastic terms, even if the novel tends to highlight those manifestations. Rather, the marvelous is linked to the irruption of *excluded otherness,* as in the perspectives and agencies hidden in the underside of any reified model of reality. In order to illustrate his view throughout the novel, Carpentier recurs to a simple but effective literary device: he systematically links verifiable, historical events of the Haitian Revolution with supernatural explanations and frames, usually related to Vodou and its vision of the world. The results are quite remarkable, as Carpentier is able to skillfully sustain throughout most of his novel a dual perspective: that of the third-person omniscient narrator, who clearly does not share the "faith-based" outlook of his characters (I will return below to this important detail), and that of the rebellious slaves whose Afro-Caribbean religion shapes and articulates their experience. The result is a paradoxical tour de force whose stitches occasionally show to the attentive reader.

As an example of the narrator's ultimately dual focalization, we can point out to the episode of Mackandal's rebellion. Although carried on through the very natural means of poison (as the novel clearly states), the revolt is presented in the following way:

> Mackandal, the one-armed, now a *houngan* of the Rada rite, invested with superhuman powers as the result of his possession by the major gods on several occasions, was the Lord of Poison. Endowed with supreme authority by the Rulers of the Other Shore, he had proclaimed a crusade of extermination, chosen as he was to wipe out the whites and create a great empire of free Negroes in Santo Domingo. (*Kingdom*, 36)

In that description the novel effectively captures what we might call an *other knowledge,* grounded in the traditional African belief in communication between two worlds through spiritual possession, as expressed in the rituals of Haitian Vodou. In the novel, that worldview is fundamental in the slaves' efforts at self-emancipation. When Mackandal is finally captured and burnt alive by the French, the slaves firmly believe that he has miraculously escaped and remains with them transformed in various animals. However, the narrator dutifully informs us: "And the noise and screaming and uproar were such that few saw that Macandal, held by ten soldiers, had been thrown head first into the fire, and that a flame fed by his burning fire had drowned his last cry" (*Kingdom*, 52). Thus, Carpentier is able to present his characters' perspective (a perspective that has total faith in Mackandal's miraculous escape; in other words, a perspective that is grounded on the "marvelous real"), while keeping his distance behind the narrator who knows what "really" happened: Mackandal was captured again and burnt. Although the prologue presents the novel as a defense (a celebration even) of a Latin American marvelous-real perspective, an examination of its narrator reveals it so be more *about* the marvelous-real than written *from* that perspective (an illustrative contrasting case, as we will see in chapter 6, is Manuel Zapata Olivella's *Changó el gran putas*).[3]

I will return to this seeming paradox below, but for now I should emphasize that I do not highlight it as a criticism of Carpentier, but simply in order to clarify his position as a writer. If his dual literary strategy points to a dilemma, then it is one that Carpentier shares with many other Caribbean intellectuals. For those intellectuals, the very awareness of the differences and inequalities between their homelands and (former or current) metropolitan centers is usually a result of their being suspended between those two worlds, between the "here" and "elsewhere," as Derek Walcott has labeled it in *The Arkansas Testament*. Thus, a writer like Carpentier may sincerely show commitment to conveying and representing the worldview of the disenfranchised masses—particularly masses from across the colonial divide. Yet that writer may come in fact from a very different, more often than not privileged position, and it is in the tension between those two perspectives that the artistic work is often created.

Carpentier's emphasis on the role of the marvelous in the events in Haiti, whether his endeavor to portray it is wholly successful or not, privileges the manifestations of a view that still regards the world as sacred. Another illustrative example of the significance of his approach is the limited role he assigns to the important connections between the Saint Domingue revolt and the ideas and events of the French Revolution. C. L. R. James and Aimé Césaire, for example, privilege those ideas and events in their accounts of the revolt in Haiti. And Carpentier certainly does not ignore that dimension. For instance, when Boukman's revolt is presented in the novel, Carpentier briefly introduces the influence of the events in France on the slaves' deliberations:

> Ti Noel managed to grasp that something had happened in France, and that some very powerful gentlemen had declared that the Negroes should be given their freedom, but that the rich landowners of the Cap, who were all monarchist sons of bitches, had refused to obey them. (*Kingdom*, 66)

However, in spite of that nod to the ideas of the French Revolution, what really makes the revolt possible in Carpentier's narrative is that "a pact had been sealed between the initiated on this side of the water and the great Loas of Africa" (*Kingdom*, 66). Calling the slaves to rebellion, Boukman declares: "Our gods demand vengeance from us. They will guide our arms and give us help. Destroy the image of the white man's God who thirsts for our tears; let us listen to the cry of freedom within ourselves" (ibid., 67). Just as Carpentier claims for the whole novel, Boukman's words are based on historical accounts. But in the novel those words frame the upcoming battle as a Homeric struggle between opposing divine beings who guide their human followers. Here it should be highlighted that Carpentier is not only confronting the Christian God but also what elsewhere in the novel he calls "the goddess Reason"—two deities from whom the slaves had received little more than sustained oppression. After Boukman's invocation, a ritual in praise of Ogoun, the god of war, formally starts the revolt.

When Boukman's rebellion is defeated the novel moves with its main character, Ti Noel, to Cuba, where we are told that "the Negro found in the Spanish churches a Voodoo warmth he had never encountered in the Sulpician churches of the Cap" (*Kingdom*, 86). Ti Noel's connection of Haitian Vodou with the particular inflections of Cuban Catholicism confirms what Carpentier had already suggested in the novel's prologue: it is in the realm of the sacred (the realm of the "marvelous-real") that the Hispanic and the Francophone Caribbeans (as represented by their black populations), along with the broader Latin America, may find their common link. Ti Noel's emotions could be regarded as an example of Edouard Glissant's distinction between what he calls "langage" and "langue" (developed throughout *Le discours antillais*). By "langue," the Martinican writer refers to French, Spanish, English and the other languages of the Caribbean region. "Langage" refers to a shared sense of history, attitudes, and worldview. Thus, he claims that even when writing in French he feels closer to other Caribbean writers writing in Spanish or English than he may to a Francophone writer from France. Similarly, in Carpentier's novel Cuba's creolized Catholicism (as opposed to the highly academic Sulpician variety that had been exported to Saint Domingue) and Haitian Vodou share a similar Caribbean worldview that Ti Noel can recognize and in which he feels at home.

We can see another example of Carpentier's attempt to frame the revolution in marvelous-real terms in his unusual approach to Haiti's final war of independence, which is diametrically opposed to most other descriptions of those events. When Ti Noel travels to Cuba with his master, Carpentier interrupts his narrative in order to focus on Pauline Bonaparte, wife of general Leclerc who had been sent to San Domingo by Napoleon to reinstate slavery. We learn little about what many readers might suppose were the essential events of that period: Leclerc's military campaigns or the former slaves' resistance. Yet just before Leclerc's death of yellow fever we see Pauline attempting to heal him through the ritual remedies of her slave Solimán:

> Those conjures, and driving nails to form a cross in the trunk of a lemon tree, stirred up in her the lees of old Corsican blood, which was more akin to the living cosmogony of the Negro than to the lies of the Directory, in whose disbelief she had grown up. Now she repented of having so often made a mock of holy things to follow the fashion of the day. (*Kingdom*, 99)

With this stab at the rationalist ideas of the French Revolution the novel marks the end of French domination in Saint Domingue. Rochambeau, Leclerc's successor, is barely mentioned, and regarding the Revolution we are told that: "Now the Great Loas smiled upon the Negroes' arms. Victory went to those who had warrior gods to invoke. Ogoun Badagri guided the cold steel charges against the last redoubts of the Goddess Reason" (*Kingdom*, 103). The next section of the novel opens many years later, with Ti Noel's return to Haiti during Christophe's rule, and concerning Haiti's independence we are only informed that

> Dessalines's victory was the result of a vast coalition entered into by Loco, Petro, Ogoun Ferraille, Brise-Pimba, Caplaou-Pimba, Marinette Bois-Chèche, and all the deities of powder and fire, a coalition marked by a series of seizures of a violence so fearful that certain men had been thrown into the air or dashed against the ground by the spells. (*Kingdom*, 109)

Critics have argued extensively about the perplexing structure of Carpentier's novel, and about the meaning of his substitution of the Pauline Bonaparte episode for the main events of the Haitian Revolution, from 1794 to 1801.[4] Several meanings have been attributed to Pauline's role in the novel. Critics like Márquez Rodríguez, Mocega-González, and Volek follow Carpentier's lead, pointing to the very presence of that European princess in Haiti as a marvelous event, in keeping with the novel's overall aesthetic project.[5] Rodríguez Monegal has pointed out that she also allows Carpentier to preserve his strategy of presenting events from "marginal" perspectives: Ti Noel's in the case of Haitians; Pauline's in the case of Europeans. Donald Shaw has astutely highlighted that, coming exactly between the section of the novel that deals with the early revolutionary heroes (Mackandal and Boukman), and the section that deals with the corruption of the revolution's ideals (Christophe's kingdom), Pauline plays the role of a hinge whose corruption and frivolity indelibly interrupts what came before her and contaminates, so to speak, what comes after (*Alejo Carpentier*, 30). While the debate remains open, most of these critics agree that, in the text, Pauline's life of hedonist pleasures and remorseless privilege perfectly embodies the hypocrisy that permeates the ideals of the so-called "Age of Enlightenment." Although herself a child of the Enlightenment, Pauline also ends up recurring to the magical remedies of her slave Solimán when her husband is sick; thus, she illustrates how underneath the ironic disbelief of Rationalism, subterranean forces of magic and religion remain always ready to come to the surface in moments of crisis. From Pauline's remedies to Dessalines war of independence (won in the end by the powerful Vodou loas), Carpentier privileges a marvelous/sacred frame in which to place Haiti's reality.[6]

Ultimately, the Pauline episode ties in with two recurrent strands of Carpentier's critique of the Enlightenment's universalist claims, which we can also see in his 1962 novel *El siglo de las luces* (translated as *Explosion in a Cathedral*, although the literal translation would be precisely *The Age of Enlightenment*). In the 1962 novel, the appeal and liberating potential of enlightened ideals is more broadly acknowledged (through the young idealism of the characters Esteban and Sofía), but that very acknowledgment serves to highlight Carpentier's two critiques. First, there is a denunciation of Europe's hypocrisy during the Age of Enlightenment—the degree to which its imperialist will to power did not live up to its enlightened ideals, and often used them to justify expansion and domination. But beyond that there is also Carpentier's view of human nature, and his suspicion that the Apollonian character of the Enlightenment dangerously ignores, and therefore represses, the darker, Dionysian side of humanity. If, as Goya suggested, the sleep of Reason produces monsters, then it is also true that the relentless wakefulness of the Enlightenment's instrumental reason creates its own monsters (*El siglo de las luces* is fascinated with that quintessential enlightened invention, the guillotine), just as it ignores monsters (the darkest human passions) that it may take more than reason to control.

But the most striking aspect of *The Kingdom of This World* is not its inclusion of Pauline as an important character, or the emphasis on Vodou's influence, but rather what the novel chooses to leave out. One name in particular comes to mind, a name that most scholars would deem essential in any account of the events of the Haitian Revolution: Toussaint Louverture.[7] But Louverture is hardly even mentioned in Carpentier's novel.[8] In a 1963 interview for "Radio Televisión Francesa," Carpentier was asked: "Did you not also feel the desire to narrate the life of Toussaint Louverture, who is perhaps better known than Henri Christophe as one of the first lords of Haiti?" (*Entrevistas,* 91; my translation). The novelist answered: "Toussaint Louverture had the disadvantage of being, in my opinion, too well known as a character who had already been the topic of a series of poems, papers, even plays and novels. The character of Toussaint has been examined several times" (ibid.; my translation). Carpentier's response, while naturally valid in its own terms, remains unsatisfactory when we consider that his whole novel relies heavily on previously written texts. In fact, the third section focuses almost exclusively on Henri Christophe, possibly the one hero of the Haitian Revolution on whom as much has been written as on Toussaint. As Emma Susana Speratti-Piñero has convincingly shown, the whole novel is an extraordinary intertextual mosaic that stitches and amalgamates numerous sources, including memoirs, historical books, and even Carpentier's own 1946 essay, "La música en Cuba" (*Pasos hallados,* 63–109).[9] Thus, it seems unlikely that Carpentier would have shied away from a character simply because it had been previously used by other writers. In fact, later in his career he would write a great novel on one truly overused character, Christopher Columbus (*El arpa y la sombra* [1978]).[10] Toussaint's exclusion from *El reino de este mundo* must be related to the fact that he does not fit Carpentier's overall concept of the novel and the events portrayed therein—his marvelous-real frame— even though his absence results quite noticeable for anyone familiar with the historical events that the novel portrays. Donald Shaw tersely states that the novel omits Toussaint's struggle against Leclerc, Dessalines's triumph and regime, and Christophe's early rule, because "these are not to Carpentier's purpose, for voodoo was less relevant to them" (*Alejo Carpentier,* 30). Moreover, Shaw significantly highlights that the gap left by Toussaint and Dessalines is filled precisely by Pauline Bonaparte, a corrupting figure in the novel. In fact, turning now to C. L. R. James's book, one could argue that the whole of *The Black Jacobins,* whose subtitle is "Toussaint L'Ouverture and the San Domingo Revolution," could be fitted between parts II and III of Carpentier's novel. Thus, an examination of James's text may help us better understand the implications of Carpentier's decision to completely exclude Toussaint from his narrative.

The Revolution Minus Vodou

C. L. R. James's *The Black Jacobins* remains to this day one of the best-known and most influential accounts of the Haitian Revolution, a necessary point of reference for most later books on the subject. James's text was published in a key historical moment (1938), when Francophone negritude and Hispanophone "negrismo," closely following the developments of the Harlem Renaissance, were re-awakening interest in, and passion for, the historical and cultural dimensions of black diasporic peoples in the New World. James is also a keen, insightful analyst who excels at connecting historical events to current circumstances at the time he was writing (not coincidentally his appendix to the 1963 edition of the book was titled "From Toussaint L'Ouverture to Fidel Castro").

But in addition to those elements that have contributed to the book's endurance as a necessary source, there is one that is easy to overlook: James was an extraordinarily gifted writer, whose prose deftly moves from sweeping epic narration to philosophical reflection, from humorous asides to effective descriptions human emotions, without missing a beat in the development of his plot. His text is written with a keen eye for detail and intrigue: it reads like a good novel.[11] This is not surprising if one remembers that earlier in his career James had published a novel (*Minty Alley*) and several short stories. Arguably it is in *The Black Jacobins* that James's narrative art achieves perfection (with the more personal *Beyond a Boundary* coming as close competitor). He implicitly acknowledges as much when, describing his method as a "historian," he comments that "traditionally famous historians have been more artist than scientist: they wrote so well because they saw so little" (x). James has clearly decided to follow that model of history/storytelling as artistic endeavor.

Examples of James's literary strategies are plentiful in every page of the book. Thus, at times he does not hesitate to employ metaphors whose fiery lyricism recalls Césaire: "In a revolution, when the ceaseless slow accumulation of centuries bursts into volcanic eruption, the meteoric flares and flights above are a meaningless chaos and lend themselves to infinite caprice and romanticism unless the observer sees them always as projections of the sub-soil from which they came" (x). He may highlight details that add to the intrigue but whose provenance is uncertain, as when Rigaud returns to France and speaks to Napoleon: "He sought an interview with Bonaparte, who listened in silence to his lengthy recital, then told him, "General, I blame you for only one thing, not to have been victorious" (James, *Black Jacobins*, 234–35). (How do we know that Napoleon listened *in silence* to the whole lengthy narrative, described by James as a *recital*?) James may explicitly guess details that have not been recorded for history: "Toussaint, usually calm, was violently agitated . . . to this personal outburst he added some reflections that so hurt the conscience of the sensitive Vincent that he would not even write them down. But we can guess what they were. Bitterness at the insults and neglect which he felt were caused by his color" (ibid., 267). One may also highlight the wonderful opening pages of chapter 13, added by James to the 1963 edition of the book, in which Toussaint's downfall is compared to the structures of classical tragedy, with the masses of slaves playing the role of the classical chorus: "But not Shakespeare himself could have found such a dramatic embodiment of fate as Toussaint struggled against, Bonaparte himself; nor could the furthest imagination have envisaged the entry of the chorus, of the ex-slaves themselves, as the arbiters of their own fate" (ibid., 292).[12]

James intended his book to be not only a historical account of the events in Haiti but also an analysis of a key period in the development of European capitalism that could yield useful revolutionary lessons for his contemporary readers. The very wealth of the colonies consolidated in Europe the position and industrial development of a bourgeoisie that eventually rebelled against the privileges of the old feudal order.[13] Once the events and ideals of the French Revolution begin to circulate, their influence becomes uncontrollable. The horrors of slavery, the contradictions between such an institution and the revolutionary rhetoric, impose themselves on the diverse historical actors. The French revolutionaries understandably (and callously) hesitate to take action against an institution that has become inseparable from France's wealth. The Saint Domingue free people of color hesitate between their position of relative privilege and their desire for more rights. The slaves, evidently, did not *need* the ideals of the French Revolution in order to fight for their own freedom, but they can appropriate them now as powerful tools in their now ongoing struggle against slavery. When the French bourgeoisie tried to stop the wheel they had in fact set in motion, it was too late: the slaves had been won for the cause of liberty, equality and fraternity.[14]

Throughout *The Black Jacobins*, explicit attempts are made to connect the events of the Haitian Revolution with current events from the time when the book was written (1938). In his short preface to the 1963 edition of the book, James proudly declares: "I have retained the concluding pages which envisage and were intended to stimulate the coming emancipation of Africa. They are part of the history of our time. In 1938 only the writer and a handful of close associates thought, wrote and spoke as if the African events of the last quarter of a century were imminent" (vii). Over and over again, throughout the minutely articulated reconstruction of the Revolution, James reminds his readers that the events portrayed are not the result of blind chance, but in fact follow the dialectical laws of history. The French revolutionaries did try for a while to remain loyal to their "ideals" while also maintaining slavery, but then, as James informs us:

> And meanwhile, what of the slaves? They had heard of the revolution and had construed it in their own image: the white slaves in France had risen, and killed their masters, and were now enjoying the fruits of the earth. It was gravely inadequate in fact, but they had caught the spirit of the thing. Liberty, equality, fraternity. Before the end of 1789 there were risings in Guadeloupe and Martinique. (*Black Jacobins*, 81)

In San Domingo, those events wake up Toussaint, a former slave who could read and write, and who had had access to some of the ideas that shaped the French revolution, particularly those of the Abbé Raynal.

For James, it is Toussaint's initial ability of channel the slaves' desire for freedom that transforms him into the protagonist of the revolution:

> The individual leadership for this unique achievement was almost entirely the work of a single man—Toussaint L'Ouverture . . . Yet Toussaint did not make the revolution. It was the revolution that made Toussaint . . . Great men make history, but only such history as it is possible for them to make. Their freedom of achievement is limited by the necessities of their environment. (*Black Jacobins*, ix–x)

It is important to notice James's emphasis on the masses of the people as the most important factor in the rebellion; this was a very important concern for him, partly as a result of the disappointing developments in Russia, where the revolutionary elite had taken control of the revolution, with catastrophic results.[15] This is one point on which Carpentier certainly agreed with his Trinidadian counterpart, as we can see in his focus on a humble slave, Ti Noel, as the center of his novel's events. Those dispossessed masses give any leader his/her legitimacy, and they also bring about the leader's undoing, if he/she should ever lose touch with their needs and support.

An important question arises for us now in the context of James's attention to the dispossessed masses, which as indicated, he *shares* with Carpentier. In the political situation that James portrays, fundamentally shaped by the tidal wave of the French Revolution that Haiti's "Black Jacobins" use to their advantage, is there any role left for the cosmogonic forces of religion that play such an important role in Carpentier's description of the same period? Or does James ignore the role of such important *popular* beliefs, not unlike the way Carpentier erases Toussaint and his "enlightened" vision out of his novel? In the same way that Carpentier cannot totally dismiss the impact the French Revolution (although his acknowledgment is cursory and dismissive), James cannot totally ignore religion in his account, even if religion is clearly not a fundamental concern for him. Religious beliefs appear particularly, and not surprisingly, in reference to the figures that Carpentier privileges: Mackandal and Boukman.

Of Mackandal we are told, in an ironic tone that foreshadows James's assessment, that "he claimed to predict the future; like Mahomet he had revelations; he persuaded his followers that he was immortal and exercised such a hold over them that they considered it an honor to serve him on their knees; the handsomest women fought for the privilege of being admitted to his bed" (*Black Jacobins*, 21). Later on, James adds: "His temerity was the cause of his downfall. He went one day to a plantation, got drunk and was betrayed, and being captured was burnt alive" (ibid.). From this less than flattering description we can gather that Mackandal, although important as a forerunner of the revolution, lacked the discipline and sophistication to really channel the agitation of Haiti's "uninstructed mass" (ibid.) of slaves.

The section on Boukman is conspicuously introduced by a Vodou chant (ibid., 85) that translates as "We swear to destroy the whites and all that they possess; let us die rather than fail to keep this vow" (ibid., 18). This is the only part of the book in which James ascribes, albeit briefly, an essential role to Vodou and religious practices in the revolution. However, James is not particularly interested in the cosmogonic dimension that Carpentier admires in Vodou, or in the persistence of an *other* worldview that could only have survived as a result of the slaves' headstrong resistance to European efforts to extinguish African cultures and beliefs. James is more interested in Vodou's tactical power to elicit cohesion and solidarity among the masses:

> They had traveled a long, long way since the grandiose poisoning schemes of Mackandal ... The plan did not succeed in its entirety. But it very nearly did, and the scope and organization of this revolt shows Boukman to be the first of that line of great leaders whom the slaves were to throw up in such profusion and rapidity during the years which followed. That so vast a conspiracy was not discovered until it had actually broken out is a testimony to their solidarity. (ibid., 86)

James is certainly right. Many of the conspiracy plans were indeed transmitted through Vodou ceremonies. Contrary to Carpentier's novel, in which slave-owners despise such ceremonies and ignore their full importance (*The Kingdom*, 78–79), James's text clearly shows that the French were perfectly aware of the danger. Regarding the chant I quoted above, James tells us: "The colonists knew this song and tried to stamp it out, and the Voodoo cult with which it was linked. In vain. For over two hundred years the slaves sang it at their meetings, as the Jews in Babylon sang of Zion, and the Bantu today sing in secret the national anthem of Africa" (*Black Jacobins*, 18). As this quote suggests, James was remarkably aware of the uses of religion in political struggles, as one could only expect from a thinker deeply interested in all manifestations of popular culture, from comic strips in the United States to cricket in Britain and its colonies.[16] However, religion receives little mention in the rest of the book, and when contrasting the efforts of a less known revolutionary leader, Hyacinth, with those of Jean Francois and Biassou, the slave chiefs under whose leadership Toussaint joined the fight, James comments: "We can judge the backwardness of the western slaves at the beginning of the revolution from the fact that both Hyacinth, and another men, Romaine the prophetess (*sic*), fortified their authority with divine attributes, while Jean Francois and Biassou in the North from the very beginning aimed at a social revolution" (ibid., 108). Like Biassou and Jean Francois, James has relatively little use for religion or for traditional African/Afro-Caribbean cosmologies in *The Black Jacobins*.[17]

In fact, it is important at this point to highlight the connection between James's attitude towards religion and that of Toussaint himself (as portrayed by James). Although steeped in the ideals of the French Revolution, Toussaint was always a devout Catholic, a fact that James explicitly acknowledges. When Toussaint rose to a position political dominion over the colony, he strictly forbid the practice of Vodou. That prohibition was resented, and occasionally had disastrous effects later on, during the war against Leclerc (ibid., 309), a period during which, James admits, Toussaint slowly began to lose touch with his people.[18] James does point out Toussaint's attitude to the religion of the masses as a strategic error; however, he partially shares that view of Vodou with Toussaint, and cannot help but celebrate a vision of the revolt as a strictly social and political endeavor that has excised any religious overtones and relies exclusively on the rational language of enlightened ideals.

Two Partial Views

It may be easier to understand now why Carpentier avoids Toussaint as a character or even as an explicit reference in *The Kingdom of This World*, even though the omission leaves a noticeable gap in his narrative. As a defender of the ideals of the French Revolution, and as a devout Catholic who in fact forbids the popular practice of Vodou, Toussaint simply does not fit into Carpentier's "marvelous-real" presentation of history and the cosmos in his novel. Carpentier's skepticism with regards to the promises and achievements of enlightened rationalism (promises and achievements that, as James compellingly argues, Toussaint largely incarnates) governs the structure and emphasis of his novel. One source of Carpentier's skepticism that Toussaint certainly embodies is the attempt of certain enlightened leaders to impose their "truths" on the masses from above.

As Richard Young suggests: "An anti-Cartesian stance is not explicitly elaborated in *El reino de este mundo*. But by showing how the history of Haiti, in the Age of Reason, is determined by myth and religion, the novel illustrates the importance of irrational forces in shaping history" (*Carpentier*, 83). I agree with that assessment, but we must remember that those irrational forces include positive elements for Carpentier, like the vitality and creativity embodied in the worldview of popular faith. Reasonable Toussaint has no place in that worldview. Carpentier does not shy away from a character like Christophe, who, although initially a "Black Jacobin" himself, comes to exemplify in the novel a degree of vanity and thirst for power that does not seek "rational" justification at all. Although condemnable, Christophe's superhuman ambition and its massive embodiment, the huge "Citadel La Ferrière" that he forces his people to build, find their place in Carpentier's marvelous universe. By contrast, Jean Pierre Boyer, whose oppressive agrarian system plays an important role in the last section of the novel (a system that distributed land among peasants, but then tied them to their land and imposed production quotas), becomes an example of the use of reason itself in order to impose authority on the dispossessed, in the name of the nation's needs in an international market. Although Boyer's system appears in the novel, he does not show up as a character.

James, on the other hand, has little use for the religious dimensions of the revolution. For him Toussaint's flaw is not his reliance on enlightened ideals, but his failure to take those ideals to their natural, truly radical conclusion:

independence for Haiti. James gives religion its due as a strategic tool in the hands of slaves, but abandons it as soon as possible. The point here is not to make an abstract critique of the values of the European enlightenment as embraced by Toussaint or James, but rather to highlight James's reluctance to include in his account what Carpentier takes for granted: first, that European enlightenment often served an imperial logic by justifying the domination of those who had not yet "attained" to European "civilized" standards; and second, that certain non-Western religious beliefs (like Vodou, which mixes Western and African elements) may have played an important ideological (as opposed to merely tactical) role in the slaves' revolt.

In this regard, it is useful to remember that Carpentier had affinities and some familiarity with Marxism during the period that he wrote *The Kingdom of This World*, but those do not appear strongly or explicitly in his works except as general claims for social justice and the elimination of inequalities, particularly with regards to the impoverished black population of Cuba. Although *The Kingdom of This World* explicitly argues for the improvement of men's lives and a struggle against injustice here on the kingdom of this world (as opposed to a vague escape to an otherworldly kingdom of heaven), its historical framework, with its cyclical, almost mythical recurrences of oppression and rebellion, has little to do with Marxism (and more to do with Carpentier's interest in the ideas of Oswald Spengler). Thus, *The Kingdom of This World* might be interpreted by some critics, as Donald Shaw suggests, as pointing to a distinction between "Carpentier's earlier and later ideological outlook" (*Alejo Carpentier*, 33). Kaisary, for example, reads the novel as exemplifying "historical pessimism" in spite of its seemingly affirmative ending (*The Haitian Revolution*, 134). Later in his career, when he became an official writer of revolutionary Cuba, Carpentier moved towards the expression of more orthodox Marxist ideas in his books, and tended to evaluate his previous works as somehow already containing his later views. Those retrospective evaluations, however, remain questionable in the light of the works themselves.[19]

James and Carpentier approach the Haitian Revolution from divergent and, to a certain degree, opposite perspectives. However, one must observe that in both cases the actual textual performance creates a more complex picture than the authors presumably intended. A more complex picture, that is, of two Caribbean intellectuals coming to terms with the legacy of the Revolution as it relates to, and illuminates, their own historical and cultural contexts. For example, one could argue that Carpentier's novel, while trying to affirm the "marvelous-real" dimensions of the New World against the decadence of European civilization, in fact re-enacts a quite European brand of exoticism by depriving the slaves of San Domingo of a clearly articulated revolutionary logic. J. Michael Dash, for example, highlights the exclusion of Toussaint from the text, pointing out that as a result we are left with a novel about revolutionary Haiti "which pits decadent France against vigorous, primitivist Haiti" ("Theater," 20), thus ignoring Haiti's "radical universalism" (ibid., 19). We already saw how the narrator of the novel, while presenting the slaves' view (grounded on a marvelous-real vision of the world), remains alien to that perspective. It is certainly true that he privileges the slaves' perspective as a corrective to an Eurocentric perspective exclusively based on "enlightened" rational categories. And yet, by eliminating the facets and characters of the historical narrative that James highlights, Carpentier seems to fall into the trap of denying the Haitian slaves the very capacity for rational political action. In the novel, deities and other cosmic forces are the ultimate actors.

James's textual performance also displays paradoxical limitations. James clearly indicates Toussaint's gradual disconnection from the masses of slaves, a disconnection that eventually contributes to his downfall, as his supporters can hardly rush to his aid when they can barely understand what his plans are. Toussaint's suppression of Vodou is certainly an example of that disconnection. As James shows, it is at this point that Dessalines, a considerably less sophisticated man than Toussaint, raises to revolutionary leadership, for it is he, and not Toussaint, who can intuit what motivates the masses, and turns the struggle into one for political independence, a concept that Toussaint never considers. One might argue that, in limiting his analysis mostly to the ways in which these leaders serve as channels for the ideals of the French Revolution and as translators of the people's desire for liberty, equality and fraternity, and in neglecting other "unsophisticated" ways in which the masses may have conceptualized their own struggle, James replicates Toussaint's gesture, and mistake, of suppressing Vodou. Vodou, here, would stand for other knowledges, other subjectivities not allowed into the Eurocentric monopoly of European modernity/coloniality. In other words, James's text performs exclusion similar to the one that it criticizes (and also implicitly celebrates) in Toussaint.[20]

Just as James's text illuminates motivations and historical circumstances that Carpentier, in his program against Eurocentric reason, tends to obliterate, at this point Carpentier's novel potentially corrects James's textual performance. For *El reino de este mundo* never loses sight of the fact that the solidarity among slaves that so impresses James perhaps owed less to the ideals of the French Revolution than to a shared vision that found its expression in the rituals of Vodou (even if it can be demonstrated that the narrator does not share that faith). I am not regarding Vodou here simply as a set of religious (and therefore "irrational") beliefs opposed to French rationalist values (for, as we have seen, Carpentier does not accept the validity of that opposition: he is particularly adept at illustrating the repressed yet always manifested irrationality that underlies European "pure reason"). Rather, Vodou emerges a syncretistic religion that in fact is neither African nor European, but Caribbean, just as the Haitian slaves cannot be considered as Africans anymore, and certainly not as fully participant parts of the European modern project. They are part of that project as its margin, its colonial underside. In this case Vodou is not a less sophisticated or illogical view of the world, but *another* view of the world, quite coherent and extremely sophisticated. As Carolyn Fick indicates in her study, *The Making of Haiti: The Saint Domingue Revolution from Below:* "voodoo was indeed one of the few areas of totally autonomous activity for the African slaves. As a religion and a vital spiritual force, it was a source of psychological liberation in that it enabled them to express that self-existence they objectively recognized through their own labor . . . Voodoo further enabled the slaves to break away psychologically from the very real and concrete chains of slavery and to see themselves as independent beings; in short, it gave them a sense of human dignity and enabled them to survive" (44–45).[21]

In her book *Haiti, History, and the Gods,* Joan Dayan makes an interesting observation that has important implications for our topic. Of all the leaders of the Haitian Revolution, it is Dessalines, to whom James grants the honor of better understanding what the masses wanted at a certain point, but whom he unquestionably regards as a less sophisticated and less enlightened leader than Toussaint, it is Dessalines and not Toussaint who eventually enters the pantheon of Vodou, becoming one of the Loas or divinities of the religion (17).[22] For James, it is clear that

> Toussaint's error sprang from the very qualities that made him what he was . . . If Dessalines could see so clearly and simply, it was because the ties that bound this uneducated soldier to French civilization were of the slenderest. He saw what was under his nose so well because he saw no further. Toussaint's failure was the failure of enlightenment, not of darkness. (*Black Jacobins,* 288)

James's very choice of words—French light and civilization versus darkness—reveals the problematic nature of his bias. However, the point I want to emphasize here is not that he is wrong, but rather that Dessalines' place in the Vodou pantheon could suggest that Carpentier's presentation of the revolution may offer significant insights into the ways *common people* might have understood it, regardless of how Toussaint (and James) understood it. This does not mean that we naively attribute to Carpentier a religious faith that, as we have seen, the tone of his text clearly denies. Nevertheless, his text does struggle to display for its readers the possibility of *an Other's* way of conceptualizing the world, even though that other way is inevitably mediated by Carpentier's quite Western perspective.

An Ecocritical Detour

The Portuguese sociologist Boaventura de Sousa Santos has argued in several of his writings that "there is no global social justice without global cognitive justice" (*Another Knowledge*, xix). What Sousa Santos is pointing to is the epistemological dimension of the coloniality of power, that is to say, the fact that Europe's global imperial expansion entailed not only military and economic domination of conquered territories, but also the dismissal of the accumulated knowledges and traditions of conquered peoples as inherently barbaric and irrational, or, at best, as primitive and "premodern," and thus destined to be replaced by Western science and rationality. This view still dominates the relations between the West and most of the globe's former colonies. Sousa Santos goes on to suggest that

> the reinvention of social emancipation is premised upon replacing the "monoculture of scientific knowledge" by an "ecology of knowledges" . . . The ecology of knowledges is an invitation to the promotion of non-relativistic dialogues among knowledges, granting "equality of opportunities" to the different kinds of knowledge engaged in ever broader epistemological disputes aimed both at maximizing their respective contributions to build a more democratic and just society and at decolonizing knowledge and power. (*Another Knowledge*, xx)

We should notice that what Sousa Santos aspires to is a "non-relativistic" equality of opportunities, not to the relativistic claim that all knowledges are equally valid for everything. Of course it may be the case that in order to cure an infection, the scientific application of an antibiotic is what is called for; however, and just as an example, in the integral care of a Indigenous patient (care of a human being, not of the disease), traditional ceremonies may play a vital and palpable role. In other conditions of dis-ease those ceremonies may play the main healing role. The point is not that all non-Western forms of knowledge are equally or uncritically valid in all circumstances, but rather that in fact they have been systematically rejected or dismissed *a priori* within a "modern" political order that in fact operates on the basis of colonial/racist assumptions.²³

Sousa Santos's suggestive metaphors—the *monoculture* of scientific knowledge and an *ecology* of knowledges—bring us to the topic I want to address in this section: how Carpentier's interest in *other* knowledges, even if limited, opens his text to issues and concerns that might easily be missed from a strictly Eurocentric perspective on the Haitian Revolution. "Monoculture" is precisely the regime imposed by colonial power all throughout the Caribbean—both literally and metaphorically. And in places like Haiti it had concrete and harrowing consequences that in his novel Carpentier aptly addresses from the perspective of those who were open to a "marvelous-real" relation to the earth as a living entity, rather than as a commodity to be exploited.

As I stated above, in the text "the marvelous real" is primordially embodied in the beliefs and practices of Haitian Vodou. However, that "marvelous-real" dimension is also highlighted by the important role played by the natural world in the text—plants, trees, animals, and landscapes. This should not be surprising, given the importance that such elements play in Vodou rituals and beliefs. Ultimately, the novel presents different modes of domination and emancipation that are clearly related to different ways of thinking about the relation between human beings and their natural surroundings. In what follows, I would like to pay closer attention to those moments in which the natural world shows its central importance for the concerns of the novel.²⁴

As a young slave, Ti Noel befriends the historically based character Mackandal, whom we first meet at the plantation's sugar mill, as he "fed in sheaves of cane, pushing them bluntly head first between the iron rollers" (Carpentier, *Kingdom*, 19). Then an accident occurs: "The horse, stumbling, dropped to its knees. There came a howl so piercing and so prolonged that it reached the neighboring plantations, frightening the pigeons. Macandal's left hand been caught with the cane by the sudden tug of the rollers, which had dragged in his arm up to the shoulder. An eye of blood began to widen in the pan catching the juice" (ibid., 20–21). Macandal's accident illuminates a setting in which plants (the sugarcane), animals (the horse that moves the mill), and humans are trapped in a colonial system sustained by slavery.

Furthermore, it was a system with an ecological impact that lasts to this day. As Lisabeth Paravisini-Gebert has aptly summarized it: "Thousands of African slaves were brought to the new world with the sole aim of making it possible to produce a luxury crop for the international market in plantations that required the complete transformation of the Caribbean's tropical landscape. The Caribbean sugar plantation grew at the expense of the dense and moist tropical forests that needed to be cleared to make way for the new profitable crop. This rapid deforestation led to soil depletion, landslides, erosion, and climatic changes that included significant decreases in levels of moisture and rainfall" ("He of the Trees," 184). Haiti still has to fully recover from the ecological and social impact of the colonial plantation system.[25]

When the slave rebellion coalesces around the practices of Vodou, Mackandal emerges as the leader and "houngan," a high Vodou priest. However, it is important to emphasize that Mackandal's contact with the world of the "loa," or gods, has its "objective correlative" in his intimate knowledge of nature:

> As he watched the slow scattering of the herd grazing knee-deep in clover, he developed keen interest in the existence of certain plants to which nobody else paid attention. Stretched out in the shade of a carob tree, resting on the elbow of his sound arm, he foraged with his only hand among the familiar grasses for those spurned growths to which he had given no thought before. (Carpentier, *Kingdom*, 23)

Among those plants to which no one has paid attention before—one may paraphrase: plants that had no use in the capitalist monoculture system enveloping the island—Mackandal finds the poisonous plants that will become the key element in his rebellion. Indeed, Mackandal's historical rebellion was characterized by a wave of poisonings that terrified the colony, and led to brutal punishment from the authorities.

Mackandal also develops the power to metamorphose himself into different animals, thus evading human surveillance:

> At night in their quarters and cabins the slaves communicated to one another, with great rejoicing, the strangest news: a green lizard had warmed its back on the roof of the tobacco barn; someone had seen a night moth flying at noon; a big dog, with bristling hair, had dashed through the house, carrying off a haunch of venison; a gannet—so far from the sea—had shaken the lice from its wings over the arbor of the back patio. They all knew that the green

> lizard, the night moth, the strange dog, the incredible gannet, were nothing but disguises. As he had the power to take the shape of hoofed animal, bird, fish, or insect, Macandal continually visited the plantations of the Plaine to watch over his faithful . . . . (ibid., 41)

Infused or directed by Mackandal, nonhuman natural creatures take revenge upon the colonial masters. Mackandal's powers question—without abolishing—strict dualistic distinctions between humans and their natural environment. Moreover, the "unnatural" behavior of some of his animal disguises (e.g., a night moth flying at noon) highlights the notion that aggression against human beings (the slavery system) is often linked to aggression against the environment (the sugar plantation system as practiced in colonial Haiti).

After Mackandal is captured and executed, the rebellion he sparks spirals into a revolution that will count among its leaders figures like Toussaint Louverture and Jean Jacques Dessalines. We have already seen that Carpentier spends little or no time on these well-known heroes. However, it is characteristic of his approach that he does give us the following information:

> The day the ship Ti Noel had seen rode into the Cap, it tied up alongside another schooner coming from Martinique with a cargo of poisonous snakes which the general planned to turn loose on the Plaine so they would bite the peasants who lived in outlying cabins and who gave aid to the runaway slaves in the hills. But these snakes, creatures of Damballah, were to die without laying eggs, disappearing together with last colonists of the ancien régime. Now the Great Loas smiled upon the slaves' arms. Victory went those who had warrior gods to invoke. Ogun Badagri guided the cold steel charges against the last redoubts of the Goddess Reason. (ibid., 103)

Carpentier's novel is a critique of the Enlightenment's hypocritical deification of reason—hypocritical inasmuch as reason's modernity was constructed on its dark underside, the brutal reality of colonial domination and slavery. Thus, the novel frames victory as the result of faith in a living pantheon of gods, as opposed to the oxymoronic deification of reason's instrumental view of both nature and human beings. That pantheon of gods acts in close alliance not only with human devotees but also with nonhuman members (in this case, the snakes) of a natural world that is also a victim of a brutally exploitative system. From an ecocritical perspective, the slaves' faith implies not simply a belief in the supernatural but a different relation with nature; a belief in the sacredness of nature and in the natural dignity of all humans.

We do not get to see the culminating events of the revolution, because as readers we follow Ti Noel, who is forced to accompany his fleeing master to Cuba. Eventually, after many years Ti Noel is able to buy his freedom from a second Spanish master, and as an old man returns to Haiti, in order to die in his home island. His attachment to that home is important in the novel's vision of the environment. "Home" is the dwelling place, the concrete location of living relations invoked by the Greek *oikos* that we still find in the word *ecology*. Through generations, and in spite of the brutal conditions of their confinement, slaves managed to create affective and culturally and socially significant connections to their lands, transforming them from mere spaces of confinement into dwelling places. Following Lawrence Buell (who quotes Yi-Fu Tuan and John Agnew in his discussion), I define *place* here as distinct from, but undeniably linked to, physical space, with place being a "center of felt value" which is "inseparable from the concrete region in which it is found"; a "discrete if 'elastic' area in which settings for the constitution of social relations are located and with which people can identify" (Buell, *Future*, 63). Haiti is Ti Noel's chosen place.

However, a bitter surprise awaits Ti Noel on his return. One of the tragedies of postindependence Haiti was the inability or unwillingness of some of its leaders to abandon the modes of production and authoritarian structures of the colonial period. Ti Noel returns to the kingdom of Henri Christophe, who created a European-style court in northern Haiti. Ti Noel now possesses a heightened awareness of his connection to both the concreteness of place and the sacredness of nature, but he only finds a landscape devastated by the greed of the colonial plantation system and the ravages of war:

> Ti Noel was never alone even when he was alone. He had long since acquired the art of talking with chairs, pots, a guitar, even a cow or his own shadow. These people were merry. But around a turn in the road, plants and trees seemed to have dried up, to have become skeletons of plants and trees in earth which was no longer red and glossy, but had taken the look of dust in a cellar . . . Everything that grew here had sharp edges, thorns, briers, evil saps. (Carpentier, *Kingdom*, 108)

In conjunction with that description of environmental degradation, we inevitably find the reinstallation of a violent labor regime, where laborers who are officially not slaves work the land for the benefit of king Christophe.

It does not take too long before Ti Noel is arrested for vagrancy, and finds himself once more condemned to forced labor in spite of his age, aiding in the construction of Christophe's monstrous "Citadel La Ferrière," a fortress that the king constructed as one last defensive bastion against a possible attack from the French. The citadel is described in the novel as "that second mountain—a mountain on a mountain" (ibid., 119), a description that at once captures the victimization of Haitians forced to serve the local king just as once they were forced to serve their colonial masters, and the environmental absurdity of building a brick and stone mountain over a natural mountain. When the people eventually turn against Christophe and overthrow him, the novel's language again links human misery and misuse of the environment: "The populace that had hailed him on his arrival was sullen with evil intentions, recalling all too well, there in that fertile land, the crops lost because the men were working on the Citadel" (ibid., 136). The fact that Christophe was not entirely wrong about France's interest in recapturing the island only highlights the extent to which the human and environmental suffering of Haiti was imbricated in the global web of European imperial designs.

Ti Noel eventually leaves the construction site (he is by now too old to be of much help), and wanders back to the ruins of the old plantation were he used to live as a young slave. He returns "like the eel to the mud in which it was spawned. Back on the manor, feeling himself in a way the owner of that land whose contours were meaningful only to him, he began to clear away some of the ruins with the help of his machete" (ibid., 127–28). The image is revealing, even if there may be some idealization of the old man humbly making a living off the land with his machete, placidly engaged in conversations with animals, the elements, and inanimate objects. That land is, again, more than a space: it becomes a *place* filled with meaning. However, it is important to notice that this fleeting harmony with nature takes place in the midst of the ruins of colonial rule that serve as concrete, spatial markers of a history that cannot and indeed, should not, be ignored or forgotten.

But of course, good things can't last. Christophe's reign is followed by the reunification of the country by Jean Pierre Boyer. Two important developments mark Boyer's rule of Haiti. First, he achieves France's recognition of Haiti's independence by agreeing to pay an indemnity to the former colonial metropolis: 150 million francs (later reduced to 90 million), a debt that would grow with time and play an important role in crippling Haiti's economic development. Second, Boyer created the "rural code" whose purpose was to tie peasants to plantations as workers and forbid them to start small farms of their own. Once again, the oppression of the Haitian people took the form of repressive control of the land. In the novel, Ti Noel is horrified as he sees

Boyer's land surveyors appear, and, unable to oppose these events, he makes a momentous decision. By now his intimate contact with nature has given him the knowledge of the metamorphosis powers of Mackandal. Given that it is impossible to find justice or compassion among human beings, he decides to transform himself into an animal. First he becomes a bird, then a horse, then a bee, and then an ant. Eventually he becomes a goose, and attempts to live peacefully in a flock of geese. However, to his surprise and that of readers looking forward to a resolution of "back-to-nature" catharsis, the geese reject him. Ti Noel is perplexed at first, but then:

> Ti Noel vaguely understood that his rejection by the geese was a punishment for his cowardice. Macandal had disguised himself as an animal for years to serve men, not to abjure the world of men. It was then that the old man, resuming his human form, had a supremely lucid moment. He lived, for the space of a heartbeat, the finest moments of his life; he glimpsed once more the heroes who had revealed to him the power and the fullness of his remote African forebears, making him believe in the possible germinations the future held . . . Now he understood that a man never knows for whom he suffers and hopes. He suffers and hopes and toils for people he will never know, and who, in turn, will suffer and hope and toil for others who will not be happy either, for man always seeks happiness far beyond that which is meted out to him. But man's greatness consists in the very fact of wanting to be better than he is. In laying duties upon himself. In the Kingdom of Heaven there is no grandeur to be won, inasmuch as there all is an established hierarchy, the unknown is revealed, existence is infinite, there is no possibility of sacrifice, all is rest and joy. For this reason, bowed down by suffering and duties, beautiful in the midst of his misery, capable of loving in the face of afflictions and trials, man finds his greatness, his fullest measure, only in the Kingdom of This World. (Carpentier, *Kingdom*, 184–85)

One should not interpret that justly famous exposition of the novel's humanistic credo as abandonment of its focus on nature and the environment, but rather as an attempt to discard naïve or romantic notions about the relation between humans and nature. Ti Noel cannot become a goose, as humans cannot turn their back on centuries of a distinct evolutionary path that puts them in quite a unique position with regards to their relation to nature. The novel seems to suggest that it is in fact quite impossible to "think like a mountain," as land ethic pioneer Aldo Leopold invited us to do, as useful and ennobling as the exercise might be. But even more important is Ti

Noel's insight that the struggle for justice among humans cannot be separated from the struggle for a more harmonious and sustainable relation with nature, and that both endeavors preclude shortsighted goals based on instant gratification.

After that realization Ti Noel can finally die in peace, and the novel's last image is one of ecological recycling of life. After "his declaration of war against the new masters" (ibid., 185), ordering his subjects (the forces and creatures of nature) to march in battle against "the insolent works of the mulattoes in power" (ibid.), we are told how the wind and the rain make the ruins of the old plantation to tumble down, and "from that moment Ti Noel was never seen again . . . except perhaps by that wet vulture who turns every death to his own benefit and who sat with outspread wings, drying himself in the sun, a cross of feathers which finally folded itself up and flew off into the thick shade of Bois Caiman" (ibid., 185–86). With the image of the cross-shaped vulture the connection between nature and the sacred is once again emphasized.

At the end of the novel, with the image of the vulture allowing for a "return to nature" of a Ti Noel fully energized in his willingness to combat oppression, two trends that are arguably inseparable but which are often distinguished in contemporary ecocriticism come together: on the one hand, ecocentrism, with nature and the protection of its bio- and geonetworks and nonhuman creatures as the priority, and on the other hand, environmental justice for oppressed populations.

The Kingdom of This World was written before the full rise of ecocriticism and environmentalism in their contemporary forms. It still works within a firm dualistic, binary, and possibly anthropocentric frame (human-nature; civilization-wilderness) that would actually come to fruition in Carpentier's following important novel, *Los pasos perdidos* [*The Lost Steps*] (1953). While the 1953 novel burns with nostalgia for a lost natural paradise that humans have irretrievably lost, the more historically grounded *Kingdom of this World* shows the human and natural world perpetually linked to each other, each interlaced with the other, without fully losing distinct contours.[26] One might also find serious limitations from ecofeminist perspective, given the limited and mostly negative role played by women in the narrative. But the novel is remarkable in its foregrounding of the natural environment as a participant—often the victim—of the dramas of human history. That vision of nature is brought to life through a foregrounding of Vodou's view of the cosmos, as opposed to the instrumental approach of colonial reason. If we think about Haiti's (and the Caribbean's) contemporary environmental problems, many of them rooted in the historical processes that Carpentier describes, the novel remains enormously pertinent to today's ecological awareness.

An Unusual View of Liberty

The differences between James and Carpentier, revealing as they are of each author's particular approach and priorities, should not make us forget what they have in common, a common element that, paradoxically, is at the origin of their differences. What both writers share is that for them Haiti works synecdochally, as a part of a larger whole that exemplifies the issues and dynamics of the total struggle. If we stay at the surface level of each work, we notice that although Carpentier's novel is missing precisely those aspects of the revolution that James focuses on, it is difficult to simply read the works as merely complementing each other. Each one seems to make exclusive claims for the whole that it takes the Haitian Revolution to be a part of. It is important to acknowledge those differences in our understanding of their unique approaches to the revolution. However, it is certainly possible to also recognize that both writers are responding to similar historical circumstances that each frames differently. That recognition results in a more nuanced appreciation of their shared concerns and different strategies.

As we have seen, Carpentier's efforts have to do with cultural self-affirmation and the defense of a Latin American view of the world vis-à-vis Europe's dominant, and for Carpentier decadent vision. In the novel's prologue, Carpentier poses his position mainly in aesthetic terms (opposing "lo real maravilloso" to European surrealism), but evidently it is a struggle with deeply rooted political dimensions. Moreover, in his insistence on applying his Caribbean observations to all of Latin America, as well as in his strategic politicization of the cultural originality of those formerly colonial regions, Carpentier is following the lead of his fellow Cuban writer and revolutionary José Martí, as expressed in the seminal essay "Nuestra América" ["Our America"] (1891). One could argue that Martí's well-known sweeping *Latin Americanist* approach to the political and cultural affairs of the Spanish speaking countries of the continent arose precisely as a result of his *particularly Cuban* (or Caribbean) experience of protracted colonialism. It is from the perspective of this lack of sociohistorical continuity between the Caribbean and the rest of the continent (which obtained its independence from Spain within the first quarter of the nineteenth century) that Martí was able to locate hidden lines of actual, or potential, continuity between the two. Those hidden lines of continuity move in two directions. First and foremost, Martí was concerned about the United States' (neo)colonial interest in Cuba and Puerto Rico, and felt that the rest of Spanish America should be on its guard against possible aggressions from the "formidable neighbor" from the North (Martí, *Selected Writings,* 295). Additionally, Martí saw in the domestic political turmoil in many of the relatively young Spanish American nations a clear warning for the leaders of the future Cuban nation.

Similarly, from the perspective of Haiti and Cuba, which were still struggling during the first half of the twentieth century to find true autonomy with regards to U.S. commercial and military interests, the marvelous real becomes for Carpentier not only a declaration of Latin American independence from European and North American imperial designs (whether cultural or political), but also the perspective from which the dispossessed masses (like Ti Noel) marked by the colonial difference can keep their faith in combating local and global oppression against all odds. Carpentier himself had been involved in local political activities against the Cuban dictator Machado. Although it is true that careful attention to the novel's narrative strategies reveals Carpentier's actual distance from the world he is describing, I would argue that one could make the case that the text does display true nostalgia for that faith that makes the miraculous possible. What saves the novel from exoticist primitivism is its steadfast focus on the ever renewed need to engage in struggle against the coloniality of power, which may operate through *both* Napoleon *and* Henri Christophe—there is no essentialist idealization of the Haitian against the European here. The novel's praise is not for Vodou merely because it is different from Western rationalism: its praise is for the spirit to combat a colonial logic that condemns all knowledge not anchored in Western rationality as primitive rubbish. In the Caribbean, the promise and aspirations of Haiti's slave revolution—which were aided by Vodou's cosmogonic vision—provide a compelling example of a decolonizing project that remains incomplete to this day.

James's Marxist reading of the revolution illuminates equally important aspects of it. As part of his effort to delineate the conditions of possibility for a world revolution, James is particularly interested in the need to dialectically take advantage of any inherent contradictions in the power structures of capitalism. This is what the Saint Domingue slaves do, as they ride the tidal wave of bourgeois discontent during the French Revolution, pushing it to limits that France could not foresee or, for a long time, accept. Moreover, James is pushing the limits of traditional Marxism itself, since his discussion of the events in Haiti shows his commitment to add to the category of class the problem of race and racism. In so doing, he highlights the essential place race has occupied in the development of European colonialism and the imperial hegemony of Eurocentric global capitalism.[27]

Here one should highlight the full implications of James's expansion of orthodox Marxism in his approach to the Haitian Revolution (in spite of his continued allegiance to a Marxist vision). James goes well beyond simply indicating that race, as a category of oppression, requires attention on its own, its own place within the Marxist revolutionary agenda. What he is actually emphasizing is that modern forms of colonial domination, from military occupation of territories to economic control of their means of production (the development of global capitalism being inseparable from Europe's colonial expansion), operate through a matrix of essentialist Eurocentric concepts, beliefs and assumptions that revolve around the *modern* category of race. In other words, one may consider James a precursor of Aníbal Quijano's insights on "the coloniality of power," as the Peruvian sociologist defines it.

James's ideas on this issue are best appreciated in a series of talks he offered in Montreal in 1968, where he insisted on *The Black Jacobins,* "I wrote it. But it is only in late years that I am able to understand and to appreciate the full significance of what I wrote in the book" (*You Don't Play,* 35). In the same lecture, James states:

> When West Indians reach a certain stage, they wish to make a complete change, and that is because all of us come from abroad. Liberty means something to us that is very unusual. There were many generations of slaves in Africa, of that we are quite sure. And in Africa they took it and no doubt fought against it at certain times. But when we made the Middle Passage and came to the Caribbean, we went straight into a modern industry—and sugar plantation—and there we saw that to be a slave was the result of our being black. A white man was not a slave. The West Indian slave was not accustomed to that kind of slavery in Africa; and, therefore, in the history of the West Indies, there is one dominant fact, and that is the desire—sometimes expressed, sometimes unexpressed, but always there—the desire for liberty; the riddling oneself of the particular burden which is the special inheritance of the black skin. *If you don't know that about West Indian people, you know nothing about them* . . . It is because being a Black man, he was made a slave, and the White man, whatever his limitations, was a free subject, a man able to do what he could in the community. That is the history of the West Indies. (ibid., 33–34; James's emphasis)

What James describes in this quote is nothing less than the coloniality of power as experienced by the black Caribbean masses, and the coloniality of being that Maldonado-Torres describes as the ontological logic of the modern European imperial self. Liberty means something "very unusual" in this context, in that it is not *limited* to overcoming an immediate constraint on one's physical freedom (as in the resistance of slaves in Africa in James's example, or the maroon flight to the mountains across the Caribbean), the formal abolition of an oppressive institution (as in the abolition of slavery), or even a formal break of ties with a metropolitan center in order to achieve full sovereignty (as in a declaration of political independence). Even when those three steps are taken (and they were in Haiti), the black Caribbean man (and woman) has to face the fact his slavery (and beyond slavery, his oppression) comes from the fact of his "being a Black man" (or woman). Again, this is not a denial of other historical dimensions of slavery as an institution, but rather an acknowledgment of an essentialist, racist, Eurocentric logic that underlies those historical events, a logic that has produced knowledges, methodologies and imaginaries that have served well the *modern* global hegemony of European (and then U.S.) expansionism, well beyond slavery as an institution. In a Fanonian twist to his Marxism, what James comes to "appreciate" in his late rereading of *The Black Jacobins* is that the Haitian Revolution and its aftermaths confront us not only with a striking moment in the history of global resistances to the excesses of capitalism, but also with "the lived of experience of the black man," as Fanon famously calls it in *Black Skins*. That experience, naturally, is not presented by James (or Fanon) as an essentialist abstraction, but as constructed by a colonial logic in which the black man's (and woman's) very *humanity* is in question. That is to say, what is in question, as James's words make clear, is the one thing white men take for granted no matter what their social position or their limitations (particularly, we can add, after the liberating humanism of foundational Enlightenment documents like the *Declaration of the Rights of Man and of the Citizen*).

From their poeticist and historicist perspectives, both Carpentier and James address that "unusual" concept of liberty that James refers to. This observation is not meant to reduce both writers to a single position, but rather to highlight an issue that neither can avoid as they deal with Haiti and its place in Caribbean history. James's main thrust is still Marxist, with its emphasis on the analysis of Capitalist modes of production; Carpentier's main interests lie in the realm of arts and culture, to the point that most of his writings include an implicit celebration of the creolized artistic forms that were developed in the Americas as a result of the confluence of so many different peoples, in spite of his clear critique of the violence of that process. But both writers are lucid enough to recognize Haiti—and by extension the Caribbean—as a particularly revealing site of the operation of the coloniality of power and the coloniality of being. What Toussaint does not fully understand (or what he is not willing to acknowledge) in James's text is Ti Noel's Vodou-inflected claim in Carpentier's novel. However, James himself perfectly and clearly articulates that claim in his 1968 lecture: abolition of slavery and independence for Haiti are necessary, yes, but it is also necessary to achieve freedom from a racist/Eurocentric logic in which Ti Noel's black skin "overdetermines from without," as Fanon would put it, his (lack of) dignity as a human being, including the worth of his worldview and religion. That racist/Eurocentric logic evidently operates though the French colonists, but also through Henri Christophe, and through Toussaint's and Boyer's attempts to mold Haiti to the needs of Europe's sugar market. Ultimately, it is James's poeticism that allows him to clearly point out the tragic nature of Toussaint's shortsightedness, and Carpentier's historicism that exposes the politically urgent character of Latin America's "marvelous-real" dimension. In both visions, Haiti and its revolution become a cautionary tale and an inspiring parable about coloniality (of power, of knowledge, of being), about its perverse and pervasive logic, and about the ever-persistent resistances to it.

Chapter 2

Between Mackandal and Tembandumba
Luis Palés Matos's Haitian Poems

Black Puerto Ricans

In 1980, the Puerto Rican writer José Luis González caused commotion in Puerto Rico's intellectual circles when he published his now classic, albeit still controversial, essay "El país de cuatro pisos" ["Puerto Rico: the Four-Storeyed Country"].[1] The essay, with others that composed the volume, attempted to define and clarify the issue of the island's national identity by paying attention to an often overlooked, if not repressed aspect of it: race. González's position, resulting from his examination of the role of slaves in the island during the colonial period, was in a nutshell:

> It is because of this that I believe, as I have said on various occasions to the embarrassment and irritation of some, that the first Puerto Ricans were in fact *black* Puerto Ricans. I am not claiming, needless to say, that these first Puerto Ricans had any idea of a "national homeland," for in fact *no one* at that time in Puerto Rico entertained, or could have entertained, such an idea. What I *am* claiming is that it was the blacks, the people bound most closely to the territory which they inhabited (they were after all slaves), who had the greatest difficulty in imagining any other place to live. (*Puerto Rico*, 10)

A corollary of González's argument is that Puerto Rican culture, as expressed in its popular manifestations from the ground up (as opposed to its portrayal by Puerto Rican elites throughout the nineteenth and the twentieth centuries), is fundamentally Afro-Caribbean in character. González is not trying to deny the multiplicity of elements from diverse cultures that have come together to give shape to what we might identify as Puerto Rican culture (although he *is* trying to give a privileged place to Puerto Rico's African legacy within that multiplicity). However, he does challenge a generalized view of Puerto Rico in which its culture is fundamentally Hispanic (that is, derived from Spain) and emblematized in the idealized portrayal of the old plantations with paternal *hacendados* [land-owners] taking care of an idyllic world built on the labor of mainly white *jíbaros* [peasants]. That view can be traced from nineteenth-century foundational works such as Manuel Alonso's *El gíbaro* (1849), through classics like Manuel Zeno Gandía's *La charca* (1894), up to the anticolonial but nostalgic works of René Marqués, such as *La carreta* (1951) and *La víspera del hombre* (1959).[2] It would not be until later in the twentieth century that such restricted (and often programmatically restrictive) views of Puerto Rican identity would be challenged by younger generations of writers, who often had to deal with the fierce resistance of writers from the older generation, such as Marqués himself (see Gelpí, *Literatura*).

González's arguments were challenged not only by the predictable reactionary perspective that indeed would attempt to deny Puerto Rico's deep links to the broader Afro-Caribbean experience but also by more sympathetic readers who nonetheless questioned González's methodology, or his seemingly harsh criticism of traditionally venerated figures such as nationalist leader Pedro Albizu Campos.[3] What seems undeniable is that González tapped into a problem that in fact has provoked deep anxiety among Puerto Rican intellectuals ever since the very idea of a Puerto Rican "national identity" began to be discussed: Puerto Rico's African roots (the issue of racial mixing plays an important role, for example, in Alejandro Tapia y Rivera's foundational play, *La cuarterona* [1867], even though Tapia y Rivera has its plot take place in Cuba). Possibly the best known expression of the national intelligentsia's dismissal of that African dimension is Antonio Pedreira's *Insularismo,* the classic early-twentieth-century essay that dismisses all influences on Puerto Rico's culture other than the Hispanic one.[4] A lesser known example that gives an idea of how pervasive Pedreira's views were among Puerto Rico's intellectuals is Tomás Blanco, who in fact did not see eye to eye with Pedreira on some issues, but who felt perfectly comfortable writing in the misleadingly titled *El prejuicio racial en Puerto Rico* [*Racial Prejudice in Puerto Rico*]: "The people of Puerto Rico live within the general norms of Western Culture. Although the mixture of blacks and whites is considerable, the African element has only had a very light influence on Puerto Rico's cultural traits. The prejudices one can find in the island are those shared by the white race in general . . . Racial prejudice, as it is understood in the United States, does not exist" (138; my translation). Arguing that there are no lynchings or actual segregation laws as in the American South (Blanco published his book in 1942), Blanco proceeds to dismiss the impact of black culture in Puerto Rico, recurring to a myth of racial democracy that resembles in some ways Gilberto Freyre's similar argument for Brazil.

It is not my intention here to argue Blanco's and Pedreira's discredited views, but rather to point out that those views were in fact pervasive throughout the twentieth century (and arguably still exert their influence on the twenty-first), and that it is against those views that González writes *El país de cuatro pisos.*[5] In the second essay of his volume, titled "Literature and National Identity in Puerto Rico," González mentions several writers who, in his view, constitute exceptions in at least trying to acknowledge the importance of the Afro-Caribbean element in Puerto Rican culture.

Among those writers, not surprisingly, the poet Luis Palés Matos occupies a privileged place. Regarding him, González indicates:

> The path followed by this great poet from "Pueblo negro" to "Mulata Antilla," or rather, the progressive refinement, without precedent in Puerto Rican literature, of a conception of the national genetics, is a path of unique and definitive discovery into the Afro-Antillean roots of our identity as a people. The unprecedented virulence of the attacks on Palés Matos's theme of *negrismo* (negritude) voiced by many of the then outstanding representatives of *criollismo* and literary "avant-gardism"—J. I. de Diego Padró, José Antonio Dávila, Graciany Miranda Archilla, and others—is yet one further example of how the Puerto Rican cultural elite was increasingly reluctant to face the problem of national identity from an unprejudiced and realistic perspective. (*Puerto Rico*, 62)

If I have begun this chapter with González's placing of Palés Matos in the context of Puerto Rico's conflictive relation to its own Afro-Caribbean legacy, it is because González's is indeed a lucid and classic presentation of the social, political and cultural milieu from which Palés Matos arose as an important poet. I agree with González's general assessment of the context in which Palés Matos wrote and with his opinion that Palés Matos's achievement has no real precedent in Puerto Rican letters, so that its importance cannot be overstated. However, as I will elaborate below, it is also clear that Palés Matos did not write from an unbiased acceptance of Puerto Rico's African heritage. As I will demonstrate, what marks Palés Matos's poetry is his own ambiguity towards his material, which causes him to embrace yet at the same time distance himself from the Afro-Caribbean realities that his poetry so vividly portrays. Palés Matos's poetry stands in paradoxical, often agonistic relation to the social and cultural crucible from which it arises, as it both challenges and reflects that crucible. As we will examine, nowhere do we see Palés Matos's ambivalence more clearly than in his approach to the Haitian Revolution, which plays a central role in several of his poems. That the events in Haiti play such an important role at all in the writings of a Puerto Rican writer immediately places him apart from the other writers of his generation—only in the last decades of the twentieth century (since the 1980s) did the non-Hispanic Caribbean begin to play an important role in Puerto Rican literature, in the works of writers like Ana Lydia Vega, Mayra Montero, and Mayra Santos Febres. And yet Palés Matos's pioneering work remains problematic and ultimately ambivalent.

Luis Palés Matos's classic book, *Tuntún de pasa y grifería* (1937; rev. ed. 1950), is rightly considered one of the classic foundational texts of Afro-Caribbean poetry in Spanish.[6] That poetic current, often called "negrismo" in Spanish, has encountered both defenders and detractors throughout the years. Palés Matos, in particular, has been the site of numerous conflictive readings. His poems generated a great deal of resistance in the 1920s and 1930s among a Puerto Rican intellectual elite that rejected them as "authentic" Puerto Rican poetry, yet also celebrated their aesthetic achievement (see, for example, Diego Padró). But there have also been criticisms from more progressive perspectives that in fact object to Palés Matos's often stereotypical, somewhat flat representation of blacks in the Caribbean, which seemingly reduces them to exotic, dancing figures without much depth or historical density (see Johnson, *Devil*; and Zenón Cruz, *Narciso*). A figure often invoked to provide contrast with Palés Matos is the Cuban Nicolás Guillén, who very early became the emblematic figure of a politically committed Afro-Caribbean poetry that takes into account the sociohistorical struggles of Cuba's black populations. The fact that Palés Matos was a white poet whereas Guillén was a man of color has certainly influenced those readings (see González Pérez, "Ballad of Two Poets"). To these assessments we must add Palés Matos's persistent sexualization of the black world, which the novelist Mayra Santos Febres has highlighted (*Sobre piel*, 153): in Palés Matos's poetry, islands are often women of color who dance and entice both tourists and colonialists, and are portrayed in such a way that often both oppressors and defenders relate to them as feminine objects of desire that must be either possessed or defended. On the other side of the spectrum we find celebratory readings of Palés Matos, both as a writer committed to the defense of Puerto Rico's national identity from an Afro-Caribbean perspective (Díaz-Quiñones, *El almuerzo*), and as ludic ironist that celebrates Puerto Rico's heterogeneous, postmodern *avant la lettre* mixture of cultures and peoples, which cannot be reduced to any one single, coherent narrative of the nation (Ríos Avila, *La raza*).[7]

Not surprisingly, there is much truth in *all* of the conflictive readings of Palés Matos described above, and they all capture important aspects of Palés Matos's personality as a writer and cultural signifier. However, those multiple conflictive sides cannot be simply smoothed out and made to fit together in a fully coherent, albeit ironic poetic subject. Palés Matos remains a composite, multifarious figure whose different sides always remain in conflict with each other, while insisting on not letting go of each other. Although it is certainly true that Palés Matos fully opened the doors of Puerto Rican literature to an Afro-Caribbean realm that many strove to keep out, the poet often comes across as stubbornly trying to keep his distance from the very realm that his poems so masterfully articulate. It is also true that, in contrast with Guillén's more populist poetry, Palés Matos's is more baroque in its inflections, insisting on rhythms and sonorities whose exoticizing effect may result "distracting" for readers looking for more programmatic political positions in his poems.[8] Palés Matos's well-known irony mocks not only the traditional centers and representatives of colonial power but also those whom many would regard as the victims of those colonial practices. All the while, the poetic voice often remains subtly aloof from all sides of the conflict.[9]

However, of all the attacks against Palés Matos's poetry, there is one that can be dismissed as inaccurate with relative ease: the notion that Palés Matos only deals with an abstract, ahistorical construction of blackness. Nicolás Guillén himself declared in an interview: "In Palés Matos, what emerges is a black, how can I put it, a superficial black, a black without any human problems at all . . . his position toward life was really limited, and he was satisfied with the rhythmic thing, which, by the way, is really beautiful, there is no doubt, but he did not go any deeper than that" (Prescott, "Conversation," 353).[10] As a matter of fact, even if one disagrees with Palés

Matos's sometimes clearly Eurocentric perspective, Caribbean history does play a fundamental role in his poetry, particularly as he examines the effects of the protracted colonialism that Puerto Rico and many of its neighboring islands still endured when Palés Matos was writing. It is true that many of his poems are not explicitly *about* history, but most of them are full of symbolic images, figures, and locations that clearly point toward that mostly conflictive history: sugar mills, pirates and smugglers, impoverished black towns, Afro-Caribbean religious ceremonies, and the often ominous, sometimes slightly ridiculous presence of European and North American interests. In this context, it is notable but not surprising that there is one foundational historical event that shows up both directly and indirectly in several of the poems of *Tuntún de pasa y grifería:* the Haitian Revolution.

Revolt in the Midst of Dancing

Before examining Palés Matos's main "Haitian" works, "Elegía del duque de la Mermelada" and "Lagarto verde," we must take a look at "Canción festiva para ser llorada" ["Festive Song to Be Wept"], in which Haiti for the first time appears as an important component of one of his poems. "Canción festiva" is one Palés Matos's great works, one in which his creolized ironic vision of the Caribbean comes to full fruition, as expressed in its recurring refrain—"Cuba—ñañigo y bachata / Haití—vodú y calabaza / Puerto Rico—burundanga" (543) ["Cuba—ñañigos and celebration / Haiti—Vodou and calabash / Puerto Rico—a hodgepodge" (my translation)]. The poem locates Puerto Rico and Cuba in the broader multilingual Caribbean with Haiti, as opposed to the traditional nineteenth-century affiliation of Puerto Rico with only the other Spanish speaking islands, Cuba and Dominican Republic. In case any doubt remains, the rest of the poem makes sure to include other Francophone and Anglophone islands such as Martinique, Guadeloupe, St. Kitts, and Jamaica.

As is often the case with Palés Matos, the very words that he uses to emblematize the islands are ambiguous in their irony: is the poet celebrating the elements that characterize the islands, or is he mocking them? Is "burundanga" (a local term referring to a heterogeneous, disorderly mix) a bad or a good thing? Characteristically, the reader cannot come to a final answer, because Palés Matos keeps his ironic distance in the midst of his celebration: his humor cuts both ways. The poem puts to rest (as do most of his poems, in any case) the myth of a Palés Matos oblivious to the historical and political realities of the Caribbean. With biting satire, the poem refers to:

> Antillean island, thick steam
> of curdled sugar cane juice.
> Constant work of the sugar-mill.
> Turkish bath of sugar cane molasses.
> Aristocracy dressed in cotton,
> whose life slides by
> among custard phrases
> and succulent metaphors.
> Stylized coasts
> tended to by sickly palm trees.
> Soft and dripping language—
> *mamey, cacao, guanábana*—
> Babbitt the tourist traps you
> as a black boy and a coconut tree;
> Sensual Tartarin dreams about you
> in your parrot and your mulatto woman . . .
>   (Palés Matos, "Canción festiva," 547; my translation)

A whole history of colonial domination is contained in these lines' images: the syrupy boiling cane juice and the sugar production machines; the presence of Europe (Tartarin) and the United States (Babbitt) as both plantation capital and tourism; and the local "aristocracy" that recalls V. S. Naipaul's notion of "mimic men," colonial subjects whom the poet mocks for their presumed inability to think creatively, and condemns for their blind imitation of the forms imposed on them by the colonial system. All of those elements are presented through the very "succulent metaphors" that the poem self-referentially evokes. In the midst of that Caribbean that the poet clinically dissects, playfully chides, and both embraces and rejects with the same poetic gesture, Haiti with its revolution will play a central role.

The first mention of Haiti is openly satirical; the poetic voice states, directly addressing the Francophone islands in an apostrophe: "In French style I slide / over your mulatto flesh / since, for lack of bread, your cake / is dark Antillean glory. / I will bring you from Haiti / a consul from the aristocracy: / the Count of Ring-in-Ear, / the Duke of Marmalade" (543; my translation). In my discussion of the book's two main "Haitian poems" in the next section, I will return to the topic of these "mimic men," Haiti's postrevolutionary aristocracy (mainly during the kingship of Henri Christophe), and of Palés Matos's problematic attitude toward them. Here the presence of the Count and the Duke is mainly the object of the poet's caricature, with the "ring in the ear" offering a primitivist image that counteracts the count's attempt to imitate the European aristocracy. After that mocking allusion to Haiti's nobility under Christophe, "Canción festiva" shifts its focus toward the actual slave rebellion:

> Mackandal beats his drum
> in the wrathful Haitian night.
> Ivory teeth gleam
> in the darkness.
> Hostile strange forms
> creep in between the trees,
> and Haiti, fierce and enigmatic,
> boils like a threat.
> It is Vodou. The tremendous
> hour of the zombie and the frog.
> Over the sugar-cane fields
> the spirits are at work.
> Ogun Badagri, in the shadows,
> sharpens his black dagger.
> —Tomorrow the little master ("el amito")
> will wear the best tie—
> Dessalines shouts: Blood!
> L'Ouverture roars: Revenge!
> while remote, hidden
> in the deep forest,
> Mackandal beats his drum
> in the wrathful Haitian night.
>   (Palés Matos, "Canción festiva," 546–47; my translation)

As a poet whose roots drink from the symbolist wells of Spanish American *modernismo*, Palés Matos gives prominence to images and metaphors: the white teeth gleaming in the dark of night (which hides the dark faces), the sound of drums, sinuous shadows advancing from between the trees, and zombies and Vodou spirits.[11] These are the kinds of details that have earned Palés Matos the reputation of focusing almost exclusively on the picturesque or exotic elements of Afro-Caribbean culture. However, Palés Matos places those details within an implicit narrative that does not shy away from foregrounding the seriousness of the events: with dark humor the poet tells us that tomorrow the master will have "the best of ties": a cut throat. Some of the main protagonists of the events (Mackandal, L'Overture, Dessalines) are explicitly identified, while the undeniable role of Vodou in framing the events in Haiti is given prominence. By condensing the events of the revolution in a few images that brood with strangeness, a sense of dread and the imminence of violent bloodshed, Palés Matos is able to convey the collapse of a system that took itself not only as fair but also as part of the natural order of things. In that context, it is significant that the emotions that dominate in the lines quoted above (fear, dread, anxiety) are emotions the white elite ("el amito") would have felt, both in Haiti and in the surrounding islands (see Geggus, *The Impact;* and Popkin, *Facing Racial Revolution*). They are not primordially the emotions of the slaves, who were fighting for their freedom and perfectly at ease with their own Vodou gods and rituals. One might find fault with Palés Matos's approach, and the question is one that comes up repeatedly as one reads his "Haitian poems:" they are *about* the revolution, but from *whose* perspective are they written? The answer is not always clear. However, in a poem like "Canción festiva" the ambiguous choice of focalization in fact allows for a compelling portrayal of the destruction of an order of things, precisely because the poem highlights the emotions of those who have most cynically benefited from it and have the most to lose from its demise.

Taken in the context of the whole poem, the Haitian section of "Canción festiva para ser llorada" stands out as a significant instance of successful Antillean revolt—a revolt that in fact contrasts with Palés Matos's dominant pessimism and skepticism regarding the political future of the islands. The poem begins, like others of Palés Matos, in a playful mood: the diverse Caribbean islands are convoked for a dance, each island's description filled with metaphorical images. However, the allusions to sugar and its derivatives, like rum, inevitably place the poem—and the archipelago—in the context of the imperial occupations that have dominated its history. We also find a reference to the region's hurricanes, and two mentions of Babbitt, Sinclair Lewis's emblematic figure of the North American ethos of conformity and capitalist self-aggrandizement without much regard for ethics. After the Haiti segment, the poem ends with the first section I quoted, with the islands steeped in sugar cane molasses and in the grasp of both Babbitt and Tartarin (hero of Alphonse Daudet's homonymous novel, who leaves his sedentary French village in order to look for "adventures" in a colonial, Orientalist Algiers), who are assisted by the local "aristocracia de dril" ["cotton-clad aristocracy"]. Thus, as is in fact often the case in Palés Matos, the festivities and the dance of "Canción festiva para ser llorada" hardly hide an undertow of political despair paired with accumulating rebelliousness.

In that regard, it is useful to remember that the Puerto Rico in which Palés Matos originally wrote the poem in 1929 (it was published in several magazines before its inclusion in *Tuntún* in 1937) shared with much of the rest of the Caribbean very similar conditions of poverty and dispossession that are linked to traditional colonial domination. The Puerto Rico of 1950, when the book's second edition appeared, was in rapid transformation, but it was still more similar than not to the rest of the region. The second half of the twentieth century would increase the political and economic distance between the islands as they moved toward different political formulas (from Puerto Rico's "Commonwealth," to the French Caribbean's "overseas department" status, to Cuba's socialism). Those differences better hid persistent neocolonial practices and continued dependence on European and North American metropolitan centers.

From that perspective, the Haiti section of the poem shines as an example of Caribbean revolt, and successful revolt at that. That dimension of the poem cannot be denied, even though, as we have seen, the poet is not quite able, or willing, to look at the Haitian Revolution *from* the perspective of the triumph it constituted against some of the evils that the poem itself presents. The rebellious slaves are still focalized from a perspective that mixes Caribbean admiration with white dread. And it is precisely that mixed perspective that leads us to the two main poems that deal with the Haitian Revolution's aftermath, specifically the reign of Henri Christophe.

A Duke and a Count

"Elegía del duque de la Mermelada" ["Elegy for the Duke of Marmalade"] is an ironically ponderous poem whose long lines and solemn rhythm enact the pretentiousness that its content parodies: the duke is a member of Henri Christophe's court. Given the excess that characterized both Christophe and his kingdom, it is not surprising that they have fascinated so many Caribbean writers, including Aimé Césaire, Alejo Carpentier, and Derek Walcott, who have approached that period from widely divergent perspectives. On the one hand, Christophe has been judged as a megalomaniacal aberration, and his kingdom as a betrayal of everything that the revolution stood for, particularly the liberation of the slaves who were, for all practical purposes, re-enslaved under Christophe's brutal regime. On the other hand, Christophe's kingdom has also been regarded as the admittedly excessive and almost picturesque form taken by several tendencies and forces that had been at work since the beginning of the revolution: first and foremost, the tendency of Haitian leaders to seize absolute power and crush dissent (a tendency, some might argue, that starts with Louverture); the uneasy compromise between the desire to affirm Haiti's Afro-Caribbean specificity and the need to court Europe's (and the United States') stamp of approval (and investment capital); and the endemic disconnect between Haitian elites and the masses.

In Palés Matos's poetry, the duke appears as the ultimate Naipaulian "mimic man" who betrays his "African" roots for the pseudo-sophisticated mannerisms and paraphernalia of the European aristocracy:

Oh my fine, my sugar-coated Duke of Marmalade!
Where have you left your caimans in the distant village of the Pongo,
and the blue and round shade of your African baobabs,
and your fifteen wives smelling of jungle and mud?

You will no longer eat your succulent roasted child,
the family monkey will no longer kill your lice during the afternoon nap,
your sweet eye will no longer gaze at the effeminate giraffe
across the flat and hot silence of the savannas.

They are over—your nights by the lit bonfires,
and the drowsy and persistent dripping of the drums,
the drumming in which you would sink as in a warm mud,
until you reached the distant shores of your great great-grandfather.

Now, wearing your fanciful French dress-coat,
you walk around receiving sugared greetings like a regular courtier,
in spite of the fact that your feet scream at you from your ducal boots:
"Babilongo, climb up the cornices of the palace."

How elegant my Duke looks with Madame de Cafolé,
all velvety and clean in the blue music of the violins,
as he contains his hands, which scream at him from his ducal gloves:
"Babilongo, throw her down on the rose-colored divan!"

> From the distant shores of your great great-grandfather,
> across the flat and hot silence of the savannas,
> why are your caimans crying in the distant village of the Pongo?,
> oh my fine, my sugar-coated Duke of Marmalade!?
>   (Palés Matos, "Elegía," 559; my translation)

The poem leaves no doubt as to why the caimans in the Duke's ancestral Africa are crying in the last stanza: by adopting the ways of the French aristocracy, the Duke has betrayed his identity, an identity grounded in an ancient landscape still inhabited by figures like his guiding ancestors (the great great-grandfather), tribal customs (his fifteen wives), and quasi-totemic animals. That dimension of the poem (its denunciation of assimilation to colonial models) should not be undervalued, and it is a reading that has been emphasized by many critics (such as López Baralt, in Palés Matos, *La poesía*, 481; Arce, qted. in López Baralt, *El barco*, 165; and González Pérez, "Ballad of Two Poets," 290). In that regard, Palés Matos is not far from other Caribbean writers who have attempted to emphasize the archipelago's connections to Africa, and who have criticized attempts to sever or hide those connections; Césaire in his *Cahier* and Kamau Brathwaite in his *Arrivants* trilogy are notable examples.

However, it is hard for the critical reader to ignore what several of Palés Matos's critics have markedly pointed out: his "defense" of the "ancestral" Africa that the duke seems to be forgetting is presented in such blatantly stereotypical, Eurocentric terms, that the effect is at best ambiguous, at worst a gallery of racist images. As examples of the "African customs" that the duke abandons, the reader finds cannibalism ("You will no longer eat your succulent roasted child"); sexual unbridling ("as he contains his hands, which scream at him from his ducal gloves: Babilongo, throw her down on the rose-colored divan!"); sheer animalistic behavior ("in spite of the fact that your feet scream at you from your ducal boots: Babilongo, climb up the cornices of the palace"); laziness and exoticism ("the family monkey will no longer kill your lice during the afternoon nap, your sweet eye will no longer gaze at the effeminate giraffe across the flat and hot silence of the savannas"). One might try to justify such images by appealing to Palés Matos's well-known irony, and by emphasizing the historical moment in which he was writing, when what we call today "Eurocentrism" was simply taken for granted not only in Europe but around the globe. Aníbal González Pérez suggests that, "as Juan Antonio Corretjer and Arcadio Díaz Quiñoes have pointed out, rather than blaming Palés Matos for being a (white) man of his time and place, the positive elements of his Afro-Antillean poems should be stressed" ("Ballad of Two Poets," 290). In that context, that Palés Matos had less than enlightened ideas about Africa is hardly surprising, and more weight would fall on the fact that he celebrates—albeit with irony—Afro-Caribbean culture at all, while also criticizing European imperialism. Taken to the extreme, that line of argumentation could even plausibly propose that Palés Matos uses those stereotypes *precisely* because they are stereotypes, as still another attack on European pretensions of superiority; after all, the luxury and customs of the European aristocracy are also mocked in the poem.

Those arguments have some value, and yet I must strongly agree with the critic Gerald Guinness when he argues, referring specifically to those who accuse Palés Matos of racism: "These are strong statements and not necessarily correct ones. It is strange, nonetheless, how little *white* defenders of Palés Matos feel they have to take such expressions of injured black pride into account when they write about Palés Matos's poetry" (*Here and Elsewhere*, 15). Indeed, while stating *only* that Palés Matos was racist may be overly simplistic or anachronistic, to simply dismiss that aspect of his work at the same time that he is celebrated as a champion of Puerto Rico's Afro-Caribbean identity is at best extremely problematic. It seems more adequate to acknowledge and carefully map the discomfort that Palés Matos's poetry provokes (or should provoke) in alert readers, particularly when the elements of that discomfort so clearly reflect the coloniality of power that still dominates, and the colonial difference that still alienates, the very Caribbean that Palés Matos was trying to dissect in his poems.

The fact of the matter is that, by the time Palés Matos publishes the second edition of *Tuntún* (1950), and by the time the last collection of his poems is prepared by Federico de Onís and revised by the poet himself (1957)—two collections that include his Haitian poems from the thirties—we may reasonably assume Palés Matos's familiarity with at least *some* developments in the process of wider self-awareness, pride, and affirmation in the African diaspora in the Americas. I am referring to manifestations such as Nicolás Guillén's poetry in Cuba, the Harlem Renaissance poets in the United States, and the *Negritude* movement in the Francophone Caribbean (the *Cahier* was translated into Spanish by Lydia Cabrera in 1943 [included in Cabrera]). We cannot tell how many of these developments Palés Matos was aware of, although he clearly knew the work of other literary figures from the "poesía negrista" movement, such as the Colombian poet Jorge Artel. In a 1937 talk on Palés Matos's poetry, Tomás Blanco (who was Palés Matos's personal friend) indicates that Palés Matos was acquainted with the work of Nicolás Guillén and Langston Hughes, that is to say, two of the most progressive black poets of the period (*Sobre Palés Matos,* 43); Palés Matos himself mentions these two poets, as well as others like Emilio Ballagas, in a 1950 essay on Artel (*Obras,* 259). We know from the "glossary" that he appended to the second edition of *Tuntún de pasa y grifería* that he knew at least Alejo Carpentier's first novel, *Ecué-Yamba-O* (1933), which in spite of its avant-garde exoticism focuses on the denunciation of the living conditions of poor black populations of Cuba in the early twentieth century.

I am not claiming that Palés Matos could have had a postmodern, multiculturally inflected, or "politically correct" view of Puerto Rican (or Caribbean) identity in the 1930s, 1940s, or 1950s; however, I am suggesting that we cannot explain away his problematic representation of black characters as merely a sign of his times, while attributing his groundbreaking celebration of Afro-Caribbean culture exclusively to his personal genius. It seems more reasonable to suppose that Palés Matos clearly had an ambiguous, sometimes even contradictory relation to the material with which his poems deal. This ambiguity was certainly not exclusive to him. Leaving aside the blatantly racist critics who would not acknowledge the importance of African culture in Puerto Rico, Palés Matos seems to have been part of a group of progressive intellectuals who were willing to acknowledge the importance of that African dimension, but who at the same time felt threatened by the need to include those hitherto marginalized perspectives. An example of one such intellectual is Tomás Blanco, a friend and early enthusiastic supporter of Palés Matos who, as I quoted in the first section of this chapter, could write a book condemning racial prejudice *as such,* while at the same time denying that it was a problem in Puerto Rico, whose culture was quite simply Hispanic.[12] Admittedly Palés Matos was way ahead of his times in the centrality he attributes to Puerto Rico's Afro-Caribbean legacy. That fact makes his limitations all the more interesting to examine, not as mere blind spots in his outlook but rather as indicators of a complex and often self-contradicting perspective that cannot be separated from a long history of colonialism and racism in the island—a long history that Palés Matos both criticized and, in spite of himself, also reflected.

We find a similar situation in Palés Matos second "Haitian" poem, "Lagarto verde" ["Green Lizard"]. The poem describes another "mimic man," another black man absurdly (for Palés Matos) trying to copy the style of the French aristocracy:

> The little Count of Lemonade,
> playful, tiny . . . Such a cute thing,
> frolicking around, tiny and playful,
> through the halls of Christophe's palace.
>
> His merry little monkey face
> says to everyone: "yes."
> "Yes, Madame Cafolé, Monsieur Haiti,
> that way, this way"
> (Palés Matos, "Lagarto verde," 561; my translation)

The description oozes irony, but once again the reader is left with the uneasy feeling that the same voice that mocks the conventions of aristocracy is also animalizing the black man who dares imitate the behavior of the white man—the comparison to a monkey being brutally racist (Palés Matos achieves an ironic effect by calling the Count "una monada," which can be colloquial Spanish for "cute," but may also mean "monkeylike"). We are offered further examples of the count's banal assimilation—"his social formula is: oh pardon! / His elegant word: volupté!"—until the poem reaches its unavoidable conclusion:

> Oh, but don't you dare say "green lizard"
> in front of His Highness,
> because he immediately loses his head
> and his fine aristocratic manners are gone!
>
> And there he goes, the Count of Lemonade,
> with his red dress-coat in disarray
> and his fierce jaw
> rigid in its epileptic tension . . .
> There he goes, with grotesque gestures
> multiplying the orangutans in the mirrors
> of King Christophe's palace!
> (Palés Matos, "Lagarto verde," 561; my translation)

Like the duke in "Elegía del duque de la Mermelada," the count assumes an aristocratic disguise that hardly conceals his "true," primitive nature. This poem results even more problematic that the other one, because in "Elegía" there was at least an explicit plea to return to a primeval world that was as exotic as it was primitive, and the lament for the abandonment of the African world of the ancestors is clearly expressed (through the crying of the caimans), even if mainly using Eurocentric language. In "Lagarto verde" the primitive nature of the count seems encoded within his very body, always ready to erupt at a minor provocation, such as the enunciation of the wrong phrase or image: here, "lagarto verde," the green lizard, which becomes a totemic figure of sorts that presumably evokes and brings to the surface a primitive, animalistic realm of grotesque impulses. Although revolving around similar topics, "Elegía" deals with an African world that can only precariously be left behind; "Lagarto" deals with animalistic tendencies that only precariously can be repressed. Both approaches are part of the repertoire of stereotyping strategies employed by European colonialism and its essentialist logic.

Again, one *might,* although with even more difficulty, find ways to justify or explain Palés Matos's choice of images. As I indicated above, such attempts seem somewhat forced, and it makes more sense to acknowledge that Palés Matos has an ambiguous, even conflictive relation to his subject matter. Such ambiguity is highlighted, not softened, by the fact his poetry was indeed groundbreaking in its foregrounding the importance of African roots in Caribbean culture, and of the Caribbean roots of Puerto Rican culture. In that context, his inability to let go of Eurocentric stereotypes about African culture should not be regarded as an incidental detail that can be brushed aside, but rather as an important, if unfortunate, aspect of his literary endeavor. It is to that literary endeavor we must turn now to shed some light on Palés Matos's paradoxes, for ultimately it is my argument that his contradictions arise from his position as a member of a local intellectual elite that is attempting to position itself against the privileges of colonial elites put in place by various imperial interventions, while at the same time attempting not to disturb too severely its own position of relative privilege within that power structure.

Africa from Haiti from Puerto Rico

We may begin by asking why Palés Matos writes about the Haitian Revolution at all, what role it plays in the overall construction of *Tuntún de pasa y grifería.* The revolution's place in "Canción festiva para ser llorada," examined above, gives us a key. In that poem, the cultural and political domination of the Caribbean are dominant themes—the region's destiny as what the Dominican writer Juan Bosch calls "a frontier between empires." In spite of the Caribbean's vitality and rhythms, the presence of Babbitt and sugarcane interests casts a shadow of unrestrained exploitation (after all, the poem is a supposedly "festive" song that is in fact suppose to be "wept" or "wept over"). In the midst of that world, the Haitian events, in spite of Palés Matos's exoticist approach, arise as the only attempt at real, concrete political resistance in the poem. It is only through Haiti that rebellion goes beyond joyous cultural survival to a militant revolt against colonial domination, a revolt that finds its ultimate expression in the extermination of the white master. Moreover, Haiti (in that poem and the others) preserves strong links to what Palés Matos seems to consider a black African culture in a state that is "uncontaminated" by European colonialism. It is, in fact, the severance of that link by the Haitian aristocracy that his two Haitian poems criticize (Aimé Césaire also regards Haiti as the place "where negritude rose for the first time" [*Notebook*, 15] in the Caribbean).

Throughout *Tuntún de pasa y grifería* Africa plays dual and complementary roles, one as cultural cradle of Caribbean identity, and one as a symbol for the region's political resistance to colonial interests. Firstly, it plays an *identitary* role. Palés Matos's defenders are certainly right in pointing out that, in spite of the limitations in his approach, Palés Matos is a foundational figure in his stubborn affirmation of Puerto Rico's roots in an Afro-Caribbean culture. It was a sign of Palés Matos's intellectual honesty, as well as of his knowledge of his context (having been born in Guayama, a town with a particularly strong and visible African heritage), which he insisted on privileging that aspect of Puerto Rican culture. In his autobiographical unfinished novel *Litoral* (included in *Obras*), Palés Matos comments on his fascination with black culture, particularly the stories of his family's black cook, Lupe. Characteristically, in the novel that black world remains somewhat alien, something close and precious but also *other*.

Palés Matos also showed a shrewdness ahead of his time by moving (occasionally) beyond a purely essentialist view of identity towards a performative view, in which identities are articulated, circulated and reconfigured in subordination and response to political and social agendas and events. Responding to an interview question about "poesía criolla" in Puerto Rico—which in the island refers to poetry about, and often modeled on traditional music and diction of, "jíbaros" or "white" Puerto Rican mountain peasants, who are emblematic figures of Puerto Rico's "true" identity— Palés Matos declared:

> Yes, there is in fact a Creole poetry in Puerto Rico. What does not exist is the Creole Puerto Rico. The palm-tree hut, the sentimental and early-rising

peasant girl, the camaguey rooster, the sensual and seductive "triple" [a traditional string instrument], all of that occupies very little space in our life, it is as distant from us as the Eiffel Tower and Napoleon's white horse. Except for Llorens, who every year produces eight or ten Creole "décimas" [popular ten-line stanza poems], and some local poets who write verses for their town's Patron Saint Feasts, nobody, as far as I know, cultivates that kind of poetry in Puerto Rico. (*Obras*, 284; my translation)

The explicit mention of Luis Llorens Torres is quite significant in Palés Matos's self-fashioning as poet. Easily the most popular Puerto Rican poet of the early 20th century, Llorens Torres was a nationalist writer who tried to preserve Puerto Rico's Hispanic heritage and identity from U.S. colonial domination, and the Puerto Rico of his poetry is in sharp contrast with the Puerto Rico of *Tuntún de pasa y grifería*. Llorens Torres's Hispanophile vision of Puerto Rican identity circulates in official circles to this day, and it was Palés Matos's merit to offer an alternative vision grounded in the island's Afro-Caribbean connections. In the interview, Palés Matos's ironically observes how the images most commonly associated with Puerto Rico's white creole identity only exist in the works of poets like Llorens Torres. Those observations in fact show a keen awareness of how the connections between identities and power (for example, the legitimization of certain identities and the exclusion of others) are meditated by cultural forms and institutions—in this particular case, the officially sanctioned poetry of Llorens Torres.[13]

Paradoxically, Palés Matos's insights into the relations between identities and power also illuminate the limitations of his concerns about colonial "mimic men," and his critique of figures like the Duke of Marmalade and the Count of Lemonade, however justified they might be at other levels. In this regard, we must highlight the ideas that Palés Matos expressed in his essay "Hacia una poesía antillana" ["Towards an Antillean Poetry"] (1932). Palés Matos wrote the essay in response to attacks from the writer José de Diego Padró, who criticized Palés Matos precisely for presenting his "black" poems as examples of Puerto Rican culture, a culture that for de Diego Padró (as for many intellectuals of that generation) was in fact "Western" or "European." Palés Matos replied:

> In general terms . . . it is true that when two cultures migrate from their places of origin and meet in a foreign environment, the one that possesses superior elements will eliminate and destroy the other one. But one must be very cautious when applying this concept, and one must not make a rigid and

unchanging law out of it. The new environment might turn out to be hostile to the dominant culture, and friendly toward the dominated culture. Or, through subtle tactics of the collective unconscious or simply in order to survive, the men who represent the dominated culture may adopt the forms and representations of the dominant culture and infiltrate it slowly, filling it with their own spirit, modifying and corroding those forms so efficiently that they can provoke the birth of a new cultural attitude. (*Obras*, 239; my translation)

The very notion of "superior" and "inferior" cultures—without questioning those categories and who gets to decide which is which—is an indicator of Palés Matos's implicitly Eurocentric approach, an approach that some might explain as an understandable sign of Palés Matos's historical period in his thought. What is striking about his words, however, is the keen awareness that cultural forms imposed on any group as part of a process of domination can be used as a disguise, as a ruse, by the dominated group, so that apparent assimilation can hide sustained resistance. In the Caribbean, syncretistic religions such as Vodou and Santeria are the best-known examples of that practice: under the guise of Catholic practices, African slaves were able to preserve the spirit of many of their ancestral religious beliefs. From our perspective in this study, what is striking is that Palés Matos's clear understanding of this phenomenon does not make him pause at the moment of writing his "Haitian" poems. Christophe's court may not constitute a good example of strategic assumption of dominant cultural forms, but a good case could be made for the need *all* Haitian leaders since independence have felt to appear "European" (thus, "civilized" in a colonial global order) to foreign capital interests that were more than ready to cut them loose. Therefore, Palés Matos's own essay makes it clear that the poetic portrayal of Haitians as mindless imitators who betray their ancestral totems is at best limited and unfair, even leaving aside its racist Eurocentric assumptions. In a collection of poems that presents many examples of strategic submission (such as the "mulata's" flirtation with Uncle Sam in "Plena del menéalo"), one might expect a more imaginative portrayal of the aftermath of the Haitian Revolution.

Even more surprisingly, Palés Matos himself, a few paragraphs later in the essay we are commenting, offers a significantly corrected portrayal of Haiti:

It is very hard for a culture that pretends to be superior to destroy the roots of a supposedly inferior culture, as long as the vigilant awareness of that other race has not lost its vitality. Haiti offers a clear example. Haitian blacks speak French, they officially practice the Catholic religion, and they created, thus assimilating themselves to the spirit of Western democratic institutions, a republic. Cult Haitians are educated in France, they read Victor Hugo, the obtain titles from the Sorbonne. The bourgeois class knows any frivolous variation in Paris's fashion, and it is said that in Port-au-Prince, during festive days, they walk around with the clothes and the solemn manners that belong to people of high status. However, inside, the Haitian remains unchanged. And there is nothing as radically opposed to the French spirit—clarity, lightness, rationalism—as the Haitian spirit—sensuality, superstition, witchcraft. (*Obras*, 240; my translation)[14]

Palés Matos's striking words encapsulate well the strengths and limitations of his approach. He clearly affirms a Caribbean culture that is distinct from that of Europe, even if Europe is evidently one of its components. That culture has survived, and has been shaped, in the process of political resistance to metropolitan interests. There is even the subtle suggestion that the "superiority" of one culture over another is far from being a clear matter—notice his reference to a "*supposedly*" inferior culture—a position that was well ahead of its times. Moreover, there is a stab at the "bourgeois class," whose attempt to display an internalized Eurocentrism (characteristic of all elites in power throughout postindependence Latin America) we may describe in terms of what Aníbal Quijano calls the "coloniality of power." However, just as in the poems, Palés Matos's "celebration" of Haiti's ability to develop and preserve its own culture as it wears the disguise of French culture is severely undermined by his description of what Haitian culture is *really* about for him: sensuality, superstition, witchcraft—the taxonomy of racist, sexist, Eurocentric categories that imperial discourse put in circulation. To Quijano's coloniality of power, we must add here Lugones's coloniality of gender, which we see displayed in Palés Matos's feminization of Haiti's racial other, and in the automatic eroticized objectification of "the feminine" that his celebration of Haiti entails.

The second role of Africa in Palés Matos's poetry is connected precisely to that awareness of the links between identity and power in a colonial context: Africa works as a symbol of *political* resistance against American and European interests in the Caribbean region, and in Palés Matos's imaginary Haiti is the Caribbean region that remains the closest to that African spirit. Throughout *Tuntún*, Africa is implicitly or explicitly associated with moments or figures of rebellion *in the Caribbean*. A few examples should suffice to illustrate that point. It is significant how the very first poem of the "Tronco" section of the book, presumably dealing with the African "trunk" of the symbolic tree of Puerto Rico's culture, offers a symbolic geography for that "trunk": "Pasan tierras rojas, islas de betún / Haití, Martinica, Congo, Camerún" (508) ["Red lands pass by, shoeshine black islands / Haiti, Martinique, Congo, Cameroon" (my translation)]. In that Middle Passage that connects the Caribbean to Africa, Haiti occupies a central role. The second poem, "Numen," a celebration, as its title indicates, of African ancestral beliefs, is built around the refrain: "African forest—Tembandumba— / Haitian jungle—Macandal." Tembandumba is a mythical matriarchal figure used by Palés Matos to represent Africa (in this poem; she becomes an embodiment of the Antillean woman of color in "Majestad negra"), but it is significant that the other pole of the Caribbean's Afrocentric resistance is Macandal (whom we already saw in "Canción festiva"), one of the main precursors of the Haitian revolution (who also plays an important role in Carpentier's *El reino de este mundo*).

Poems like "Ñam ñam" and "Ñáñigo al cielo" also present Africans or characters connected to African belief systems emblematizing resistance. "Ñam ñam," a poem about cannibalism, could be criticized for its stereotypical representation of African cannibals, but it can also be read as an allegory of political resistance when one realizes that in the poem Africa devours "its meal of explorers and missionaries" (518; my translation), that is to say, emblematic figures of European colonial penetration. In "Ñáñigo al cielo" the ñáñigo, a member of an Afro-Cuban syncretistic religion, subverts and carnivalizes the heavenly hierarchies established by Christian authority. In "Lamento," black men from Havana to Zimbabwe lament the malefic influence of a "white shadow" in their world. And in "Plena del menéalo" a personified Caribbean island dances and shakes its body to African rhythms with "goce rumbero" ["with rumba joy"]; the political implications of that dance are explicit: "Keep shaking your stern as you dance / because it is that dancing / that saves you / from the monsieur who leers at you / from beyond the sea" (616; my translation). At the end of the poem we find the American counterpart of that European "monsieur" (humorously Hispanicized in the poem as a "musiú") who also surveys lasciviously the island-woman; the poet's advice is: "shake it, shake it, / so that you drive Uncle Sam mad!" (616; my translation).

In all of the examples quoted above, and in other subtler ones throughout the book, one finds the Caribbean's African roots playing an important strategic role as a symbol of the region's cultural autonomy and political resistance to European and U.S. colonial interests. In that context, it makes sense that Haiti, as a prime example of that resistance, should have a significant place in Palés Matos's poetry, from the very first poems of the book, as we have seen. It is also in that context that Palés Matos's condemnation of the Haitian "mimic men" of Christophe's court acquires its full scope: for Christophe and his minions are not only oppressing Haiti but also corrupting the symbolic importance of Haiti's revolution for a Caribbean realm still under the chains of imperial domination. It is precisely because of the important cultural and political role Africa plays in Palés Matos's poetry that the ambiguity towards the African elements in his own poetry should be taken seriously, as a paradoxical but constitutive dimension of his work, rather than simply an accident or a mere remnant of the prejudices of his times.

The ambivalence that Palés Matos shows towards the African element in Caribbean culture—which becomes almost synonymous with Haiti in some of his poems, as the "Mackandal—Tembandumba" axis shows—is clearly shown in his "Haitian poems," but is also noticeable in several others. One example is "Preludio en boricua" ["Prelude in Boricua"], an extraordinary poem that opens the collection and introduces the aesthetic and political project of the book, displaying and performing all the stylistic and thematic trademarks of Palés Matos's poetry. However, the poem mysteriously ends by self-reflectively invoking the book's title (*Tuntún de pasa y grifería*, which I translate below as "black and mulatto tom-toms") and declaring:

> Black and mulatto tom-toms,
> this book that is delivered to your hands,
> I composed one day with Antillean ingredients. . . .
> . . . and when all is said and done: wasted time
> that ends up boring me.
> Something that I glimpsed or sensed,
> little that has been actually lived,
> much that is made up and concocted.
>   (Palés Matos, "Preludio," 503; my translation)

The poem's striking end can be (and has been) read ironically, as a mischievous indicator of the ultimate textual nature of the poetic material that follows—a reading that would highlight Palés Matos's awareness (as indicated in the quotes above from "Hacia una poesía antillana") of the constructedness of identitary images.[15] In a context of U.S. colonial domination to which many members of the local intelligentsia were responding by an affirmation of Puerto Rico's "true" Hispanic identity, Palés Matos was very much rehearsing and "concocting" Afro-Caribbean images as an antidote to the Hispanophile ones. However, taking into account several important moments in the book itself, it is also legitimate to read the poem's ending somewhat more "literally," that is to say, not simply as a tongue-in-cheek pointer to the textual, "concocted" character of its content but rather in terms of the *affective distance* it establishes between the poet and his material.

The disclaimer that the book is in some ways "wasted time," that not much in it comes from lived experience, and that it ultimately bores the poet, allows Palés Matos to keep some *distance* from the universe his poems articulate. Such a reading is supported by the poet's attitude in other poems in the book, with his Haitian poems constituting prime examples. But there are other compositions that reveal Palés Matos's conflicted relation to his surroundings, such as the somber "Topography," which is not part of *Tuntún*'s main structure but was included by the poet in both editions of the book (in a section titled "Other poems"):

> This is the barren, stepmother land
> where the cactus grows.
> Chalky saltpeter land
> that birds traverse, broken by thirst . . .
> Fear. Desolation. Asphyxia. Everything here
> sleeps smothered . . .
>   (Palés Matos, "Topografía," 421; my translation)

There is also the well-known "Pueblo" (a word that may mean both "town" and "people" in Spanish), constructed around the refrain: "Pity, oh Lord, pity for my poor town / where my poor people will die of nothing!" (424; my translation). In these poems and others, the poet's personal malaise becomes entangled with what he perceives as the stagnation of his island, a stagnation with clear political dimensions rooted in a colonial history. The Afro-Caribbean-centered poems certainly bring a more rebellious attitude to that political situation, but as we saw in the ending of "Prelude in Boricua," they do not eliminate the poet's skeptical distance from his surrounding universe.

We can see another example of the poet's ambivalent position in the poem "Kalahari" (541–542), structured around the persistent repetition of the refrain, "Why now, the word *Kalahari?*" The word "Kalahari," which mysteriously and obsessively keeps arising in the poet's mind, invokes "a bay with clear coconut trees, / with hundreds of monkeys engaged in / a disorderly series of acrobatic leaps" (541–42; my translation), in one word, Africa (an Africa whose coconut trees constitute a symbolic link to the Caribbean). But Africa in the poem is sheer sonority, a perplexing word, a vague nostalgia, a reminder of something important that insists on imposing itself on the poet but never quite becomes a *presence* in the poem or for the poet. In many ways "Kalahari" captures Palés Matos's relation to Africa in his book. When it is a matter of facing "Uncle Sam," the poet does not hesitate to invoke that Africa; when it is matter of the claims that Africa makes on him, the poet hesitates, and takes a step back.[16]

The poet writes about Africa in the Caribbean, he even celebrates it, but at the same time maintains an ironic detachment that betrays an anxiety not to be too closely identified with his material.[17] Palés Matos often seems caught between his commitment to take a stand against the historical injustices against the black populations of the Caribbean, and his own position of racial and cultural privilege. He remains constant in his commitment while at the same time retaining a distance that never quite gets to talk to power *from* an Afro-Caribbean perspective, but rather *about* it.[18]

Palés Matos declared quite explicitly that he never intended to write "black poetry" but rather "Antillean poetry."[19] However, it is evident that he considered the African presence in the Caribbean to be fundamental and foundational. *Tuntún de pasa y grifería* strongly suggests that no aesthetic celebration or political defense of the region can even be considered without privileging that African dimension. Throughout the text, African cultural elements (such as the percussive rhythms and dancing) and black struggles for emancipation (such as the Haitian Revolution) are given thematic privilege in the articulation of the region's cultural and political personality. Europeans and North Americans often appear as greedy tourists, or colonialists, in poems like "Intermedios del hombre blanco." The presence of Africa in the Caribbean also governs the book's structure: the text is divided in three sections, and the first one, "tronco," is composed of poems that refer to Africa (the same Africa that the duke of Marmalade and the Count of Lemonade "betray") as the trunk or ground of Caribbean culture. In many regards, what Palés Matos intuited in his poems is what C. L. R. James expressed quite transparently in his 1962 appendix to *The Black Jacobins*, where he writes:

> The West Indians were and had always been Western-educated. West Indian society confined black men to a very narrow strip of social territory. The first

step to freedom was to go abroad. *Before they could begin to see themselves as a free and independent people they had to clear from minds the stigma that anything African was inherently inferior and degraded.* The road to West Indian national identity lay through Africa. (402; James's italics)

Palés Matos also feels the need to "go abroad" in his poems, particularly to those other West Indian islands (the Anglophone and Francophone Caribbean) which, although having histories that are very different from Puerto Rico's in many regards, also share an element to which Palés Matos gave as much importance as James does: the African presence. Palés Matos's Africa lies primordially in those other Caribbean islands (including Haiti). What the mirror of those other islands reveals to Palés Matos's Puerto Rican eyes is not only the fundamental presence of Africa's culture all throughout the Caribbean but also the coloniality of power and the *coloniality of being* that have systematically marked anything African as *"inherently degraded and inferior."* Any road toward self-emancipation (regardless of how we define it, and Palés Matos was certainly a supporter of Puerto Rico's political independence) must overcome that stigma, which Palés Matos saw not only in the colonial metropolis (Babbitt and Tartarin) but also encountered among Puerto Rico's local cultural elite.

Thus, although Palés Matos has been accused of portraying exotic, ahistorical black figures, the fact is that his main interest lies in Africa as a cultural and political symbol of resistance from the perspective of the colonized Caribbean region. One could argue that the center of gravity of his book is the axis created by the refrain of his poem "Numen:" "African forest—Tembandumba / Haitian jungle—Macandal" (516). In other words, *Tuntún de pasa y grifería* takes as its point of departure the Middle Passage and the historically grounded experience of the Black diaspora, rather than some mythical, precolonial Africa.

However exotic and picturesque Africa's rhythms, customs, and beliefs may look to a poet who, after all, had links to the avant-garde movements of the early twentieth century, the poems suggest that Palés Matos was quite aware that, in the Caribbean, "Africa" can only be contemplated through the lens of (and for Palés Matos it remains symbolically inextricable from) "Haiti" and all it represents, with its misery and revolt. Palés Matos's Caribbean perspective grounds the black experience in the historical legacies of imperialism, colonialism, and slavery, on the one hand, and resistance and rebellion, on the other. Haiti with its revolution becomes the embodiment of those historical, pan-Caribbean realities. Moreover, for Palés Matos the violent events in Haiti and the seemingly benign tourist showcase of Puerto Rico are two poles of a spectrum of Afro-Caribbean experience forged by the racist imprint of colonial interests deeply imbricated in the development of Euro-American capitalism. (In "Prelude in boricua" he describes the "golden Niagara of tourists" that endlessly wander the Caribbean by pointing out, "tomorrow they will be stockholders / of any sugarcane mill / and then they will get off with the money" [502; my translation]). Thus, the aesthetic celebration of the Caribbean, as well as its political defense, point towards Africa: an Africa linked to both Haiti and Puerto Rico by imperial designs, and by the logic of the coloniality of power and the ontological claims of the coloniality of being.

Colonial Ambivalence

How to read, then, a poet who expresses quite openly, albeit often ironically, his anticolonial stand, who shows awareness of the significance of the Haitian Revolution in the context of a Caribbean resistance to imperialism, yet who voices his criticism of Haiti, however justified at some levels, from such a blatantly Eurocentric perspective? At this point, rather than easily lean towards one of these two readings, Palés Matos as Caribbean critic of colonialism vs. Palés Matos the Eurocentric racist, I want to stay with the tension, because I think it encapsulates his position as a Caribbean intellectual.

Palés Matos's poetic performance in *Tuntún de pasa y grifería* is a rhetorical balancing act that creates a precarious logic of exclusion/inclusion—the poet participates in the carnival he creates, but he also keeps his ironic distance. That distance, one should also remember, is also *aesthetic:* one often has the impression, when reading Palés Matos, that he is simply unable or unwilling to let a striking image or metaphor go by (particularly if it is appropriately "African sounding"), and that he never forgets to articulate his own location/role first and foremost as *a poet*.[20] His virtuoso performance allows the poet to remain in agonistic tension with regard to his conflictive imperatives. On the one hand, the poems articulate his political resistance to the imperial designs for the archipelago, a resistance that in Palés Matos often takes the forms of satire and irony. On the other hand, the poet attempts to find a balance between participation in the Caribbean's heteroglossic, plural, Afro-Creole performance, and lyrical distance anchored in ironic disdain. Palés Matos articulates a space for himself as a poet and intellectual by remaining at a safe distance from all his possible roles. He writes against white colonizers but seems to feel the need to distinguish himself from that black world that he attempts to defend. We can see the poet's anxiety in the surprising ending of "Preludio en boricua," and the paradoxical "Haitian poems" that we examined.

The point I would like to emphasize here is that we can link the ambiguity of Palés Matos's poetic performance to the colonial context and logic that his work quite clearly addresses. Although the way Palés Matos articulates his position (through the elaboration of an ironic distance that bizarrely combines anti-imperialist commitment with racist and sexist stereotypes) is unique, his performance in fact reflects the conundrum of other Caribbean and (post)colonial intellectuals. Constantly shifting between worlds and languages; speaking in favor of subaltern populations from positions of relative privilege; often silencing those they defend by the very act of speaking on their behalf; frequently at an impasse between politics and aesthetics, (post)colonial intellectuals constantly face the anxiety of betraying one or more of their multiple and, for them, equally valid commitments. As one short example from another Caribbean island, we can think of the Nobel prize-winning Saint Lucian poet Derek Walcott, who, although writing well after Palés Matos, occasionally expresses similar concerns, the main difference being that Walcott explicitly thematizes them in his poetry. In a dramatic passage from his 1990 epic poem *Omeros*, this potential conflict between political commitment and aesthetics, on the one hand, and between solidarity and privilege on the other, is taken to its ultimate consequences:

>   Didn't I want the poor
> to stay in the same light so that I could transfix
> them in amber, the afterglow of an empire,
> preferring a shed of palm-thatch with tilted sticks
> to that blue bus-stop? Didn't I prefer a road
> from which tracks climbed into the thickening syntax
> of colonial travelers, the measured prose I read
> as a schoolboy?
> . . . .
>   Had they waited for me
> to develop my craft? Why hallow that pretense
> of preserving what they left, the hypocrisy
> of loving them from hotels, a biscuit-tin fence
> smothered in love-vines, scenes to which I was attached
> as blindly as Plunkett with his remorseful research?

> Art is history's nostalgia, it prefers a thatched
> roof to a concrete factory
> . . . .
> Hadn't I made their poverty my paradise?
> (Walcott, *Omeros*, 227–28)

In a disturbing twist of the logic behind the ideal of *littérature engagé*, the poem feeds on the reality it is presumably trying to transform. Torn between divided loyalties, the poem may not turn its back to the wretched of the earth, nor truly commit to their deliverance. Each (post)colonial artist or intellectual finds his/her own precarious solution, or lack of solution, for that conundrum. While Walcott attempts to address the problem explicitly thematizing it in his poem, Palés Matos attempts to give both aesthetics and politics their due, remaining committed to both and alienated from both.

Thus, one may argue that in spite of its joyous immersion in the heteroglossic and politically charged realities of the Caribbean, *Tuntún de pasa y grifería* is partly (but very importantly) about the articulation of a "safe" space for the poet himself at the same time that colonial politics in the Caribbean are confronted and the archipelago's creolized heterogeneity celebrated. That "safe" space is not clearly defined in the book, or perhaps it is more accurate to say that it is defined by omission, by default. Every time Palés Matos marks his distance from his surroundings, as he does in the end of "Preludio en boricua," or in the racist rhetoric of his "Haitian poems," what emerges is a space of relative "stability" and aesthetic distance that attempts not to be ultimately defined or governed by history with its legacy of colonial, racial, and cultural conflicts. "I address those issues but I am not defined by them," the poet seems to say, as he seeks refuge in an ironic distance that naturally is also a manifestation of historically inherited privilege. As is the case with many colonial and postcolonial writers, there is a sense of nostalgia that pervades Palés Matos's poetry and that of many his Caribbean peers: nostalgia for a space of stability (with regard to political struggles) and unity (with regards to identity) that the colonial history of the Caribbean has rendered impossible. And by colonialism here I do not refer specifically to the political status of Puerto Rico (which Palés Matos opposed[21]), but rather to the imperial legacy of dispossession and dependence that still governs most of the Caribbean region, sometimes in neocolonial forms, from the blocked Cuba to the French "departements d'outre mer."[22]

But if colonialism has made the dream of stable and unified identity impossible, it has also made the wish for its fulfillment unavoidable. As I discussed in the introduction, it is the colonial condition itself, and the colonizers' *claim* to a stable and unified self, that fuels that desire in the subaltern, in spite of the fact that such a self was always already a fiction for both colonizer and colonized.[23] There was never a happy Edenic time when the self was not fractured by difference and conflict, rather than actually articulated by them. The colonial condition, however, revolves around the myth of that "lack" which affects the colonized but not the colonizer—what Mignolo calls "the colonial difference." Palés Matos strives in his poetry to attack the system that perpetuates that myth while still partially believing it himself: his poetry bravely defends a creolized, heterogeneous, rebellious Afro-Caribbean space while refusing, or remaining unable, to fully inhabit that space.

In *Tuntún de pasa y grifería*, Palés Matos's poetic subject is characterized precisely by an avoidance of definition that attempts to remain politically committed while also staying ironically aloof. In a difficult to sustain (but masterfully sustained) performance, the poet attempts to articulate himself as a unified and stable subject impermeable to the mighty tensions of the Caribbean while also articulating and voicing the all-encompassing heterogeneities and colonial conflicts that have shaped the region. I agree with most contemporary critics of Palés Matos's poetry who point out to his irony and playfulness as clear indicators that he does not truly believe in the possibility of such a stable, impermeable self. But I do suggest that his clear engagement with (and disappointment with) Caribbean colonial politics, combined with his very problematic representation of the "identity" of those Caribbean Afro-descendants who have been at the center of the region's history, present us with a Caribbean intellectual deeply troubled about his own position in the universe that he is representing. Palés Matos's irony not only mocks essentialist metropolitan certitudes or (equally colonial) Hispanophile alternatives but also shields him from their pull and betrays an unfulfilled desire to find a "safe" location from which to address the coloniality of power and the coloniality of being in the Caribbean.

As I suggested earlier, it is not surprising that the role of Haiti in Palés Matos's poetry reveals so clearly the gaps and contradictions in the poet's lyric self-fashioning, for Haiti itself, with its misery and its rebelliousness, has become for the whole Caribbean an emblem and embodiment of the colonial condition and its discontents, past and present. Palés Matos's ironic alienation from both the political arena and the ivory tower is certainly not a "solution" to his impasse, but it remains a compelling representation of the dilemma in a very specific context. From several of his poems it seems that Palés Matos would be happiest if able to remain "position-less," dancing and arguing from a safely cut off position. That, of course, is impossible, and Palés Matos is forced to perpetually shift positions throughout his poems, sometimes within the same poem: Eurocentric mocker of black attempts to both inhabit and challenge the European "myth of modernity," and committed defender of the Caribbean's African dimensions in the face of that myth. Although such a strategy provokes little but perplexity in the reader at times, it is a perplexity that adequately captures the paradoxes and insights, the agony and hope of the region's (post) colonial legacies and continuing struggles. Palés Matos's poetry remains, often in spite of the poet himself, even in the aspects that one may justifiably criticize, undeniably Caribbean in its performance.

Chapter 3

Between Louverture and Christophe
Aimé Césaire on the Haitian Revolution

Best known as one of the foundational poets of the Negritude movement in the Francophone Caribbean, Aimé Césaire remains to this day a very influential voice in the colonial and postcolonial world. Beginning with the publication of *Cahier d'un retour au pays natal* (1939; rev. ed. 1956), his poetic masterpiece and de facto manifesto of negritude, Césaire cultivated poetry and drama, and produced significant nonfiction works that range from essays to speeches, prefaces, declarations, and even a major historical study. In addition to that distinguished career as a writer, Césaire also had an important career as a politician. From 1945 to 1993 Césaire held simultaneously the positions of Mayor of Fort-de-France and deputy to the French Assembly. He was also instrumental in the transformation of Martinique into an official "Département d'Outre-Mer" after World War II, although as time went by he became disillusioned with some of the restrictions and impositions of that status, and for many years he struggled for more local autonomy.[1]

As a writer and as a political leader, Césaire explored and attempted to reconcile the needs of his people with the problematic and evolving relationship between his island and France. Such exploration entailed an unrelenting examination of the legacy of colonialism and slavery, which to this day inevitably mediates the interactions between Martinique and the metropolis. Césaire's examination of that colonial legacy has made his work intensely pertinent to other countries and regions that have shared aspects of Martinique's historical experience, just as the experiences of other countries (from Patrice Lumumba's Congo to Henri Christophe's Haiti) have given Césaire rich material and examples in order to ponder questions of immense importance to himself and Martinique. Fundamental among Césaire's works that explore the (anti)colonial experience of other countries are the two books he dedicated to Haiti in the early 1960s. As we will see below, Haiti remained an inspiring yet agonizing presence in Césaire's thought from the beginning to the end of his career. However, it seems clear that, by the 1960s, political events—of which we must give priority to the wave of anti-colonial and independence movements throughout Africa and around the world—had brought to the foreground questions and anxieties that Césaire saw best embodied in Haiti's history. Without lapsing too far into biographical criticism, one may ask then, what is the relationship between the struggle for nationhood in the Haiti of his historical study *Toussaint Louverture: La révolution française et le problème colonial* (1961), the newly independent Haiti of his first play, *La tragédie du roi Christophe* (1963), and Césaire's concerns for his own island since he became the leading politician there in 1945. This chapter attempts an answer to that question by conducting a comparative study of both works and examining the diverse imperatives facing the poet and political leader, a man who, until his death in 2008, still met with visitors in his office in Fort-de-France and voiced strong opinions on political and cultural affairs.[2]

Although separated by only two years, Césaire's works on Toussaint and Christophe approach the Haitian Revolution from very different perspectives. In general terms, it may be argued that *Toussaint Louverture* attempts to explain the Revolution, and the figure of Toussaint Louverture, in terms of the "enlightened," universalist ideals that shaped the French Revolution. *La tragédie du roi Christophe*, on the other hand, attempts a balancing act that is harder to sustain. On the one hand, it clearly displays Christophe's despotism and the corrupting effects of power. On the other hand, the play attempts to highlight the tragic, albeit frustrated, nobility of the aspirations behind Christophe's actions. For even in his authoritarian blindness the king is guided by an attempt to affirm the historical greatness of the black populations in Haiti (and by extension, everywhere). From that perspective, Louverture and Christophe emerge, both in severely partial ways, as forerunners of negritude, as Césaire conceives it. Christophe tries to reach the universal via a celebration of the particular (in his case, the black people of Haiti), rather than subordinating the particular to the claims of the "universal" enlightened values upon which France, and other European powers, have justified their colonial enterprises. Louverture, on the other hand, departs from those "universal" values, as expressed by the French Revolution, and "concretizes" them in the Haitian context. Both the play and the essay offer Haitian history as a Caribbean embodiment of the colonial condition, with its multiple possibilities and contradictions. But even though it might seem that both works simply reach the same end from different perspectives, there are in fact considerable tensions between their approaches, which have very different ideological implications. Those tensions clearly reveal the diverse imperatives that the poet struggles with as a Caribbean intellectual and politician.

The Lure of the Universal

In referring to Césaire's engagement with universalism and particularism, I am in fact addressing what Naomi Schor has aptly referred to as the oxymoron of "French Universalism." As Schor clearly indicates, even though "universalism is defined as the opposite of particularism, ethnic, religious, national, or otherwise," nevertheless "French national discourse has for centuries claimed that France is the capital of universalism" (43). Schor compellingly traces the evolution of "French universalism" from its religious origins based on France's role as defender and purveyor of Catholicism, to its incarnation in claims to linguistic universalism (French as the language of reason and transparency), to the rational and ethical universalism of the Enlightenment and the French Revolution. All of those conceptions of "French universalism" (or more appropriately, as Schor also names it, "the Frenchness of universalism" ["Crisis," 43]), naturally carry with them the legitimization of France's time honored "civilizing mission."[3] I will return to such claims to universal reason at the end of this chapter. However, it is important to remember that, from the perspective of subjugated peoples whose cultures and natural resources were shattered by colonialism and by the shameful reality of the slave trade, France's "civilizing mission" was a justification for, and therefore cannot be separated from, that nation's colonial endeavors. It is that colonial framework that Césaire confronts in his works, even when he agrees with some of the tenets of "universalism" as presented by the French enlightenment.[4]

It may be useful to clarify that what is at stake here is not a philosophical discussion of the universal "as such," in the abstract. One might concede the need and inevitability of such a notion coming up in discussions of human affairs, and even its potential usefulness in discussions of human rights and global justice. However, what we are addressing here are the concrete discursive incarnations that the concept has taken in the long history of Europe's global imperial expansion. In that concrete and ineludible context, the notion of universalism has frequently served as a justification for the domination of cultures that were deemed inferior or primitive, lagging behind a Europe (or France, or the West) that had the duty to redeem or civilize them. Inevitably, and beyond any potential value of the universal "as such" (if one may talk about such a thing), the *history* of the values and norms presented and often violently imposed as universal is full of self-servingly Eurocentric ideas.

The paradoxical nature of Césaire's engagement with France's claims as stronghold of universal values in *Toussaint Louverture* and *La tragédie du roi Christophe* is highlighted when we pay attention to the concrete historical moment when both the essay and the play were written. Césaire breaks with the French Communist Party in 1956 and creates his own party, the "Parti Progressiste Martiniquais," in 1958: his well-known *Lettre à Maurice Thorez* explains his reasons, chief among which is the inability of the Communist Party's framework to take into account the specific plight of black peoples in the colonial world. In 1958, Charles de Gaulle inaugurates the Fifth Republic, which Césaire supports on the assumption (based on promises by de Gaulle) that it would bring more autonomy to the French Overseas Departments: he is soon disappointed with the actual results. The events in France eventually lead to the Algerian crisis and the wave of independence movements in Africa; Césaire's writings from this period, as well as his speeches in the French Assembly, show his support for those decolonizing developments. His literary works from that period are marked by a renewed emphasis on the history of the Antilles and on the topics of colonization and slavery from the perspective of those recent events.[5] One can appreciate that renewal of the writer's focus in poetry collections such as *Ferrements* (1960), whose title plays on the French words "fers," referring to the iron shackles that were put on slaves, and "ferments," referring to the revolutionary ferments arising all throughout the colonized black world.[6]

Césaire's passionate interest in contemporary anticolonial movements also found expression in essays such as the preface to the writings of Guinean independence leader and first president Sekou Touré, where his praise for the Guinean president echoes the concerns that drive him to study the two heroes of the Haitian Revolution:

> One sees many erroneous statements about him. Some of his French admirers say with satisfaction: "He is a product of our culture." Others, the reactionaries, say: "Do not trust him, he has been formed by Prague and Moscow." The truth seems altogether different to me. One only has to observe his style: abandonment of self and control of self, vehemence and wisdom, particularism and humanism—he has created in politics the African style, but it is Africa, its millenary past, that has taught him all that. ("Preface," 6; my translation)[7]

In Césaire's preface, Touré becomes the embodiment of the balance between "particularisme et humanisme" that will also guide his exploration of Toussaint Louverture and King Christophe.[8] An aspiration to a never fully achieved equilibrium between those two principles will guide Césaire's political and literary output, shaping his compromises and spurring his rebelliousness. Of course, there is no reason why particularism should be opposed to humanism, except within a Eurocentric, colonial framework that regards the non-European as not fully human. As I will suggest below, Césaire's inability to completely let go of that Eurocentric assumption (a valorization of *the human* over *the particular* that overlooks the particular "Frenchness" of France's colonial version of "the human"), even as he dissects its racist premises, is one of the underlying dramas of his anticolonial activity.

That Césaire possessed a deep insight on the issue of particularism and universalism is clearly shown in his *Letter to Maurice Thorez* (1956), one of the documents that most clearly exposes his political philosophy. Beyond its immediate purpose of breaking with the French Communist Party, the letter presents Césaire's mature positions on some of his most cherished political concerns. Toward the end of the text, Césaire states:

> I shall anticipate an objection. Provincialism? Not at all. I am not burying myself in a narrow particularism. But neither do I want to lose myself in an emaciated universalism. There are two ways to lose oneself: walled segregation in the particular or dilution in the "universal." My conception of the universal is that of a universal enriched by all that is particular, a universal enriched by every particular: the deepening and coexistence of all particulars. ("Letter," 152)

In "Letter to Maurice Thorez," Césaire displays a remarkable awareness of the universal and the particular as relative points of a spectrum whose main characteristic is its continuity, none of whose points can be imposed as the summit that simply transcends those that come before and exist around it. In fact, the "universal," as defined by Césaire in the letter, has a striking resemblance to Ernesto Laclau's categorization of the universal (in *Emancipation(s)*) as an "empty signifyer," an ever receding horizon whose main purpose is precisely to always avoid and escape "walled segregation," but whose content cannot be prescribed or imposed.[9]

My point here is that, in spite of Césaire's insightful ideas on these issues, as revealed in the quote above from "Letter to Maurice Thorez," in fact throughout his career he experienced the relation between the universal and the particular as a *tension,* a source of anxious concern. This, as I will show below, is most clearly seen in his two works on Haiti. And the reason for Césaire's discomfort, I venture, is that he was trying to dismantle from the inside a colonial logic that ontologizes Europe's claim as sole or main possessor of the universal and the human. In conjunction with the coloniality of power and knowledge, the coloniality of being operates precisely by racializing (essentializing) cultural differences that are also fitted neatly into Europe's narrative of what Enrique Dussel calls the myth of modernity: everything non-European falls outside of, or at best comes before, Europe's *universal* narrative toward its own modern self. Stuck in their colonial difference, Europe's Others are condemned to perpetually aspire to that universal presence, while remaining eternally condemned to the partiality of their particularity. What we observe in Césaire is not only a critique of this model but also the drama of a colonial subject partially caught in it. This, I should clarify, I do not present as criticism of Césaire, but rather in order to insist on why his work remains so vital, so necessary, so engaging for us still today. Even at his most political, Césaire is never merely programmatic: his doubts, hesitations, and shifts reveal the humanity that makes him first and foremost a poet.

Where Negritude Rose for the First Time

The events of the late fifties and early sixties certainly made Césaire's examination of the issues mentioned in the previous section particularly pressing (to the point of making him choose drama as his main literary medium of expression, in order to reach wider segments of the population). However, it is also true that the poet's main preoccupations remained fairly constant throughout his career, for his concern, from his very early works, was an exploration of (with a view to overcoming) the colonial condition. Thus, it is not surprising that Haiti is present in Césaire's work from the very beginning.

Already in his foundational *Cahier*, Césaire refers to Haiti as the country "where negritude rose for the first time" (*Notebook*, 15), and in a well-known passage from the poem he evokes:

> What is also mine: a little cell in the Jura,
> a little cell, the snow lines it with white bars
> the snow is a jailer mounting guard before a prison
> What is mine
> a lone man imprisoned in whiteness
> a lone man defying the white screams of white death
> (TOUSSAINT, TOUSSAINT LOUVERTURE)
> a man who mesmerizes the white sparrow hawk of white death
> a man alone in the sterile sea of white sand
> a coon grown old standing up to the waters of the sky
> Death traces a shining circle above this man
> death stars softly above his head
> death breathes, crazed, in the ripened cane field of his arms
> . . . .
> Swellings of night in the four corners of this daybreak
> convulsions of congealed death
> tenacious fate
> screams erect from mute death
> the splendor of the blood will it not burst open?
>   (Césaire, *Notebook*, 16–17)

Those lines contain Césaire's first literary allusion to Toussaint Louverture, the heroic "black Jacobin" who became the leader of the slave rebellion in Haiti, but who was ultimately betrayed by his own generals (including Christophe) and taken prisoner by Napoleon. Toussaint dies in solitary confinement in a prison in the Jura Mountains, and already in his lifetime he was considered by some what he is in Césaire's poem: an emblem of an oppressed people who dared show their oppressors that, in oppressing them, they were betraying their own loftiest principles.[10] As C. L. R. James made clear in *The Black Jacobins*, Toussaint was greatly inspired in his revolutionary actions by the very principles of the French revolution—liberty, equality, and fraternity—principles whose radical implications he could see more clearly than the empire that destroyed him in order to re-enslave his people.[11] In Césaire's poem, Toussaint becomes a martyr of negritude, whose spilled blood awaits the moment when black peoples will burst toward freedom. Politically, that aspiration was a somewhat distant hope when the poem was first published in 1939, but it was well within reach at the publication of the poem's final and definitive edition in 1956.[12]

In spite of that invocation of Toussaint as the founding hero of the country "where negritude rose for the first time," already in the *Cahier* we can see the tensions that will also appear in Césaire's later works on Haitian Revolution. In the lines quoted above, Césaire carefully constructs Louverture's death through images of ominous whiteness, and the Haitian independence hero's ordeal is presented as part of a more generalized battle against racism. To be sure, from its very origins the Haitian revolution was interpreted as a racial threat by European *racist* colonists throughout the rest of the slave-holding Caribbean.[13] And indeed, one cannot deny the importance of the struggle against racism in Haiti's slaves' battle for emancipation, for it is clear that racism underlay and articulated the logic of European colonial domination at a global level. Racist essentialism is at the center of the coloniality of power and the coloniality of being that govern and order the colonial/modern world system of which Saint Domingue was an important node. The struggle against such racial logic implies, for Césaire, not simply the material struggle against slavery and colonialism but also the affirmation and celebration of African (and Afro-Caribbean) cultures, customs, and worldviews, which have been reduced to marginal status, at best, by the primacy of Eurocentrism.

However, throughout the *Cahier* Césaire is careful to balance his justified attacks on the colonial legacy of racism, and the resultant affirmation and celebration of the *particularity* and *specificity* of black experience, with exalted (and perfectly consistent with his antiracist stand) declarations that the liberation that he aspires to should be *universal,* that is to say, apply to all races. Thus, in a celebrated passage (one that Edward Said was particularly fond of [Said, *Power,* 220]) we read: "no race has a monopoly on beauty, on intelligence, on strength, and there is room for everyone at the convocation of conquest" (*Notebook,* 44). Interestingly, in that passage Césaire's invocation of "universal" virtues ("beauty," "intelligence," "strength") comes clothed in the militant (and military) rhetoric of "conquest," a charged and provocative word in a colonial context. This new "conquest," we must assume, will only target obstacles or challenges shared by the whole human race.[14]

My point here is not to minimize in any way the centrality of the struggle against racism and colonialism in Césaire's work or in his portrayal of Haiti's battle for emancipation. Rather, I am emphasizing that Césaire's rhetorical strategy in the *Cahier* tends to alternate between Afrocentric pride and a somewhat abstract universalism in his attempt to ground his movement toward liberation. Thus, we find universalist passages like the one on everybody's place "at the convocation of conquest" quoted above, and multiple passages like the following, in which the poet becomes one with a particularly African setting:

> Who and what are we? A most worthy question!
> From staring too long at trees I have become a tree and my
> long tree feet have dug in the ground large venom sacs ...
> from brooding too long on the Congo
> I have become a Congo resounding with forests and rivers
>   (Césaire, *Notebook*, 18)

The *Cahier* consistently alternates between those two approaches. Even as it invokes a collective encounter of all humanity at the convocation of conquest, it does not forget how Eurocentric definitions of the human have denied the humanity of black peoples ("I am of no nationality recognized by the chancelleries. I defy the craniometer. *Homo sum, etc.*" [ibid., 29]). In fact, at moments the poet flatly refuses to partake of the "achievements" associated with Europe's aggressive culture: "my negritude is not a tower or a cathedral / it takes root in the red flesh of the soil / it takes root in the ardent flesh of the sky" (ibid., 35). Not surprisingly, Césaire's ambiguous use of those two paradigms (abstract universalism and affirmation of his black specificity) has occasionally made him the object of criticism and misinterpretations. Negritude itself has been accused of essentialism (by critics like René Ménil), whereas Raphaël Confiant, from the *Créolité* movement, accused Césaire of being too disconnected from the specific realities of his native Caribbean in his constant attention to both France and Africa.[15] On the other hand, in his famous essay "Black Orpheus," Jean Paul Sartre, a supporter of negritude and its anticolonial claims, felt quite comfortable subsuming the movement under a universal dialectic that in fact reduced its specificity to a dialectical moment of negativity (Sartre *What is Literature*)—an approach that was later criticized by Fanon in *Black Skin*.[16]

Those accusations and interpretations of Césaire's ideas may not always be fair, but they do point to tensions in his work, tensions that find clear expression in the two works on the Haitian Revolution and its aftermath that Césaire wrote in the 1960s. What I want to highlight here is that Césaire's alternations between "universalism" and "particularism" are intimately related to the colonial context in which he writes, which locates him, as a colonial intellectual, in a paradoxical situation: he condemns the exclusionary logic of Eurocentric colonial "humanism," yet he is unable, and unwilling, to completely let go of paradigms learned from that colonial framework, and which are often used to justify colonial domination. Césaire constantly struggles to open up the notion of universalism, while at the same time using as his point of departure the tenets of *"French* Universalism," which then force him to defensively proclaim and affirm his excluded particularity (in a way that seems too essentialist to his critics). Those tensions already form the cradle for that initial invocation of Toussaint Louverture in his first poem, and they will naturally come to the foreground in his subsequent explorations of Haiti's history.

Christophe's Pride and Césaire's

La tragédie du roi Christophe is a play full of ironic humor.[17] The object of its irony is the attempt on the part of Henry Christophe (as he spelled his name), former general in the Haitian revolution and self-proclaimed king of Haiti, to create a Haitian royal court in the French style. That attempt is accomplished at the expense of the working masses, who must support Christophe's nobility, just as before they sustained the French colonialists. However, the play, as its title indicates, is supposed to be a tragedy, and its protagonist, Christophe, a tragic hero. What, then, makes Christophe a tragic hero in Césaire's portrayal? As in the case of other tragic heroes, there is something noble and grand about him, even as the play reveals his tragic flaw and the way he oversteps his rightful boundaries in unrestrained hubris.

In order to better understand what makes Christophe tragic in Césaire's eyes, therefore admirable in spite of his excess, we can turn to one famous scene of the play in which Christophe's wife blames him for being too harsh on the Haitian people. Christophe responds:

> I ask too much of men? But not enough of black men, Madame. If there is one thing that riles me as much as slaveholders' talk, it's to hear our philantropists proclaim, with the best of intentions of course, that all men are men and that there are neither blacks nor whites. That's thinking in an armchair, not in the world. All men have the same rights? Agreed. But some men have more duties than others . . . Does anyone believe that all men, all I say, without privilege, without special exemption, have known capture, deportation, slav-

ery, collective reduction to the level of animals, the monstrous insult, the total outrage that we have suffered, the all-denying spittle plastered on our bodies, spat into our faces. We alone, Madame, do you hear me, we blacks . . . And that's why I have to ask more of blacks than of other people, more faith, more enthusiasm, a step, another step, and still another, and never a step backward. (*Tragedy*, 41–42)

Here we see another version of the distinction between "humanism" and "particularism" that we saw above in the *Letter to Maurice Thorez*. Yes, all men have equal rights; but no, all men are not simply men. The disjunction between those two statements comes from the fact that one is an abstraction; the other one, an assessment of a long history of colonial domination in which Africans have been not only materially dominated by European empires but also relegated to a subhuman status, both culturally and existentially. Moreover, as Christophe bitterly points out (when he implicitly links the abstract humanism of philanthropists and the rhetoric of slave-owners), Western colonial powers have claimed to purvey the truth of the universality of the human just as they deny or minimize the humanity of their colonized subjects. Even more: knowledge of, and access to, "the human" is that which Europeans presumably bring to those dominated cultures, the white man's burden, a justification of a colonial process that also keeps full access to "the human" perpetually out of reach for the colonized. It is the recognition of that twisted logic that makes Christophe noble in Césaire's play, even if as readers and spectators we recognize the way in which he translates his insight into an occasion for his self-aggrandizement.

Christophe articulates the meaning of the Haitian Revolution and his own kingdom as a vindication of the black race. More than once throughout the play he affirms his identity as a black man with regard to both European whites and Haitian mulattoes and free people of color (*Tragedy*, 12, 26, 56, and others).[18] Moreover, Christophe attempts to clarify the meaning of the new nobility titles and names, which could be easily misconstrued as simple imitation of Europe, in the following way:

These new names, these titles of nobility, this Coronation! In the past they stole our names, our pride, our nobility. They, I repeat, stole them. Pierre, Paul, Jacques, Toussaint. Those are the humiliating brand marks with which they obliterated our real names. I myself, your king, can you sense a man's hurt at not knowing the name he's called by, or to what his name calls him? Only our Mother Africa knows. Since we can't rescue our names from the past, we'll take them from the future. With names of glory I will cover your slave names, with names of pride our names of infamy, with names of redemption our orphan names! (*Tragedy*, 25–26)

Thus, in the context of the slaves' history of material and cultural dispossession, Christophe's obsession with nobility titles is more than mere personal vanity; it is an admittedly perverse way of restoring pride (recovering Africa) for his black people. Throughout the play, the link between the revolution's victory and the recovery of that lost Africa is made explicit: during Christophe's crowning ceremony we hear a song to Shango, the Yoruba god of thunder and lightning (*Tragédie*, 40), and the king himself says at one point: "Poor Africa! Poor Haiti, I mean. Anyway, it's the same thing" (*Tragedy*, 36). Just before the rebellious masses take over his palace and he kills himself, Christophe invokes the African gods, and finally exclaims:

Africa! Help me to go home, carry me like an aged child in your arms. Undress me and wash me. Strip me of all these garments, strip me as a man strips off dreams when the dawn comes . . . Strip me of my nobles, my nobility, my scepter, my crown. And wash me, oh, wash me clean of their grease paint, their kisses, wash me clean of my kingdom. (*Tragedy*, 90)

Displaying the same Afrocentric sensibility that has exasperated some critics of Césaire among the members of the *creolité* movement in the Caribbean, Christophe's final apotheosis finds him equaling his *true* identity with a primordial Africa rather than with Haiti. In Césaire's imaginary, Christophe's European trappings and even his Haitian history as mere temporary disguises that cover his fundamental Africanness.

If I have insisted on these examples of Christophe's Afrocentric vision, it is because that vision, that desire to exalt his oppressed race, is what redeems him in Césaire's play, what makes him not simply a vulgar despot but a tragic hero. However, there is a paradox in Christophe's attempt to vindicate Africa, a paradox that is at the heart of the tragedy. Christophe attempts to vindicate Africa in the Americas *by mimicking the splendor of imperial Europe*. Clearly, one explanation for this would be to accuse Christophe of simply drawing on a populist rhetoric of African pride in order to better impose his authoritarianism as an expression of the will of the masses. Indeed, there may be much truth to that reading, and one might find examples of similar conduct throughout the postcolonial world. But I would suggest there is something subtler is going on in this play. There are no indications that Christophe does not believe his own rhetoric, and some of his most exalted moments of Afrocentric pride come clothed in a language that reminds us of the intensity of Césaire's best poetry.

The point I am trying to make is that the play does not simply present the corruption of Christophe by power. It presents the blindness of a colonized subject who, even in his attempt to recover the dignity of an identity denied by the colonial condition, finds no other model on which to articulate his pride than the very colonial frame that deprived him of his dignity in the first place. Christophe looks for agency and greatness, but European splendor is the only *available* model of grandiosity in his (post)colonial environment. This tragic dilemma had already been articulated by thinkers like Frantz Fanon, who in *Black Skin, White Masks* writes, "Out of the blackest part of my soul, across the zebra stripping of my mind, surges this desire to be suddenly *white*" (63). The meaning of that desire is further clarified by Fanon: "I will compel the white man to acknowledge that I am human" (ibid., 98), because "all I wanted was to be a man among other men" (ibid., 112). By the desire to be white, Fanon means the desire to be a man, to be *human*, but if in the logic of coloniality only a white man has the material benefits and the *ontological wholeness* that come from being human, then Fanon's black subject must become white, wear a white mask that puts him in an existentially and politically untenable situation, since it is the white man who has denied the humanity of the black man. And yet, the impulse to become white is compelling, for within the logic of coloniality the alternative is nonbeing.

Similarly and in a more farcical key, Christophe's mimicry of the signs of European power becomes for him the only (yet untenable) means of recovering a dignity that has been denied. The grammar of colonial authority and power remains oblique and malleable: for Christophe, it becomes a sign of black greatness when a black man uses it. Thus, one could argue that he is sincere, even righteous, in his desire to reinstate black greatness, but blind in attempt to attain it through the white masks of a Eurocentric aristocracy. That aspiration and that blindness make Christophe tragic, not merely evil, in Césaire's play.

Throughout the play, Césaire portrays clearly enough how Christophe has overstepped his legitimate boundaries, but the poet cannot help being moved by the emperor's commitment to glorifying his African roots in Caribbean soil.[19] We can see the basis for this fondness in an important interview from 2004, in which Césaire commented on the play and read sections from it, emphasizing how aspects of the Haitian drama in fact remain relevant to the rest of the Caribbean. At one point Césaire reads Madame Christophe's objections to her husband's relentless ambition: "Christophe! I am only a poor woman, I am queen, but I have been a servant at the Crown Inn! A crown on my head will not turn me into anything other than a simple woman, a good black woman who tells her husband: beware!" (*Tragédie*, 58; my translation). Then the interview presents Césaire's comments: "Isn't that very Martinican? I can almost see the person I have just described," at which point the interviewer adds : "Césaire continues reading Madame Christophe's part with a '"woman's" voice'" (*Nègre je suis*, 60; my translation). After finishing his reading, using a "woman's voice" to imitate Madame Christophe that the interviewer carefully registers, Césaire observes: "Madame Christophe is calling on us to use our common sense. My grandmother expressed herself in that way. I have written from what I knew. Imagine, at that period, a woman who had been a slave. She could be tempted by acceptance ["résignation"], by caution ["prudence"]. That is quite understandable. In fact, it is an old tragedy" (*Nègre je suis*, 63; my translation). Interestingly, Césaire's words acknowledge the tension between Christophe and his wife's positions (his violent pathos and her cautious call to prudence) as a source of tragedy, which implies that, as in any truly tragic conflict, both characters present legitimate claims. However, the poet cannot stop himself from describing Madame Christophe's position as a "temptation" that comes from *a woman* who had been a slave. In Césaire's language, "bon sens" (common sense), "résignation" (resignation, acceptance) and "prudence" (prudence, caution) become weak, "feminine" temptations, in spite of their legitimate claim in the face of Christophe's brutality. For a few moments Christophe's *manly* strength, however violently applied, is worthier than *feminine* resignation.

Here we must highlight that, as indicated in the introduction, gender has been one of the dimensions of coloniality that is often neglected in theoretical formulations and literary critiques. Given Césaire's long fascination with the rhetoric of tragic "masculine" heroics (as expressed most vehemently, perhaps, in his early dramatic poem *Et les chiens se taissaint*, whose protagonist is simply called "the rebel"), it is not surprising that such language is most valued in the poet's assessment of his Christophe tragedy.[20] However, for us as contemporary readers such masculinist rhetoric becomes a revealing example of what María Lugones has called "the modern/colonial gender system." The point here would not be merely to criticize Césaire for that rhetoric (although there is no reason not to do that), but also to highlight the pervasiveness, within the thought of a writer clearly committed to anticolonial politics, of a language that ultimately legitimizes "the naturalizing of the identities and relations of coloniality" (Lugones, "Heterosexualism," 192) when it comes to gender. Thus, the cautionary call here is for all of us engaged in decolonial thought and action.

In spite of Césaire's proud affirmation of Christophe's masculinist heroics, it is clear that he is also aware of the fact that his play portrays a historical character whose excesses he cannot condone (in the same interview, he refers to Christophe's monarchy as "grotesque" [*Nègre je suis*, 57]). However, it remains revealing that Césaire does feel that Christophe's passion for Africa's glory, as portrayed by Césaire himself, still brings something to an anticolonial struggle that no criticism of his excesses can deny. And in spite of Césaire's universalist rhetoric, Christophe's flaw is not the particularism he fiercely tries to embrace. In fact, his violence is partially linked to the fact that he is not particular enough, since he invokes his hurt pride but seems to find no other way to repair the hurt than embracing Europe's oppressive colonial models.

Regarding Christophe's court, Césaire states: "All of that is grotesque; but behind the etiquette, behind that man, there is a tragedy that poses very deep questions about the encounter of civilizations. These people take Europe as a model. And yet, Europe frantically mocks them" (*Nègre je suis*, 57–58; my translation). Césaire's comments perfectly illuminate the tragic intensity of his play. And yet his words do not fully capture his literary achievement, for Christophe's tragedy is not simply that of a "mimic man" who is convinced that anything European is better. As suggested above, Césaire's Christophe is actively engaged in recovering the dignity of his black people but cannot find any other way of doing it than imitating Europe's models. He is not trying to be European, but rather to be black (which in the play ambiguously stands for both African and Haitian) through European means. His tragedy is that of the victims of the coloniality of power, which goes well beyond colonialism itself—the double bind in which the colonized thirsts after a fullness of presence that remains perpetually out of reach yet always enticing. Ultimately this logic implies, as Maldonado-Torres reminds us, a coloniality of existential being itself. Later in the same interview, Césaire comments: "One must liberate the black man, but one must also liberate the liberator" (*Nègre je suis*, 63; my translation). His Christophe stands out as an exemplary representation of that recurrent figure in all anticolonial and emancipation movements: the liberator in desperate need of liberation. This clearly implies for Césaire not a rejection of the West (no one can really accuse Césaire of that), but rather a rejection of the West's claim to ontological, essential superiority: the coloniality of power and the coloniality of being.

Toussaint's Compromises and Césaire's

Césaire's other work on the Haitian Revolution is the historical essay, *Toussaint Louverture: la révolution française et le problème colonial* [*Toussaint Louverture: The French Revolution and the Colonial Problem*] (1961). The alert reader may pause at the book's subtitle: surely Césaire means the *Haitian* Revolution? Not quite, for in this book Césaire's approach to the events in Haiti is dramatically different from that of the *Tragedy*. (By contrast, C. L. R. James's *Black Jacobins*, which Césaire lists among his references, is subtitled "Toussaint L'Ouverture and the San Domingo Revolution.") There is certainly no question about the close relation between the French and the Haitian Revolutions: as Césaire compellingly demonstrates and C. L. R. James had shown before him, the full implications of neither revolution can be thoroughly understood without considering the other. However, the way Césaire arranges his material in this book has significant implications for what his priorities are. As a noteworthy detail, one should notice that, in a 345-page book titled *Toussaint Louverture,* Toussaint himself does not appear as a central actor until page 194, more than half way through. Thus, the whole text is organized as a progression of increasingly radical *reactions* not only to the events of the French Revolution but also, and more importantly, to its guiding principles, particularly the ideals of liberty, fraternity, and equality, and the Declaration of Rights of Man and of the Citizen. As we suggested in the introduction when commenting on Hayden White's ideas, the way writers *structure* their events matters; in Césaire's book on Toussaint, universal principles radiate from France, and France's others follow suit.

The first part of the book, titled "La fronde des grands blancs" ("The White Uprising"), focuses on the French colonists in Haiti, and their demands for autonomy and fuller control of their own commercial interests, until that moment subordinated to those of metropolitan France. As Césaire clearly indicates, the white colonists claim rights for themselves while at the same time trying to exclude not only the slaves, who are considered property, but also the growing class of free people of color. The second part, titled "La révolte mulâtre" ("The Mulatto Revolt"), shows how mulattoes and free people of color, realizing they cannot expect anything from the racist whites, decide to take matters in their own hands. Before the free people of color finally have to resort to an armed revolt, Césaire fills many pages with debates in the French National Assembly, debates that revolve around the fact that people of color are free citizens, many of them landowners, but are not receiving the same rights as the white landowners. It should be clear, however, that the free people of color wanted the same "universal" rights that *white* men enjoyed: they also regarded slaves as property.[21] It is in the third part, titled "La révolution nègre" ("The Black Revolution"), that the obvious (for our contemporary eyes) question is asked: if all men have equal and natural rights by virtue of being human, how can some human beings be slaves? Not surprisingly, only the slaves "get" that simple point; they rebel, and soon find their leader in Toussaint Louverture, a former slave who could read and write, and who had absorbed the main ideals of the French Revolution.

It is important to emphasize that, in Césaire's structuring of his narrative, the revolting slaves do not bring anything fundamentally *different* or new to a revolutionary movement that *starts in France*. Their contribution, and Toussaint's in particular, is to radicalize it, to push it to its logical consequences (the abolition of slavery). As Césaire indicates: "The abolition of slavery was within the logic of the [French] revolution; but it was necessary to brutally shake up that historical actor, so that he would consent to play his role" (*Toussaint Louverture*, 215–16; my translation). In a rhetorical move that reveals the poet behind the historian, Césaire personifies the French Revolution in a theatrical metaphor, turning it into a historical actor that leads the march towards freedom, with the other human characters, including the Haitian revolutionaries, following behind (one is reminded of Delacroix's similarly structured "Liberty Guiding the People"). It is not surprising that in a later interview Césaire refers to "my book about Toussaint Louverture, which in reality is a book about the French Revolution" (Louis, *Conversation*, 66; my translation).

Of course, whether the liberation of the slaves was within the logic of the French Revolution is itself open to debate, and that statement may be regarded Césaire's concession to a frame that he is struggling to preserve. One might equally argue that the French Revolution unfolded within a *colonial logic* that, while breaking some untenable social barriers in the metropolis, left untouched the divide of the colonial difference between white Europeans and racialized Others from around the world. In the abstract, Césaire is right: to state that "men are born free" (as the first article of the 1789 *Declaration* states) logically includes all men. The question is what does this mean for slaves whose very humanity is in question.[22]

In the conclusion of his essay, after still another extended reflection on the French Revolution, Césaire rhetorically asks, as if foreseeing a query from a confused reader: "Mais alors, où est la part de Toussaint-Louverture dans tout cela?" (*Toussaint Louverture*, 343) ("But then, what is Toussaint's role in all of that?" [my translation]). It is then that Césaire conveys his views on Toussaint's quite significant contribution to the whole emancipating process:

> When Toussaint arrived, it was to take the declaration of Human Rights literally; it was to show that there is no pariah race; that there is no marginal country; that there are no excluded people; it was to incarnate and particularize a principle; that is to say, to bring it to life. In the history and the realm of the rights of man, he was, on behalf of blacks, the agent and intercessor. That is his place, his true place. Toussaint Louverture's combat was for the transformation of a formal right into a real right, a combat for the acknowledgment of man, and that is why he, and the black slave revolt in Saint Domingue, are inscribed in the history of universal civilization. If there is a negative side to his character—which is hardly avoidable given the situation—it lies precisely there: above all he attempted to deduce the existence of his people taking an abstract universal as his point of departure, rather than seizing the singularity of his people in order to promote it to universality. (*Toussaint Louverture*, 344; my translation)

Here we see again the tension between the "universal" and the "particular," a tension that Césaire occasionally acknowledges as an untenable, deconstructible fiction (as in the quote from his *Letter to Maurice Thorez* presented above in section II), but which recurs in his work as a source of considerable anxiety.

In Césaire's reading, the Declaration of Rights of Man leads, and Toussaint concretizes its abstract ideals; that process gives Toussaint his true place in history. However, Césaire's discomfort with his own assessment is clearly revealed in his immediate criticism of Toussaint. While Toussaint's "true place" in history comes from his incarnation of an abstract principle, Césaire is clearly uncomfortable with the gesture of "deducing" the existence of the Haitian people from "an abstract universal," rather than departing from the people's concrete singularity in order to elevate it to the universal (while at the same time insisting that the Haitian leader could hardly avoid his behavior "given the situation"). Césaire does not elaborate on how the second gesture would differ from the first, but one may assume that the result would look more like the universal as he defines it in his *Letter to Maurice Thorez:* a confluence of particulars. However, the point I want to emphasize here is that the conundrum that Césaire describes comes, to a large extent, from his own structuring of the narrative as that of universal principles that find their first and most complete articulation in France. By subordinating Toussaint to that dialectical development (for it is a dialectic between France and the former slave that clearly invokes Hegel's dialectic of the master and the slave), Césaire subordinates the Haitian Revolution to a teleology that is anchored and has its origin in France's relation to its colonial others. Paradoxically, as he subordinates the Haitian slaves' revolt against France's brutal imperial regime—which was also linked to an emerging global system of colonial capitalist accumulation—to an abstract dialectical process, Césaire in fact reproduces the deductive gesture he criticizes in Toussaint (as portrayed by him).[23]

Another consequence of Césaire's presentation of Toussaint as a leader who incarnates universal principles appears in chapter 10 of the third section of his essay. In an extended comparison of the revolutionary leaderships of Toussaint and Lenin, Césaire attempts to explain and contextually justify Toussaint's authoritarian moves when he forces former black slaves to work in their plantations while respecting the rights of white land owners: "the ideas were good, the method much less so" (*Toussaint Louverture*, 269; my translation). We may remember here that in Christophe's tragedy we find a parallel situation, with the playwright also keenly aware of flaws in the king's methods, even if those flaws are somewhat softened by his grand vision. Toussaint was engaged in his own tragic dilemma, which operates as a mirror image of Christophe's tragedy: Toussaint is too involved with the universal at the expense of the concrete, even though that involvement constitutes his glory; Christophe is too involved with his attempt to make his particular people glorious, seemingly at the expense of universal values.

It is of course not coincidental that Césaire presents these two characters as mirror images of the same conflict, since they represent two poles that he himself felt compelled to pay homage to throughout his career, even as he showed keen awareness of their eminently deconstructible character. Just as Christophe tries to celebrate his "particularity" within a colonial frame that a priori rejects the worth of that particularity, Toussaint clings to a universal that (as portrayed by Césaire) is little more than Schor's "French Universalism"—the universality of Catholic religion, the transparency of the French language, and later the self-evidence of French enlightened secularism. To this we could add the Western Universalism of Capitalist global production, whose first waves Toussaint was trying to remain part of, in his attempts to preserve the colonial plantation system. In other words, each from an opposite end of the same spectrum, both Christophe and Toussaint are still partially operating within the logic of coloniality.

I should emphasize again that, in describing Césaire's portrayal of these two foundational characters as still operating within the logic of coloniality, I do not necessarily mean a criticism of the Martinican poet. In fact, the point I am trying to highlight is Césaire's lucid representation of the colonial intellectual's (or revolutionary's, or politician's) struggle with the lure of the universal *as defined by the coloniality of power.* As indicated above in the section on Christophe, Fanon has provided a masterful description of this condition. In his depiction, the white mask does not simply promise to make the black man white—it promises to make him *a man.* Both Fanon and Césaire excel in the presentation of the *affective* dimension of the colonial condition, wherein social, economic and political conditions, disguised as a natural ontology, are internalized as structures in the cognitive and behavioral patterns of the colonial subject. Even the struggle for liberation, then, must unburden itself of seemingly self-evident colonial assumptions. Existentially, the liberator must be liberated.[24]

The question here is not the desirability of universalism as such, in the abstract, and in fact a case could be made for the usefulness of such a concept along the lines of Césaire's statements in his *Letter to Maurice Thorez,* quoted above. The issue is how Western universalism developed historically in conjunction with colonial projects, more often than not providing a justification for such projects. For universalism, as conceived by the logic of coloniality, is not an ever-expanding addition of particularities, but the transcendence of all particularities, which naturally translates into the universalization of one particularity, whether that of Hegel's Prussia in the 1830s or global hegemony of neoliberal capitalism today. In Césaire's representation, both the glorification of the particular (Christophe) and the appeal to the universal (Toussaint) must purge themselves of the colonial frame that has produced the better-known versions of those concepts.

Behind the Times, or Too Far Ahead?

As I indicated earlier, the dilemmas that Toussaint and Christophe incarnate touched Césaire very closely as an intellectual and as a politician, at a moment when he attempted to redefine Martinique's relation to France in a context of global anticolonial movements. Regarding Christophe, Césaire has said: "In *The Tragedy of King Christophe,* I have described the difficulties of a man who must lead a country like Haiti, a very complex country, and one can certainly find that in the Caribbean" (*Nègre je suis,* 53; my translation). While

Césaire is being disingenuous in his concise description of what he is doing in a play about a man who virtually re-enslaved his people, it is clear and accurate that in the context of a postcolonial Caribbean still operating within a global neocolonial logic, Haiti's case becomes exemplary in an extreme manner, both as luminous example and as cautionary tale. Christophe's luminosity, in Césaire's portrayal, is his commitment to *négritude*.

Toussaint Louverture presents still another aspect of the "complexity" of the Caribbean that was very close to Césaire's personal experience. Throughout the text, one can clearly notice Césaire's ambiguous position toward the fact that Toussaint never tried to turn his revolution into an independence movement. While at one point Césaire recognizes, following C. L. R. James, that it was probably a mistake on Toussaint's part (304–307), he is very understanding of Toussaint's desire to retain the ties with France, provided that France would live up to its own ideals: "There is a magic word that Toussaint always refused to pronounce: the word *independence* . . . Did he think it was premature? In that case, he was behind with regard to the masses" (ibid., 304–5; my translation). But Césaire's assessment at that point of the book comes after a slightly different one with regard to Toussaint's 1801 constitution. Commenting on the plans that Toussaint seemingly had for an autonomous Haiti with French representatives who would operate almost as ambassadors, Césaire states: "Genial intuition. The idea of a French Commonwealth was there in seed. Toussaint was wrong in only one count: he was ahead of his times by a good century and a half" (ibid., 283; my translation). Toussaint was either behind his times or too far ahead of them—Césaire in the 1960s does not seem quite sure, just as he seems uncertain of where to find the right balance between his anticolonial positions and his prudent (to use the word he uses to describe Madame Christophe) pursual of political compromises. Martinique's situation as a French "Département d'Outre-Mer" already seemed stagnant to Césaire, and in fact, some sort of "French Commonwealth" (*not* independence) was precisely what he proposed as a possible solution to the disappointments and failures of that status throughout the years: the development of more autonomy for the island within the context of political union with France. Thus, Césaire's portrayal of Toussaint clearly reflects his anxiety about his own role in Martinique's political history: a man behind his times at a moment when so many colonial territories around the world were seizing the opportunity of independence, or a visionary who realized that Martinique's economic stability and decolonized future could both be achieved without independence, in union with France? Indeed, it could be argued that while the structure of the essay on Toussaint is peculiar as a portrayal of the Haitian Revolution (no other text examined in this book spends as much time in the meetings of the French Assembly), it is a structure that coincides with Martinique's relation to France at the time Césaire was writing. It was a France-centric structure that Césaire in many ways dreaded, but also hoped could be turned around for Martinique's benefit.[25]

As was indicated earlier in the chapter, *La tragédie du roi Christophe* and *Toussaint Louverture* are by no means irreconcilable works, and one may find ways to make them complementary in spite of their differences in tone, emphasis, and implications. Taken together, they both tackle the issues of particularism and universalism discussed above, and the fact that they come at it from different directions is a sign of Césaire's keen (if agonistic) insight into their interplay in colonial societies and subjectivites.[26] Edward Said, a great admirer of Césaire, emphasized the complementary character of both approaches when he stated, commenting on a passage by C. L. R. James in which the Trinidadian writer quotes Césaire's *Cahier*:

> "There's room for all at the rendez-vous of victory" [C. L. R. James quoting Césaire]—is a very important phrase for me. It's impossible to talk about the sides of the opposition between Oriental and Occidental separately. I talk about what I call overlapping areas of experience. The whole point is that imperialism was not of one side only, but of two sides, and the two are always involved in each other. That's where the contrapuntal method comes in. Instead of looking at it as a melody on top and just a lot of silly accompaniment down here, or silence, it's really like a polyphonic work. In order to understand it, you have to have this concept of overlapping territories— interdependent histories, I call them. That's the only way to talk about them, in order to be able to talk about liberation, decolonization, and the integrative view, rather than the separatist one. I'm totally against separatism. (*Power*, 220)

In referring to the "melody on top, silly accompaniment down here" perspective, Said is certainly describing the cultural logic of the coloniality of power. His musical metaphor also brings to mind Enrique Dussel's notion of colonized territories and peoples as constituting the "underside of modernity," always there as marginalized and repressed part of official histories (Dussel, *Underside*). Said's concept of "interdependent histories" attempts to correct that exclusivist historical narrative, even if its suggestion of mutuality fails to highlight the violent power disproportion between the different sides of those interlocking histories.

Said is right in invoking Césaire as a champion of the "integrative" perspective that does not seek to essentialize the distinctions between "the West" and its colonial territories throughout the world. What Said does not emphasize, by quoting just one phrase from the *Cahier*, is the degree to which that "integration," which also entails the interaction between universalist abstract ideals and particularist affirmation of identity, is a site of tension and anxiety in Césaire's work. The anxiety is, as we have seen, understandable, since in practice there has been little universal in the Western colonial export of universalism, and Césaire's limitation has often been his willingness to take Western universalism at face value, even as he acknowledges the colonial violence that has been exerted in the name of that universalism.

The complexity and paradoxical character of Césaire's engagement with Western universalism are probably best appreciated in an interview offered late in his life (the same one in which he revisits his *Tragedy of King Christophe*), in which he confronts the subject, and his own critics, directly. The Martinican poet states:

> It matters little to me who wrote the text of the Declaration of the Rights of Man; I couldn't care less, it exists. The criticisms against its "Western" origin are simplistic. Why would that bother me? I have always been irritated by the sectarianism I have found even in my own party. We must appropriate that text and we must know how to interepret it correctly. France did not colonize in the name of the rights of Man. One can always invent something about what happened: "Look at how unhappy they are. It would be a kind deed to bring them civilization." Besides, Europeans believe in *Civilization,* whereas we believe in *civilizations,* in plural, and in *cultures.* (*Nègre je suis*, 69–70; my translation)

Césaire's words clearly indicate his allegiance to what Said would call the "integrative' approach. Like the "rendez-vous of victory" that so enthuses Said, the Declaration of the Rights of Man becomes for Césaire a neutral space of encounter for all peoples, regardless of origin. In this view, the Declaration is eminently valuable in itself, in the abstract, independently of the specificity of its origin (for example, the fact that France was a slave holding country when the document was produced), and any attempt to reduce it to the limitations of its historical context becomes an irritating sectarianism.

However, the tensions that underlie Césaire's defense of the document and the universality of its ideas are quickly revealed in his attempt to immediately qualify his statement. The document is European, affirms Césaire, and yes, Europe colonized much of the planet, but Europe did not colonize "in the name" of the principles of the Declaration (but rather, we must assume, in *spite* of them, out of greed and other base motives). Except that perhaps they *did use* those principles as justification (as in the notion of the white man's burden of "civilizing" natives): "it would be a kind deed to bring them civilization." But those justifications are excuses provided after the fact (in order to, we must again assume, justify the greed that motivated conquest and colonization). Then, in just a few sentences, Césaire moves from insisting on how unimportant the European origin of this document is, to the need to clearly and sharply distinguish *his* position from that of Europeans—Europeans believe in *civilization* (singular, universal), whereas "we" (nonwhites, non-Westerners, formerly and currently colonized peoples, we must assume) believe in plural *civilizations*. In the end, Césaire's "integrative" perspective is so carefully qualified by his corrections to the Western model that, although the necessity to integrate universalism and particularism is not questioned, their conjunction can only be proposed as an unfulfilled aspiration, as a space of hardly reconciled conflict. I would suggest that both Césaire's aspiration to fulfill the dream of universality and his anxious misgivings about its potentially lethal effects on a true ethos of pluralism are a reflection of his location as a colonial subject.

Césaire's words in the interview bring to mind Said's own assessment of Toussaint Louverture as presented by C. L. R. James in *The Black Jacobins*: "James shows Toussaint's sincerity and also his latent flaw, his willingness to trust European declarations, to see them as literal intentions rather than class and history-determined remarks of interests and groups" (*Culture*, 246). In spite of his devotion for the rhetoric of Western universalism, it would not be accurate to suggest that Césaire suffers from the naiveté that Said, rightly or not, attributes to Toussaint. His works remain in often-precarious balance between a universalism which is boldly declared (and seemingly trusted as Europe's "literal intention") and a fundamental mistrust of a "universalist" rhetoric that, at best, did not stop the march of colonialism and slavery, and, at worst, often served as their ideological justification (in Europe's civilizing mission). Here we must remember that Césaire always refuted the accusation that his idea of negritude implied any sort of essentialism, and always found his way back to a universalism that attempts to include all particularities, as when he suggests in an interview with the Haitian poet René Depestre: "We bore the imprint of European civilization, but we thought that Africa could make a contribution to Europe" (Césaire, *Discourse*, 92). However, he consistently returned to topics and figures (like Christophe) whose purpose is to poetically embody an Afrocentric defense of the oppressed populations of the Caribbean and Africa, celebrating a particularity that does not need to justify itself in universalist terms, and that indeed should look suspiciously at all demands for such justification.[27]

In this regard, it is important to mention the poem "Le verbe marroner" ("The Verb 'Marroner'"), published in the 1976 collection *Noria,* and dedicated to his friend and younger colleague, the Haitian poet René Depestre. The poem was written when Depestre and Césaire were engaged in a debate on the character of political art and literature. Depestre, assuming the more orthodox approach prescribed by Louis Aragon in France, leaned toward the need for straightforward, clearly committed Marxist poetry. In his poem, Césaire invites Depestre not to allow himself to be subsumed under such doctrinaire models, and to pursue his own unique way, just like the old maroon slaves used to do. "Marronerons nous Depestre marronerons nous?" asks Césaire (*Collected,* 368) ["Shall we escape like slaves Depestre like slaves?" (ibid., 369)]. In the poem, Césaire invokes Boukman, the Vodou priest and initial leader of the slave revolt in Haiti, and Dessalines, proposing them as models of revolutionaries who did not take instructions from their enemies. "En verité le sang est un vaudoun puissant," he declares (ibid., 368) ["Blood is truly a powerful vodun" (ibid.)]. The paradox I want to highlight in this poem is that maroon slaves, Vodou priest Boukman, and fierce enemy of whites Dessalines play little to no role in Césaire's two main accounts of the revolution. Even more, when he introduces Toussaint to his readers in his historical study, he establishes a clear contrast between him and those other leaders. About the famous Vodou ceremony at Bois Caiman presided by Boukman he states that it was "moving and picturesque" (*Toussaint,* 196; my translation). It is Toussaint who brings "what neither Boukman nor Mackandal had: a political head" (ibid., 205; my translation), by which Césaire means, evidently, a mentality steeped in the enlightened ideals of the French Revolution. Once again we see Césaire vacillating, here between Toussaint's appeal to an abstract universal order and the particularist ethos of maroon rebelliousness.

The point here is not to indict either of the two "poles" in Césaire's critique of colonialism, or to suggest that he actually had the alternative of giving either up. My emphasis is on the fact that they do not merely coexist in his work, or even less come together to form a harmonious whole. They coexist in tension, in conflict, as the expression of mutually exclusive yet unavoidably linked historical perspectives and aspirations. That tension, which might be considered a contradiction or a weakness from a purely programmatic political reading (and Césaire's works have often been read in such a manner), are not a problem or limitation in Césaire's work, but rather the opposite: they are an example of the extreme lucidity of his exploration of the colonial condition and its discontents, and of his own position within that colonial context. The white mask is always available for the colonial subject as the clear marker of a humanity that grants access to the universal; the black (or any similarly constructed shade of nonwhite) skin is always already a sign of irredeemable (picturesque and folkloric at best, barbaric and subhuman at worst) particularity. The fact that these poles are constructed by the logic of coloniality does not make them any less real in their effects, and their deconstruction and eventual overcoming often imply multiple visitations of their dead-end promises and enticements.[28]

It is a struggle with, and an expression of, those unavoidable tensions that I see lucidly expressed in Césaire's "Haitian" works. The black Martinican poet recognizes himself in the universal aspirations of European enlightenment, as expressed in the oxymoronic notion of French universalism, but as a product of Europe's imperial endeavors he inevitably recognizes his exclusion from that project. Césaire clearly expresses the colonial subject's relation to French universalism when he writes about the colonial society in Saint Domingue: "Such was the colonial society: more than a hierarchy, an ontology. Above, the whites—*being* in the fullest sense of the term—below, the blacks, without juridical personhood, chattel; a thing, which amounts to saying, *a nothingness;* but between that all and that nothingness, there was a formidable in-between category: the mulatto, the free man of color" (*Toussaint*, 33; my translation). The ontological dimension that Césaire highlights in his description dramatically captures the dynamic of what Walter Mignolo has called the "colonial difference." The logic of coloniality does not simply regard the difference of the colonial other as merely one of civilizational degree, even if it uses that argument to justify Europe's civilizing mission; when the colonized subject attempts to join the colonizer "at the rendezvous of victory," the racialized essentialism of the difference comes to the foreground, creating what Césaire describes as a hierarchy/ontology. Homi Bhabha has aptly described this tension when he suggests that the colonial subject is condemned to be "almost the same but not quite" as the European, a formula that he then astutely translates as "almost the same but not white" (*Location*, 89). Because, as we saw in the introduction, the "colonial difference" is grounded on that ontological dimension, the subaltern is trapped in a sinister double-bind: either (s)he becomes a "real" subject within the European framework, thereby making no distinctive contribution and effectively disappearing, or (s)he refuses to participate, thereby losing any claim to any real, or legitimate, "being." We find that "double bind" expressed—not simply criticized—in Césaire's attempts to capture both the legitimacy of the universal and the self-evidence of the particular in his works.

The fact that Césaire's works embody those colonial contradictions and tensions does not deny their rebellious and emancipating thrust. That liberating impulse is still central to both *La tragédie du roi Christophe* and *Toussaint Louverture*. But like Césaire's other literary writings, his "Haitian" works should not be considered simply (programmatically) as confrontations of the Caribbean's colonial legacy but also as performances of that very colonial condition, which certainly includes the struggles for emancipation, but also false starts, dead-end streets, and sheer exhaustion at the constraints imposed by the coloniality of power. The books do not come together to offer a simple, coherent anticolonial strategy or vision, but they offer a compelling and relentless illumination of the complex and often contradictory location from which they arise.[29]

Caribbean Existential Anguish

It is not surprising that the role of Haiti in Césaire's works reveals so clearly some of the gaps and paradoxes in the poet's self-articulation as a Caribbean intellectual, for Haiti itself, with its tragedy and its rebelliousness, has become throughout the Caribbean an emblem and embodiment of the colonial condition and its discontents, past and present.[30] In the 1960s, Haiti's struggle for nationhood allows Césaire, who at that point was Martinique's leading writer and political leader, to examine the colonial problem in its philosophical depth and historical breadth, particularly at a moment when global anticolonial movements seemed to be moving in a different direction from his chosen path of departmentalization for his country. Haiti offers concrete examples of the virtues and limitations of Afrocentric particularism and universalism in the French tradition through the figures of Christophe and Louverture, each construed by Césaire as an embodiment of one of those poles. Césaire clearly saw his path as a middle ground, a third way, between both extremes—and that still seemed to be his position when he died in 2008.

Haiti's history shows a spectrum of roads taken and not taken that, observed from Martinique, offers both a model to imitate and a cautionary tale to avoid. Haiti's proud affirmation of its own culture should be imitated, but Christophe's disregard of the means to achieve such an end must be avoided. Louverture's awareness of the practical usefulness of retaining links to the old metropolis should be imitated, but it must be complemented with a proud defense of one's culture and autonomy. All of those issues were of paramount importance to Césaire at a moment when France was redefining its relation to its former colonies, and it seemed as if Martinique might be able to find a middle way between total assimilation on the one hand, and independence, with the economic consequences of the total withdrawal of French aid, on the other. Such a balanced middle way did not come to fruition, but it was Césaire's ideal until the end, and his last interviews still reveal an intellectual, and a politician, deeply attached to the principles that both Christophe and Louverture incarnate for him.

In concluding this chapter, I want to refer to still another late interview with Césaire, in order to highlight the fundamental but agonistic role that Haiti's history plays in his thought. In 1993 the Puerto Rican novelist Edgardo Rodríguez Juliá interviewed Césaire. Rodríguez Juliá is himself interested in the Haitian Revolution and in what it might mean from the perspective of Haiti's almost polar opposite in Caribbean history, Puerto Rico. In fact, in the 1970s he wrote a series of novels that deal with fictional slave revolts (not unlike the nonfictional revolution in Haiti) in eighteenth-century Puerto Rico. These novels explore the symbolic importance of events like the Haitian Revolution in an island where, to the chagrin of some of its most radical anticolonial thinkers, such a decisive break with colonial domination never happened.[31]

In his interview with Césaire, Rodríguez Juliá was very aware of similarities that link Puerto Rico and Martinique in spite of their evident differences (*Caribeños*, 275–90). Particularly similar is each island's protracted connection with its colonial metropolis, France in Martinique's case and the Unites States in Puerto Rico's. Not surprisingly, in his chronicle of his visit to Césaire, Rodríguez Juliá connects the Martinican poet's role to that of Puerto Rico's Luis Muñoz Marín, the architect of Puerto Rico's status as a "commonwealth" (Estado Libre Asociado) (ibid., 277). In spite of the differences between that status and Martinique's departmentalization, both islands and their populations remain in a vague anxious limbo regarding their ultimate destiny. Yet it is also true that both Martinique and Puerto Rico, in spite of formidable and ever increasing economic difficulties, have relatively high standards of living when compared to the rest of Caribbean.

Rodríguez Juliá reflects: "In Martinique you find an anxiety similar to ours: how economically viable would Martinique be if France gave it its independence? Uncertainty about the future is an obsession that Martinique shares with Puerto Rico" (ibid., 278; my translation). Curiously, in his conversation with Césaire, Rodríguez Juliá does not ask about the relationship between these two islands, but rather about Cuba first, and then about Haiti, two islands that share histories of successful revolutionary struggles. Césaire avoids a direct answer with respect to Cuba, which prompts Rodríguez Juliá to ask about Haiti, thus drawing a revealing albeit vague answer from the old poet: "Is there any hope for Haiti?, I ask him when I see him avoid the topic of Cuba . . . Césaire lowers his voice, folds his hands, places only his fingers on the desk and turns somber: he points out that big racial divisions—blacks and mulattoes—and the big class differences have not allowed democracy to emerge in Haiti . . . It is a primordially peasant county . . . given to Vodou . . ." (ibid., 289; my translation). We must trust here Rodríguez Juliá indirect representation of Césaire's words (the ellipsis in the quote are in the original), but his description captures elements we have already observed in Césaire's works on Haiti. Most problematic is the apparent link between Haiti's problems (tremendous racism and economic inequalities) with the fact that many of its inhabitants are peasants ("campesinos") who practice Vodou ("entregado al vudú"). Concrete material and cultural problems whose cause is certainly (though not exclusively) linked to Haiti's long colonial and neo-colonial history are subtly connected to forms of livelihood that do not fit into the mainstream globalized capitalist model of the West, and to belief systems that deviate from the Western standard of secularism or Christianity. Thus, the diagnosis of the ills of colonialism still partakes of the logic of coloniality.

Césaire's cautious critique not simply of Haiti's problems but also of some of the practices and existential outlook of its inhabitants (thus, his sympathetic but firm rejection of an island whose great claim to history lies in its successful slave rebellion) is certainly connected to Rodríguez Juliá's questioning of his political compromises, his rejection in real life of a great revolutionary tradition that his writings celebrate. When asked about Martinique's political status, Césaire insists that "the difficulty of this relation [with France] consists of defining by themselves a relation to their own Martinicanness, while remaining within the French state of law, which guarantees them security and liberty" (*Caribeños*, 287; my translation). Yet he insists that the struggle for more autonomy must continue (ibid.). Rodríguez Juliá concludes:

> It seems that in the Caribbean all complex formulas of relation to the metropolis (Commonwealth, a Federated Statehood that preserves Puerto Rican

cultural identity, more autonomy within the frame of union with France proposed by Césaire) acquire a ghostly, rarefied, overly complex aura. Only the mention of one word—independence!—makes the discourse more sober and categorical. When I ask him about the possibility of an imposed independence, he repeats again that Martinique has no economic foundation. It is impossible to compete with Africa and Central America in the sale of sugar and bananas . . . Besides, Martinicans fear independence . . . He repeats the word 'fear' (peur) with an insistence that borders on anguish . . . And they fear it, he adds, because Martinicans live well above their economic possibilities, above their real means. In this moment the Martinican economy is going through a crisis . . . . (ibid.)

For the old poet, no amount of celebration of Haiti's *symbolic* role as "the country where negritude rose for the first time" can overcome the necessary caution about its tragic history—in which he highlights the ignorant practice of Vodou (remember the characterization of Boukman's Bois Caiman ceremony as "picturesque"), but not (at least in his conversation with Rodríguez Juliá) details like the crippling effects of Haiti's debt to indemnify its former colonial metropolis. Martinicans fear independence for good reason, since their standard of living is higher than that of most of the Caribbean; France (again the purveyor of a particular brand of universality) guarantees security and, most paradoxically, liberty.

Towards the end of his chronicle on Césaire, Rodríguez Juliá dramatically comments:

> There is for Césaire a tragic conception of the Caribbean, because we were born from "historical violence, racism, slavery" . . . However, one could talk about a re-encounter of sorts with hope, in spite of that *Caribbean existential anguish* . . . I am fascinated by that last phrase. I repeat it in Spanish and he repeats it in French. We look at each other with the sorrow of acknowledging ourselves as children of the same illusions, the same defeats. (*Caribeños*, 288–89; my translation)

Against the ghostly presence in the horizon of Haiti and Cuba—roads that were deemed too perilous to follow, and which in any case it may be too late to follow now—Martinique and Puerto Rico remain suspended in a relative privilege whose long-term sustainability both writers suspect. Equally important, both islands remain linked to metropolitan centers whose *respect* (the respect one reserves for an equal) they can never count on.

Caribbean existential anguish is certainly what *La tragédie du roi Christophe* and *Toussaint Louverture* are about. The phrase—so characteristic of Césaire, the poet engaged with the thought of Nietzsche, Sartre, and other thinkers of the alienation of modern man—loses its abstract quality when one considers its historically and geographically specific referent, the Caribbean. In that concrete realm, generated by the forces of "historical violence, racism, and slavery," we find colonialism and its exclusionary logic crippling not only the development of oppressed masses but also that of would be liberators. This is the realm of the coloniality of being, which Maldonado-Torres vividly describes as "racist/imperial Manichean misanthropic skepticism" ("On the Coloniality," 245). In Césaire's representations, Christophe and Toussaint are very different men, but they share a fatal inability to see themselves beyond the models offered to them by the logic of coloniality. In this regard, they incarnate tensions, contradictions and aspirations that Césaire shared with them, even if clearly in a more lucid way.

Ultimately Césaire's invocation of existential anguish (sympathetically shared by Rodríguez Juliá) brings to mind Lewis R. Gordon's seminal discussions of Africana existential thought. Following Sartre, Gordon reminds us that "anguish is a confrontation with the self; it is a confrontation with one's responsibility for making choices in one's situations" (*Existentia*, 124). In that case, Césaire's doubts may be related to Gordon's discussion of Frederick Douglass's narrative of his own education, as he learned to read against his master's will. As Gordon indicates, through Douglass's act of transgression:

> He became aware that there was nothing *inside him* that precluded reaching beyond his circumstance. His self became, as Sartre would put it, a project. He faced himself in existential anguish. But this realization, that disobedience raised an anguish-riddled relation to the system of oppression, also raised the question of how far he *should* go. Being secretly disobedient draws the weight of existence onto the self. Public disobedience needs to be waged at some point as absolute disobedience. (ibid., 51)

As we have seen, Césaire always struggled with that question: how far should he go? As one of the leading writers and intellectuals against colonialism in the 20th century, he cannot be accused of merely being "secretly disobedient." However, as a politician he was definitely haunted by that possibility of moving closer to some form of "absolute disobedience," whether expressed as the struggle for Martinique's political independence or in some other way, and much of his anguish resided precisely in his keen ability to imagine himself "beyond his circumstance," while remaining unable or unwilling to actually translate those possibilities into concrete political action. Regardless of how we evaluate Césaire's ambivalences, it seems clear that they were a deep source of existential anguish for him.

In conclusion, I insist one last time that my assessment of Césaire's Haitian heroes as black leaders who, in spite of their extraordinary achievements in the Haitian emancipation project, were unable to fully articulate their freedom and humanity beyond the white masks offered by the logic of coloniality (with Toussaint somewhat naively assuming the neutrality of the white mask, and Christophe tragically assuming the white mask in an effort to affirm his blackness) is not presented as a criticism of Césaire. Not that Césaire is beyond criticism, for he certainly is not, and has received it from early colleagues like René Ménil to more recent figures like Raphaël Confiant. However, what I am emphasizing here is his keen examination of the existential (by which I mean psychological and sociological, internal and external) constraints faced by those whose outlook was shaped by the logic of coloniality. If his works on Haiti are regarded in this way (and not merely as programmatic texts), they show themselves to be as insightful phenomenological descriptions of the coloniality of being as Fanon's *Black Skin, White Masks* is, and they are clearly diagnosing the same condition, the same impasse—that of the *colonial difference*. It is a condition that clearly touched Césaire closely, up to the end of his life, as can be seen when he states about his first visit to Haiti: "In Haiti I saw above all what one should not do! A country that had supposedly acquired its freedom, that had conquered its independence, and which I saw more miserable than Martinique, a French colony!" (*Nègre je suis*, 56; my translation).[32] One could hardly find better words to describe the paradoxical, even tragic tensions that face an intellectual confronting the coloniality of power and the coloniality of being. That Césaire assumed those tensions and conflicting imperatives not passively, but rather as challenges that spurred him to keep on re-examining what freedom meant for him and his people, is why he remains one of the truly necessary names in decolonial thinking.

Chapter 4

A Tragedy of Success
Derek Walcott's Haitian Heroes

Towards the end of Derek Walcott's *The Haitian Earth*, his 1984 play on the events of the Haitian Revolution, Jean-Jacques Dessalines declares: "I am the beginning. And I am the end. Haiti is me" (*Haitian Trilogy*, 426). Coming from him, it is a curious phrase in the context of the Haitian Revolution. In the chronology of events, Dessalines usually makes his appearance mainly after Toussaint Louverture, and also after precursors like Mackandal and Boukman. On the other hand, many histories of the revolution also focus on what comes after him: particularly Henri Christophe—his kingdom and conflicts with Pétion. It is true that Dessalines's importance, as the one who brought his country to independence, cannot be underestimated. But that climatic event usually finds its place towards the end of the narrative, after much else has happened, if we are dealing with a history of the revolution (that is the case in C. L. R. James's *Black Jacobins*); or it occurs in the *second* chapter, after Louverture's struggles, if we are dealing with a broader narrative of Haiti's history as a nation. In the chronology and the symbolic hierarchy of Haitian heroes, Dessalines often occupies a second place, after Toussaint, and even after Christophe.

However, Dessalines's words are true about Walcott's play: *The Haitian Earth* does begin with Dessalines, and in doing so it is different from all other accounts of the Haitian Revolution. The play opens with Dessalines, fictionally presented as a buccaneer, alone on a beach. A wild boar attacks him, and after a fierce battle Dessalines kills the animal, exclaiming: "My friend, I think God send you as a sign. Nothing can kill me. My name is Dessalines. Jean Jacques Dessalines. Nothing can kill me. [. . .] I will drive the French pigs into that sea. And when I come back here, on this same beach, I not going to look like this. The next time you see me, I will be a king! The hills, the sea, will echo with my name. Dessalines! Dessalines!" (*Haitian Trilogy*, 302–3). From that moment on, Dessalines's presence in the events that follow is ubiquitous: sometimes overt, sometimes in the shadows. He finds his way to the initial rebellions of free people of color, saying: "I'm walking to my throne" (307). Thus, there is a sense of almost supernatural determinism in Dessalines gradual takeover of Haiti's destiny.

In order to fully appreciate Walcott's gesture in *The Haitian Earth*, we must remember that, somewhat paradoxically given his seminal role, Dessalines has rarely occupied the central stage in Caribbean accounts of the Haitian Revolution. Commenting on this curious phenomenon, Joan Dayan highlights the fact that Francophone Caribbean writers like Aimé Césaire and Edouard Glissant turned their attention to Louverture and Christophe (both of them in Césaire's case), and suggests that the reason may have to do with Dessalines's reputed brutality, and that perhaps "they had difficulty (in spite of their rhetoric or their desire) acknowledging the chief who called his people to arms with the command, "Koupe tèt, boule kay" ["Cut off their heads, burn their houses"], a command recast by Haitians today as "Koupe fanm, boule kay" ["fuck their women, burn their houses"] (*Haiti*, 20). In *The Kingdom of this World*, Alejo Carpentier barely mentions Dessalines in passing, characteristically attributing the final defeat of the French to a great coalition of Vodou loa (gods). On the other hand, C. L. R. James does not hide his limited appreciation for the figure of Dessalines. Even as he acknowledges that Toussaint gradually lost touch with the people while Dessalines rose as their natural leader, James is careful to declare: "Yet Toussaint's error sprang from the very qualities that made him what he was . . . If Dessalines could see so clearly and simply, it was because the ties that bound this uneducated soldier to French civilization were of the slenderest. He saw what was under his nose so well because he saw no further. Toussaint's failure was the failure of enlightenment, not of darkness" (*Black Jacobins*, 288).

To be sure, this does not mean that Dessalines has been totally absent as a protagonist in literary accounts of the revolution, although, interestingly enough, it is easier to find him in that role in works written by African American authors in the United States. Chief among these is Langston

Hughes in his play *Emperor of Haiti*, from 1936, which was also performed under the title *Troubled Island*, becoming an opera with that second title in 1949. Before Hughes, African American author William Edgar Easton published a play titled *Dessalines: A Dramatic Tale* (1893), offering an idealized version of the Haitian emperor; and writer John Matheus, also linked to the Harlem Renaissance, wrote the libretto to the opera *Ouanga: a Haitian Opera in Three Acts* (c.1929; performed in concert version in 1932; staged in 1949), which also centers on Dessalines. An interesting aspect of these works is that, in the context of African American struggles against racism during the late nineteenth and early twentieth centuries, Dessalines, as the hero who finally achieves Haitian independence, becomes a source of black pride in spite of (and in Hughes's case, arguably because of) his fierce resolve to eliminate white oppression in Saint Domingue by any means necessary. Phillip Kaisary suggests that

> *Emperor of Haiti* should be considered a prescient and significant attempt to secure and rehabilitate Dessalines's place in black history, making it clear to an African American audience that accepting the prevailing opinion of Dessalines as a butcher and an embarrassment could no longer be accepted. (*Haitian Revolution*, 52)[1]

Perspectives on Dessalines in the Caribbean (leaving aside his gradual rehabilitation within Haiti itself, to which I will return in the next section) have been more skeptical, and literary works of the region tend to either place him in a secondary role or display the traditional hostile view of the emperor. The portrayal of Dessalines most often than not reflects his reputation for blind violence, racial hatred, and sheer brutal ambition.[2]

Whether that reputation is fully deserved has been questioned, and I will return to that issue below. However, it is in the context of that negative symbolic valorization that Dessalines's central and unusual role in Walcott's play reveals its full significance. For Walcott's play does not attempt to vindicate Dessalines; in fact, it takes his violent reputation as its point of departure, thus presenting through him a somber assessment of the revolution and its aftermath. Moreover, even though Dessalines's role in *The Haitian Earth* becomes almost unbearably cosmic—he is indeed the alpha and omega of the revolution—it is in fact a logical expansion and deepening of the role he plays throughout Walcott's *Haitian Trilogy*, the series of dramas the Saint Lucian poet wrote on the Haitian Revolution, and which were published together in one volume in 2002.[3]

In 1948 Walcott became one of the first major twentieth-century Caribbean writers to address the revolution and its protagonists in a literary work, his play *Henri Christophe*. As the title indicates, the play focuses on the figure of Christophe; however, Dessalines already plays an essential role in it, one that in some ways encapsulates his symbolic embodiment of all that was "barbaric" or corrupt in the revolutionary struggle. *Henri Christophe* opens with the news of Toussaint's death in France, as Dessalines takes control of the revolution. It is a beginning that is already full of ominous implications for Haiti, but it is still more traditional than that of *The Haitian Earth*, which opens with a prescient Dessalines *before* the initial slave revolts. Throughout the first half of *Henri Christophe*, Dessalines's acts of violence multiply: his massacre of whites after independence, his contempt for common people (he rejects "talking politics to savages" [14]), his thirst for power, his vanity, and his virtual re-enslavement of the newly freed slaves. So appalling is Dessalines's rule that it horrifies Christophe himself, even though he is also quite ambitious and ruthless. While conspiring against Dessalines, Christophe declares: "Blood grows into a habit with a born butcher; / He has grown into something monstrous" (41). Pétion, who is already engaged in a power struggle with Christophe which will divide the country in two halves, replies: "To think that for two days he has been / Martyring children with a tired sword! He is a model / Of horror. Dessalines is only a beast; / He goes to blood with the joy that I go to a feast" (41–42). Thus, Dessalines figure stands apart from those of Christophe, Pétion, and most definitely Toussaint. Dessalines comes across as irredeemably bloodthirsty and cruel.

Drums and Colours (1958), Walcott's epic pageant written to mark the opening of the first West Indies Federation, includes a segment on the Haitian Revolution in a play that traces historical moments from the "discovery" by Columbus to the execution of George William Gordon in nineteenth-century Jamaica. Although Dessalines does not have a lengthy role in the Haitian segment, he represents again the blind barbarism of a general guided at best by a desire for revenge against whites, at worst by personal ambition.

We see Dessalines in the midst of the conflict between Toussaint and the mulatto Rigaud, celebrating and drinking as he states: "Up in the north two thousand whites are slaughtered" (Walcott, *Haitian Trilogy*, 239); "It is a new age, the black man's turn to kill" (240). In addition to Toussaint Louverture, who embodies a higher moral ground in Walcott's plays, Christophe plays again the counterpart to Dessalines. Addressing Dessalines during the war against Rigaud, Christophe complains: "This butchering of mulattos you call assault" (238); and he replies to Dessalines's enthusiasm at "the black man's turn to kill" by stating: "Then we are no better. Revenge is very tiring" (241). Of course, such moral misgivings will not stop Christophe from joining Dessalines in the betrayal of Toussaint and from pursuing power relentlessly himself. However, Christophe comes across as an initially noble soldier who is gradually corrupted by power; Dessalines's animalistic violence seems to be his true nature. In the last section of the chapter I will return to Christophe's words about revenge being tiring, for they connect to ideas that run deep in Walcott's work, and they constitute one of the core issues explored in his Haiti plays. A concern with the place of revenge, justice, and forgiveness in emancipation struggles links those plays to several of Walcott's major essays, particularly "The Muse of History" (1974), a piece that in some ways works as the interpretative key to his Haitian plays. But first I want to make a small detour into some alternative perspectives on that figure that incarnates all brutality and despotism in so many accounts of the revolution, including Walcott's plays: Jean-Jacques Dessalines himself.

A Maligned Hero?

It would not be fair to evaluate Walcott's portrayal of Dessalines *exclusively* on its historical accuracy or lack thereof: the character allows the playwright to make important points about what, in his view, went wrong, or not, in Haitian and Caribbean history. Of course, the question of fidelity to historical sources is not unimportant either, even as it necessarily begs the question of the reliability of those historical documents themselves, particularly when they deal with figures whose historical role has provoked strong passions for and against them. In this regard, even with the best intention not to distort the historical records, both historians and creative writers must inevitably deal with interpretations of historical events and figures (including the very notion of what and who constitute significant events or figures).

In the case of Dessalines, the fact is that the negative portrayal is not exclusive of Walcott—as indicated above, it is a fairly generalized assessment of the revolutionary hero that Walcott incorporates into his plays. Given Dessalines's importance as the figure who led Haiti to independence and whose name still reverberates in the nation's national anthem, *La Dessalinienne*, it is appropriate to examine at least some of the objections to such a lopsided view of Haiti's first emperor. Needless to say, many of the negative portrayals of Dessalines were in fact produced by Eurocentric or racist historians, both in Europe and in Haiti.

Joan Dayan has made the interesting point that, of all the heroes of the Haitian Revolution, Dessalines was the only one that was deified in the Vodou pantheon. After his murder, he was brutally dismembered, but as Dayan indicates:

> Popular vengeance turned Dessalines into matter for resurrection. Dessalines, the most unregenerate of Haitian leaders, was made into an *lwa* (god, image, or spirit) by the Haitian people. The liberator, with his red silk scarf, was the only "Black Jacobin" to become a god. Neither the radical rationality of Toussaint nor the sovereign pomp of Christophe led to apotheosis. Yet Dessalines, so resistant to enlightened heroics, gradually acquired unequaled power in the Haitian imagination. (*Haiti*, 17)

Thus, in spite of his reputed cruelty, Dessalines achieved a unique lasting place in his people's imagination and devotion.

Two factors contribute to a more positive assessment of Dessalines and of his hallowed place in his people's imaginary (without in any case totally erasing his violent legacy): his views on race, and his intended policies of land distribution. With regard to race, Dessalines was uncompromising in his attempt to vindicate the pride and dignity of the former black slaves. The slaveholding society that the French imposed on the island was brutally racist; it kept a strict hierarchy in which whites were are the top and black slaves at the bottom. Free people of color made intense efforts to dissociate themselves from the slaves and be accepted as legitimate members of white society.[4] After the French Revolution, free people of color sent delegations to France in order to have authorities recognize their rights as land and slave owners. Their role in the Haitian Revolution was consistently ambiguous, and in 1799 Toussaint was engaged in a bloody war against free people of color in the south led by André Rigaud. It was during that war that Dessalines gained his reputation as slayer of free people of color and whites, as a hater of everyone nonblack. Pétion himself (with Rigaud and Boyer) came back to the island as part of Leclerc's expedition (one of whose purposes was to reinstate slavery), and he did not join the revolution until he realized the French could not defeat the former slaves.

It is certainly true that Dessalines was brutal in his subjugation of people of color during the war against Rigaud. However, the question remains of whether he was violent out of sheer racial hatred or whether he would have been as violent against *any* enemy attempting to challenge the liberation struggles of the slave masses. The popularized story goes that Toussaint himself was appalled by Dessalines's violence in the south; when faced with the results of Dessalines's handling of the people of color rebellion, he quipped: "I said to prune the tree, not to uproot it" (James, *Black Jacobins*, 236). However, Berthony Dupont suggests that such a position on Toussaint's part might have been either a political ploy or quite simply "opportunistic and contradictory" (*Jean-Jacques Dessalines*, 100). Toussaint ordered, or was presumably aware of, many of the executions he later criticized, and it is not impossible that he might have benefited from having Dessalines get the blame while he, Toussaint, reaped the benefits. In *The Haitian Earth* Walcott has Dessalines say of Toussaint: "Ho, ha! He kills ten thousand mulatto citizens / And shrugs his shoulders and says he hates excess! / I love this hypocrite!" (365). The phrase also appears in almost identical form in *Drums and Colours* (*Haitian Trilogy*, 242).

Another detail that problematizes the view of Dessalines as a racial butcher is his attitude towards race after independence. It is true, on the one hand, that he allowed, and perhaps encouraged, massacres of whites after the end of the war. But such violence occurred mainly against landed colonists, who still held claims of ownership over the land and of racial superiority (and implicit ownership) over the former slaves. Such claims could play into the ever-present threat of a French expedition coming to reclaim the former colony for France. In his attempt to vindicate the identity of those who were for centuries mere owned objects within the colonial society, Dessalines declared that all Haitian citizens, without distinction, would be officially "black." But Dessalines made sure that that racial category honorifically included the Polish soldiers who had defected from the French Army and taken the side of the revolting slaves during the war. He was also quite willing to gain the favor and protect the business interests of American and British merchants, white powers that could strengthen his position against the French. Such moves suggest a more cunning and flexible view of race than the essentialist stance that is usually associated with him.

In her lucid examination of Haiti's early constitutions, Sibylle Fischer writes about Dessaline's 1805 document that

> [the constitution] performs one of the most troubling paradoxes of modern universalist politics—the paradox that the universal is typically derived through a generalization of one of the particulars. Calling all Haitians, regardless of skin color, black is a gesture like calling all people, regardless of their sex, women: it both asserts egalitarian and universalist intuitions and

puts them to a test by using the previously subordinated term of the opposition as the universal term. (*Modernity Disavowed*, 233)

Indeed, in conjunction with some of his political gestures after independence, Dessalines's constitution becomes, as Fischer aptly calls it appropriating Doris Sommer's term, a "foundational fiction" (229): a document notable for expressing and trying to articulate the aspirations of a people who, up to that point, had been relegated to the very margins of humanity. As such, Dessalines's attitudes to race display a vision that attempts to both appropriate and subvert the relation between the universal and the particular which, as we have seen in previous chapters, is deeply imbricated in the logic of coloniality and has preoccupied numerous anticolonial thinkers.

The second factor that may have contributed to a more positive view of Dessalines in popular imagination is his attempt to deal with the land problem in Haiti by expropriating lands from former colonists and by strictly tossing aside spurious claims to land ownership from people of color descendants of former colonial owners. In Dessalines's view, such lands would become property of the state. That approach gained him the enmity of both people of color who claimed hereditary rights to lands owned by former slave owners, and of military officers who wanted personal rewards for their participation in the Revolutionary War. It may have been that attempt to redefine land ownership that ultimately cost Dessalines his life.

Again, it must be realized that much of the "bad press" against Dessalines comes either from French sources or from a discontented Haitian elite unwilling to give up privileges after independence. Even seemingly arbitrary acts like crowning himself emperor become more difficult to judge when one realizes that, as Berthony Dupont indicates (*Jean-Jacques Dessalines*, 297), Dessalines became emperor when he learned that Napoleon was about to do the same thing in France (this is a connection that Fischer also highlights [*Modernity*, 231]). The act can be interpreted then as an attempt to send a clear message that Haiti and France were now two sovereign countries on equal footing: both had emperors to lead them. In this regard, it is significant to notice that Dessalines did not create a royal court with its nobility, as the slightly less maligned Christophe did after him, and that he always made a point of displaying his lack of refinement.

Within Haiti itself, the fortunes of Dessalines's reputation were initially uncertain. For decades there was little mention of, or sympathy for, the slain "Liberator." Gradually, and often in conjunction with political ploys and interests of the moment, Dessalines's figure took its place among the officially celebrated founders of the nation (Dayan, *Haiti*, 16–29). In 1904, *La Dessalinienne*, written by Justin Lhérisson and composed by Nicolas Geffrard, was adopted as the national anthem of Haiti.

It is possible that none of the later attempts at reinterpretation, or his lofty rebirth as a Vodou loa, amount to a full exoneration of Dessalines's violent acts, of which there were definitely plenty. By all accounts he was fierce and ambitious, but a case can be made for a more careful and balanced examination of his life and possible motives, an examination that more likely than not would diminish the moral distance between him and figures like Christophe, Pétion, and even Toussaint Louverture. In the meantime, we are left with the reality that Caribbean literature, in spite of often running ahead of historiography and scholarship in the reassessment of the past, has not yet fully come to terms with the figure of Jean-Jacques Dessalines and what he represents. In Walcott's plays, as we will see below, Dessalines occupies one pole of a moral spectrum that finds Toussaint Louverture at the other extreme, with Christophe and other revolutionary leaders occupying diverse slots in the space between. From that partial perspective, the fact that Dessalines moves from a secondary role in *Henri Christophe* to a cosmic ubiquitous presence in *The Haitian Earth* can only imply an increasingly tragic view of the Haitian Revolution and its Caribbean aftermath in Walcott's oeuvre.[5]

However, one may also take a different approach and suggest that Dessalines and Louverture represent opposite ends of a spectrum that must be deconstructed: the spectrum of Caribbean heroism. From that perspective, Dessalines's excesses simply constitute the tragic summit of the authoritarianism and blindness that are implicit in the very worship of heroes that has dominated Haitian and Caribbean history. It is that rhetoric of violent and mostly masculine heroism as the only solution to the region's historical problems that Walcott confronts in his Haitian plays. In that regard, Toussaint is not that far from Dessalines, and indeed in two of the plays Dessalines refers to Toussaint's "hypocrisy" (242; 365). The problem then is not a contrast between enlightened heroes and barbaric heroes, but the violent narrative on which heroism as a model depends. For Walcott, Dessalines is simply the most revealing example of a violent grammar that includes all the other heroes and which, even if one acknowledges its historical successes (Haiti's independence, for example), needs to be questioned and challenged in the contemporary Caribbean. Not surprisingly, as we will see in the next section, it is also a problem that brings to the foreground the often-invisible category of gender in discussions of coloniality, since the rhetoric of heroism often devalues and excludes any concepts or approaches constructed as "feminine."

". . . for a future without heroes" (*Another Life*)

In his foreword to *The Haitian Trilogy*, the volume that compiles his three plays that deal with the Haitian Revolution, Derek Walcott states: "The Haitian revolution, as sordidly tyrannical as many of its subsequent regimes tragically became, was an upheaval, a necessary rejection of the debasements endured under a civilized empire, that achieved independence" (viii). Walcott's words reveal tensions that are in fact part of his outlook on much of Caribbean history beyond the Haitian Revolution.[6] It is not hard to agree with the basic idea conveyed by Walcott's statement, for it simply acknowledges that the revolution's excesses (particularly those of its subsequent regimes) can be regretted even as the achievement of independence and liberation from slavery can be celebrated. I do want to highlight, however, Walcott's choice of two words in that context: "necessary" and "tragically."

On the one hand, a retrospective look on history inevitably regards its events as necessary, for once they happen they are inalterable. That in itself might be a banal statement (although, as we will see in the case of Glissant, inalterable is precisely what history is not, and the Martinican writer sees his literature precisely as an attempt to accomplish a "prophetic vision of the past," in which a reassessment of the meaning of past events and the unveiling of roads taken and not taken open up the possibilities of freedom in the present). However, the need to accept what is already history, not to turn the present into a resentful struggle with what cannot be undone is far from banal for Walcott, but rather one of the constant obsessions in his work, and an issue that has often found him at odds with his Caribbean peers. As I will explore in more detail in the next section, the need to find peace with the past in order to unleash the creative possibilities of the present is one of the main issues that the Haitian Revolution brings up for Walcott, and it is the basis for his criticism of figures like Christophe and particularly Dessalines.

The "necessary" upheaval of the revolution is also related to its "tragic" character. "Tragic" here refers both to its generic meaning as sad and unfortunate and to its meaning as a literary genre. Both *Henri Christophe* and *The Haitian Earth* are tragedies (as is Césaire's *Tragedy of King Christophe*): both present heroic figures that, while not lacking nobility and pathos, possess insurmountable tragic flaws. Moreover, in both plays characters fight against the unbendable will of indifferent, sometimes cruel gods: mainly the historical forces of war and empire, but also the demons of the human soul—ambition, cruelty, desire, and cowardice. Like the classical tragic heroes, the characters in these plays fight against forces that they have little chance of defeating. To be sure, there are tentative and not unimportant victories—just like Oedipus frees Thebes from the plague by solving the sphinx's enigma or Prometheus manages to bring the divine fire to humanity, these men are instrumental in the deliverance of thousands of slaves, and in the renewed deployment of the possibilities of their human dignity. But just as in classical tragedies, these men's downfall is often provoked by inner demons that are often inextricably intertwined with their heroic virtues. In *Henri Christophe,* Vastey, Christophe's secretary, tells the king as they wait for the rebel forces that will exterminate them: "Hither a new king, and another archbishop, / Monotonies of history . . . / We are finished, Majesty, / We were a tragedy of success" (103). What makes Christophe (and Haiti) truly tragic is that their tragedies are not those of defeat (which would be merely sad), but rather brought about by the very qualities and conditions that made their success possible.

In that regard, more readily than James's *The Black Jacobins,* Walcott's plays may reflect David Scott's praise of tragedy as the genre that can most eloquently portrays "the paradoxical reversals that can unmake and corrupt our most cherished ideals" (*Conscripts of Modernity,* 190). Although in her important work on West Indian drama, Judy Stone follows the lead of *Henri Christophe*'s Shakespearean epigraph (from *Hamlet*) in suggesting that, in contrast to James, "Walcott chose for his Hamlet the enigma, the lesser man bur more complex mortal" (*Theatre,* 95), John Thieme aptly points out that "the play incorporates intertexts from both *Richard III* and *Macbeth,* and Christophe has more in common with the protagonists of these plays than with Hamlet. Like both of them, he is a killer-poet who walks to a throne through blood" (*Derek Walcott,* 48). And while I agree with Scott that Hamlet's self-reflective doubt makes him a better figure for Toussaint as an embodiment of the "historical conflict between the old and the new" (*Conscripts,* 133), at least as represented by James, the distance between Hamlet and Macbeth serves as a cautionary warning about the use of wide categories like "tragedy" in the description of events like the Haitian Revolution. Which notion of tragedy or which tragic character we are talking about, as well as which precise moment, historical character, or vision of the revolution are important considerations to keep in mind.

Another detail in Walcott's foreword's assessment of the revolution deserves closer attention. The "debasements" of colonialism and slavery were apparently inflicted by a "civilized empire." Walcott's words could be read as ironic, and indeed they are. Like Carpentier and many others before him, Walcott is fully aware of the hypocritical claims of an enlightened Europe that has inflicted so much misery on its colonial dominions around the globe, sometimes using the spreading of those enlightened values as justification. But Walcott's words are not merely ironic, for he remains clearly steadfast in his unwillingness to totally discount a European culture to which he owes so much in all realms of human experience, not the least the aesthetic. It is another topic that has remained constant throughout Walcott's career, from the "The Muse of History," in which the daffodils of colonial education were more real in his young imagination than any Saint Lucian flower (*What the Twilight*, 62), and the early poems in which he remained divided "between this Africa and the English tongue I love" (*Collected*, 18).[7] In the next section I will focus on how Walcott's Haitian plays are an integral part of his polemics against both Eurocentrism and Afrocentrism. In the rest of this section I want to return to Walcott's confrontation with a Caribbean tradition of "tragic heroism" in his Haitian plays.

In his essay "What the Twilight Says: An Overture," originally published as the prologue to his collection *Dream on Monkey Mountain and Other Plays* (1970), Walcott comments on his youthful fascination with heroes of the Haitian Revolution. Such fascination was not without its somber overtones; it came, according to Walcott, from his frustration with the insular colonial world around him:

> At nineteen, an elate, exuberant poet madly in love with English, but in the dialect-loud dusk of water-buckets and fish-sellers, conscious of the naked poverty around me, I felt a fear of that darkness which had swallowed up all fathers. Full of precocious rage, I was drawn, like a child's mind to fire, to the Manichean conflicts of Haiti's history. The parallels were there in my own island, but not the heroes . . . those slave-kings, Dessalines and Christophe, men who had structured their own despair. Their tragic bulk was massive as a citadel at twilight. They were our only noble ruins . . . Now one may see such

heroes as squalid fascists who chained their own people, but they had size, mania, the fire of great heretics . . . To put it plainer, it was something we could look up to. It was all we had. (*What the Twilight*, 10–13)

One can certainly recognize the attitude of the young Walcott in his first play, *Henri Christophe* (1948). Edward Baugh has aptly and succinctly traced the development of Walcott's vision in Haitian plays, from the tragic and grandiose heroism of that first play, through the focus on Toussaint's more rational form of heroism (an equally brave but more enlightened leadership) in *Drums and Colours* (1958), to the focus on common people as the true heroes of history in *The Haitian Earth* (1984). While I definitely agree with Baugh's account, we must not discount the remarkable consistency and continuity of Walcott's positions through several decades.

Already in the first play Dessalines appears as a bloodthirsty butcher, criticized by no other than Christophe himself for his use of race as a justification for his violence. Dessalines tells Christophe: "You mock my color. You cannot think a black king real" (48), to which Christophe replies: "I am black, too, but today I am ashamed. You have red work in your hands" (48). In this first play, the representation of Dessalines, with his vengeful concept of race, establishes a pattern that will remain consistent until and throughout the third play. In spite of his misgivings, Christophe himself will virtually re-enslave his own people, and the contrast and continuity between those two characters will continue in the other two plays. Provocatively, in *Henri Christophe* it is the white Archbishop Brelle who pleads for reason and reconciliation. He blames Christophe for "with hammer and hatred breaking / What Toussaint built, exploding / Where he created" (91). Toussaint never appears as a character in this first play, but he already embodies the role of rational builder and constructor that he will retain in *Drums and Colours* and *The Haitian Earth*.

We will return to the subject of racial politics in the next section, but for now it must be emphasized that, regardless of the validity of any criticism of the revolutionary leaders, their use of racial categories was certainly not arbitrary: racial essentialism was built into the very fabric of the colonial regime and, beyond that, into the very logic of coloniality. In a regime where slaves were racialized objects and non-Europeans were at best racialized subjects, it is not surprising that the turning upside down of received, oppressive racial categories would be deployed as a central strategy of emancipation, even if that approach might be criticized from a contemporary perspective as simply inverting, not dismantling, the oppressive structure. As John Thieme has pointed out, one limitation of Walcott's first play on Christophe is that in its fascination with the "Manichean conflicts" of Caribbean history it does not clearly present that Manichean worldview "as an attribute of colonial discourse . . . a *psychological* trap, a product of colonial brainwashing" (49). Walcott's later works will increasingly focus on highlighting that corrupting effect of that colonial logic.

Leaving momentarily aside racial politics, the pressing question that Walcott's Haitian plays pose is: What is the relation of history's self-appointed heroes to *their own people,* Haiti's newly freed black slaves? We find one answer in a poignant scene in *Henri Christophe,* when two nameless murderers are waiting to ambush and kill Dessalines. One of them expresses misgivings about taking a man's life with such ease; the other one replies: "Ask the generals of the wars that are supposed to buy liberty and peace; ask them why they use ordinary people, worksmen, niggers, and smiling boys with sonnets in their eyes dying like Greece on vulgar cannons; ask the man who hired us" (53–54). Already in the first play we see the critique of heroic leaders for whom the lives of ordinary people are expendable in the context of their own grandiose plans. That critique will come to full form and fruition in *The Haitian Earth,* but it is already there from the beginning, as an indictment of Dessalines and Christophe.

It is true, however, that Walcott allows Christophe to have his moment of grandiloquent glory before he meets his tragic fate in this first play. Dessalines receives a similar but briefer honor from one of his murderers, who laments as he is about to perform his deed: "I have no authority to cut the throat of light" (54)—a phrase that links Dessalines to the sun and may honor Aimé Césaire's book *Soleil cou-coupé,* published precisely in 1948 (the phrase itself, "sun cut throat," comes from Apollinaire's poem "Zone"). Asked skeptically by his secretary Vastey if it was for racial hatred that they fought, Christophe replies:

> Yes, fool; for that Haiti bled,
> And spilled the valuable aristocratic blood
> To build these citadels for this complexion
> Signed by the sun.
> Yes, for that we killed, because some were black,
> And some were spat on.
> For that I overturned the horn of plenty,
> And harvest grey hairs and calumny;
> It is I who, history, gave them this voice to shout anarchy

> Against the King. I made this King they hate,
> Shaped out of slaves . . .
>   (Walcott, *Haitian Trilogy*, 101)

Christophe appears here as one of those heroes who have "structured their own despair" indeed, as Walcott suggests in "What the Twilight Says." He gives a tragic and violent shape to lives that, according to him, lacked any dignity, form, or purpose before. Christophe takes it upon himself (and this is both his greatness and his hubris) to rewrite the meaning of Haitian history, using the Haitian people themselves as his alphabet. When the king says "it is I who, history," there is a clear conflation of Christophe and history—either the black king embodies the movement of history, or he addresses history directly in an apostrophe. Either way, he is linked to an impersonal stream of events that has achieved the liberation of Haitian masses just as it also has been relentless in their enslavement.[8]

In this regard, it would not be out of place to emphasize here that Césaire's portrayal of Christophe in his own 1963 tragedy, as we saw in chapter 3, corresponds quite neatly to Walcott's. When confronted about his treatment of men by his wife, Césaire's Christophe replies:

> I ask too much of men? But not enough of black men, Madame . . . All men have the same rights? Agreed. But some men have more duties than others. Does anyone believe that all men, all I say, without privilege, without special exemption, have known capture, deportation, slavery, collective reduction to the level of animals, the monstrous insult, the total outrage that we have suffered, the all-denying spittle plastered on our bodies, spat into our faces. We alone, Madame, do you hear me, we blacks. (*Tragedy*, 41–42)

Like Walcott's character, Césaire's Christophe's abuses are closely intertwined with his attempts to avenge the humiliations of black masses. His vision grants him his tragic nobility, even as his ambition poisons his actions almost beyond redemption.

Paul Breslin has highlighted how, in "What the Twilight Says," Walcott engages in a wordplay that links C. L. R. James's black Jacobins to his own black Jacobeans (*What the Twilight*, 11), thus moving from James's revolutionary fervor to the high literary style but fatal flaws and corruptibility of Walcott's heroes. As Breslin indicates (*Nobody's Nation*, 76), this gesture clearly marks the difference between James's enthusiastic and Walcott's much more skeptical perspectives on Caribbean emancipation movements—a skepticism, it should be clear, about the way those movements may have betrayed their own ideals, not about the ideal of emancipation itself. However, as we will see in the next section and Breslin also highlights, both writers agree on the notion that "revenge has no place in politics" (James, *Black Jacobins*, 373). In that regard, *Henri Christophe* already points in the direction of Walcott's later, more mature reflections.

In spite of pointing to Christophe's tragic grandeur, *Henri Christophe* certainly does not shrink from highlighting the delusional dimension in the king's dreams. However, as is clear from Walcott's autobiographical assessment in "What the Twilight Says," his younger self was precariously balanced between horror of Christophe's cruelty and admiration for his daring, a daring that, as Christophe describes it in the passage quoted above, is not very dissimilar from the literary and artistic achievement to which the young Walcott aspired. One can appreciate how such a figure might appeal to the young poet who saw himself as engaged in a similar endeavor: giving shape and meaning (through poetry) to lives that he perceived as left behind by history. Christophe "gives voice" (his own) to the voiceless; he "made" his kingdom, "shaped" it out of the amorphous magma of slaves. Of course, etymologically the "poet" is the supreme "maker," and Walcott has clearly expressed several times how his younger self felt compelled to give shape and voice to the chaos and poverty he perceived around him.[9] And certainly, the elitism of that view of the poet or artist makes him a lofty, regal figure.

Although *The Haitian Earth* implies more a shift of emphasis than a full about-face with regards to *Henri Christophe*, it is certainly a significant one, and mediating them is *Drums and Colors*, organized around four important figures in the history of the Caribbean: Christopher Columbus, Walter Raleigh, Toussaint Louverture, and George William Gordon. Written as a pageant for the inauguration of the West Indian Federation in 1958, its performance included participation of actors from different islands, thus showing that "the many local governments and peoples of the Federation could work together" (King, *Derek Walcott and West Indian*, 21). Moreover, and appropriately for an Anglophone author with a protestant upbringing from a mostly Catholic island where most of the population speak French creole, Walcott's presentation of Caribbean history included segments on Spanish and French imperialisms (Columbus and Haiti). Paula Burnett has pointed out that such a strategy shows how, although the play was written for a federation made up exclusively of former British colonies, Walcott "declined the narrow definition of the region and its history" (*Derek Walcott*, 224). I would add that it also points to an awareness of how, in spite of the differences between the diverse empires that found their ways to the Caribbean, one may identify in all of them recurrent patterns that place Europe/the West, narrowly conceived, at the center of a global colonial hegemony that rapidly solidified after the "discovery" of the Americas in 1492, and which Dussel has called the "myth of modernity," and Mignolo "the modern/colonial world system."

In the Haitian segment of the long play, the emphasis on Louverture marks a significant evolution from Walcott's initial assessment of Caribbean heroics in his first play. As Walcott tries to articulate what intelligent leadership (as opposed to chauvinistic heroism) might look like in a time of crisis, Dessalines and Christophe recede to the background as brutal and ambitious generals (Dessalines more so than Christophe, as usual). Toussaint appears as the enlightened leader anguished by the violence he is forced to exert, always unwilling to let the struggle for justice and freedom degenerate into mere revenge. Moreover, the play tries to give more prominence to the importance of common people in the development of Caribbean societies by focusing on a lengthy, centuries-long panorama of historical events. It also structures its plot within a carnival frame; that is, within the play, everyday people in the context of a carnival celebration perform the historical episodes. The result is a highlighted role for the masses that is often erased by an emphasis on heroic figures.[10]

Several central scenes from the Haitian episode of *Drums and Colours* were used again, with some rewriting, in *The Haitian Earth*. Not surprisingly, paramount among those scenes are those in which Toussaint confronts his generals, particularly Dessalines, expressing his loathing for unnecessary violence. However, and tellingly, Walcott also moves from one play to the other the scene in which Dessalines accuses Toussaint of hypocrisy (240; 365), and also of being power thirsty (240; 389). The scene may represent Dessalines' duplicity in order to justify his own betrayal, but it may also represent an instance in which Dessalines voices Walcott's doubts about how different Toussaint was from the other revolutionary heroes, if not in his intentions, certainly in the violent results of many of his decisions.

As I pointed out in the beginning of this chapter, *The Haitian Earth* opens with Dessalines, who eventually declares: "I am the beginning. And I am the end. Haiti is me" (426). However, elsewhere in the play, Pompey, a black peasant trying to convince his beloved Yette, a mulatto prostitute, that they should leave the city and return to the countryside to work the earth, says to her: "You and I, we is Haiti, Yette" (386). As Edward Baugh has compellingly shown, the tragic events of the play take place between the symbolic implications of those two phrases, one revealing the megalomania of power, and the other one the promise of shared work and responsibility. Thus, the third play develops themes and possibilities that were only implicit in the ambivalent, skeptical view of heroic leaders that dominates the first two plays.

As indicated above, Walcott's use of Dessalines's perspective and ambition to trigger and frame the action of *The Haitian Earth*, compounded by his almost supernatural ubiquity throughout the plot, in which events move inexorably towards his ascension to the throne, transform the revolution into a veritable tragedy. We meet him at the beginning as a buccaneer, then he foretells his own future kingship, joins the rebellion of Boukman, and calmly walks through the plot with the confidence of a man whose destiny is certain. It is (although Walcott does not state this) as if the violent aftermath of the revolt had been written before the events even get in motion. Dessalines's self-characterization as the beginning and the end, with religious echoes of Christ as the Alpha and Omega, dominates the play, which then becomes, in spite of its celebration of the efforts of common people like Pompey and Yette, one of Walcott's most pessimistic assessments of Caribbean history. Similarly to the narrative of Jesus Christ in the New Testament, Dessalines is murdered, but what he "truly" is—what he represents in the play—resurrects almost immediately in Haiti's long succession of tyrannical regimes.

In the play, Dessalines freely admits that he knows nothing about the art of war (a statement that does not do justice to the historical Dessalines) but he immediately clarifies, "I know plenty about the art of revenge (350). When Toussaint Louverture comes to the forefront of the story, still the coachman of the slave-owning Breda family, he reluctantly finds his way to a plot already dominated, from the beginning, by Dessalines's ambition.

Toussaint joins the revolution, but is horrified by its violence. His nephew, Moïse, later a general under his command replies: "They did us worse" (352). Toussaint insists: "We are supposed to be fighting a war. To kill a child, that's a childish thing . . . The soil itself is bleeding . . . I don't want revenge. There's no strategy in revenge" (352). And while these warriors fight their battles, Pompey, the peasant, insistently ploughs the earth, telling Yette: "Somebody have to plant for people to eat. Not everybody can be a soldier. And they burning down this country" (356).

Later, in a scene transferred from *Drums and Colours*, Toussaint, already the leader of the Revolution, will state: "I hate excess" (364). It is Dessalines who, either projecting his own defects on Toussaint, or displaying keen insight, will exclaim: "Ho, ha! He kills ten thousand mulatto citizens and shrugs his shoulders and says he hates excess! I love this hypocrite!" (364). Until the end of the play, Dessalines will insist that Toussaint's political oscillations are a sign of hypocrisy: first he is aligned with the Spanish army against the French republic (and declares himself monarchic), then he switches back to France but expels the representatives of the French government in order to retain his control of the colony, and then he tries to reach a deal with Napoleon (who will take advantage of this in order to imprison him). Although the play remains sympathetic to Toussaint's anguish and consistently marks the distance between his aspirations and Dessalines's cynicism, Dessalines's words destabilize attempts to simply idealize Toussaint's historical role, particularly in a story dominated by the suffering of innocent civilians like Pompey. Although quite different from each other, both Toussaint and Dessalines come to embody historical processes that are indifferent to the fate of ordinary, specific individuals.

As we saw above, Berthony Dupont suggests Toussaint was not above hypocrisy at least in his attempt of blame Dessalines for the free people of color massacre (in the conflict with Rigaud) that he, Toussaint, had implicitly authorized. In *The Black Jacobins* C. L. R. James justifies Toussaint's fluctuations by indicating that they were political maneuvers under which his actual convictions remained constant: liberty and equality for everyone in Saint Domingue. In James's reading, even though Toussaint would not shy away from shifting alliances according to circumstances, his guiding principles, those of the French Revolution, did not falter. Walcott's play points in a similar direction. When confronted by Leclerc, who has been sent by Napoleon with the mission of capturing Toussaint and reinstating slavery, Toussaint insists: "I have served France" (392). When Leclerc exclaims: "I am talking about civilization!" (394), Toussaint replies: "I am remembering civilization. All those glorious white marbles in your museums, all your Gothic arches, your embroidered books. What do they mean to a slave whose back is flayed so raw that, like a book, you can read the spine" (394). It is not that Toussaint does not believe in France's "civilized" ideals; his argument, and the basis of his sarcastic parallel between a slave's back and a book, is that France has betrayed, or never lived up to, those ideals. Confronted with France's principles he clearly states: "I have always appreciated that. But those are ideals, as much as the Christian Church is an ideal. The empire wasn't built on that, General" (394). Here Toussaint appears pretty much as C. L. R. James portrays him: committed to the ideals of the French Revolution, fighting to push them to their logical implications farther than the French would care to envision, much less admit, yet insisting on maintaining Haiti's links to the nation that had given them faith in liberty, equality, and fraternity. Unwilling (and, according to James, unable) to follow Toussaint's lofty principles, Dessalines and Christophe betray him. Thus, Toussaint's indecision, and his insistence on linking his claim for justice to the interests of those who would enslave him again, opens the door precisely to what he has been trying to avoid: brutal revenge and absolute despotism.[11]

It is not without irony that Toussaint's relative weakness, even if it is what James called "the failure of enlightenment, not of darkness" (*Black Jacobins*, 288) (as opposed to the insights of Dessalines, who "saw what was under his nose so well because he saw no further [ibid.]), ends up opening the way to such despotic violence. In both James's and Walcott's accounts, Toussaint's attempts at fairness and evenhandedness do not go far enough, whereas Dessalines's brutal excess and suspect essentialist rhetoric get the job of achieving independence done. After all, one should not forget that, in spite of Dessalines' "brutality," what the Haitian slaves were up against was the even more brutal, cynical force of France's slave holding, colonial, racist empire. For it to be perfect, Dessalines's energy would have had to include within its own momentum a sense of its legitimate limits, which it did not. But all of this, of course, implies that we agree with James's view of Toussaint and Dessalines. Overall, Walcott seems to, but astutely and provocatively puts another, not wholly disposable possibility in Dessalines's lips: that Toussaint might have also been ambitious and violent, albeit more politically shrewd and rhetorically cautious.[12]

Pompey and Yette are dragged by the force of events. In a sinister scene near the end of *The Haitian Earth*, Dessalines rapes Yette before being betrayed by Christophe. The play ends with the beginning of Christophe's kingdom: he is using forced labor to build his gigantic Citadel Laferriere, and he has Yette killed for stabbing a little voodoo doll in his shape with needles. Pompey is left to bury her, to help her "join the Haitian earth" (433), having had his chance to tell the king first: "my life is one long night. My country and your kingdom, majesty. One long, long night. Is kings who do us that . . ." (431); "When was I ever free? Under you all?" (432).[13]

It is not totally surprising that Pompey refers to the former revolutionary heroes, now kings, as "you all," just as before he had said "they" are burning down the country (356), without even making a distinction between the black leaders, the free people of color, and the French. From his own position, of course, he is right. From a bleak perspective that differs significantly from the optimistic thrust of many of his other works, Walcott offers through Pompey his critique of a Caribbean ethics/aesthetics of heroism that has pervaded many anticolonial and anti-imperialist works from the region. What that rhetoric forgets, for Walcott, is central role of humble citizens in struggles for emancipation, and in the (re)construction of society after the violent phase of such struggles is over. The fact that the play ends with Christophe's execution of Yette offers a bleak vision of the possibilities of breaking the cycle of violence, a vision that, unfortunately, is solidly grounded on Haitian history to this day.[14]

Here it is important to highlight that, through the character of Yette, the important but often-neglected role of gender in the logic of coloniality comes to the foreground. In other words, in addition to the marginal position that she occupies because of her race and class, the fact that she is a woman adds still another dimension to her exploitation. Before joining Pompey, we meet her as a prostitute; as such, her body is a sexual commodity for both white men and free men of color. She is then raped by Dessalines, and her experience as a victim of that violent act is shared by countless female slaves and indigenous women throughout the Americas, for colonial domination has walked hand in hand with sexual domination since the conquest. Although Yette herself is a free woman of color, she is still a victim of the sexualization of racialized otherness in a colonial context in which sexuality becomes a vehicle for the exertion and display of violent domination; this is part of what María Lugones has called "the coloniality of gender." As part of this perverse dynamic, we should notice that when Dessalines retains Yette with him and expels Pompey, the latter lingers outside of the palace, crying, which prompts Dessalines to question his manhood, and Yette to defend it (416). This "feminization" of male victims is part of the gendered racial logic of coloniality; it coexists with the hypersexualization of women of color, and both display the role of gender categories in the normalization of colonial relations. The paradoxical fact that the victimizer here is Dessalines highlights Aníbal Quijano's point about the pervasiveness of the coloniality of power in postindependence societies.[15]

Although Pompey, in his misery, does not greatly distinguish between French colonizers, Dessalines, and Christophe, he does make an exception for Toussaint. He states: "It had one talk then, I remember, under the old coachman, and that talk was not who was king but who would make each man a man, each man a king himself; but all that change" (431). Pompey's words resonate with extraordinary acuity in the way they link, yet also differentiate, the ambitions of "the old coachman," Toussaint and those of later leaders like Dessalines. Toussaint wants to make each man a man; Dessalines wants to be king. But Pompey inadvertently points to a possible key in Dessalines's and Christophe's behavior, at least as they are presented by Walcott (and arguably, Césaire). Because if to be a man is to be one's own king ("each man a king himself"), then perhaps when the trauma of a dehumanizing, brutal institution like slavery damages some men beyond repair, it is only by becoming kings, in spite of the violence that such a gesture may mean to *other men*, that those men can feel that they become men. To be a king here becomes a figure for possessing agency, dignity, freedom, respect from others: everything a slave lacks. It is a white mask in a white world in which a black man wants to be not a king but rather "a man among other men" (Fanon, *Black Skin*, 112). The importance of this connection between the illegitimate grab of absolute power on the part of men like Dessalines and the legitimate aspiration to full humanity on the part of every slave cannot be underestimated. One of the corrupting effects of the racial axis of the coloniality of power, which makes a legitimate aspiration illegitimate, is to facilitate and embolden the substitution of an illegitimate goal (absolute power) for a legitimate one (full humanity and agency). Here, the Fanonian link leads us to another important dimension of Walcott's Haitian plays: the racial politics they explore, which have been recurring preoccupations in Walcott's oeuvre.

Revenge or Nothing

In his 1974 essay "The Caribbean: Culture or Mimicry?," Walcott famously declares: "We owe the past revenge or nothing, and revenge is uncreative" (Hamner, ed., *Critical Perspectives*, 57). That essay, along with the contemporaneous and equally well known "The Muse of History" (1974), presents some of Walcott's most definitive positions on issues such as Caribbean identity in relation to its colonial past, the Caribbean artist's connections to both Europe and Africa, and equally important, the Caribbean intellectual's responsibility toward the injustices inflicted on the region by centuries of imperial domination. In some ways, those essays could be used as interpretive keys for Walcott's Haitian plays, since those plays are concerned precisely with those questions of identity and justice, as they are emblematized by the Haitian Revolution and its aftermath. The phrase quoted above almost encapsulates Walcott's answers to many of those questions, but his plays also demonstrate that no absolute answer can be easily reached that is not made unstable by the implications of the opposite answer.

Walcott's essays were written during the height of "Black Power" cultural and literary movements in the Caribbean and the United States, and they reflect his mistrust, and sometimes open antagonism, to all forms of cultural nationalism (understood by him as being too often not simply about pride in one's culture or nationality, but rather as an ethnocentric, sometimes racist, unwillingness to be "tainted" by other cultures, with the implicit claim of the uncontaminated purity of one's own identity).[16] Thus, in "The Muse of History" he provocatively states:

> That all blacks are beautiful is an enervating statement, that all blacks are brothers more a reprimand than a charter, that the people must have power almost their death wish, for the real power of this time is silent. Art cannot last long in this shale. It crumbles like those slogans, fragments and shards of a historical fault. Power now becomes increasingly divided and tribal when it is based on genetics. (*What the Twilight*, 57)

Although Walcott is responding to his immediate context, his mistrust of racial essentialism (or anything that might be construed as such) runs throughout his whole career, from well before the Black Nationalist movements of the 1960s and 1970s. Walcott has always regarded himself as a "mulatto of style," as he defines himself in another essay, "What the Twilight Says" (*What the Twilight*, 9). "Style," in that phrase, does not refer merely to aesthetic concerns and his views on writing, but to a whole cultural outlook. That outlook is often experienced as the precarious balance between conflicting commitments and loyalties, which leave the poet "divided to the vein . . . Between this Africa and the English tongue I love" (*Collected*, 18), as he expresses it in one of his best known poems, "A Far Cry From Africa." And it is important to notice the ambiguity in the very choice of words in both the essay and the poem: "mulatto" and "vein" refer to biology, whereas "style" and "love," refer to actions/approaches and emotions/affects. Although Walcott attributes no essentialist content to the mix of races in the Caribbean, he is certainly aware of the role that "biology" has played in the region's historical relations, inasmuch as biology has been part of the ideological racist arsenal that Europe used to justify its imperial expansion. But precisely for that reason, he is suspicious of any attempts to challenge that colonial history that take as their point of departure a similar essentialism, even if now with its poles inverted.[17]

Walcott's early response to the dangers and possible performative contradictions that may underlie racial politics can be clearly seen in *Henri Christophe*, where both Dessalines and Christophe justify their oppressive regimes by deploying racial essentialism and appealing to the quite justified resentment of the masses against colonial Europeans. However, already in that first play Christophe confronts Dessalines by attacking precisely the latter's misuse of race: "You kill offenders because of their complexion; / Where is the ultimate direction of this nation, / An abattoir of war?" (39). Dessalines remains unconvinced: he shows the marks that the whip has left on his body, claiming, "for every scar / Raw on my unforgiving stomach, I'll murder children, / I'll riot" (39). However, when Christophe turns despotic himself and is confronted by his white Archbishop Brelle, "Your smell of blood offends the nostrils of God" (91), Christophe readily responds by invoking racial categories as justification for his actions:

> Perhaps the smell of sweat under my arms
> Offend that God, too, quivering His white crooked nostrils.
> Well, tell Him after death that it is honest
> As the seven words of blood broken on His flesh; tell Him
> The nigger smell, that even kings must wear,
> Is bread and wine to life.
> I am proud, I have worked and grown
> this country to its stature . . ."
>   (Walcott, *Haitian Trilogy*, 91)

One should notice Christophe's insistence on the material, even physiological, fact of his blackness. In doing so he invokes a whole array of racial categories that constellated Europe's gradual domination of the globe (since the "discovery" of the Americas in 1492). Those categories were intimately linked with the development of what Walter Mignolo calls the "modern/colonial world," in which Europe's colonial domination is implicitly and explicitly justified as resulting from an inherent, essential superiority of Europeans to inhabitants of colonized territories.[18] Thus, it makes perfect sense for Christophe to invoke those categories in his defense of his vision, but in Walcott's play such racial rhetoric energizes rebellion at a high prize: it also keeps those who use it entrapped in Eurocentric models.

However, even that criticism—that a discourse of rebellion that relies on racial essentialism ends up replicating the abuses it is trying to undo—is only part of the problem that Walcott's plays attempt to address. The question that these plays pose most insistently (and understandably leave unanswered) is to what degree these men actually believed their own essentialist rhetoric, and to what degree it was a ploy to justify their own personal ambition.

On the one hand, Walcott's comments in "What the Twilight Says" would suggest the former: "Those first heroes of the Haitian revolution, to me, their tragedy lay in their blackness" (*What the Twilight*, 12). In that interpretation, as I suggested at the end of the previous section, the megalomania of these heroes would be a twisted attempt to overcome the dehumanizing effect of centuries of slavery and abuse. These men attempt to become men—to regain their agency and dignity—by becoming kings, as Pompey's words suggest at the end of *The Haitian Earth*. If the attempt is misguided to the point of transforming them into tyrants, then that much clearer is our insight into the almost insurmountable trauma they have to overcome.

In *Henri Christophe*, Dessalines presents his violence as "a necessary horror" (48). It is not surprising that in addition to Fanon's observations on the black man's need to wear a white mask when all he wants is to be acknowledged as human (to be "a man among other men" [*Black Skin*, 112]), the actions of the revolutionary heroes in Walcott's plays also invoke the purging effects of violence that Fanon examines in *The Wretched of the Earth*. Violence is the abject reality of the slave, who suffers it every day of his/her life; it is also the means by which the slave can recover his/her freedom. Says Fanon: "At the level of individuals, violence is a cleansing force. It frees the native from his inferiority complex and from his despair and inaction; it makes him fearless and restores his self-respect" (*The Wretched*, 94). However, it is equally true that "there is no native who does not dream at least once a day of setting himself up in the settler's place" (39). The danger here, for Fanon, is not violence itself, but that the only option—or aspiration—for the colonized becomes simply to occupy the position of the colonizer. For that reason, the conclusion of *The Wretched of the Earth* is a plea to "find something different. We today can do everything, so long as we do not imitate Europe, so long as we are not obsessed by the desire to catch up with Europe" (312); "Humanity is waiting for something other from us other than such an imitation, which would be almost an obscene caricature" (316). Arguably, both Dessalines and Christophe, as portrayed in Walcott's plays, incarnate that "obscene caricature" that Fanon warns against, just as they also (and paradoxically) embody the "cleansing force" of a violent revolt—its "necessary horror."

Walcott may implicitly acknowledge Fanon's thoughts on violence's cleansing potential when he calls the Haitian Revolution, for example, a "necessary upheaval" (*Haitian Trilogy*, vii-viii). But it is important to highlight that Walcott's is a very different sensitivity, and that violence itself is more often than not a suspect force in his works, an approach that is frequently self-defeating even when it seems justified. As he states in a 1990 interview:

> If Black power oppresses the white victim, it is no different from a white power oppressing a Black victim. Now you can say that it is justified on the

basis of revenge and it is justified on the basis of history. But it is the very idea of history as revenge that does nothing for humanity. . . . But if, for instance, you consider Gandhi's or even Martin Luther King's idea of history as not containing revenge, then you have change. (Baer, *Conversations*, 166–67)

Walcott does not ignore that from certain perspectives revenge may seem justified by the historical oppression of one group over the other. From that perspective, "black violence" (say, Dessalines) exerted against a white victim (say, a former French slave holder) is not the same as its opposite, and to suggest so would bring one dangerously close to bad faith. Even if one grants that distinction, the question becomes, for Walcott, what is the end result that is been pursued through that violence—how to achieve what Walcott calls "change." The uplifting of oppressed groups (as opposed to the satisfaction of individuals) is rarely served well by "revenge." And here it is important to distinguish violence as such from revenge—even if violence may sometimes be regarded, in retrospect, as a "necessary horror," it is not so if its motive is simply revenge. Even when violence seems justified, the ends can hardly justify the means if the means threaten to destroy the ends. For Walcott, violence rarely knows when to stop once its immediate objective has been reached, and it rarely chooses its objectives with precision. Both Dessalines and Christophe exert their violence not only against whites but also against other blacks, against their own people.

All of the concerns described above still assume a genuine concern for oppressed racialized groups, even when ethical dilemmas remain. But another possibility that Walcott's plays insistently raise is that racial essentialism may be, at least in part, mere rhetoric in lips of these ambitious men, a way of rousing the masses to support their leaders' self-aggrandizement. Already in *Henri Christophe* Dessalines is described as "vain," more interested in power and its outer ornaments than in any political agenda (8). Christophe, who refuses any comparison to Dessalines (82), is also described as vain (59) and then as worse than Dessalines (92); in the last scene, while he waits for Pétion's troops to raid his citadel, he has a "witch doctor" work on his sick legs, but soon enough dismisses him, commenting: "It is useless. Christ and Damballa, or any god" (97). Christophe does not believe in Africa or Europe; he only believes in his own ambition.

It is in *The Haitian Earth* that the fully disenchanted reading of these leaders' motives comes to dominate. Therein lies the importance of Dessalines overpowering presence in this play. The full ambiguity of his motives is made clear from the beginning; when a young slave expresses surprise at seeing him alive, thinking he had been burned, Dessalines replies: "Black magic, boy. Black magic. Keep walking. / What could be safer than this? Don't worry. / Tonight you'll be free. I'm walking to my throne" (307). Dessalines's suggestion that he may have indeed been burned but has survived by "black magic" links him to the figure of Mackandal, the precursor of the revolution whose myth (which plays such an important role in Carpentier's *The Kingdom of this World*) he thereby appropriates. In Mackandal's legend, even though the maroon leader is captured and burnt by the French colonial authorities, his magical ability to transform himself into any animal saves him. But Mackandal, like Boukman after him, had genuine links to the beliefs and rituals of Haitian Vodou. Whether the historical Dessalines had such links or not is a question open to debate. Those links have been claimed for him and for Toussaint, whose adopted name, "L'ouverture" ("the opening") could be associated to the *lwa* Legba, who opens the way in Vodou ceremonies. However, Toussaint is best known as a devout Catholic who persecuted Vodou practitioners, and it was Dessalines who carried out his orders. Moreover, in the play Dessalines uses the Eurocentric, disdainful term "black magic," suggesting a distance from actual belief in those practices, and the possibility that he merely wants to impress his listener's credulity. Is Dessalines genuinely promising freedom to the young slave, or is he enlisting him as an aid on his way to his throne? Both, perhaps? Does the difference even matter if, as a result of Dessalines's ambition, the young slave conquers his own freedom too? This last possibility inevitably begs the question, is the young slave really free if once he obtains his freedom Dessalines becomes a despot on his throne?

Both Dessalines and Christophe appear in Walcott's plays as ambitious figures who only believe in their own seizure of power, and who manipulate their people's justified resentment in order to enlist aids to their egotistical plans. In this, they may emblematize other postcolonial leaders. However, it should be clear that, although Walcott is concerned about the way racist and essentialist rhetoric can be used to manipulate the masses, he is not any more sympathetic toward that rhetoric when it is *genuinely* embraced as a philosophy, even as a response to Western aggressions on the cultures of Africa and the African diaspora. I referred above to his ambivalent response to pressures on him during the height of the "Black Power" movements in the 1970s, and his unwillingness to renounce or denounce an European dimension of his cultural identity that, even if the result of colonial violence, he claims as legitimately his. In *The Haitian Earth,* Walcott's dilemma as a man between two worlds is most powerfully incarnated by Anton, a young mulatto man who is torn between his loyalty to the European and African sides of his identity. Anton complains:

> Perhaps I'm very tired of Western culture
> And its privilege of ideas, perhaps,
> Except for art, I see the whole technological
> Experience as failure, but true or not,
> I have no wish to go back to the bush.
> I think their African nostalgia is rubbish.
>   (Walcott, *Haitian Trilogy*, 306)

Anton is almost anachronistically talking about twentieth century issues that have always been of vital importance to Walcott. It is not at all evident that Haitians wanted to "go back to the bush" (a *racist* way of saying, "back to Africa") during the revolution; they wanted emancipation, which, more often than not, Haiti's black Jacobins understood in the terms made current and popular by the French Revolution. All the same, even if Anton's words encapsulate some of Walcott's concerns (or prejudices) about Black Nationalism, we should also notice his mistrust of Europe's claim to greatness. Walcott's position is not one of blind celebration of Eurocentric "civilization." However, one cannot bypass the fact that the contrast is very unevenly represented in Anton's words: the alternative to "Western culture" is "the bush," rather than a different, even if conceived as less advanced in some respects, culture.

Anton, the character, is certainly not Walcott, but it would be naive not to recognize in his words a summary of Walcott's preoccupations. Walcott's language, if not his full-fledged position, is problematic indeed, and, fairly or not, he has been called to task for it. At the level of identity politics, his general point may not be difficult to accept, and it may not be particularly controversial today: the Caribbean and the Americas are not simply African, nor simply indigenous, nor simply European. They are heterogeneous, creolized, hypersyncretistic and chaotic (to use A. Benítez Rojo's terminology) combinations of multiple cultural elements that also include Asia and the Pacific. But what Anton's words lack (and some may lament Walcott's essays do not highlight enough) is, first, a historically grounded awareness of the colonial context in which injured black pride attempts to find a voice, any voice, even as it may fall into dead-ends like essentialism; and second, enough emphasis on the racist ideological worldview that not only justifies the colonizer's domination over the colonized but also allows even critics of colonialism the easy identification of "civilization" with Europe, a view that relegates Africa—with its rich histories, cultures and civilizations—to "the bush."

It is not surprising that Anton, whose voice follows Walcott's so closely in this play, exempts art from his willing condemnation of Europe. Already in "The Muse of History" Walcott presented the great poets (and artists in general) of the Americas as the clairvoyant articulators of a new culture that is "Adamic," new, original. Paradoxically, that Adamic gift comes to the New World artist from a willingness to imitate and incorporate (that is, embrace) all of his/her influences, whether African or European. The essay, nonetheless, is a polemic piece particularly stressing the need to accept the European side of that cultural legacy, written in a moment when its author felt that the injunction to create political, anti-colonial, Afrocentric art was too constraining for true artists. Not surprisingly, it is in this essay that we find Walcott's defense of Wordsworth's daffodils as windows to the life of the imagination. Walcott is not flippant in his defense of artistic autonomy, and his genuine anguish at his ambiguous position between European historical oppressors and the historical victims of imperial expansion clearly comes across in his essays, as it does in Anton's words. What one might have expected from Walcott, in his essays at least, would be a more nuanced, more compassionate representation of why artists from populations that had been vilified for centuries might feel the imperative to reject the influence of those who had performed the vilification for centuries with impunity and even with a sense of condescension (the "white man's burden"), even if that imperative is ultimately rejected as misguided or self-defeating. But those essays were written in the heat of then current debates, when Walcott himself felt under attack for the kind of poetry *he* wrote.[19]

The Haitian plays are more explicit on the historical reasons that feed into Afrocentric sentiments, essentialist or not, justified or not. Anything Dessalines—and to a lesser degree, Christophe—might say is suspect, for as we have seen, it is in question to what degree they use such rhetoric to manipulate the population's resentment. But Toussaint Louverture remains in Walcott's plays a voice for reason, a man who is dragged to violence in spite of his best judgment and inclinations. In *The Haitian Earth*, just before he makes the heartbreaking decision (for him) of condemning his former master to death, Toussaint states:

> Do not speak of God, Monsieur Calixte.
> I cannot think of God. Where was God in those years
> When we were shipped and forced to bear our excrement,

Were peeled alive, pestered with cannibal ants,
Where was God?
  (Walcott, *Haitian Trilogy*, 366)

Calixte remains silent for an instant, and the stage directions indicate: "Calixte-Breda is also weeping. The love between them pours out its bewilderment" (367). In spite of a love for his former master that some critics might find implausible, Toussaint, the character, uses words that clearly show Walcott's keen awareness of the arguments against white callousness (well justified by their "God") that "Black Power" advocates could have used against Walcott's own defense of Western culture.[20] Referring to the "white man's burden" of bringing "civilization" to the men he enslaves, Toussaint responds to Leclerc when he is taken prisoner: "I am remembering civilization. All those glorious white marbles in your museums, all your Gothic arches, your embroidered books. What do they mean to a slave whose back is flayed so raw that, like a book, you can read the spine?" (394). The powerful image that transforms the slave's back in a book that allows us to read the real good that Europe did to its colonies during the period of slavery (and after) is another example of Walcott's awareness of the kinds of well-justified historical examples an Afrocentric critic of the West could use (and against some of Walcott's own occasionally over-dismissive criticisms of "Black Power" movements).

However, Walcott is careful to distinguish Toussaint from Dessalines and Christophe, and in spite of his historical role as liberator of the black slaves and the words that Walcott puts in his mouth, Toussaint in *The Haitian Earth* is closer in spirit to Anton than to Dessalines and Christophe. Both Toussaint and Anton are full of doubts and internal conflicts, both avoid gratuitous violence. However, all of this changes when both Anton and Toussaint are forced to take a position in spite of their doubts. At that point, Toussaint clearly chooses to join and lead "the wretched of the earth;" Anton does not. In that regard, they represent the possibilities and perils of Walcott's own ambivalent position.

In *Drums and Colours*, which as I have indicated shares several scenes and characters with *The Haitian Earth* (Walcott calls his recycling of the material "a repetition in a slightly altered context" [vii]), the revolting slaves kill Anton before he makes up his mind about where his true loyalties belong. The play clearly highlights the links between Toussaint and Anton. When Anton describes the brutal punishment of slaves, he identifies himself in the following manner: "Because I am torn to pieces with them, I am myself a division. / By the fact that I am half African and half French, / I must become both spectator and victim" (226–27). Shortly after he refers to Toussaint, who is still the coachman of his family, and states: "I have seen his black face tormented with division, / Between duty to his people and the love of our family. / How am I better than Toussaint, greater than his anguish?" (228). Anton's words link him to Toussaint in that both of them are marked by internal "division" and anguish at the choices the events force them to make, which imply severing ties to what up to that point they have regarded as part of their heritage. Eventually Toussaint will lament, over Anton's dead body, "This poor boy hated nothing, nothing" (235).

Like Anton in *Drums and Colours*, Walcott's essays from the 1970s expressed not only indecision and anxiety ("division") but also a steadfast openness to *both* cultures. In the darker but more realistic *The Haitian Earth*, Anton joins the forces of the mulatto Rigaud (fighting against Toussaint), warning his father "Do not trust a single black" (359). Anton's decision to join the free people of color army against the slaves is significant precisely to the degree that his words on European and African culture—his indecision between their pull on him, his resistance to privilege an Africa to which he does not feel fully connected over a Europe of whose hypocrisy he is only too well aware—closely reflect Walcott's positions in his essays from the seventies. However, in spite of its sympathy for Anton's cultural dilemma, *The Haitian Earth* indicts Anton's predictable rejection of a world he racistly describes as "the bush." Is Walcott unsaying himself in the 1984 play then? Not precisely, but the later play considerably complicates Walcott's earlier position by acknowledging that the conflict goes well beyond daffodils. What makes Anton's arguments about having to choose between Europe and Africa self-defeating and self-complacent to the point of bad faith is that the problem is not simply about cultural *identity* but about *ethics* and *justice*.

At the level of identity, Anton's anguish, so similar to Walcott's in the sixties and seventies, could find resolution in the Adamic vision expounded in "The Muse of History." Ultimately, there is no such thing as an original or isolated culture. All drink from the past and transform it creatively. Anton, like Walcott, does not (and indeed, should not) have to choose between Europe and Africa. Moreover, a defense of identity that relies on essentialism or ethnocentrism becomes divisive and even violent, thus replicating the very oppressive logic it is rebelling against. After all, even in the age of postmodern "multiculturalism" fixed views of identity have not lost their power to divide and justify violence and prejudice. If anything, there is more atomization and attachment to essentialist ethnocentrisms. Edouard Glissant refers to this when, in texts like *Poetique de la rélation,* he contrasts the emphasis on a unique root as the basis of identity to a rhyzomatic identity that acknowledges its indebtedness to many sources. Glissant's "poetics of relation" points precisely to that desirable balance between preservation and enjoyment of the unique, particular, individual forms that multiple elements take in specific cultures, and the need not to enclose oneself within the boundaries of that culture in fear of all change and development, for change through multiple contacts is the way *all* cultures develop.

It is certainly the case that identity still has considerable importance in debates about colonial and postcolonial justice, and that defenses of particularism play an important and necessary role. This becomes increasingly clear as marginal and subaltern populations around the globe attempt to resist the unequal domination exerted by metropolitan centers of globalized power (not coincidentally, the old centers of colonial power). From that perspective, attempts to vindicate *other* traditions, perspectives, customs and priorities are important gestures against the push of globalized capitalism to transform as many countries as possible into homogenized obedient consumers or cheap labor. These attempts are part of what Sousa Santos calls the need for an "ecology of knowledges" based on "epistemological justice" (*Another Knowledge,* xix–xx). That such efforts to privilege heterogeneity and otherness are important attempts at resistance is clearly shown by the violent backlash in Europe and the United States, for example in the anti-immigrant movements recourse to essentialist myths about the purity of European and Euro-American identities, whether focusing on the Christian roots of that identity, or on its modern secular developments. The racial component of that identity, its explicit or implicit whiteness, is fundamentally shared.

However, identity is only one set of problems. From the point of view of identity, Anton may feel closer to free people of color, blacks or whites; it does not really matter. But in a society in which whites are *enslaving* blacks, his choice to join the free people of color who have joined the whites in their attempt to repress the slaves' struggle for emancipation is clearly the wrong ethical choice. In that regard, *The Haitian Earth*'s treatment of the character of Anton constitutes a significant evolution in Walcott's emphasis (and the difference is mostly of emphasis, for it would not be accurate to state that Walcott was uninterested in ethical questions before that point). Identity questions, important as they are, are not the only or the ultimate concern in struggles for liberation—and the most genuine links of solidarity are often articulated not around identities, but rather around shared visions of justice and inclusion. Thus, in *The Haitian Earth* Toussaint has little in common with Anton, whereas in *Drums and Colours*, with its stronger emphasis on Anton's identity crisis rather than his ethical choices, the two of them share the same internal "division." For the same reason—the primacy of ethics over identity—in both plays Toussaint has little in common (and here we must decide whether Walcott is being fair or not) with Dessalines.[21]

Evidently, transposing the conflict from identity questions to ethics and justice does not make it easier to find the right course of action. Certainly it cannot be argued that Dessalines and Christophe make the right ethical choices; at least, not entirely, in these plays. Toussaint comes closest in his careful attempt to measure the consequences of his actions. But as we have seen, Toussaint is as tormented about his ethical choices in the plays as Anton is about his identity. For the real question is: What is the right course of action? Furthermore, when does justice cross the line unto revenge, how can we tell them apart, and is the latter ever justified?

Naturally, Walcott cannot offer easy answers to such questions. The closest he comes to certainty is in his steady negative answer to the last question: revenge is uncreative, a dead-end that locks everyone, but particularly the original victims, in the past. The temptation is always there. It could be argued that in Walcott's masterpiece, *Omeros* (1990), the redemption of the Fisherman Achille comes from his ability embrace his past without resentment, claiming his whole historical experience as legitimately his. Not surprisingly, the other character in that poem who comes to terms with the past through a similar act of acceptance is Plunkett, the descendant of the white colonizers. In Walcott's Haitian plays, the most violent leaders, Dessalines and Christophe, who quite consciously practice a politics of vengefulness, enact the "wrong" choice. And it must be emphasized that their choice is not "wrong" from a position of abstract moralism, but rather from its concrete results: in their obsession with racial vindication (assuming it is a real motive and not a disguise for personal ambition), Dessalines and Christophe bring misery to themselves and their own people.

How, then, can we tell justice from revenge? It would be naive to expect a definite answer to such a question (and it is very much the question that the Haitian Revolution, in Walcott's representation, poses to us), but *The Haitian Earth* points in two important directions to explore: one is a politics of inclusiveness in which subaltern subjects can find effective voices; the other is the mystery of forgiveness and reconciliation.

Pardon or Revenge

In "The Muse of History" Walcott states, "Who in the New World does not have a horror of the past, whether his ancestor was torturer or victim? Who, in the depth of conscience, is not silently screaming for pardon or for revenge?" (*What the Twilight,* 39). The three Haitian plays offer powerful negative warnings, from the early ambiguous figure of Christophe in the first one to the full-fledged demonic dominance of Dessalines in the last one. In *Drums and Colours,* Toussaint (whose role is limited in the last two plays and does not appear in the first one) is adamant in his opposition to revenge: "Revenge is nothing. Peace, the restoration of the burnt estates, the ultimate rebuilding of those towns war has destroyed, peace is harder" (241). Toussaint names his alternatives to revenge "peace" and "restoration." In his essay, Walcott refers to "pardon," and although the differences between "pardon" and "restoration" have important consequences to which I will return below, it is clear that Walcott is pointing toward the problem posed by the possibility or impossibility of forgiveness (pardon). Forgiveness is one of the dominant (albeit sometimes implicit) themes in Walcott's Haitian plays and in "The Muse of History," as it is indeed throughout his whole oeuvre.

Even as he invokes forgiveness's healing power, Walcott remains aware of the dangers of tossing that concept around too easily. In the last paragraph of "The Muse of History," the writer states:

> I accept this archipelago of the Americas. I say to the ancestor who sold me, and to the ancestor who bought me, I have no father, I want no such father, although I can understand you, black ghost, white ghost, when you both whisper "history," for if I attempt to forgive you both I am falling into your idea of history which justifies and explains and expiates, and it is not mine to forgive, my memory cannot summon any filial love, since your features are anonymous and erased and I have no wish and no power to pardon. (*What the Twilight,* 64)

Forgiveness is indeed a slippery term, and its content can be trivialized and become complicit with the logic of violence it tries to overcome. Forgiveness is not supposed to "justify, explain and expiate," and it stands in relation to "justifying" much as justice stands in relation to revenge. Once that important clarification is made, Walcott can write in the sentence that immediately follows (the last one in the essay), "But to you, inwardly forgiven grandfathers, I, like the more honest of my race, give a strange thanks" (64). There is forgiveness, but almost as a surplus of love and willfulness that is not, cannot be, part of the same logic of violence that has dominated so much of Caribbean history. Paradoxically, forgiveness must be gratuitous to be effective, because the historical crimes committed have been too egregious, and the claim to justify or explain them, to offer expiation, would be too arrogant. The poet's inward, not ostentatious forgiveness is neither a necessity nor a favor: it is a gift.

In that sense, Walcott's conception of forgiveness resembles Jacques Derrida's well known reflections on the topic, in which forgiveness is indeed true forgiveness only if attempts to forgive the unforgivable, if it does not become a comfortable part of a transaction that justifies and expiates:

> If one is only prepared to forgive only what appears forgivable, what the church calls "venial sin," then the very idea of forgiveness would disappear. If there is something to forgive, it would be what in religious language is called mortal sin, the worst, the unforgivable crime or harm. From which comes the aporia, which can be described in its dry and implacable formality, without mercy: forgiveness forgives only the unforgivable. One cannot, or should not, forgive; there is only forgiveness, if there is any, where there is the unforgivable. (*On Cosmopolitanism*, 32–33)

Derrida pushes his argument to suggest that true forgiveness cannot depend on the repentance or confession of the guilty party, if only because he who is forgiven at that moment is already a changed person, he who is forgiven is no longer the same as the one who committed the crime. Walcott's words reflect Derrida's in their radical call to face the unacceptable. In the George William Gordon section of *Drums and Colours,* Deacon Sale, while talking to the rebellious slave Aaron, makes the point clear while also highlighting Walcott's view of the Haitian Revolution's lesson to the Caribbean:

> The man who whips you cuts his own flesh, Aaron. For you are a piece of that man. Do not hate him. Twenty years ago, in Haiti, the slaves turned on their masters and butchered them. When the great generals of the Haitian revolution came to power, their cause was corrupted by greed. Even that great general Toussaint caught the contagion of hate. But those that followed him, Dessalines, Christophe, from free slaves turned into insane emperors. Toussaint died in a cold tower in France, his dream ruined. Betrayed by his own generals, sold to his enemies. Do not hate, Aaron, however hard it seems.

Revenge is easier than love. That is why I tell you to pray continually, for God delivers us from evil and from hatred in the end. (255–56)

It would be inaccurate to suggest that Deacon Dale's words encompass the totality of Walcott's thoughts on Toussaint, Dessalines, and Christophe, for the rest of his works clearly attest to his awareness of the difficulty and often paradoxical nature of movements of historical emancipation. His preface to *The Haitian Trilogy* does call the revolution, in spite of its violence, a "necessary upheaval" (vii-viii). However, the Deacon's ideas appear with enough frequency in Walcott's poems and plays to suggest that they are indeed an essential trend in his thought, and an integral part of his partial discomfort with the Haitian Revolution's legacy for the Caribbean archipelago. Like Derrida in his musings on forgiveness, Deacon Dale emphasizes the difficulty of love and the easiness of hatred. Even more: at least in some circumstances, hatred may feel more human or logical; love (which I am linking to forgiveness here) can only come from "praying," as a gift from God, not a natural response. I am not interested here in the use of God in a traditional religious or Christian sense.[22] I am trying to emphasize that love, in those conditions, like forgiveness for Derrida, can only come, if it comes at all, as a gift that achieves the impossible, following not the logic of historical causality of retribution but of gratuitous grace.[23]

Both Derrida and Walcott are aware that such divine love, such pure forgiveness, exists as a horizon of possibilities that is never fully actualized. In the words that I quoted above, Toussaint opposes "revenge" with the need for "peace," "restoration," and "rebuilding" (*Haitian Trilogy,* 241). Toussaint's goals are eminently worthy, but they are different from forgiveness as such, as understood by Derrida and Walcott. Within the unattainable (but always dimly posed) horizon of forgiving the unforgivable, Toussaint proposes more concrete goals toward which practical, specific steps can be taken. Derrida also acknowledges the need to combine the lofty vision of forgiveness with such more attainable goals. Toussaint's objectives could fall within the realm of what Derrida calls *conditional* forgiveness.

Derrida's distinction between "conditional" and "unconditional" forgiveness follows a logic similar to that of Emmanuel Levinas's understanding of ethics. Inconditional forgiveness may be compared to Levinas's ethical relation, which is the original source of subjectivity itself, but which only occurs in its purity in the face-to-face encounter between two subjects. For Levinas, once a *third* person whose rights must be considered appears, the imperative for *justice* is added to that original ethical intersubjective relation. Similarly,

Derrida's understanding of forgiveness is altered when we need to consider the rights of third parties. In those circumstances "forgiveness" requires certain conditions, such as the "repentance and transformation of the sinner" (*On Cosmopolitanism*, 44). Derrida states:

> In principle, therefore, always in order the follow the vein of the Abrahamic tradition, forgiveness must engage two singularities: the guilty (the "perpetrator" as they say in South Africa) and the victim. As soon as a third party intervenes, one can speak again of amnesty, reconciliation, reparation, etc., but certainly not of pure forgiveness in the strict sense. (42)

> These two poles, *the unconditional and the conditional,* are absolutely heterogeneous, and must remain irreducible to one another. They are nonetheless indissociable . . . It is between these two poles, *irreconcilable but indissociable* that decisions and responsibilities are to be taken. (44–45)

It is not a coincidence that Derrida refers to South Africa, for the Commission for Truth and Reconciliation presided over by Desmond Tutu was part of the issues he was trying to address in his essay.[24] Walcott's Haitian plays also bring up questions related to conditional forgiveness, justice, truth and reconciliation, and they do so from the perspective of colonial, postcolonial, and neocolonial experiences. For in a colony built upon the blood and suffering of thousands of slaves, wherein the metropolis was willing to fight to death in order to cling to its monstrous privileges, it may be difficult and perhaps hypocritical to ascertain how much violence was too much violence in the slaves' struggle for liberation. However, from a "post"colonial perspective, a valid critique may be made of the violence that Haitian leaders used against their own people after independence, regardless of how necessary or not that violence might have been during the emancipation struggles. And then there is the "neo"colonial perspective, for the fact is that, regardless of how one addresses the previous two points, France did not willingly give up its most prosperous colony, and Dessalines's and Christophe's anxiety about a new invasion from France was certainly not unjustified. Moreover, when Boyer finally achieved France's "recognition" of Haiti as a nation, it was at the price of an indemnity that contributed to cripple Haiti's economy. If unconditional forgiveness can only happen in the ethical encounter between two subjects, then one could argue that history is nothing if not a perpetual overflow of "third persons" claiming for justice.

In Walcott's plays, we may see a paradoxical glimpse of the possibility "unconditional" forgiveness in the relation between Toussaint and Calixte Breda. The intersubjective relation is suggested by the stage directions, which indicate: "The love between them pours out its bewilderment" (367). But Toussaint is not deaf to the claims of history's "third persons," in this case those at the very bottom of dispossession: the Haitian slaves. For them, justice is necessary—not revenge, as Toussaint insists. They also need truth, and ultimately, reconciliation. All of those elements are part of what Derrida calls "conditional forgiveness." Skillfully, Walcott's plays invoke the presence of unconditional forgiveness as a ghostly horizon whose utopian glow fills the wisest men in the revolution with unease at the inevitable compromises that the practicalities of reality entail. Only the conditional is ever satisfactorily attained, if at all. Yet, invoking that tenuous, disquieting pressure that the possibility of the unconditional (in Derrida's sense of the word) exerts on the revolution's most lucid actors is one of Walcott's most enduring achievements in his Haitian plays.

Of course, the question that Walcott's plays most insistently pose is whether even those conditional goals—"peace," "restoration," "rebuilding," as Toussaint calls them—were achieved by Haiti's former slaves. The immense achievements of emancipation from slavery and independence cannot be underestimated or diminished. But inasmuch as Haiti went from the ambition of two emperors to becoming what Robert Fatton calls a "predatory republic" that feeds upon its own citizens, it betrayed, for Walcott, many of its promises. This topic leads us to the second of the issues that I suggested above that Walcott presents as responses to an over-emphasis on identity politics. The first one was an inquiry into the possibilities of forgiveness. The second one is the need for a politics of inclusion, which paradoxically finds its fullest expression in the most pessimistic of the three plays, *The Haitian Earth*, through the figures of Pompey, the black peasant, and Yette, the mulatto prostitute; and particularly through Pompey's understanding of his own situation.

Pompey is a slave at the beginning of the play; at the end he is a free man, but such freedom is merely formal, for Pompey, like thousands others, does not count as a *subject*. As we have seen, Yette is trapped in a triple knot of victimization—class, race and gender. She is poor and a prostitute; she is presented in the play as a mulatto woman, which in spite of the relative privilege it represents in her society makes her the target of race purists, whether black or white; and she is a woman. The brutal scene of her rape by Dessalines highlights that gendered dimension of her colonial condition. I have already referred to Pompey's indictment of Haitian rulers—"My life is one long night. My country and your kingdom, majesty. One long, long night. Is kings who do us that" (431); "When was I ever free? Under you all?" (432)—in which he does not even try to make a distinction between the black leaders, the free people of color, and the French. Earlier in the play he similarly states that "they" are burning down the country, without making distinctions (356). However, he keeps working the earth, because "somebody have to plant for people to eat" (356). As I stated earlier, it is hard to question Pompey's assessment if one examines it from the perspective of the events he has experienced as an anonymous "everyman."

Although the erotic coming together of Yette and Pompey might seem a facile emblem for racial unity in Haiti (and the Caribbean), the play ends in a note of tragic hope that is grounded in realism. While a better future is invoked by the shift of focus from military heroes to humble peasants, in fact Yette is dead and Pompey is at least temporarily defeated. He does not know it, but we as readers know that much of what is still to come to his country (at least for people like him, that is, the majority) is not much better than what came under Dessalines and Christophe. Decades of problems still lay ahead, ranging from endemic internal political corruption and constant external intervention to natural disasters like the 2010 earthquake, with the understanding that all of those spheres, and others like ecological depletion, are intimately linked.[25] Even after "independence" and emancipation the Haitian masses have remained subordinated to economic interests and essentialist racial categories that remain firmly in an international colonial logic. Moreover, that logic and its implementation found welcoming agents in Haiti's elite.

In his response to the colonial logic that governs Haiti's history, Pompey praises Toussaint's ideal (as portrayed by Walcott), that the important thing was "not who was king but who would make each man a man, each man a king himself" (431). As I noted above, those words make "being a king" a figure for human agency and freedom. When Pompey suggests that the ideal is not to become a king but to become a man, that in that sense each man is a king, he is talking about a politics of inclusion of others *as subjects*. Those others may be others in terms of class, of race, of gender, of religion, etc. However, such inclusion cannot be simply granted from above: in Walcott's account, Dessalines will not allow that inclusion any more than Napoleon. It is the other agencies and voices that *push* their way to the stage, following diverse tactics or strategies, just like at the end of *Drums and Colours* the Carnival group in charge of representing historical events virtually takes over the play and transforms it into a carnival, as Edward Baugh aptly observes ("Of Men and Heroes," 52).

Moreover, in the play Pompey tries to pose a politics of inclusion that does not define exclusion only in racial terms. This is interestingly revealed when Pompey explains the events of the *French* revolution that preceded the one in Haiti: "It was only poor people, it was slaves, and those who work and die as if they was white niggers under the sixteen kings of France" (431).[26] By that point of the play, race and origin are not as important for Pompey as a subaltern position before the authorities. Evidently, race and origin *are important* inasmuch as the coloniality of power and the coloniality of being have inextricably linked them to a subaltern position, both before and after political independence. But Pompey has realized that black leaders can be as effective agents of (neo)colonial violence as white Europeans, and that gender, poverty, and any other category may be used as a tool to exclude certain people, and to justify violence against them. The point here is not create a hierarchy of which form of exclusion is worse, but to remain vigilant of the manifold ways in which exclusion and oppression operate and justify themselves, with a view to persistently try to incorporate those marginalized subjects.

But how is that to be done? In *The Haitian Earth,* what is Pompey to do after he buries Yette? Would a struggle for inclusiveness justify violence? Would it *require* it? Would not an overcoming of the "coloniality of power" (and the ontological claims of the coloniality of being) imply the paradoxical need to include the voice of the former oppressor, the need for the reconciliation, and perhaps the mysterious workings of forgiveness? Walcott, by insistently posing those questions, considerably deepens our appreciation of the implications of the Haitian Revolution for both Haitians and everyone from the Caribbean and the rest of the post/colonial world. As an event, it not only marked a Copernican turn in what was believed possible for colonized and enslaved peoples, and thus foreshadowed the great decolonizing struggles of the twentieth century, but also—and equally importantly, in its failures and successes—clearly pointed to many of the ethical and political questions that always lie at the heart of all movements of liberation.

Chapter 5

Maroons in the Tout-Monde
Edouard Glissant's *Monsieur Toussaint*

The Maroon and the General

In the preface to *Monsieur Toussaint,* a play first published in 1961 and then republished in a shorter "version scénique" in 1978, Edouard Glissant states:

> The present work is linked to what I would call . . . *a prophetic vision of the past.* For those whose history has been reduced by others to darkness and despair, the recovery of the near and distant past is imperative. To renew acquaintance with one's history, obscured or obliterated by others, is to relish fully the present, for the experience of the present, stripped of its roots in time, yields only hollow delights. This is a poetic endeavor. Of course this attempt seems incomprehensible, indeed useless, if not harmful, to those who, far from feeling an absence of history, may on the contrary feel that they are laboring under the tyrannical burden of their past. Struggling with, and in, history is our common lot. Thus, often from opposing sides, the literary work strives to diminish the same basic insecurity of being. (*Monsieur,* 15–16)[1]

Interestingly Glissant does not try to solve or attenuate the keen tension, contradiction even, that the two views of history that he invokes imply. Is the Caribbean world that he describes and addresses in his play suffering from too much history, or too little? The exploration of history (particularly its silenced voices and perspectives) is liberating and enables the present to imagine a better future while attempting to avoid the mistakes of the past—thus the "prophetic vision of the past," to which I will return below. On the other hand, history is a prison, a nightmare with no awakening in sight for those who have been internally and externally, psychologically and socially, *overdetermined* by centuries of colonial domination and by the legacies of slavery and racism.

Glissant's preface confronts us with the tensions and anxieties that underlie what Walter Mignolo calls the colonial difference, or "difference articulated by the coloniality of power" ("The Geopolitics," 236; see also *Local Histories*), which also imply the ontological claims of the "coloniality of being" as described by Maldonado-Torres. The logic of coloniality attempts to *naturalize* (through essentialist and racialized categories and imaginaries) the positions and identities of those who have endured historical structures of violent domination. Within that colonial logic, even attempts at liberation may not be able to release the colonized from that perceived *ontological* lack that Glissant quite accurately refers to as a "basic insecurity of being." Here we could quote Frantz Fanon's famous statement from *Black Skin, White Masks*, when he states: "When people like me, they tell me it is in spite of my color. When they dislike me, they point out that it is not because of my color. Either way, I am locked into the infernal circle" (116). Color, in Fanon's quote, operates like Glissant's "history," for colonial history is indeed a *racialized* essentialist history that will not release its prisoners. That history cannot (and indeed, should not) be ignored, but it attempts to foreclose resistance by defining the colonized as its objects, never as subjects, even when they resist. Thus, colonial subjects constantly face the double bind that Glissant describes: the need to confront inherited historical categories and demonstrate agency, but also the claustrophobia of being always already defined by those categories, even in their oppositional roles as challengers of it.

Not surprisingly, Derek Walcott has declared, in "The Muse of History," that it is precisely history that condemns artists from the Americas to uncreative vengefulness, and he figuratively opts for the creative blank slate of an Adamic aesthetics. Evidently, we need not take Walcott at face value: what is significant in his gesture of denunciation is the acknowledgment of the historical double bind that Glissant foregrounds in his introduction to *Monsieur Toussaint*. In fact, Walcott's work is nothing if not an exploration of the many dimensions of Caribbean history, framed precisely by his condemnation of the objectified position in which that history has placed its Caribbean *subjects*.

The ambivalent relation to history that Glissant's preface presents is reinforced by the stage directions in his play. The action takes place in Toussaint Louverture's prison in the Jura Mountains and in Toussaint's memory of the events in Haiti; the directions indicate that "there is no clearly indicated frontier between the world of the prison in France and the lands of the Caribbean island" (21). The Caribbean, in the play, is a prison whose inmates struggle for their freedom; and the prison, which throughout the play is visited by loas (Vodou gods) and the dead, is precariously Caribbeanized. On a stage that metaphorically stands for Caribbean history, the spaces of freedom are always just a few actor's steps away from renewed, metamorphosed oppression (a sad reality of Haitian history), and the spaces of oppression (Toussaint's prison) are populated by half realized possibilities—ghosts—that point the way to possible inroads toward liberation.

In terms of its plot, *Monsieur Toussaint* is deceptively simple. The play takes place in Toussaint Louverture's jail in the Jura Mountains. There, as he waits for the French authorities to dispose of him, and as he uselessly attempts to send messages to Napoleon in which he insists on his loyalty to the principles of the French Republic, Toussaint remembers the events of the revolution, from the moment he joins the troops of Biassou, through his raise to leadership and the difficult decisions he has to make as a military chief, to his fall as he is increasingly isolated from his people and his generals, to the final betrayal that leads to his capture and deportation. Toussaint's cell is visited by Vodou gods and dead spirits who work, in many ways, as embodiments of his troubled conscience. Mackandal and Macaïa, in particular, represent the rebellious spirit of the maroons, always willing to fight to death for freedom. They feel betrayed by Toussaint's approach to the Revolutionary War, which always made sure that ties to France were not permanently severed, attempted to maintain the plantation system so that Saint Domingue could retain its place in the world sugar economy, and tried to maintain law and order even if it meant imposing them violently. The tension between the maroon libertarian impulse and Toussaint's reasonable planning for the future makes for much of the drama in the play. The story ends with Toussaint's death; the only person by his side is Manuel, a young soldier from Piedmont who, in spite of the distance between their historical positions, has come to develop some sort of respect, perhaps affection, for the ailing black general. (Towards the end of the play, Toussaint acknowledges his link to that humble soldier who feels compassion for him and who also comes from a marginal region of Napoleon's empire: "Your land speaks, your land sings, Manuel. I can hear it in your voice" [114–15].)

In his preface to the play, Glissant explicitly acknowledges that C. L. R. James's *Black Jacobins* and Césaire's *Toussaint Louverture* are the main sources for his view of the Haitian leader. And indeed, the play could be regarded as a dramatization of James's and Cesaire's books on Toussaint. One may particularly see Glissant's indebtedness to James in the way the play describes Toussaint's gradual alienation from the people who follow him: an alienation that is due to his inability or unwillingness to explain the vision that guides his actions. That vision leads to unfair actions like that execution of his nephew Moyse for his radicalism (a key event in both the play and James's book), even though Moyse was, according to James, more attuned to the desires of the Haitian people. Toussaint's character flaws in Glissant's play can be best explained in terms of James's memorable contrast of Toussaint to Dessalines "Toussaint's error sprang from the very qualities that made him what he was . . . If Dessalines could see so clearly and simply, it was because the ties that bound this uneducated soldier to French civilization were of the slenderest. He saw what was under his nose so well because he saw no further. Toussaint's failure was the failure of enlightenment, not of darkness" (288).[2]

From Césaire, Glissant takes the tragic twist of Toussaint's realization that his presence has become an obstacle to the revolutionary process; thus, he intentionally removes himself from the scene. James's book already highlighted the tragic dimensions of Toussaint's predicament, but Césaire's historical essay (published the same year as Glissant's play) adds to the pathos by suggesting that Toussaint decides to open the way to those who can take the revolution to its ultimate consequences.[3] Thus, historiography mimics literature as Césaire in his essay draws a Toussaint in the image of his own "Rebel" character from *And the Dogs Were Silent* (1946). Glissant's play subtly suggests a similar rationale for Toussaint's willingness to accept General Leclerc's treacherous invitation to a rendezvous, even against the pleas of his friends.

Where Glissant departs from James and Césaire is in the fact that, for the two older writers, Toussaint's position, in spite of its limitations, is clearly the most appropriate one, precisely because it is the most "enlightened" one. While James and Césaire indulge the "tragic" dimensions of Toussaint's dilemma, and both have to face the fact Toussaint indecisiveness opens the way to Dessalines, neither gives much symbolic weight to the other black leaders and positions surrounding Toussaint. Glissant, on the other hand, clearly constructs his play around the conflict between equally legitimate positions, at least a priori, before the revolution is won. On the one hand, there is Toussaint's need to insure that order, progress and commerce will survive the abolition of slavery (and independence, if that thought ever crossed his mind). On the other hand, we have the libertarian maroon impulse (to which Glissant adds the figure of Dessalines), which wants to break off all chains and links to slavery and colonial domination, even if it means relying on a local, subsistence basis. Toussaint is opposed to slavery but wants Saint Domingue to remain part of global networks of commerce and cooperation; the maroons see those global networks as already colonial, already exploitative of the labor and lives of former slaves. They have no reason to believe that the regime that enslaved them will want their international success once they violently liberate themselves from slavery. In the play, Glissant alternatively gives legitimate arguments to both Toussaint and his maroon objectors.[4]

Ultimately Glissant's play directly and indirectly addresses a series of problems that remain important not only for Haiti but also, not surprisingly, for his native Martinique. The critic Jack Corzani, in his multivolume *La littérature des Antilles-Guyane françaises,* provocatively suggests that the Dessalines-Toussaint tension in the play stands for the Glissant-Césaire tensions with regard to Martinique's future. Césaire followed the moderate path of departmentalization coupled with attempts to preserve some autonomy for the island. In 1959 (that is to say, not long before the publication of *Monsieur Toussaint*) Glissant formed, with Paul Niger, the separatist Front Antillo-Guyanais pour l'Autonomie, as a result of which Charles de Gaulle barred him from leaving France between 1961 and 1965.[5] Corzani suggests, somewhat dramatically: "Facing Toussaint-Césaire, Glissant places the brutal silhouettes of the maroon slaves and those willing to take things to their ultimate consequences ("jusqu'auboutistes"). He is clearly seduced by Dessalines, that Frantz Fanon of older times, a warrior incarnation of that ideal that Glissant attempts to defend with his pen" (217; my translation). Provided one does not accept it in a reductive way, Corzani's reading is at least partially plausible given Glissant's political circumstances at that point of his intellectual career, and it is highly suggestive in the way it links Fanon to previous Caribbean figures like Dessalines.[6]

However, Corzani's reading must be modified to include the considerable weight Toussaint's arguments do have in the play. As Corzani ultimately acknowledges, "Dessalines acknowledges his final debt to Toussaint, just as Glissant and Fanon admit their debt to Césaire" (218; my translation). That acknowledgment of the important links between Glissant and Césaire (in spite of their profound differences) is essential, for it suggests that even during his most radical political period Glissant was never wholly blind to the expediency of Césaire's political compromises (as opposed to his exalted rhetoric). This gives us a more nuanced perspective on Glissant's own change of heart later in his career, when he modifies his position on Martinique's independence not unlike the way Césaire did before him. As *Monsieur Toussaint* suggests, that change of heart (criticized by some critics as a gradual *depolitization* of Glissant's work from the 1990s onward) was already implicit in the 1961 play, with its inability, or unwillingness, to solve the tensions incarnated by Toussaint on the one hand, and Dessalines and the maroons on the other. From there, there is only a step to Glissant's later more explicit lost of interest in *nationalist* politics, clearly expressed in a 1998 interview: "it seems to me we are beyond the old quarrels over independence, autonomy or departmentalization" (Couffon, 51; my translation). The later position is rooted in the earlier impasse that the play expresses so effectively. I will return to this topic in the last section of the chapter.

From the above, it seems clear that Haiti works for Glissant (as for the other Caribbean writers we have examined) as a master narrative where key issues and problems of Caribbean history can be vividly observed. Some of those problems include: the fate of newly independent nations after anticolonial struggles (an area in which Haiti works as a cautionary tale and distorting mirror for islands such as Martinique and Puerto Rico, each of which remained linked to its metropolis [see chapter 2]); the persistence and replication of colonial hierarchies among local elites; the tensions between local cultures and traditions and Eurocentric models, including the "marooning" temptation of isolation vis-à-vis the neocolonial demands of global markets; and, self-referentially, with regard to the play's function as a cultural artifact, the primacy of *cultural* action when viable *political* options are not readily available.

Postcoloniality and Its Discontents

The Future (Haiti after Independence)

Near the beginning of the play, Mackandal, now one of the spirits talking to Toussaint in his cell, describes how, years before, he prophesied to his fellow slaves how Toussaint would come and successfully lead them to freedom from slavery; however, as he talks of future freedom the slaves think that he is talking about the past, "for these slaves could not conceive the future" (26). Mackandal's poignant observation captures the state of mind of those who have been so utterly crushed by brutal oppression that they have a hard time merely imagining a brighter future. That predicament, the need or desire to imagine a future out of the morass of the present, in fact permeates the whole play, and torments Toussaint more than any other character. It is also a question that plagues all struggles for liberation—nationalistic or otherwise—and it possesses the aggravating quality of not allowing itself to be ignored. The avoidance of the task of imagining a future often invites chaos and random violence, while the compulsion to dwell too obsessively on what the future should look like can lead to paralyzing inaction in the present.

In the play, there are two radically different positions about the future, which are represented by Toussaint and the maroon slave Macaïa. Mama Dio, a Vodou priestess who is now one of the spirits in Toussaint's cell, pleads with him: "Let your people to get used to the land, be patient, don't go and put a new yoke around their necks" (50). Mama Dio is referring to Toussaint's insistence on the need to preserve the large plantations if Saint Domingue is to survive economically. To be sure, there were at the time, in addition to former slaves unwilling to return to a labor regime that was simply too similar to their previous enslaved condition, abolitionist thinkers (like Condorcet) who believed that the island's economy could be rebuilt on the basis of small plots of land, where the newly freed peasants could grow cane individually and then bring it to state run sugarmills for processing (Dubois, *Avengers*, 192; Dubois, *Haiti*, 47–48; 65–68; 104–112). But Toussaint never gave any serious consideration to that option. Moreover, he seemed disturbingly willing to allow former plantation owners return to control over their old plantations, which would now operate with the former slaves as laborers. And indeed, many of those plantation owners returned to their lands after Toussaint seized control of the colony, figuring they could still make good profit out of a difficult situation. The slaves, understandably, resented and resisted those developments, through historical leaders like Moyse, and the maroon leader Macaïa.[7]

This tense drama culminates in 1801, when Toussaint announces his constitution and makes proclamations on the labor regime in the island whose authoritarian content display his attempt to gain full control of the situation. He not only proclaims himself Governor for life of the colony, but also imposes severe limitations on the freedom of the former slaves: "Every individual will have to serve at his post. The field hands will be confined to their plantations, not allowed to leave without a temporary, special permit . . . Runaways will be put in chains and in this manner sent to work" (74). This (historically accurate) authoritarian dimension of Toussaint's figure is more sharply highlighted by Glissant than by any of the writers we have examined in this book.

However, it would be a mistake to regard the play as fundamentally a critique of Toussaint Louverture, in spite of the intensity of Macaïa's, Mama Dio's, and Mackandal's denunciations. It is strongly emphasized throughout the story that, in spite of his heavy-handedness, Toussaint has the best interests of the island in mind (as he understands them), and that, like Walcott's Toussaint, he is concerned about the revolutionary war turning into mindless destruction: "The gun and the hoe; don't forget the hoe! Find a soldier who can plow, who can reap" (79). The dilemma of how to infuse the struggle with the ideals he envisions without oppressively stifling the common people who constitute the soul and ultimate arbiters of the revolution brings up the old problem of revolutionary leadership, an issue that C. L. R. James regarded as one of the lessons of the Haitian Revolution. James himself, an ardent admirer of Toussaint, acknowledged the disconnection between the visionary leader and his people toward the end of his career (*Black Jacobins*, 286–288).

From Macaïa's perspective, the deeper problem is not simply Toussaint's authoritarianism, but rather that the leader's vision of the island's future is irredeemably flawed from the very start. Toussaint is attempting to reinsert Saint Domingue into a productive regime that is inherently exploitative, based on a world market that after squeezing the slaves dry is more than willing to prey on them as salaried workers. And indeed, it must be remembered that, in spite of public declarations of horror at the events in Haiti, the United States and even France were still quite willing to engage in profitable trade with the former colony, provided there was indeed a profit. Toussaint was aware of this:

> He understood that, however principled France's leaders had been in 1794, ultimately the French nation would stick to the principle of emancipation only if Saint-Domingue continued to send the commodities it had produced for the past century across the Atlantic. Freedom was sweet, but it had a cost. France still needed the sweetness of sugar, and the coffee to go with it. (Dubois, *Avengers*, 192)

In Glissant's play, Macaïa and the maroon slaves represent the refusal of that new form of enslavement. The confrontations between Toussaint and Macaïa multiply throughout the play, with the maroon slave openly accusing the general of betraying his people (29), of betraying his old leader the rebel Biassou (41), of allowing his obsessive "thinking of tomorrow" stifle the present ardor of rebellious slaves (56), of displaying too much zeal in protecting and restoring the properties of white land-owners (67), of oppressing his own people (76). Mama Dio, the Vodou priestess, also joins the maroons in their accusations. Early in the play she declares that, in spite of Toussaint's worship of the "white god" (Toussaint was a devout Catholic), the African warrior god Ogoun has always protected him (44–45). However, Mama Dio feels later compelled to state: "Warrior Ogoun has gone far away from you—ever since you began to give commands as governor, and no longer like a brother among brothers" (48). Thus, the maroons' critique is devastating and, in spite of Toussaint's justifications and ultimate redemption at the end of the play (when after death he follows Ogoun back across the ocean in order to rejoin Macaïa in the struggle for freedom), the reader is left with the impression that, of the two arguably justifiable positions, Glissant has undoubtedly given the most impassioned arguments to Macaïa.

The problem for Macaïa and the maroons is: what alternatives do they present to Toussaint's pragmatism? The play focuses on the tension between the maroon's desire for immediate liberation, a liberation that suffices by itself and does not require further planning or delay, and Toussaint's insistence that such freedom must be employed toward some predetermined goal. Ultimately, Macaïa insists: "I am a man of the forest. So that means I am anarchistic and sterile. Ah! The time in which I dwell is not the time that takes you forward!" (63). Macaïa's "anarchism" does not receive further elaboration in the play, but his allusion to two different concepts of time is suggestive: Toussaint's is "the time that takes you forward," anchored on notions like progress, development, economic growth, as defined by the interests on an increasingly global capitalism. Macaïa's anarchistic forest time ("sterile" from the perspective that Toussaint represents) may be linked to the former slaves' desire to cultivate small plots of land without being tied (or re-enslaved) by the interests of international markets which have their own profit as ultimate motivation.[8]

As Paul Farmer aptly writes of the early post-independence period: "The new elite insisted that the emerging peasantry produce commodities for an international market, but the peasants—the former slaves—wished to be left alone to grow foodstuffs for themselves and for local markets" (*The*

Uses, 65). Carolyn Fick, in addition to linking the former slaves' view of the land to a traditional African outlook, which must have been familiar to many of them, forcefully elaborates:

> A personal claim to the land upon which one labored and from which to derive and express one's individuality was, for the black laborers, a necessary and an essential element in their vision of freedom. For without this concrete economic and social reality, freedom for the ex-slaves was little more than a legal abstraction. To continue to be forced into laboring for others, bound by property relations that afforded few benefits and no real alternatives for themselves, meant that they were not entirely free. (249)

While Haiti's situation and the circumstances of its independence are certainly unique, these dilemmas are familiar to all newly independent countries. Ultimately, as Farmer indicates, the Haitian elites got their way in their attempts to reintroduce the island into those world markets, and the history of Haitian poverty is deeply linked to a world economy always already dominated by metropolitan interests (including, first and foremost, France, which forced Haiti to pay a millionaire compensation to its former masters), which had no interest whatsoever in Haiti becoming an "equal." This is not to say that small scale or subsistence agriculture would have led to Haiti's economic and political success (again, any country needs relations of some sort with its neighbors, and Haiti was born into an extremely hostile international community). But we will never know what might have developed from following that route. The broader question, then and now, is whether one can feasibly imagine models of economic stability and sustainability that are not tied to the dogmas of winner-takes-all capitalist globalization.[9]

The Macaïa-Toussaint conflict is not unique in Haitian history (or in other independence struggles, for that matter), and diverse permutations of similar tensions, with different characters, come to the foreground at different moments. The well-known conflict between Toussaint and Moyse, which we will highlight in the next section, comes to mind. Such conflicts may be related to what Michel-Rolph Trouillot has called the "war within the war" (40) in the Haitian Revolution; in other words, the fact that the war was not simply between Haitians and French, but sometimes, tragically, Haitian against Haitian, depending on diverse power struggles between multifarious groups and leaders. Trouillot highlights the case of colonel Jean-Baptiste Sans Souci, who originally fought under Christophe but refused to follow him and Dessalines when they joined Leclerc (thus betraying Toussaint).

With his skillful guerrilla tactics, Sans Souci created a lot of trouble for Leclerc, and even after Dessalines started his war against the French, Sans Souci refused to join him and Christophe, considering them traitors. When he finally acquiesced to recognize Dessalines's leadership, Christophe called him for a meeting; when Sans Souci appeared, Christophe's soldiers killed him.

In Trouillot's reading, Christophe's well-known luxurious palace of Sans Souci *may* reference the king's enemy in its name: thus, it simultaneously erased the name of the man by making it the name of the palace, and the construction of the palace near the place where Sans Souci was killed became Christophe's "transformative ritual to absorb his old enemy" (65). Trouillot is particularly interested in how Sans Souci is mostly absent or minimized (other than in a construction like the palace that actually *silences* his presence) in official accounts of Haitian history as produced by the Haitian elites, such as the history by Beaubrun Ardouin. Such histories, Trouillot argues, minimize "the war within the war" and the abuses of the Haitian elites against the Haitian people, in order to present a heroic, epic portrayal of Haitian history grounded on heroic figures. It is through such operations, I might add, that the coloniality of power intersects with the coloniality of knowledge—perspectives, figures and events from across the divide of the colonial difference are not simply ignored, but rather actively silenced (although rarely in a completely successful manner). From our perspective in this discussion of Glissant's play, it is most significant that one of Sans Souci's guerrilla allies against Dessalines and Christophe was, precisely, the historical Macaya (Trouillot, 43).

The Present (Local Elites, Coloniality of Power)

Evidently not all of Haiti's problems can be attributed to the interests and interventions of foreign powers, although one would be hard-pressed to find one that was not deeply tied to or complicit with those forces. In the play, Toussaint replies to Dessalines, who asks him to choose a successor:

> Let's see, Christophe dreams of nothing but palaces, Clairveaux sees only plumes and gold braid, Belair must devote himself to his young wife, and Dessalines is too fond of wars. For a soldier-farmer, you must admit, there is only Moyse . . . General Moyse is popular, the workers applaud him, he is the one to carry on after me. Send for Moyse! (79)

This particular scene shows the effectiveness of Glissant's strategy of linking the cell space of Toussaint's last days to the island space of the revolution. In this instance, as he talks to Dessalines, Toussaint thinks he is in the present of the island, but in fact he is remembering the past from his cell. The answer to his command comes from the spirits in his prison cell: "General Moyse is dead, O Toussaint. You executed him without a hearing" (80). In what C. L. R. James regards as one of Toussaint's most grievous mistakes, Toussaint executed his adopted nephew Moyse because the latter led the peasants who rebelled against the oppressive labor regime imposed by the black general, and attacked white planters whose privileges Toussaint wanted to preserve (*Black Jacobins*, 278–79). Thus, in Glissant's play Toussaint can foresee that most of his possible successors will betray the liberation struggle they are engaged in by creating local elites that preserve the exploitative privileges that the old colonial elite possessed, yet he executes Moyse, the one figure who, at least symbolically, stood up not only against colonialism but also against what Aníbal Quijano calls the coloniality of power.

As we have seen, Quijano's definition of the "coloniality of power" revolves around a Eurocentric view of essentialist racial differences in which the colonized is not only militarily conquered and economically dominated, but also considered to be inherently (biologically, ontologically) inferior to the colonizer. That Eurocentric essentialism continues to exert its influence after the former colony achieves independence and attempts to establish commercial links and attain "recognition" from its former metropolis, and it also pervades the worldview of local elites that maintain colonial structures and institutions of power and domination under the guise of the new nation.[10] As Quijano states, "European culture became a seduction; it gave access to power. After all, besides repression, seduction is the main instrument of all power. Cultural Europeization turned into an aspiration. It was a means of participating in colonial power" (qted. in Castro-Gómez, "(Post)coloniality," 282). How this coloniality of power weaves together local elites and former colonial (or new neocolonial) masters is most tragically illustrated in *Monsieur Toussaint* through the figure of Toussaint himself.

Throughout the play, a marginal but essential subplot involves the efforts of the colonial landowners (represented by the characters Désortils, Blénil and Pascal) to destroy Toussaint and his threat to their interests. Their ally is Granville, Toussaint's white secretary, who betrays him by providing information to the white landowners. However, Granville is critical of their methods—they feel they must annihilate Toussaint, whereas Granville understands that history cannot be undone, and that there is no going back to the old regime based on slavery. Granville's plan is actually more insidious. As he informs his fellow conspirators:

> He has only one weakness, gentlemen, through which we can get the better of him. He believes in order and prosperity. The blacks will desert Toussaint if you put your trust in him. Appoint him the lord of the plantations . . . When Toussaint forgets his people, when he is again overcome by his passion for planning and pruning, his people will abandon him and he will be in your hands . . . Only Toussaint Abreda can defeat Toussaint Louverture. (49–50)

The cynicism of Granville's words is matched by their insight. His keen observation is that the logic of coloniality (here applied to its fundamental economic dimension) does not necessarily depend on formal political or military control of a territory. Metropolitan capital can exert as effective a control, provided the local elite of the (former) colony also benefits from that control. Moreover, control is more effective when that local elite benefits not only in economic terms but also when it is truly immersed in the modern/colonial myth of Europe's *inherent* superiority (cultural, racial) to its colonies. Whether the historical Toussaint had ambitions for his own enrichment is open to debate (after all, he did sacrifice much to the struggle for liberty), but the play suggests that he was unable to think of Saint Domingue's future development outside of the paradigms offered by the colonial metropolis.

It should be clear that when Granville refers to Toussaint's love of "order and prosperity" as weaknesses that make him easily controllable, he (and Glissant with him) is not talking about those principles "as such," in the abstract. Of course there may be nothing inherently wrong with them. Rather, through the character of Granville, Glissant is referring to those notions as defined by colonial authorities: order and prosperity as an exploitative regime that benefited white planters by enslaving black workers. Toussaint opposes slavery but is still unable or unwilling to acknowledge that the oppressive character of the plantation system goes well beyond slavery. It is to that side of Toussaint as (perhaps unintentional) purveyor of the logic of coloniality that Granville refers when he suggests that only Toussaint Abreda (the name Toussaint received as a slave) can defeat Toussaint Louverture (his revolutionary name).

In the play, Moyse criticizes the colonial logic of Toussaint's postslavery economic plans in these terms:

> You say, "the people," I say, "the disadvantaged." You say "the people" with your republican highmindedness; I see only those who weed, cut, and bundle sugarcane. In sackcloth, sweating, their heads turning giddy under the sun . . . You say "the people," I shout in reply, "the wretched ones." (82)

Moyse's fleshing out of Toussaint's abstraction, "the people," implies more than a change of register. It challenges and highlights the erasures in the language of coloniality, particularly when that language draws upon pseudo-universal abstractions. The objection is not to the notion that the former slaves form part of "the people," but rather to the fact the use of such notions hide the fact that, throughout the many liberal, democratizing upheavals that dominated the Western "Age of Revolution" (as Eric Hobsbawn refers to it), including the American and French revolutions, in order for some in the metropolis to gain access to the privileges (material and otherwise) that come from being "the people," others were submitted to (or allowed to remain in) subhuman conditions. Moreover (and this may be more pertinent in Macaïa's critique of Toussaint), once those former subhumans are "granted" the symbolic privilege of becoming part of "the people" (as the French Revolution presumably did by abolishing slavery), that abstract, formal concession in itself can hide the reality of the concrete, material injustices that persist. As part of "the people," the former slaves should be counting their blessings; as "those who weed, cut, and bundle sugarcane," they know quite well that their conditions have hardly improved.

A further, important implication of Moyse's words relates to what the Argentinean philosopher Enrique Dussel calls "the myth of European Modernity" ("Europe") and Walter Mignolo refers to as the "Modern/Colonial World system" (*Local Histories*). In opposition to the myth that modernity (whether the scientifically driven industrial modernity or the philosophical-political modernity of the secular democratic Western nations) developed as an exclusively *intra-European* affair, Dussel insists that European colonial expansion to other parts of the world (led by Spain in the sixteenth century, then followed by other countries after the seventeenth century) was at the center of the development of "modernity:" not necessarily as its cause, but as an integral part of it (see Dussel "Europe"). The discovery and exploitation of the Other in a context of *global* domination is an intrinsic part of the developments associated with European modernity. What this means is that the colonized, the subaltern, the Other, have never been outside of Europe's modern project, but part of it as what Dussel calls its "underside" (*Underside*). When Moyse refuses the abstract language of Eurocentric modernity, and instead focuses on the oppressed masses laboring day in and day out under the scorching sun, he is highlighting that underside of modernity, the concrete details that its rhetoric hides. This does not imply the rejection of any liberating principles that "modernity" might offer (for example, its particular articulation of the notions of liberty, equality, fraternity), but rather the exploration of what those *excluded* from the myth of modernity might have to say about those, and any other values.

Symbolically, Moyse is not against modernity "as such," or for modernity as Eurocentrically defined by the logic of coloniality. His is what we might call following Dussel a transmodern perspective. By that term, Dussel refers to the emancipatory irruption of those subjectivities that have been denied by the "modern/colonial" project, and whose purpose is not to naively deny any value to the principles of modernity in the abstract, but to *decolonize* the world created by that modern project, confronting it from an underside that in fact was never not part of it, although it was (paradoxically) an excluded, marginal part (Dussel, "Europe"; see also Dussel, "Transmodernity").[11]

The Past (Eurocentric Values vs. Local Traditions/Africa)

Another issue, closely related to that of the Eurocentric myth of modernity and Haiti's modern/colonial history, is the tension between allegiance to "European" (French) values and rootedness in African (or Haitian of African origin) customs and traditions. As we have seen, one of the play's main structuring devices is the extended dialogue Toussaint has with the spirits in his cell. Those spirits are closely related to the cosmos of Vodou beliefs and, as Glissant explains in his preface, "Toussaint's relations with his deceased companions arise from a tradition, perhaps particular to the Antilles, of casual communication with the dead" (16). It is certainly true that casual communication with the dead is not a prevalent custom in the West that Toussaint tried to espouse, either in its secular scientific strand or in the traditional Catholicism that Toussaint practiced. Thus, the spirits that surround him highlight his seeming disconnection from the traditional beliefs most of the Haitian people held dearly, and it is not surprising that many of those spirits have an adversarial, recriminating relation to Toussaint throughout the play.

In fact, when Toussaint is organizing his army near the beginning of the revolution, he states: "There is no Legba, there is no Ogoun. There is science and knowledge now. When we march, even the dust will be disciplined" (35). In the French version, a soldier responds that those who die will go back to Guinea to join their brothers, thus highlighting even more sharply the contrast between Toussaint's worldview and that of many of his followers.[12] When Mama Dio wants to honor Toussaint, she finds no better praise than stating: "Toussaint worships the white god, but in his heart Ogoun is all powerful" (44).

At a certain level, the tension could be regarded as overly simplistic, given that Haiti, like other Caribbean societies, is a creolized culture that incorporates both European and African elements, as well as many others. However, the issue at hand is not the cultural identity of Haiti in the abstract, but the oppressive hegemony of one cultural worldview (that of European "modernity") in a colonial context. This aspect of the play highlights its connection to cultural debates closer to Glissant's own context in the late 1950s and 1960s. For instance, it is in the context of those debates that movements like Césaire's negritude find their full meaning: they advocate a return of sorts to Africa precisely because it is the African dimension of that colonized population that is being construed as worthless, uncivilized, exotic at best. Regardless of one's ultimate assessment of it, the cultural project of negritude must be understood in the context of those *anticolonial* struggles that swept the world after World War II. Glissant always kept his distance from what he regarded as the overgeneralizing aspects of negritude, but even he participated in those "counter-balancing" efforts against a colonial logic that taught blacks to "despise themselves" (Couffon, *Visite*, 35; my translation).[13]

It is questionable whether Césaire himself saw negritude much differently than Glissant. Regarding the important issue of struggles for liberation, Césaire states, as we saw in chapter 3: "It matters little to me who wrote the text of the Declaration of Human Rights. I don't care; it exists. The criticisms against its "Western" origin are simplistic. Why would that bother me? One must appropriate that text and know how to interpret it correctly" (*Nègre je suis*, 69; my translation). Part of interpreting the text "correctly" would be to flesh out what the French were reluctant to accept: that its principles must also apply to all colonized peoples regardless of race.

But again, the battle is not usually to demonstrate that European concepts and formulations are an important or useful part of the Caribbean experience; the struggle is more often to dismantle the myth that *only* European notions have provided anything of value to that experience. In *Monsieur Toussaint*, we can see this conflict played out in the two different concepts of the revolution that Toussaint and Macaïa hold. Toussaint attempts to justify his loyalty to the French Republic by stating that "the Republic began in 1792, and we, who once endured so many kings on our heads, we were born with her!" (Silenieks, *Monsieur Toussaint*, 36). By "we" Toussaint is referring to the revolutionaries, the black Jacobins who took the principles of the French Revolution and, as Césaire suggests, appropriated them and knew how to interpret them, that is to say, pointed out that, to be consistent, those principles entailed the liberation of the slaves.

Macaïa takes Toussaint to task not over the worthiness of the enlightened ideals of universal emancipation, but over the implication that the black slaves needed to be taught how to aspire to freedom. Now Toussaint has *not* said that, but Macaïa seems quite aware of the logic of the coloniality of power, by which even the slaves' ability to articulate their own desire for freedom is construed as a gift from the colonizer. Under such logic, even the former slaves who have liberated themselves remain the *others* of rationality and agency, to which they attain precariously through the civilizing efforts of the Europeans, as the colonizers had always declared (thus justifying their colonizing mission: the white man's burden). To this, Macaïa replies:

> Before the whites even knew the word revolution, we maroons already had the run of the forest. Their dogs could smell us a mile away, in the very midst of a peaceful crowd. Maroons had the smell of freedom. We were building our own republic . . . Freedom cannot be taught! . . . Freedom has grown in the forest ever since the slave trade began. Come reap it if you wish. (42)

I will not reproduce here the debate over the influence on European "enlightened" ideas and the French Revolution on the revolting slaves, and what shape their rebellions would have taken without those European developments. From the very title of his book, C. L. R. James laid the ground for an appreciation of the influence of those ideas on the slaves, with the important caveat that those slaves were never the submissive or irrational savages that European accounts would present (and thus, blank slates of sorts upon which those ideas were imprinted), but oppressed *subjects* longing for freedom since the very beginning of the slave trade, who were able to identify very valuable tools for their liberation in the concepts of the European Enlightenment. Césaire's essay on Toussaint also privileges the influence of French revolutionary ideas, while some later historians attempted to balance the picture by privileging the role of illiterate masses in the revolt (Fouchard, Fick, Thornston), or at least the extraordinary complexity of the factors that led to it (Geggus, *Haitian Revolutionary*). Nick Nesbitt also offers valuable insights in his attempt to clarify that the European Enlightenment itself was not a monolithic tradition, an important fact when trying to ascertain its impact on the Haitian revolutionaries (*Universal Emancipation*).

Naturally no contemporary writer that I am aware of would deny that the slaves' struggles for freedom did not start with, or needed in order to exist, the ideals of European Enlightenment. This is quite clear from the long history of slave revolts and escaped slave maroons since the conquest of the Americas. By the same token, there is no denying, when one considers the evidence, that the ideals and the rhetoric of European Enlightenment, appearing when they did, played a fundamental role in the way the revolting slaves articulated and gave form to their struggles for freedom.

However, it is equally important to consider the notion that the slaves' participation in the ideals and events of Enlightenment politics was not something clearly foreseen in the ideals themselves as first articulated by Enlightenment thinkers, or in the initial political upheavals of the "age of revolution." As historian Laurent Dubois aptly suggests, even after the French Revolution, with its enlightened principles, the abolition would not have occurred as swiftly, if at all, without the slave revolt (*Haiti*, 29).[14] The "appropriation" of enlightened ideas by the slaves represents the irruption of an *other subjectivity* into the scene, which wants to contrast/join its own ideas/desires of freedom to those that had been developed in Europe, and which creates something new out of that encounter, not something already contained but somehow not yet manifested in European discourse. On the other hand, to consider the slaves as simply the absolute Others of those European developments plays into the logic of coloniality. The slaves were always already part of those modern developments, as their marginalized symbolic border and exploited labor. From that perspective, what the slaves bring to the scene are transmodern subjectivities that engage in what Mignolo has called "border thinking:" their desires and projects are not merely something wholly other than the desires and projects of European Enlightenment, but they are not mere passive recipients of what Europe had already figured out without them (and then bestowed upon them).[15] They had been linked to Europe for centuries, and had been part of the modern project since the beginning as its excluded, colonial outer border.[16]

In Glissant's play, at times Toussaint seems to believe that the freedom he has attained he does owe to France (a logical assumption if one believes that France bestows the very idea of freedom on ignorant slaves). In his cell, he pleads with his jailers, protesting that his loyalty to the republic should not be questioned, and that it has guided all his actions (66). Mama Dio moans and the other spirits in his cell express their disapproval of Toussaint's submissive attitude. Of course, C. L. R. James would argue that there is no reason to take Toussaint at face value given the daring defiance of his actions up to that point, and that we should regard his seeming submission as still another ploy. That may be the case; however, in Glissant's play Toussaint comes across as a man who was indeed too devout of the French republic as the true purveyor of emancipating projects. In a scene of tragic pathos, French soldiers remove his uniform and his insignias, since "you have no right, except in your own stupid pride, to the uniform of an officer of the Republic" (Silenieks, *Monsieur Toussaint*, 81). Toussaint is reduced to complain: "was it necessary to add humiliation to my misfortune?" (ibid., 82). He is paying for his tragic mistake: what France grants, France can easily take away.[17]

Again, it would be incorrect to conclude that Toussaint's error is in believing in liberty, fraternity, and equality as such. Yet, in his enthusiasm about those values as formulated by revolutionary France, he neglects the fact that those values have been made to coexist with the logic of coloniality. It is not that the values are wrong, or that they are "Western," but rather that the very humanity of the slaves (and therefore the applicability of those values to them) is still very much in question. In the play—and one might engage in a Jamesian critique of Glissant in order to show that his portrayal of Toussaint is much too lopsided and partial—Toussaint seems too invested in the belief that, in spite of their duplicity and deceit, the French as purveyors of enlightened ideas *must* play a salutary role in Saint Domingue's future. To this one must add his concerns about the island's plantations in the world economy, which he rightly believes would require the cooperation of France and other imperial powers.

In this context, and in spite of Glissant's dislike of Afrocentric essentialism, it is not surprising that Toussaint's redemption at the end of the play should come through a reconciliation with the spirits and deities of Vodou. As he is about to die, Mackandal sustains him, praising his epic role in the liberation of his people as he invokes Legba, the opener of the way (121), and Toussaint tells Macaïa he is about to cross the ocean again, an action that replicates, in a liberating key, the slaves' middle passage.[18] Toussaint dies speaking Creole and invoking Ogoun: "Man lé la libeté pou Sin-Domingue! Ogoun, Ogoun!" (121).

The end of *Monsieur Toussaint* is not a return to Africa, but rather a return to a Caribbean reconciled with the African dimension of its history. The "Caribbeanness" of the ending is certainly highlighted by Toussaint's use of Creole. Throughout his career, and unlike his younger colleagues of the *creolité* movement, Glissant never favored the use of Creole in his own literary production, preferring the use of a Creole-inflected French. One may question the reasons for his approach, which probably range from aesthetic preferences to the marketing constraints of a Paris-centered publishing world.[19] In the play, the use of Creole by Toussaint at the end and by certain characters (slaves and spirits) throughout the play enhances the significance of Macaïa's anti-French arguments—those arguments are not being made from an essentialist Afrocentric position, but rather from a creolized, Caribbean reality that fully integrates its African components. The Creole language, developed through the fusion of French and African languages, concretely embodies that creolized reality. In his preface to the 1978 version, Glissant indicates that he resisted the temptation to "creolize" the language of the whole play because the artificiality of that procedure would have been obvious (which is itself a questionable, potentially Eurocentric assessment, except from the practical point of view of performing the play in France). However, he does invite producers and actors to incorporate any such creolizing elements through improvisation if the performing situation allows it.

The play makes sure to include a revealing example from Haiti's history that demonstrates the precariousness of all essentialisms in the Caribbean. It is well known that Dessalines, a much fiercer leader than Toussaint, not only led his people to independence by fighting the French to the death; there were also massacres of whites after the French had been defeated. However, Dessalines famously spared the Polish and Germans who had refused to carry on Rochambeau's orders (*Monsieur*, 111), and he excluded them from the prohibition that his Constitution imposed on white men owning land in Haiti. Dessalines is not interested in attacking an essentialist whiteness whose very nature is defined by the tenets of European colonialism, but rather in loosening the grip of that colonial logic: anyone who joins him in that struggle is an ally, regardless of race.

Totalité-Monde or Globalization?

In the previous section, my examination of the problems that Glissant's representation of Toussaint poses started with concrete, material concerns about possible avenues of subsistence and development in the world economy for postslavery Saint Domingue. Toussaint does not consider the possibility of an independent Haiti, but Dessalines will face similar problems after his victory, as does every newly independent nation. Toussaint's error, as portrayed in the play, is his inclination to reinsert the island in global markets that, in their very structural setups, already followed a colonial logic. Are there any other possible models for livelihood, Macaïa and the maroons seem to ask. From there I moved toward questions of cultural legitimacy, to the tension between the primacy of Eurocentric notions and values in a colonial society such as Saint Domingue (notions and values that are internalized by the colonized themselves) and the need to reconnect with African (in this case) dimensions of identity that the colonial logic has condemned to the realm of the animalistic and the subhuman.

The point I want to emphasize here is that although the order of my analysis was arbitrary (I could have started with the cultural and ended with the economic), in recent years several critics have pointed out—sometimes with frustration or downright indignation—that Glissant's own career as writer and theorist followed a similar path, from more concrete economic/political concerns that find their most coherent expression in 1981's *Le discours antillais* to more cultural, identitarian (albeit in a postmodern, antiessentialist vein) preoccupations. For critics like Peter Hallward, those developments are parallel to Glissant's abandonment of his projects for an independent Martinique, and his acceptance of the island's somewhat permanent political ties to France, in one form or another. Although I will not reproduce the lengthy debate here, I must allude briefly to it because, as we have seen, both concerns, the economic and the cultural, play an important role in a play that was written toward the beginning of Glissant's career (1961), revised and shortened during a middle period (1978), and then co-translated (and further revised) toward the end of his career (2005).

According to Hallward, Glissant's work since *Poétique de la relation* (1990) became progressively disengaged from concrete political commitments that found their clearest expression in his support of Martinique's independence (or at least national autonomy). Hallward accuses Glissant's thought of moving toward a banal, politically ineffectual, Deleuzean "incorporation into the univocity of a new world order based on nothing other than constant internal metamorphosis, dislocation and exchange" (68). In other words, where before we had concrete political action based on universal principles that coalesce around anticolonial struggles anchored in the need for national independence (Hallward approvingly refers to this position as "neo-Jacobin" nationalism), Glissant's late emphasis on notions such as "relation," "tout-monde," "chaos-monde," and many others constitutes a celebration of a singular world where each part exists through and in connection with all other parts, and which calls for an acknowledgment of such always-already-there relations as the main act of engagement with it. This "postmodernization" of Glissant's views is also confirmed, somewhat approvingly first (1998) and then disapprovingly (2008), by Chris Bongie.

Not surprisingly, many critics have attempted to "defend" Glissant, either by pointing out concrete political projects that the Martinican author has been engaged with regardless of how abstract and aestheticized his books have become (see Forsdick, "Late Glissant"; and also Nesbitt's praise [in spite of his general agreement with Hallward] of Glissant's proposal to turn Martinique into an "ecological nation" in *Voicing Memory*), and also by questioning Hallward's premises, and showing how Glissant's late positions, whether one agrees with them or not, were developed out of the need to address legitimate political concerns. Thus, Eric Prieto suggests that Glissant's notion of "Tout-Monde" addresses the apparent dichotomy between the local and the global by invoking a "principle of interrelatedness" that "has the effect of releasing us from the too-abstract/too-specific binary" and whose challenge is "to represent individual events in ways that highlight their participation in this larger, global scheme, to find a language of representation able to capture simultaneously the relatedness and the uniqueness of every individual" (118–19). The task at hand may still be as specific as founding a nation or protecting an endangered forest—but neither can be accomplished in naive or stubborn blindness to the global forces that weight on it and are affected by it.

Similarly Celia Britton argues that Glissant's late works are not only political (if one allows for a broader definition than Hallward's) but also that their progressive distance from the nation as solution for political problems is a result of Glissant's engagement with the concrete conditions of the contemporary world. Thus, Britton suggests, "in a world of multinational economies and US neoimperialism, gaining national independence does not guarantee freedom from oppression; Glissant's late texts repeatedly argue that the nonlocalized "invisibility" of the multinationals, situated nowhere and everywhere, eludes conventional resistance and requires us to find new ways of opposing them" ("Globalization," 7). Certainly, one need not agree with Glissant's diagnosis or approach in order to recognize that his late works constitute an attempt to address global systemic forms of domination that his earlier ones did not always tackle directly, focused as they were on the colonial relation between France and Martinique.[20]

The realities of nonlocalized multinationals and metropolitan neocolonialism return us to the concerns we have explored in *Monsieur Toussaint*.

After all, many of the tensions that feed the debates on Glissant's "late style," are already included, in one form or another, in his only play. Hallward himself acknowledges that the changes that he is criticizing are possibly more changes of emphasis than an absolute break in Glissant's work (67); however, he finds that the change of emphasis is significant enough to allow us to talk about two distinct periods (at least) in Glissant's writing. Although I agree that increasingly dense neologisms of late Glissant do mark a transition in his work, my suggestion here is that the *impasse* at the end of *Monsieur Toussaint* points to many of the conflicts that the later neologisms will try to bridge, if not solve.

After all, the end of *Monsieur Toussaint*, in spite of Toussaint's redemption and symbolic return to Haiti, is a failure of sorts, or at least a tragic denouement. Toussaint has a hard time imagining Saint Domingue outside of the international circuit of the sugar market, which foreshadows the realities of globalization. Macaïa and the maroons might have represented the beginning of a viable new direction, but they did not have a chance to test it. Moreover, they are unable to articulate it beyond the romantic exaltation of libertarian freedom. Those two "failures," if one might call them that, will haunt the leaders of the future nation, or at least those whose main concern is not their own enrichment. The play ends with the inability to name a third way that might combine and/or surpass Toussaint's and Macaïa's concerns. That impasse points to the need of a language, an imaginary that might incorporate the local and the global, sovereignty and cooperation, opacity and relation. And while *Monsieur Toussaint* is unable to create that imaginary (not the least because of historical accuracy: Haiti's history has not been able to find such a way), it is not surprising that Glissant returned to the play twice throughout his career (in 1978 to shorten it and in the early 2000s to co-translate it). In many ways, Glissant's work (after, but certainly also before, *Le discours antillais*) has been an attempt to articulate and productively *imagine* a fruitful conjunction of what Prieto calls the "interrelatedness" of the local and the global. That interrelatedness would imply a conjunction of the imperatives that Toussaint and Macaïa represent and are unable to reconcile in *Monsieur Toussaint*.

Glissant's best known attempt to provisionally *name* that interrelatedness that evades both Toussaint and Macaïa is the neologism *tout-monde*, which takes its place among many concepts in his oeuvre that work over decades like variations on a very specific set of concerns and obsessions, from the confluence of "opacity" and "relation," to the exploration of the contemporary "chaos-monde," to the imaginary cartography of a "new region of the world."[21] The tout-monde refers both to the reality, and to our awareness of that reality, that the totality of the world is indeed connected and interdependent, so that no group or individual can claim to exist or aspire to succeed without taking into account the rest of the world. This view does not invalidate the realities of specific identities, but it does move identity away from any essentialist grounding toward an awareness that all specificity is the unique and unpredictable result of the coming together of those multiple elements. Any group or individual can still claim a "right to opacity" (*Poétique* 203), because the many factors that make up their identity can never be fully sorted out and reduced to simple, clear-cut "explanations" (indeed, the reductive transparency of such explanations is usually part of the epistemic violence of colonialism, through which the colonizer always pretends to know what the colonized *is*, and *is not*). As Glissant lyrically puts it:

> What I call Whole-World [Tout-monde] is the universe as it changes and endures through changing, and, at the same time, the "vision" that we have of it. The Totality-World [totalité-monde] in its physical diversity and in the representations that it inspires in us. We would no longer be able to sing, enounce, or painfully work only from our place, without plunging into the imaginary of this totality. (*Traité*, 176; my translation)

If it is certainly easier to criticize, perhaps even to parody Glissant's late style, it is in part because his poetic, abstract musings can have a diluting effect on the points he is trying to make, points that become much more intense when incarnated in a tragic historical drama like that of Toussaint.[22]

However, the pertinence of his points (that is to say, the connection between his late abstractions and important historical and political dramas in the real world) becomes clearer when we read them through the lens of our previous observations on the coloniality of power. That matrix of political inequality became a truly *global* phenomenon with the expansion of modern empires (beginning with Spain in the sixteenth century and culminating with France and England through the twentieth, with the United States frequently operating in a neocolonial economic key, but just as often ready to engage in military interventionism). As we have seen, the coloniality of power operates through an essentialist Anglo-Eurocentric ontology whereby other "races" are regarded as less and/or other than fully human. In order to operate, that matrix requires an imaginary, a series of images, stories, beliefs, myths, and other disciplinary knowledges and practices, which both articulate and spread the coloniality of power not only among, but also within, individuals. At the existential level, as Maldonado-Torres compellingly argues, one may even refer to a coloniality of being, which excludes from full humanity certain races or human groups. As mentioned before, this matrix continues operating even after the formal ending of colonial domination; in fact, it dominates much of contemporary neoliberal globalization. Thus, for Glissant, that battle at the level of the imaginary is fundamental (to the point that sometimes he may be criticized with good reason for seemingly underestimating the importance of struggles at other levels).

As Glissant states in *Poétique de la relation:* "Most of the nations that gained freedom from colonization have tended to form around the idea of power—the totalitarian drive of a single, unique root—rather than around a fundamental relationship with the Other. Culture's self-conception was dualistic, pitting citizen against barbarian" (Glissant, *Poetics*, 14). We can see clear links between these words from *Poetics* and the dire realities of the coloniality of power as highlighted in *Monsieur Toussaint*. Toussaint's authoritarian imposition of the plantation labor regime on his people enacts, at the level of economic production, the "totalitarian drive of the single root" that still dominates the postemancipation Saint Domingue, as it will dominate postindependence Haiti. Needless to say, the European nations that are anchored in the totalitarian certainty of their ontological superiority, and thus saw no contradiction in the enslavement of their inferiors, will not ultimately object (in spite of initial resistance) to a change of regime (salaried workers instead of slaves) as long as they keep receiving the goods to which their superior nature entitles them. Thus, the development of a different, alternative, decolonizing matrix of images and knowledges that will counteract the "totalitarian drive of the single root" (which responds to the coloniality of power, as well as to the coloniality of knowledge and being) is of vital importance for Glissant, even if their practical applications in concrete situations may not always be immediately evident.[23]

Glissant is not naive (although admittedly he seems to be sometimes) about the fact that oppression continues in the "tout-monde," precisely because the logic of coloniality does not need the mechanisms of classical colonialism to operate. However, an essential part of his project is to shake and demolish the claim to *legitimacy* that attempts to anchor the coloniality of power, knowledge, and being (see Glissant, *Introduction*, 68 and 77; and also Britton, "Globalization"). He tries to combat the imaginary of coloniality (fundamental to its operation) with an alternative imaginary that consistently diffuses and disseminates all claims to ontological essentialism. Again, a critic might with some justification attack that approach as irredeemably insufficient, but one could equally argue for the necessity of such a project in any struggle against not only the material realities of colonialism and its legacies but also against the logic of coloniality.[24]

In the links that I am suggesting between *Monsieur Toussaint* and Glissant's later works, those late, often perplexing neologisms should not be regarded as *solutions* to the play's conflicts (as if uttering the word "tout-monde" somehow exorcised its dilemmas), but as *extensions* of the play's final impasse—as attempts to turn that impasse into something productive rather than paralyzing. They are attempts, yes, of imagining new ways of articulating notions and concepts (such as identity) that have been fundamental in the long history of colonial relations, but they are not final solutions. They cannot be because, as we have seen in previous chapters, the logic of coloniality locates the colonized in a double bind in which even resistance often puts those who resist in the self-contradicting position of "confirming" their oppressor's prejudices. Faced with this impasse, this uncertainty as to viable *clear* political options, the play offers itself, with its "prophetic vision of the past," as a form of *cultural* action. Thus, the importance of *Monsieur Toussaint* is not merely in what it says or prescribes but also in what it does, in the way it *performs* the tensions and contradictions of the colonial condition. Its power for spectators and readers is to enable their reflective participation in the story's unsolved dilemmas, rather than the expository solution of those dilemmas.

Naturally, action is still required in the real world, action that will necessarily be partial and not take into account important dimensions (ultimately, the totality of the *tout-monde*) of the situation at hand. Glissant does not deny the need for such action—Toussaint must act according to his best judgment, as must Macaïa. But Glissant does seem to believe that there is a salutary and humbling effect with *ethical* dimensions in acting, first, with the awareness that the "tout-monde" around us (not just our small parcel of it) claims our commitment, and second, with the awareness and the regret that we cannot do full justice to that call. At any given moment Toussaint's and Macaïa's actions might be enhanced or limited by their ability or inability to *imagine* a broader or different totality (for Glissant always composed of a multiplicity of interrelated parts) beyond their immediate concerns. Readers and spectators also learn the same lesson through their participation in the play's action, and that is one of the effects of Glissant's "prophetic vision of the past."

The notion of a "prophetic vision of the past" entails more than the examination of past events from the perspective of the problems of the present. It also involves, as Glissant makes clear in the preface to the play, a recovery of dimensions of that past that have been hidden and marginalized by official (read: colonial) versions of history. But even more, the "prophetic" aspect of that view logically implies the impulse to announce a future, and moreover a future in which, as with the prophets of the Old Testament, the iniquities and injustices of the present are duly rectified. Evidently, Glissant is not thinking in literal religious terms, and in many ways it is not surprising that when he again invokes the notion of a prophetic vision of the past in 1996's *Introduction à une poétique du divers* (86), it is in the context of a discussion of another concept dear to him, that of the *erratic* (a term he takes from chaos theory) or *unpredictable* character of the tout-monde (81–107). For Glissant, this unpredictability is primordially a positive value, because he associates predictability with the tendency to organize the world in well-defined, essentialist compartments that are then naturalized as "the way things are," which has characterized colonial thinking for centuries.[25] Thus, even the "new" world "discovered" by the Europeans was organized through the use of old categories, and while that does not surprise us in the case of the almost medieval minds of Spanish discoverers, as a *modus operandi* it did not particularly change with the French and English empires up to the twentieth century. Coloniality always entails a foreclosure of novelty, as knowing is controlling.

Glissant's notion of unpredictability implies that, regardless of the strength with which the logic of coloniality set in motion and was infused into the history of colonized territories and peoples, such regimes are never tightly closed systems. Coloniality and colonialism cannot control everything, least of all the colonized's responses and resistances. These occur at multiple levels, including the political (wherein developments like the principles and events of the French revolution can become useful tools in hands of those enslaved by the French) and the cultural (wherein colonial societies, in spite of efforts to distinguish metropolitan "civilization" from native backwardness, become *creolized* societies to multiple degrees in multifarious ways). Although Glissant does not explicitly emphasize this aspect of unpredictability, one consequence of his concept is the opening of multiple (though often minimal) spaces of freedom in which groups and individuals can act in ways unforeseen by the power structures that constrain them.[26]

Glissant's "prophetic vision of the past" is paradoxically linked to unpredictability because one of things it does is to introduce *imagination* into *history* through *literature* [or art] in order to illuminate *spaces of freedom*. Those spaces of freedom, moments when events could have taken a different turn, are of course only visible to us in the present, but they can inform and inspire that present as it moves toward the future. In returning to a series of foundational events in Caribbean history, the play illuminates roads taken and not taken. What the play does better than much of Glissant's later theorizing is to highlight that those unpredictable junctures in history are always related to (albeit not totally dependent on) individual and collective *choices*. And the quality of those choices is deeply influenced (although not determined) by the richness of the imaginary of those who make them.

From this perspective, it makes sense that the play revolves around a series of key moments when certain characters (observed from our present) could have made a different choice. Those moments include Toussaint's joining the revolution, which happens after overcoming his wife's objections (26–27); his execution of Moyse (79–81), a moment in which, interestingly, it is Madame Toussaint who intervenes on Moyse's behalf, reminding Toussaint that it is *his* decision whether Moyse lives or not, while Toussaint claims (with Sartrean bad faith) that it is Moyse who has sealed his own fate; ultimately, Toussaint's decision to accept Leclerc's invitation to meet (again, against Madame Toussaint's advice), even when he suspects he will be taken prisoner (this last decision is given tragic overtones by Glissant's acceptance of Césaire's thesis: Toussaint removes himself from the stage so that the revolution can follow its course under Dessalines and Christophe). In addition to those moments, the long dialogue between Toussaint and Macaïa throughout the play illuminates the unpredictable implications of roads taken and not taken. The point here is not that Toussaint made the wrong choices—maybe he did or he did not—but that at certain key moments he chose, and that those choices were (and always are) greatly affected by the individual's (or group's) ability to *imagine* what totality they are part of. Each choice closes certain possibilities, but also opens numerous unexpected ones. The illumination of those possibilities in the past by the literary imagination opens up the exploration of similar possibilities hidden in the present. From this perspective, Glissant's later copiousness of neologisms may be found lacking in focus or clarity, but it was not banal or apolitical.

Naturally, those "spaces of freedom" are not absolute, and I am not suggesting them as metaphysical claims to Kantian free will. But Glissant's prophetic vision of the past works as hermeneutical tool that, in highlighting the myriad possibilities that the present situation can divine with hindsight when examining the past, opens up the multiple futures that could depart from the present, even if we must always opt for only one of those futures. Of course, the past cannot be changed and the future *is* unpredictable, and the myriad possibilities open to us in the present are never fully available to us (nobody can act from a full apprehension of the tout-monde). But if we are not absolutely free to decide, we are not absolutely overdetermined by the overwhelming logic of coloniality. It is that overdetermination that Glissant is combating, rather than proposing some unlimited freedom in the abstract. Glissant's angel of history sees not only ruins behind him, but a multiplicity of roads not taken that imaginatively illuminate the possible presence of many productive untaken roads in the present, even if they are not visible. It is imagination (through literature and art) that makes the invisible partially visible.

This chapter's inquiry began with the apparent paradox in Glissant's preface to the play: are the Caribbean peoples deprived of their histories, or trapped by them? The answer that emerges from *Monsieur Toussaint* is "both," or more accurately, "neither," since the issue at hand is not history in the abstract, but a colonial logic that denies some the ability to engage history as *subjects*. In the Caribbean context, the Haitian revolutionaries constituted a dramatic irruption of those denied subjectivities into realms that refused to acknowledge them, and which indeed made them pay dearly for their daring, up to this day. But once the irruption occurs, other problems to be solved begin, as the tension between Toussaint and Macaïa throughout the play shows. The core of many of those problems is aptly summarized by Glissant in his *Introduction a une poétique du divers*:

> The location from which one emits one's word, from which one produces the text, from which one emits one's voice, from which one emits one's scream, that location is immense. But one can close that location, and lock oneself inside . . . The important thing today is precisely to be able to discuss a poetics of relation that is able to open the location without undoing it, without dissolving it. Do we have the means to do that? Is it something that man, that the human species, that the human being can do? Or should we consider once and for all that in order to preserve the location it is necessary to preserve its exclusiveness? I have not denied that there is a question there. (29–30; my translation)

Glissant does not answer his question in *Introduction* or in any of his other books, just as *Monsieur Toussaint* does not solve the impasse between Toussaint and Macaïa. But the question remains fundamental, and Glissant's whole oeuvre is an attempt to *imagine* approximations to an answer. That is, for Glissant, one of Literature's main gifts to History. What *Monsieur Toussaint* shows more clearly than most of Glissant's theoretical works is that, in places like the Caribbean, both the impulse toward preserving the concreteness of one's location and the impulse toward the openness of relation are crossed by colonial designs that are always ready to take advantage of *both* impulses.[27] In this, Haiti remains, not only for the Caribbean but also for the rest of the world, both an inspiring story and a cautionary tale. *Monsieur Toussaint* compellingly explores both sides of that Haitian gift to those who want to reflect upon liberation and its discontents and possibilities.

Chapter 6

An Afrocentric Theodicy of Liberation
Manuel Zapata Olivella's *Changó el gran putas*

The Horses and Their Riders

Changó el gran putas (1983; *Changó, The Biggest Badass*, 2010) remains to this day one of the least studied masterpieces of Latin American narrative, just as its author, the Colombian Manuel Zapata Olivella (1920–2004), remains one of the most underrated writers of the hemisphere.[1] Zapata Olivella started publishing in the 1940s and had his share of international and national prizes and recognition; his most important works have been translated into English and other languages; and he has been favorably (and inevitably) compared to the writers of the Boom generation. However, international recognition beyond specialized academic circles has somehow eluded the Colombian writer.

The reasons for the neglect are probably multifarious and complex, but they may be related, in part, to the idiosyncratic path of his literary production. His first novels from the 1940s through the early 1960s (*Tierra mojada* [1947], *La calle 10* [1960], *Detrás del rostro* [1963]) fall within the category of social and political narratives where the plots are explicit vehicles for the denunciation of economic, political, and racial injustices. In terms of style, those works mostly adhere to a traditional realistic approach, but they were published during a period when writers such as Alejo Carpentier and Miguel Angel Asturias (along with Jorge Luis Borges, Juan Carlos Onetti,

Juan Rulfo, and others) were already pushing Latin American fiction in a different, more experimental direction, even when addressing political and social issues. Two intermediate, more stylistically complex novels, *En Chimá nace un santo* (1964) and *Chambacú, corral de negros* (1967), could have broken Zapata Olivella into literary fame, and indeed *En Chimá* was a finalist in the influential "Premio biblioteca Breve Seix Barral." International recognition still lagged but seemed imminent.

Then Zapata Olivella stopped publishing fiction for almost twenty years, as he patiently worked on his masterpiece *Changó*, a huge novel that is both stylistically and thematically ambitious, attempting nothing less than an epic history of African diaspora in the new world, narrated from the perspective of Yoruba and Bantu spirituality and mythology. The novel is not only very long and stylistically complex, elements that make it a challenging read, but it also requires an encyclopedic knowledge of black history for its full appreciation. For those willing to put in the effort, ideally having reference sources at hand for quick consultation of obscure historical characters or deities in African pantheons, the novel offers a veritable magical voyage, as it weaves its epic narrative through a prose that frequently dazzles in its poetic intensity and imagery. However, one can easily understand that it is not the type of novel that easily becomes, or aspires to become, a bestseller.[2]

It has been argued that the neglect of Zapata Olivella's work has a simpler explanation: covert racism. For not only is Zapata Olivella a Afro-Colombian writer, he has also made the experiences of the African diaspora in the Americas (and particularly in his native Colombia) the main object of both his fiction and his important work as an essayist and anthropologist.[3] It is hard to argue with the very strong likelihood that such prejudice may have played a role in the reception of Zapata Olivella's work: just in Colombia, the attempts to erase the very important presence in the country's black history and heritage constituted one of Zapata Olivella's main objects of study throughout the years.[4] In the way Latin American literature has been marketed internationally, an exotic, vaguely magical "mestizaje" has always dominated as *the* definition of what Latin America is all about—the market may have even been receptive to stories about local dictators who torture their own people, but not to tortuous examinations of racial prejudice and a history of the slave trade that directly implicates European and U.S. imperial designs, and which explicitly link the fate and histories of African Americans in the United States to those of Afro-Latin Americans.[5] Still, it is also true that even among scholars who would be sympathetic to Zapata Olivella's political project, and who are familiar with the important work of African American,

African, and Afro-Caribbean novelists, the work of Zapata Olivella remains relatively unknown.[6] Thus, it may well be that his initial lack of circulation was a bump that the author was not able to overcome. Hopefully, the acknowledgment of his significance will gradually increase with milestones like the translation of his chef d'oeuvre in 2010, for Zapata Olivella represents one of the truly innovative attempts to explore a fundamental aspect of the history of the Americas and the very construction of the modern/colonial world: the experience of the Middle Passage for millions of human beings, and the long, centuries-lasting struggle for liberation of the peoples of the African diaspora.[7]

In order to fully comprehend the fundamental role that the Haitian Revolution plays in Zapata Olivella's *Changó el gran putas*, and how that work offers us an innovative perspective on the significance of the revolution, I must start with a very succinct summary of the novel's massive "plot" and complex structure. As indicated above, the novel attempts to narrate the experience of the black diaspora in the Americas, conceived as one long, epic struggle for liberation: liberation from slavery to begin with, but then also liberation from racial prejudices and economic disadvantage, and eventually spiritual liberation from the many alienated versions of selfhood that imperialism and slavery have imposed on black peoples. The narration of black emancipation struggles across centuries is accomplished through a poetic prose, full of images and metaphors, that freely moves back and forth in time and space, and which constantly switches narrative persons in order to better capture the collective, prolonged character of the struggle.[8]

The novel is divided in five sections. The first one, "Los orígenes" ("The Origins") narrates, in free verse, the origins of the world from a perspective that combines Yoruba and Bantu religions. The African gods, or orishas, play an important role in this section, particularly the figure of Changó, the powerful and violent god of thunder and war. As a result of his excesses, his followers and other orishas rebel against him, sending him to exile. In his anger, Changó condemns his human followers to slavery and exile, fiercely commanding them that they must prove their worth by reconquering their own freedom. Thus, a mythical explanation for the enslavement and diaspora of the African peoples is provided, and also a divine grounding for the struggle for freedom. I will return to this topic below, since it constitutes one of the most unique, and certainly most problematic, aspects of Zapata Olivella's recounting of black emancipation struggles. In this first section we also witness the beginnings of the slave trade.

In the second section, "El muntu americano" ("The American Muntu"), we find the first experiences of the enslaved Africans in the Americas. And here I must briefly define this term, "Muntu," which plays such a fundamental role in the novel. Throughout the narrative, "Muntu" is used mainly to refer to people of African descent, both the African diaspora in the Americas and the many generations of African ancestors. But the term has deeper implications, and the novel's glossary defines it as meaning "man" or human being, clarifying however that

> the concept implicit in this word transcends the connotation of man, since it included the living and the dead, as well as animals, plants, minerals, and things that serve these. More than entities or persons, material or physical, it alludes to the force that joins in a single knot mankind with its Forebears and offspring, all immersed in the present, past and future universe. (449)[9]

Thus, the novel's preferred name for the members of the African diaspora contains within it philosophical and political implications that point to the unity of black experience, which the rest of the narrative tries to exemplify. A second recurrent term for Afro-descendants in the Americas is "ekobios," defined in the glossary as "'fellow member' or 'brother' among the Ñáñigos or Afro-Cuban priests" (452), another word that grounds the unity of blacks in the Americas in ancestral spiritual beliefs. I will return in the final sections of the chapter to the fundamental importance of that religious framework in the novel's political agenda.

An important aspect of Zapata Olivella's approach to the history of slavery in the new world is his emphasis on the fact that, from the very beginning, this is not a story of submission, but a story of resistance: sometimes spiritual resistance and resilience, but just as often violent revolt. Slave attempts to rebel and the struggles of runaway maroon slaves (like the Colombian Benkos Biojo) are highlighted in the narrative. Also important for Zapata Olivella's view of the Americas as "tri-ethnic" lands are the connections Africans were able to establish with the also enslaved indigenous peoples of the continent.

The third section, "La rebelión de los vodús" ("The Vodou Rebellion"), deals with the Haitian Revolution. As the title indicates, much emphasis is put on the role of the loas, or Vodou gods, in the revolution. The fourth section, "Las sangres encontradas" ("Rediscovered Bloodlines"), focuses on important figures from the colonial period to the wars of Spanish American independence, all of whom were either Afro-Latin Americans, or connected to their struggles: Simón Bolívar, the great liberator who nevertheless lacked the political will to achieve the abolition of slavery in his newly liberated countries; José Prudencio Padilla, a heroic free man of color officer of Bolívar's army who rebelled against the liberator when the latter delayed the liberation of slaves, and who as a result was executed by Bolívar; "the Aleijadinho," the colonial Brazilian sculptor and architect who embodies the syncretistic creative genius of the African diaspora; and José María Morelos, the man of color who was one of the heroes of the Mexican independence wars. The fifth section, "Los ancestros combatientes" ("Ancestral Combatants"), creates a fictional character, the revolutionary Agne Brown (very loosely inspired by Angela Davis), in order to travel in time and space through the emancipation struggles of blacks in the United States, from the achievements and conflicts of figures like Marcus Garvey, Booker T. Washington, and W. E. B. Du Bois, back in time to figures like Nat Turner and Harriet Tubman, to later martyrs like Martin Luther King and Malcolm X. In this section we have one of the few white characters with a significant role in the novel: the revolutionary abolitionist John Brown.

The summary above can only offer the faintest glimpse of the novel's complexity, which is enhanced by richly dense language and by the fact that throughout its pages orishas and ancestors participate in the action, comment on it, and establish connections between the past and the present. The experience is not unlike that of reading Homeric epics, in which the universes of gods and humans constantly interlock; this is, as indicated above, part of the philosophical and metaphysical implications of the concept of "Muntu." Not surprisingly, the author includes a glossary of terms at the end of the novel, which includes many of his more obscure historical references and many of the allusions to African religions.[10]

It is in the context of this epic, Afrocentric adventure that *Changó el gran putas* situates the Haitian Revolution. More than any other author in this study, with the possible exception of Glissant, Zapata Olivella locates the revolution in the context of the black diaspora or Middle Passage. The revolution is a neuralgic node in the long diasporic experience that the novel tries to capture. Thus, the text portrays the African/Afro-Caribbean/African (Latin) American experience as situated between the two vectors of diasporic identity defined by Stuart Hall as "the vector of similarity and continuity; and the vector of difference and rupture;" the first one providing "some grounding in, some continuity with, the past," and "the second reminds us that what we share is precisely the experience of a profound discontinuity" (395) as a result of slavery and violent relocation. Although the novel is very much about the *survival* of Africa in the midst of a violent diaspora, it is not shy about the fact that survival does not imply a simplistic retrieval of one unchanged African tradition, but the *imaginative reinvention* of that tradition at every turn of the way, for if there is something that the imperial violence exerted against Africans was intent upon, it was the elimination of any such cultural integrity. The novel itself as a literary and cultural artifact performs that retrieval through reinvention.

The Haitian Revolution is central to the novel's celebration of Afro-diasporic survival, and it becomes an essential locus to examine the physical and spiritual violence that was integral to the coloniality of power and the coloniality of being exerted against Africans and their descendants. The implications of that violence, which go well beyond the actual physical violence against the slaves, can be clearly ascertained in one of the monologues spoken by an already dead, yet alive-in-the-realm-of-the-spirits Toussaint Louverture, who comments:

> Even in death I still suffer the lies of those who will vainly attempt to darken the Muntu's victories. Our struggle for liberation has been reviled with the false stigma of a racial war. If the White Wolf oppressed, murders, and will despoil, his cruelty, always perfumed with incense, is adjudged as civilizing. When the slave resisted, exploded his chains, and defeats the master, his action is homicidal, racist, barbarous. For the Wolf's forgetful scribes, the history of the Republic of Haiti will always be the fanaticized and hate-crazed blacks' massacre of their white brothers, never the slave owners' genocide against a defenseless people. (175)

Toussaint's words capture the conundrum of what Walter Mignolo calls the "colonial difference" as they poignantly point to the slaves' position: they inhabit an always already racialized space where their oppression is justified by their inherent inferiority, and in which their attempts to liberate themselves are attributed to that same inherent inferiority and barbarism. Most definitely overdetermined from without, as Fanon would put it, the slave or descendant of slaves cannot point to that overdetermination without being accused of being obsessed with race. As Fanon states in a different context, "When people like me, they tell me it is in spite of my color. When they dislike me, they point out that it is not because of my color. Either way, I am locked into the infernal circle" (*Black Skin*, 116). By bringing the white outrage at the revolution's violence to the foreground, *Changó* points to the truly epic struggle for liberation of which Haiti is just a chapter: liberation not only from slavery but from the racialized framework of the modern/colonial world in which even the desire for freedom, enthroned in the founding documents of the West's liberal political orders, becomes a symptom of barbarism when incarnated in a black body.

The novel attempts to transcend this imperial asymmetry by framing its events wholly in an Afrocentric universe in which the opinion or judgment of racist whites is treated with the indifference and contempt it deserves. However, the novel's Afrocentric universe is porous and rhyzomatic. It does not attempt to create an essentialist black narrative, but rather to overcome an already existing white racist (not *white*, but *white racist*) epistemology. Furthermore, in the novel, as in history, the African diaspora will find allies of many ethnicities. Thus, the novel does not advocate for the subaltern to blissfully ignore the colonizer's prejudice and judgment, but rather for the subaltern to create their own narratives of selfhood, and to stick to those narratives in their struggles against oppression. It is that kind of creative reframing that the novel attempts, even as it acknowledges that, in the real world, Haiti, like other former colonies later on, cannot avoid dealing with the lingering presence of former colonial powers and their allies.[11]

The section on Haiti moves back and forth in time, following some of the main heroes of the revolution: Mackandal, Boukman, Toussaint, Dessalines, and Christophe. An important dimension of this section, which it shares with the rest of the novel, is that those heroes are always presented as acting under the guidance of, and often directly as instruments of, ancestors and Vodou gods, or loas. The longest chapter of the section is titled "The Horses and Their Riders Speak"—an allusion to the fact that in Vodou (as in Santeria and other Afro-Caribbean religions), when a god possesses a priest or priestess and speaks through them, it is said that the god is "riding" them. Thus, in this section, the revolutionary heroes are horses that African gods ride in the struggle for freedom.

In addition to the African gods, the revolutionary leaders are intimately connected to the ancestors, and this allows the novel to develop a spiritual link (which again, is insisted upon throughout the whole text) between the African slaves and the native indigenous inhabitants of the island. In planning his revolt, Mackandal declares: "We Africans will liberate the Indians and mulattoes of this island from all oppression" (159), and after he is burned by the French he states: "After dying I continued the war because those who fall in combat are promoted to the rank of general in the army of the deceased... Our war has endured and has no end in sight. We fugitives have been invincible since 1522, when the Indian rebels of Caonabó were already putting up resistance in the mountains" (160). During the Boukman rebellion the narrative breaks into verse and reinforces the connection:

> Muntu
> Who search for your lost home
> In alien lands,
> Do not forget that these lands,
> These forests
> Are the dwelling of the dead,
> Behequio,
> Cayacoa,
> Guarionex.
> Eyá! Yesterday the Indian's,
> Tomorrow your blood spilled!
>   (Olivella, *Changó, The Biggest*, 166)

European imperialists—to whom the novel refers collectively as "la loba blanca" ("the white wolf"), a sinister presence that often lurks in the dark waiting for its chance to devour the ekobios—are finally defeated with the aid of all ancestors, African and Indigenous. In the novel, ancestors are in fact the compass of freedom: "Without the experience and support of the Ancestors—the compass of the living—our actions in the face of the onslaught of so many enemies would have strayed from the path of freedom" (182). I will return to this topic below, but it is important to highlight that the emphasis on ancestors not only reflects the belief systems of many traditional African religions but also grounds and roots the violent struggle for freedom, shifting it from mere freedom *from* oppression to freedom *into* a fuller articulation of renewed selfhood through the imaginative recovery of the past.[12] The endeavor is not only emancipatory (from an oppressive present) but also unitive (with the experience of past generations moving through the present into the future).

I must highlight briefly a parallel that easily comes to mind when examining Zapata Olivella's version of the Revolution: Carpentier's *Kingdom of This World*, where, as we saw in chapter 1, Vodou loas also dominate some of the key moments and events. There are undeniable links between both visions, as there are links with Glissant's *Monsieur Toussaint*, which is also framed by the action of supernatural beings. Of course, Vodou played an important role in the slaves' conceptualization of their own rebellion, not to mention its importance as a disguise for the organization of the revolt. The main difference between Carpentier's and Zapata Olivella texts is that the narrator of the Cuban novel, in spite of his genuine fascination with the universe of the loas, remains the Other of that universe. The reader gets two versions of Mackandal's death: what the slaves think happened, and what actually happened. The novel remains (and that is its power as a fiction) stuck between those two worlds: that of traditional magical beliefs and that rational analysis. Zapata Olivella's text attempts to fully embody a perspective that looks at the world from the standpoint of traditional African spirituality. Many of the events are in fact narrated from the perspective and through the voice of Yoruba deities, or ancestors, who can move freely in time, or through their chosen human instruments.

Now, in pointing out the contrast between Carpentier's perspective and Zapata Olivella's, I am not necessarily attributing a naive religious faith to the latter. As we will see in the next section, I think that question remains unclear and one can detect an evolution of Zapata Olivella's views on religious beliefs. What is certainly true is that his main concern is political—the struggle for liberation that has consumed Afro-descendants in the Americas for centuries. He is mainly interested in myth and religion to the extent that they have been an integral part of that struggle. Yet, myth and religion are not merely incidental, since they also give those struggles a deeper spiritual character that goes beyond material liberation to a full recovery of pride in one's identity and history, whether those beliefs are taken in a literal manner or as inspiring allegories. As a *literary* artifact *Changó* is able to sustain its narrative voice and focalization admirably, immersing the reader in an Afrocentric spiritual universe that is very different indeed from even magical realist or marvelous-real portrayals of Latin American history.

Magical Keys to the Americas

Changó gives fullest shape and development to several concerns that recur in Zapata Olivella's works from the beginning, and that were to remain central in the texts he published after the novel. Among those, one could highlight: 1) A fundamental unity in the experience of the African diaspora in the Americas. That unity is not naively founded on an essentialized "African identity," but rather in the shared experience of enslavement and deportation, and on the persistent resistance to that oppression, sometimes through cultural creations, sometimes through violent means. 2) The important role of myth and religion as ground and means for the expression of black resistance, and as expressions of cultural identity and creativity that deepen the meaning of those struggles for emancipation, expanding them from the immediate concern with material circumstances to the need for psychological and spiritual liberation for *all* of the oppressed (not only blacks). 3) Zapata Olivella's concept of "tri-ethnicity," which refers to the African, Indigenous, and European dimensions of the cultural and ethnic identities of the inhabitants of the Americas. Zapata Olivella's "tri-ethnicity" is certainly limited—for sure there are more than three components in the composition of the Americas, and each of those three can be complicated and problematized. However, the concept points to a delicate balancing act that Zapata Olivella tries to maintain throughout his works. First, the novelist complicates his own emphasis on the black experience by acknowledging that black identity is articulated through its relations, oppressive or not, with other groups. Of those groups, Zapata Olivella is particularly interested in Native Americans, who have shared a history of dispossession with Africans in the context of modern European colonialism. Second, moving beyond any one ethnicity aids Zapata Olivella in tying racially motivated discrimination to other sources of oppression and injustice, particularly those related to class inequalities.

In his autobiography *¡Levántate mulato!* the author tells the revealing anecdote of his mother recriminating him for prioritizing his black Zapata heritage over his white Olivella heritage. The writer responds: "If those who are exploited and persecuted were white, I would be engaged in combat by their side" (180; my translation). Here oppression and marginality take priority over race, as they do in fact throughout Zapata Olivella's works. However, there is a catch: in the modern/colonial world created in the Americas, race and ethnicity cannot by simply abandoned for the sake of wider categories of resistance, because they have been, and continue to be, central devices in justifying the exclusion of certain groups. Thus, Zapata Olivella's view of ethnicity could be regarded as an attempt to retain race as a fundamental site of oppression and resistance, without falling in the trap of identifying only one race as essentially oppressed or oppressive, and without deploying race as the only site that generates oppression (class being another important concern of his). As we will see, the Haitian Revolution plays an important role in all three of the concerns summarized above.[13]

The Unity in the Experience of the Black Diaspora

One important theme that links *Changó* with Zapata Olivella's other works is the concern with the commonalities in experience and in rebelliousness throughout the African diaspora. From that perspective, the Haitian Revolution is quite simply one link among many in the long chain of pan-African revolts that the author has either examined or alluded to.

His second book, *He visto la noche* (1953), was a travelogue that documented his experiences in the United States during the Jim Crow era of the 1940s. The African American resistance to such indignities, including the efforts of Black Renaissance writers like Langston Hughes to instill a renewed sense of ethnic pride, constitutes an important dimension of the book. *Chambacú, corral de negros* (1967), one of Zapata Olivella's best-known novels, deals with popular rebellion and resistance among the primordially black poor community in the slum of Chambacú, just outside of the city of Cartagena. In the novel, black characters attempt to combat the interference and aggressions of official state authorities (an important part of the plot deals with the recruitment of poor young men for Colombia's involvement in the Korean war). At the same time, the marginal place of Afro-Colombians in the official symbolic cartography of the nation is examined and challenged. Through the character of José Raquel, however, the novel also presents a black character who is eager to assimilate to the official white establishment, joining the army and then proudly flaunting his Swedish girlfriend. Albeit somewhat lacking in subtlety or complexity, the character of José Raquel embodies what *Changó* calls the "dog shadow" that is attached to many members of the African diaspora: namely, the internalized shame and racism that centuries of colonial domination have inflicted on many blacks; in other words, he displays what Fanon called a black skin with a white mask.[14]

In *Changó*, the struggles of the Haitians in the third section are preceded in second section by the struggles of Benkos Biojo, leader of the San Basilio Palenque ("palenque" is the Spanish word for the maroon or runaway slave community) in the late sixteenth and early seventeenth centuries in Colombia (near Cartagena de Indias, one of the main ports in the influx of slaves to Spanish America). In his last book-length essay, *El árbol brujo de la libertad* (2002), Zapata Olivella calls the "palenque" "the first free territory of the Americas" (173; my translation), suggesting that Benkos should "take the place he deserves next to such precursors as Gunga Zumbi, L'Ouverture, Petion, Bolivar, Piar, Morelos and Padilla" (173), who are, not coincidentally, some of the main figures in *Changó*. The idea of that long Afrocentric tradition/history of liberation struggles, which welcomes and incorporates emancipating efforts of other victims of the racist Eurocentric articulation of the modern/colonial world, is a cornerstone of Zapata Olivella's universe. In *Changó*, we may read the words of Manuel Piar, a *mestizo* general in Bolívar's armies who forcefully protested against the lack of rights for mestizos in an army mostly led by white creole officers; foreshadowing his own death (he was executed on Bolívar's orders), Padilla states: "At the other end . . . my maroon brothers await me, free since long before the créoles began to parrot the word 'freedom' picked up from the French" (239; modified translation). Piar's words have important consequences, for they attempt to challenge a Eurocentric concept of the struggle for freedom, which ties it exclusively to the principles of European enlightenment. As we saw in chapter 5, dismantling that myth was also an important dimension of Edouard Glissant's *Monsieur Toussaint*. The slaves undoubtedly came to the Americas as prisoners, but, as Zapata Olivella suggests in a 2001 interview, the chains themselves should be regarded as a symbol of freedom because "if they came in chains, it was because they refused to accept their condition of prisoners or slaves" (Krakusin, "Conversación," 18; my translation). Although the ideas of the European Enlightenment became a tool in the hands of slave leaders (as C. L. R. James clearly shows in *The Black Jacobins*), the saga of the African diaspora's search for freedom begins with the enslavement of the first African, and while the slaves often used European concepts as tools and inspiration, just as often they were guided, as *Changó* suggests, by fidelity to ancestral memories and precepts.

When I state that the struggle for freedom starts symbolically with the enslavement of the "first" African, I refer more precisely to the beginning of the modern/colonial European slave trade, in the context of the development of European global imperial hegemony since the "discovery" of the Americas. Evidently, the history of slavery extends well beyond that, both in and out of Africa, but its modern/colonial manifestation marks the first truly organization of the globe in terms of a fundamentally racist coloniality of power.[15] As to the role (or not) of enlightenment ideals, the point, as indicated in previous chapters, is not to make an either/or proposition: they certainly played an important role but evidently cannot be supposed to have instilled a love of freedom to men who were brutally enslaved.[16]

If Haiti's rebellion is linked to a long previous history of black liberation struggles, it is also connected to later acts of resistance. When the novel moves to the United States in the 1960s and the protests against conscription during the Vietnam War (a subject that brings echoes of Zapata Olivella's previous *Chambacú* and conscription for Korea in Colombia), an anonymous black protester states:

> "My black grandparents and parents have all died in those wars instigated and won by the whites, but we have never enjoyed a victory: we remain slaves! That is why, ekobios, I exhort you to destroy this uniform that the Wolf has given us and to keep the weapons." The ritual . . . started with the drumbeats of Papaloi Bouckman announcing the fires. We new recruits, deserters, draftees begin to get undressed, tossing our military clothes into the flames: caps, trousers, epaulets, the lizard skin that masked our true color. Blacks, yellows, whites, we recovered the faces of our forgotten parents. (441)

This liberating ritual against the Vietnam draft begins with the drums of Papaloi Boukman, precursor of the Haitian Revolution in the famous gathering of slaves at Bois Cayman. However, and equally important, Boukman's call and symbolic importance, like that of the Haitian Revolution, transcend the interests and needs of one race and incorporates the others ("blacks, yellows, whites"). That motif—the solidarity of all oppressed peoples regardless of race—persists throughout the whole novel, even as the text also consistently emphasizes the tragic trials specific to the black diaspora.

The novel does not attempt to solve the tension between those two imperatives, but rather prefers to weave their dialogic relation through different moments and characters. In fact, the productive tension between them—a drive towards *universal* emancipation that nonetheless prioritizes the needs of those most brutally repressed by the system, namely black slaves—is one of the main legacies of the Haitian Revolution in the novel. Again in the section on the United States, we read:

> The White Wolf . . . is also alert. Ever since the blacks of Haiti expelled the whites from the island and L'Ouverture demonstrated to the Europeans and the Americans that we blacks could successfully govern a nation, the masters of the South feel their heads float above their shoulders. I don't think it was an informant who induced the governors of the Southern states to request reinforcements. The Lord does not let them sleep by stirring their guilty conscience: "I have created all nations with the same blood." (346)

The narrative maintains the balance between the moral imperative of the fraternity between all human beings (God created them "with the same blood") and the historical reality that white Europeans did indeed enslave black Africans. The project of black liberation (emblematized by Bouckman's drums and L'Ouverture's victories) cannot ignore the need to address the second reality even as it keeps in sight the first imperative. While there may be, to quote Césaire, "room for everyone at the convocation of conquest," it is still tragically true that the clearing the space for that room may require the struggle of some against some. And the main reason for this, and this also appears quite clearly in the passage above, is that the struggle for black liberation is a *response* to an imposed injustice that will not go away on its own: white slave-owners, like white racists and colonial powers ("the White Wolf"), are willing to cling to their privileges by any means necessary. The novel, nonetheless, is quite consistent in its insistence that, as that other great scholar of pan-African revolt, C. L. R. James, wrote precisely in his *History of Negro Revolt*, "the African bruises and breaks himself against his bars in the interests of freedoms wider than his own" (qtd. in Nielsen, *C. L. R. James*, 81).

In this regard, we must highlight the dialogue between race and class in Zapata Olivella's works. As noted above, his persistent effort has been to keep both as priorities without letting one subsume the other. Although his early novels display a social realism whose main focus is economic and political disenfranchisement, already in the first novel, *Tierra mojada* (1947), we find descriptions like this: "The dark skin of Gregorio's body glistened next to the dry and rusty skin of Próspero, who was an Indian without knowing it. His friend, who was a mulatto, was also ignorant of his African ancestors. They were simply peasants, born and raised on the banks of the Sinú River" (23; my translation). Race is not the center of attention here, but it is not allowed to simply disappear either. In the Americas, where class differences were built upon and around a "colonial difference" that essentialized the inferiority of a racialized other, race and class are never too far apart.[17]

In *Chambacú* and then in *Changó* (as later in *El fusilamiento de diablo* and *Hemingway, el cazador de la muerte*) race comes to the forefront, but always and only to the degree that it is imbricated in the marginalization of certain groups and individuals. In other words, even though Zapata Olivella spent much of his life investigating and publicizing the important role of African culture in Colombian (and Latin American) identity, his approach is different from that of many of the contemporary celebrations of multiculturalism. Of course, he might have wholeheartedly supported any attempts to celebrate diversity, but his focus is on a history of subjugation, exclusion, and discriminatory practices that did not simply disappear with abolitions or independences, but rather have been inseparable from the ways in which the coloniality of power operates in Latin American nations to this day.[18]

In *Las claves mágicas de América Latina*, an essay that in many ways offers fundamental interpretive keys to *Changó*, Zapata Olivella tackles the issue directly:

> It has been argued, in an attempt to reject the use of the word "race," that there are also white people among the exploited classes in the Americas. Yes, indeed, there are many whites among them, just as there are a few blacks among the rich in this country. This is evidence that when it is a matter of imposing their class interests, exploiters equally oppress whites, Indians and blacks, without ethnic or economic distinctions. The inclusion of the white proletariat in the group of the oppressed does not alter the old conditions of exploitation that have always plagued blacks and Indians . . . That is why we do not oppose the use of a class categories. Let that be understood, and let no one insist on a debate that can only be useful to racists: we accept the notion of class as more general, more adequate to describe the increase of surplus value that the new capitalist society imposes on the old serfs and slaves of the colonial regime. But we demand that to the noun "worker" one adds the adjective "black" or "Indian" when we are referring to the great masses of those ethnicities, because in leaving them without their surnames [that is to say, their ethnicities], we are only serving exploiters who are interested in hiding the survival of a caste system. (151–52)

What Zapata Olivella calls a "caste system" corresponds to what I have been referring to as "the colonial difference" embedded in the "coloniality of power," following Mignolo and Quijano. The nonreductibility of racial discrimination to class inequality is evident for its victims, and in his attempt to acknowledge both categories as essential to an understanding of oppression and subalternity in colonial societies, Zapata Olivella is following the steps of important figures like C. L. R. James and Aimé Césaire. In him as in them, the fact that race has no biological reality as a determinant of human character and culture does not invalidate the fact that it has a long history as a construct that has been deployed for exploitation and discrimination.

Thus, we can read in *Changó* words that, in their essentials, could have been written by either James or Césaire:

> Changó's chosen one to preserve the memory of the Muntu, do not forget that whatever mistakes have been made in the fight for freedom, it has always

been the firm mission of our people to defend this land as the common patrimony of all mankind. There will be no free America, nor Africa, nor any other part of the world, as long as there remains in our country a single oppressed individual—black, Indian, or white. (420)

Such an ecumenical attitude at the level of economic and social disenfranchisement is joined by an equally forceful acknowledgment of a different form of dispossession: "Black Power is not just a demand for social, civil, and economic equalities, but also for the equality of identities. The power to be Black!" (405; modified translation). The coupling of those egalitarian and identitarian demands is what Zapata Olivella and his novel strive for: not only more power *for* blacks (economic and political power: the kind of power that all whites do not necessarily possess) but also the basic power (or right) *to be black,* that is to say, not to have their ethnic and cultural identity as an a priory determinant-from-without that denies them access to full respect and participation in society (a kind of power that whites, no matter how disenfranchised, already possess in an antiblack racist society). Even as he acknowledges the urgency of addressing economic inequalities, Zapata Olivella highlights the existence of a colonial difference, imbricated in the modern/colonial world order, that simply cannot be reduced to (albeit it is often connected with) other forms of inequality.

Like James before him but through a different route, Zapata Olivella attempts to solve the seeming tension between race and class by grounding his vision on a more general notion that includes them both: the pursuit of self-determination and happiness, which locates both Marxism and Black Power as concrete manifestations of a humanist reflection on the human desire to be free of unfair constraints.[19] No one would dispute James's commitment to Marxist revolutionary politics, and yet he was adamant in affirming that "it is utterly false to draw the conclusion that the independent struggle of the Negro masses for their democratic rights is to be looked upon merely as a preliminary stage to a recognition by the Negroes that the real struggle is the struggle for socialism" (*James on Negro Question,* 74).[20] Zapata Olivella would agree: the question of black liberation does not precede, but rather coincides with, the struggle for economic justice as defined by Marxism, and the victory of one without the other (as well as, one might add, other struggles for emancipation organized around any axis other than race and class) is of necessity incomplete. Where Zapata Olivella moves in a different direction from James (and clearly leans toward what Paget Henry might call a "poeticist" approach) is in his attempt to imaginatively articulate a mythic foundation for those struggles for liberation. Almost as if suspicious of the superficial conflicts that different sociological perspectives can provoke, his novel moves toward a religious world that, as I will argue in the last two sections of this chapter, attempts to provide an ontological basis for the universal struggle for freedom at the same time that it preserves what I call "a preferential option for the oppressed black diaspora."

"Tri-Ethnic" Unity: Haiti's Impact on Latin America's Independence

The relation between black struggles for emancipation and other similar battles raises another important topic I want to highlight in this section. Zapata Olivella's view of Latin America as a primordially "tri-ethnic" continent brings to the foreground a dimension of the Haitian Revolution that no other creative writer has explored as explicitly: its impact on the Spanish American wars of independence. Here the key figure is one that usually does not come up in a starring role in most accounts of the revolution, although his historical importance is not in question: Alexandre Pétion. Pétion was a free people of color leader who allied himself with Rigaud against Toussaint, then left for exile in France, returned with Leclerc's expedition but then joined Dessalines, and went on to become Christophe's enemy and president of the South against Christophe's northern kingdom. His life embodies many of the complexities of the revolution, not the least of them being the ambivalent role of free people of color or "gens de couleur" in Haitian history. But Zapata Olivella's main interest in Pétion lies elsewhere: in his important assistance to Simón Bolívar during the Spanish American independence wars.

In 1815 a defeated and exhausted Bolívar sought sanctuary in Haiti, and Pétion not only received him, but also provided him with material and military support. After his military campaign fails, Bolívar seeks refuge in Haiti for a second time, spending a good part of 1816 in Port-au-Prince, and once again securing the help of President Pétion. That support was instrumental in Bolívar's later battles, but there is an aspect of it that is often not highlighted in the historical accounts. In exchange for his help, Pétion asked Bolívar to abolish slavery in the liberated territories of the Spanish empire. Bolívar agreed to do so.[21]

The chapter on Bolívar in the novel opens with the voice of the ancestors telling an already dead Bolívar: "Little Simón, I want you to remember what you have forgotten" (205). What Bolívar has forgotten is the promise he made to Pétion: because of his lack of political will, or because it was not strategically expedient, he did not officially abolish slavery, even though he often paid lip service to that ideal in speeches and writings. In the dreamworld of the after-death, a young Bolívar tells his black wet nurse (inspired by "la negra Hipólita," the real wet nurse who took care of Bolívar as a child): "I hear them bark at me in my mulatto blood" (210), to which she replies:

> My little master Simón, it is the Dog Shadow that you half-breeds carry within you, the impure part that tyrannizes the Indian and black brothers and sisters. It is that which opens kitchen doors for a stranger to enter the house. It barks along with the neighbor's dogs, chasing the ekobios. Only when the different bloodlines, mixed and united, manage to smother it will Changó's curse be lifted. (210)

As we saw earlier, the image of the "Dog Shadow" represents the internalized racism that victimizes many blacks and other "nonwhites." There is no denying that the language of this passage, with its emphasis on "half-breeds" and "bloodlines," may seem too close to biological essentialism for comfort. It can only be rescued from a historicized perspective, in terms of the ideological prejudices associated with skin color. By the same token, one can argue that the "Dog Shadow" of racial self-hatred does not confront people of mixed blood exclusively, or even primarily, as Fanon has made abundantly clear in *Black Skin, White Masks*. However, again from a historical perspective and in contexts like that of Haiti or colonial Latin America, it is true that in a society where every minor gradation of skin color counts, men of mixed racial ancestry like Simón Bolívar strongly feel the incentive to minimize or hide their African heritage. In fact, the link between Bolívar and Pétion is even stronger (and their dilemma more pan-Latin American) when one remembers that Pétion, in spite of his request to Bolívar, spent much of his career privileging the "white" side of his identity over the black one.

In the last section of the chapter, Bolívar must face a tribunal of ancestors who lay bare his betrayal. The independence hero is forced to admit: "Protected twice in Haiti by Pétion, the victorious general, I trembled as I dealt the blow to the chains that oppress my ekobios" (211). Bolívar's wet nurse responds: "Retreat before Changó awakes and spits on you in wrath. You will be assigned to collect the blood of the ekobios Piar and José Prudencio, shot by you, in order to close their wounds" (211–12). Manuel Piar and José Prudencio Padilla were generals in Bolívar's army, both of them men of color, and both of whom rebelled against Bolívar's authority. Among the reasons for both insubordinations was the discontent with the way Bolívar's white officers treated their "mestizo" or people of color officers, and concern about the ultimate destiny of slaves and free people of color in the new republics. In the case of Padilla, there was an open response to Bolívar's inability to ensure the freedom of blacks. Both were executed on Bolívar's orders. (As an interesting aside, the character of Bolívar in García Márquez's *The General in his Labyrinth* is also tormented by his actions against Piar).

In the section about Padilla, the novel imagines him in Haiti with Bolívar and Piar during the independence leader's sojourn in the island under Pétion's protection. Padilla himself narrates:

> Bouckman's drums convoked the Vodous to celebrate the thirteenth year of independence . . . There is dancing on the beaches, and the water of sweaty bodies buries in another sea the entire island of Haiti. Piar and I spend the day dancing in the streets with black and mulatto women who sweated the same perspiration that moistens our blood. At night, invited by the deceased Bouckman, we gather secretly in the patio at the house of the governor of the Keys. His lover, like all the ekobio women on the island, is a daughter and priestess of Yemayá. The candles are lit, and on the ground the effigies of Changó, Ogún, Osún, and Ochosi, the orishas of war, are drawn with chalk. On other occasions I had heard the weeping of these drums when the rebels of Benkos Biojo bury their dead in the Palenque of San Basilio. (241)

The imaginative thread that links ancestors, orishas, and humans manages to bring together the rebelliousness of maroon leaders like Benkos Biojo and the mulatto leaders of the independence wars in the drums of Mackandal. As always in the novel, the momentum of the struggle is provided by black rebels who constantly fight, to paraphrase C. L. R. James, "in the interests of freedoms wider than their own" (Nielsen, *C. L. R. James,* 81).

Zapata Olivella's writings, beyond *Changó*, display a conflicted view of Bolívar's role in the liberation struggles in the Americas. And here one must distinguish liberation, or freedom, from independence. As Padilla says in the novel: "Few creoles in Venezuela believe that fighting for the country's independence is fighting for freedom. They think that if they die, the blacks surviving them will impose a caste government as they did in Haiti" (231). In *Las claves mágicas* Zapata Olivella offers his harshest indictment against Bolívar, stopping short of accusing him of political opportunism. The author clearly states that when it comes to Spanish American independence,

> Any narrative or interpretation is racist if it forgets the decisive importance of the antislavery revolution in Haiti, whose victory influenced not only the organization of Miranda's and Bolívar's armies, but also the thought of all the peoples of America. It was that revolution that demonstrated that European colonialism, in spite of its great armies and alliances, could be defeated. (145; my translation)

In the essay Zapata Olivella mentions the concrete material help that Bolívar obtained from Pétion, and the promise he made regarding Spanish American slaves. Indeed he suggests that in Bolívar's gesture of liberating his own slaves, and in his words at the Angostura congress, Bolívar's abolitionist ideals shine through. But he cannot help but conclude that it is "unjustifiable" that "when his acts did not respond to immediate interests of the fight, when the national constitutions of Cúcuta, Lima, Quito and Paz were established, Bolívar left the decision on the abolition of slavery to the creole aristocracy, knowing quite well that they would refuse to do it, so that they could use the slaves in their lands and mines" (145; my translation). Zapata Olivella even suggests that in seemingly generous acts like the abolition of his own slaves Bolívar may have been simply calculating, trying to increase the numbers of his army (148). Ultimately,

> silence becomes complicit if one knows but does not condemn Bolívar's attitude when, quite intentionally, he did not invite the Republic of Haiti to the Panama Congress (1826). There is only one reason that can clearly explain that attitude: Bolívar did not want to encourage the increasing discontent among blacks and Indians against the constitutions allowing slave holding of the new republics. (146; my translation)

As a corollary to Zapata Olivella's words, one could add the actual dates for the abolition of slavery in the countries that were liberated by Bolívar, all of them well after his death: in his native Venezuela, 1854; Colombia, 1851/1852; Ecuador, 1852; Peru, 1855; Bolivia, 1851.

Without putting as much emphasis on the topic, Zapata Olivella mentions Bolívar's inability to fulfill his promise to Pétion in his two other major book-length essays, *La rebelión de los genes* (38) and *El árbol brujo de la libertad* (250), which indicates that the problem was in his mind until the very end of his life. The topic is controversial, not only because of Bolívar's hallowed place in the pantheon of Latin American heroes but also because of many examples that one could quote in his writings and speeches that would testify to his belief in the ideal of the emancipation of slaves.[22]

Sybille Fischer has also made a compelling case in favor of the notion that Bolívar's stay in Haiti had a significant impact on his political thinking, particularly in matters regarding the organization of the newly independent nations ("Bolívar"). All of that may seem insufficient in light of the realities that Zapata Olivella highlights, although one must also keep in mind that, not only on the topic of slavery but also on many others, Bolívar found himself entangled in multiple contradictions and conflicts after the end of the independence wars, when in fact he was often unable to impose, or even to effectively communicate, his will and vision to his previous, precarious supporters. His fall from power and his partly (but only partly) self-imposed imposed decision to go into exile just before his death clearly show this, without necessarily invalidating Zapata Olivella's points.[23]

Ultimately, the independence project of what is usually called Spanish America could be partially (albeit not entirely) linked to the interests of creole elites that aspired to political and economic control of their territories, but which had little interest in yielding their own privileged position. In that regard, political independence in the nineteenth century kept in place the Eurocentric logic of the coloniality of power, as it manifested in actual institutions (like slavery) and in mental and cultural attitudes. From that perspective, Zapata Olivella's critique of the interests that Bolívar represented (both politically and symbolically) throughout much of his career seems justified. As we have seen repeatedly throughout this book, even in the case of the Haitian Revolution, which was openly led by revolting slaves, local elites and international interests kept colonial priorities firmly in place after Haiti's independence. By the same token, one might regard "Spanish" or "Latin" America's independence in the nineteenth century as significant step in a still incomplete process of liberation, that keeps moving forward as Afro-descendants and Indigenous peoples (among others) keep struggling for clearer voices and increased agency in the control of their own destinies.[24]

One important point that Zapata Olivella is making in his analysis of Bolívar's actions and their effects on the future of Latin America, is that they acquire their full meaning in the context of Bolívar's literal and symbolic dialogue with Pétion. The Colombian novelist declares explicitly that "the Americas are a product 'made in' the Caribbean" (*Las claves*, 169; my translation), and that many of the social and political conflicts that trouble the broader region can be better understood by studying the colonial history of those islands. Moreover,

The antislavery revolution of Haiti is the best example to illustrate the origins and repercussions of social conflicts in the Americas and European ideologies in our continent. Contrary to what is usually stated, that it was the French Revolution that ignited the rebelliousness of blacks in Saint Domingue, the fact is that that rebelliousness had its origins in in the aggressive resistance to the conquistadors that was led by the cacique Caonabo, and which increased its firmness and ideals with the later war of the Haitian maroons. (ibid., 70; my translation)

Zapata Olivella goes on to say that, predictably, the Haitian triumph horrified not only the French, who immediately attempted to reconquer the island, but also all of those globally who were invested in what we could call the racist logic of a Eurocentric modern/colonial world.[25] Haiti suffered the dire consequences, but not without its struggle and victories becoming a model for all similar aspirations throughout the Americas. For Zapata Olivella, the Haitian Revolution is both a unique turning point and just one more example of many liberation struggles that stretch back all the way to the very beginning of the conquest. It is precisely that kind of "nested singularity," an idiosyncrasy that acknowledges itself as a river that feeds on multiple previous and concurrent tributaries of experience, and which itself flows into a larger main stem, that characterizes the vision presented in *Changó*. That historical vision is further enhanced by the novel's emphasis on ancestors and orishas shaping the contours of the future out of concrete fights in the present that are fed by the mythic assimilation of the past.

The Role of Myth and Religion

In his 1964 novel *En Chimá nace un santo*, Zapata tells the story of an invalid man to whom the impoverished people of his town attribute miraculous powers. Extraordinary events do occur around Domingo, although the narrative always leaves open the possibility that they might be coincidences. As a popular cult develops around him even after his death, the local priest intervenes in an attempt to re-establish the traditional authority of Catholic orthodoxy. The story then becomes, in a characteristic manner for Zapata Olivella's fiction, that of the struggle between dispossessed masses attempting to preserve their traditional worldview and official authorities trying to impose a disciplinary regime that may facilitate the control of bodies and thoughts. While the story clearly betrays Zapata Olivella's sympathy for the downtrodden, it is preceded by a revealing epigraph from a book on magic by Arturo Castiglioni:

> Myths are a necessary product of the infantile mentality as well as the mentality of primitive peoples. They originate as an escape into the field of magic, as an apparently acceptable explanation, as a hope for salvation. (Zapata Olivella, *En Chimá*, 1; my translation)

In a somewhat obvious manner, the epigraph shows an appreciation for the "hope of salvation" that guides mythical thinking at the same time that it distances itself from such a mindframe, condescendingly relegated to infantile mentalities and primitive peoples. Given its location as a threshold to the story, the epigraph works as a privileged perspective designed to filter, if not determine, the reader's interpretation of the story that is about to follow.

Some 26 years later, in his essay *Las claves mágicas de América Latina (The Magical Keys to Latin America)*, Zapata Olivella comments on the struggle of the Haitian masses against the immense resources of the French Empire:

> Against them, it was enough for one-armed Mackandal to invoke the orishas born and recreated in Haiti; for Bouckman to loudly play his bewitching drums, so that the living and the dead would leave their houses, their mountains, their cities, their rivers and their beaches, in order to join the maroon guerrillas . . . In order to understand the deep motives of the African religions in the Americas—Vodou, Candomble, Santeria, Rastafarianism, Macumba, Myalism, "Alabados," Lumbalu, etc.—it is enough to acknowledge that a people can only preserve their life, their ethnicity, their liberty and culture, if they turn themselves, their urgent needs and dreams, into the myth of their own divinity. (112; my translation)

Here one may find echoes of Derek Walcott's approving allusion to T. S. Eliot in "The Muse of History": "Eliot speaks of the culture of a people as being the incarnation of its religion" (*What the Twilight*, 43)—religion referring to the deepest beliefs held by a community. If *Las claves* shows an evolution from *En Chimá* that brings it closer to *Changó*, it is not in any firmer belief in the metaphysical content of religion, but rather in its attempt to understand religion as an expression of the concrete, existential situation of its believers. In other words, it need not be an infantile regression or primitive wish-fulfillment that is superimposed on that situation, but rather a creative attempt to symbolically embody the higher aspirations, as well as the deeper fears, that arise from that situation.[26]

Again in *Las claves,* the author states:

> To talk about religion in the tragedy of the Africans violently uprooted from their cultures to a burning world is to face naked human beings, but not arising from primeval jungles. In the middle of the storm, with Europe colonizing America, blacks had to create their own compass, improvising it out of their pain, their ancestral memory, their creative power. That is what they did with their philosophy, their myths, their experiences. The analysis of the religious thought and cults of Blacks in the Americas must depart from a concrete reality: slavery, threatened lives, the loss of freedom, family and land, and from all that, the attempt to fly toward supernatural forces, gods, and miracles. (110; my translation)

The text reinforces these ideas in the concrete case of Haiti:

> That is how Vodou was born in Haiti, where under the sun and under the moon the slaves had to sow, to harvest, to grind, to carry. Once they died, they had to wait for the gods to make them alive in death again, so that they could dedicate the rest of eternity to avenge and liberate their descendants and living brethren. No matter what the words, the drums, the vevés, the offerings, the dances or the sacrifices—decapitated goats, headless roosters or black dogs—of Vodou might be, they had only one goal: freedom. (111; my translation)

Without insisting on the metaphysical or supernatural aspects of religion, *Las claves mágicas* regards it as a fundamental aspect of the cultural identity of the black diaspora in the Americas. To say that religion becomes an embodiment of the black aspiration to liberation is no longer to regard it as a simple tool or even less as an escapist distraction, since for Zapata Olivella the aspiration to freedom is *the* existential constant that governs the lives of generations of slaves and their descendants in the New World. Thus the importance of clarifying that the religious views of enslaved Africans and the great syncretistic systems that they gave birth to (like Vodou) should not be regarded as "arising from primeval jungles" (a typical approach anchored in the colonial view of Africans as premodern or out of history altogether), but rather as a concrete expression of the historical experience of bondage.

As indicated above, that respectful approach to the existential dimension of religion dominates the whole organization of *Changó el gran putas,* which is entirely narrated from the perspective of African deities and ancestors.

I will return to the topic of religion and myth in the next two sections of the chapter, but for now it is important to highlight that even in the last section of *Changó,* which deals with the history of Africans in the United States, the novel retains its overall frame and perspective, making figures like Nat Turner, Harriet Tubman, John Brown, Martin Luther King, and Malcolm X into instruments and coworkers of the African orishas, Vodou loas, and ancestors. While Christianity and Islam are not downright rejected, the novel's emphasis is on a pan-ancestral Afrocentric view of the black saga against oppression. Now, it is evident that, particularly in the United States, both Islam and Christianity have played a fundamental role in African American narratives of emancipation, and the novel acknowledges that reality. However, even those characters most closely associated to Christianity or Islam (Martin Luther King, Malcolm X) appear as agents of ancestral African deities, which are regarded throughout the text as the deeper strata of black aspiration to freedom. This should not be construed as the text naively attributing a quasi-biological connection to Yoruba or Bantu beliefs to Afro-descendants in the Americas. Rather, the text draws on those traditional African religious systems, and imaginatively deploys them as symbols of Black resistance and solidarity. What unites Afro-descendants in the Americas is not an abstract set of beliefs or dogmas, but a shared history and the aspirations that arise from that history.

Afrocentric Theodicy

One inescapable aspect of Zapata Olivella's narrative strategy is his use of the Changó myth as the framing device for his story. The reverence of ancestors plays at least as important a role as the orishas and loas do. As suggested above, I do not believe that the novel is naively suggesting that a return to Yoruba/Bantu religious beliefs can unite Afro-descendants in the Americas. Zapata Olivella uses those concepts as a source of inspiring symbolism grounded in traditional African cultures, which can be used in spurring a spirit of rebelliousness. Moreover, they represent evidence of African creativity and philosophical depth that European colonial interventions have consistently attempted to deny or trivialize.

Although it is of very relative importance to our analysis, it should be remembered that, as I mentioned in the first section of this chapter, Zapata Olivella's own religious convictions remain, at best, ambiguous. In the first part of his autobiography ¡Levántate mulato! the novelist describes in sometimes humorous fashion the religious tension in his childhood home, with his mother and paternal grandmother preserving a traditional religious worldview (centered on African traditions in the grandmother's case), and his father adopting a fierce, freethinking atheistic stand, regarding religion as mere superstition (which he tolerated in others as long as they did not try to impose it on him) and desiring his children to grow up with a rational mindframe. Moreover, he regarded religion as often complicit in the manipulation and oppression of poor people.

It was partly as a result of that rationalist impulse that Zapata Olivella's father encouraged his son to study medicine, so that he could help people through rational, scientific methods. Zapata Olivella does not comment on his own attitude toward those influences, but he did study medicine and his initial political activities and exposure to Marxist thought strongly suggest a general agreement with his father. Such a perspective seems to dominate up to a novel like *En Chimá*, with its explicit warnings about people with "infantile mentalities" turning to myth and magic in their need to escape oppressive situations. However, as also noted above, *Changó* is permeated by a voice that seamlessly presents events from an Afrocentric mythical perspective: if it is only a literary device, it is certainly masterfully sustained.

The picture is further complicated by a 2000 interview in which Zapata Olivella explains, in plain expository language seemingly devoid of metaphorical ornaments, that he felt sections of the novel were "dictated" by higher forces, probably related to the Ifa Oracle that keeps a spiritual record of African experience.[27] During a visit to Dakar, the novelist spent the night in one of the prisons where slaves were kept just before being forced into ships bound for the New World, and there he felt the visit of ancestors and spiritual forces; in the interview he gets into details such as: "I do not dare to say that it was Ifa who dictated [the poems that appear in the book] to me, I think there must have been some intermediary. Maybe it was the intermediary that I saw that night" (Krakusin, "Conversación," 22). I do not include these details to comment on the veracity or not of his account—which can be clearly explained as a metaphorical portrayal of poetic inspiration—but simply to highlight that it is hard to ascertain what Zapata Olivella's own religious convictions were, if any. *El árbol brujo de la libertad*, the last book-length essay he published very few years before his death, opens with an "Introduction for the Ekobios and Siblings of All Ethnicities" which invokes orishas and ancestors, and could come right out of *Changó*. The term "ekobios," defined in the glossary of the novel as "'fellow member' or 'brother' among the Ñáñigos or Afro-Cuban priests" (452), again puts the emphasis on ancestral African spirituality as a uniting link within the black diaspora in the Americas. In fact *El árbol brujo* is subtitled "Historical Mythical Essay." So regardless of what Zapata Olivella's personal beliefs were, it seems clear that he had come to regard such appeals to the cosmos of African spirituality as an essential part of his poetics of emancipation.

By the same token, it seems fairly evident that Zapata Olivella was never a total insider of these belief systems—if he was ever initiated into the rituals of Santeria, Vodou, or any similar system, he kept it secret. What we do have are references to his research work both in libraries (for example, at Harvard University [Krakusin, "Conversación," 21]) and during his important fieldwork as anthropologist and folklorist. As we saw earlier, myth and religion interest him mainly and primordially as creative means and expressions of the struggle for freedom, and as repositories of besieged African identities. That prioritization of political and historical struggles raises the questions: Why focus on religion at all, then, if evidently freedom can be adequately pursued in a secular, humanist context? What useful tools does religious discourse bring to Zapata Olivella's project?

First and foremost, the emphasis on a religious framework results from an attempt to be faithful to the historical experience of Africans in the new world. For it is a fact that religious beliefs have been integrally linked to many black struggles for liberation. We see that clearly not only in the role of Vodou in the Haitian Revolution but also in the religious commitments of figures like Malcolm X and Martin Luther King. Zapata Olivella is adamant in his insistence that, while such religiosity reflects "the religious character of African cultures" (*Claves*, 98; my translation) that the slaves brought to the new world, the later syncretistic and Christian manifestations of black spirituality should not be regarded as signs of the cultural subjugation of those slaves. For even though it is true that many of them adopted the Christian idiom, they did so only to the degree that it allowed them to articulate their aspirations to freedom. In the greater Caribbean region, we have the great syncretistic systems like Vodou, Santeria, and others, in which saints are identified with the gods of diverse African religions. In Santeria, Christ is usually identified with Olofi, the Yoruba creator god, who usually does not intervene in everyday human affairs. In the Anglo-Saxon Protestant world, with Christ (and no saints) as the only manifestation of the divine, the slaves "transform him [Christ] into a Messiah, a Changó of sorts for their libertarian aspirations" (ibid., 104; my translation).

All of the above brings us to the figure of Changó in the novel, which incarnates many of the potentialities and pitfalls of Zapata Olivella's mythopoetic strategy. In a 1983 interview, shortly after the publication of his novel, Zapata Olivella stated: "Changó in African mythology is the god of fertility, dance, and war. Well, I think that those three powers that Changó joins clearly identify the black community: it is a vital community, it is a dancing community, it is a warring community" (Captain-Hidalgo, "Conversación," 30). There is little to criticize in Zapata Olivella's words as far as they go; however, they do not accurately describe Changó's role in the epic novel. At the beginning of the narrative, it is clearly indicated that, as a result of his subjects' betrayal, Changó condemns them to exile and slavery: the entire experience of the middle passage and slavery in the new world is explained as a result of Changó's curse on his people.

It is true that Changó also prophesies that the Muntu (the African slaves and their descendants) will eventually achieve liberation—by their own efforts—but the reader cannot help being surprised by the callousness of the orisha, by the disproportion of his punishment against his people, and by the central place that *that* aspect of the myth occupies in Zapata Olivella's narrative. It is important to point out here that there is an ambiguity to Changó's character that is part of the original African myth. Scholars seem to agree that the attributes and stories of this orisha were inspired, at least in part, by a real "alafin" or monarch of the Oyo Kingdom in fourteenth-century Nigeria who was, indeed, resented for his violence and abuses, who was eventually expelled by his people, and who was later deified by popular belief.[28]

Interestingly, there is in Yoruba lore a story that is almost identical to that of Changó's curse used by Zapata Olivella, but it refers to a later monarch of the Oyo empire—Awole, a late eighteenth century alafin who, as a result of his flawed military decisions, was betrayed by his generals. In the story, before committing suicide Awole shoots arrows to different cardinal points, and curses his people: "the Yoruba people will be taken as slaves all over the Earth" (Abimbola, *Ifá Will Mend*, 101). This story is so similar to the one Zapata Olivella uses that one is tempted to propose that possibly the Colombian author was aware of it and conflated Awole's legend with the figure of Changó in his novel. However, we have no evidence for this, and it would still leave us with the question of why transfer the actions of the eighteenth-century monarch (a story still remembered in Yoruba oral tradition) to the deified orisha, in the process making Changó, the beloved albeit feared god, a deity who curses his people.[29]

It would seem then, that the transformation of Changó into a vengeful orisha who is responsible for the enslavement of African peoples by Europeans is Zapata Olivella's invention. At the very least, if he did find a little known version of Changó's myth that includes the story of the curse, it is the novelist who gives it such a prominent place in a mythical explanation of the African diaspora. This raises the question of what purpose such a fiction might serve. While I do not think one can offer an entirely satisfactory answer to that question—in fact, one should be weary of attempting to do so, given the unspeakable obscenity of Changó's actions if taken at face value—I will attempt a symbolic interpretation of the role of Changó in the next section which will remain of necessity tentative and open to debate. In the rest of this section I would like to comment on some of the negative implications of Zapata Olivella's specific recycling of the Changó myth.[30]

Considering the disturbing implications of Changó's curse in the novel, it is surprising that more critics have not found it a formidable stumbling block, if they notice it at all. For the most part, Changó is merely celebrated as the fierce instigator of the black impulse toward emancipation. Jonathan Tittler highlights the problem I am describing when he suggests, in a discussion of the novel's Afrocentric critique of Catholicism's alliances to colonial powers: "The Church is characterized as a sham designed to disguise imperialist, territorial, materialistic aims. Despite the injustice implicit in Changó's wrathful vengeance—and indicative of the tragic mode of the novel's historical dimension—the false spirituality of Catholic conquest prevails" ("Catching the spirit," 108). Thus, the implication seems to be that although Changó *is* unjust, at least he is an African tyrant. This is hardly an acceptable solution for a character that embodies black aspirations to emancipation, although one might argue that it unfortunately reflects the attitude of many postindependence tyrants, both in Africa and the Americas, such as Henri Christophe. Several other critics mention the Changó's curse as they summarize the novel, but they do not seem to find it problematic enough give them pause.

In her important book on Zapata Olivella, Yvonne Capatain-Hidalgo also acknowledges the problem that I am describing. In the context of a discussion of Changó's status as a god, she suggests that his divine status does not imply that he is perfect and good, as divinity would imply in a Christian context. Like many gods in other religious systems, Changó is a god but not perfect. Captain-Hidalgo states:

The idea of Changó's godliness and conversely his imperfectibility brings this reader to a puzzling conceptual premise informing Zapata's text. It is impossible to analyze *Shango* without recognizing that the deity is responsible for his own fall . . . If we were to remain solely at the surface level of the text's action, this fact would constitute a highly difficult concept for all readers of African descent. On a superficial level, Changó's fall would mean that the deity is to blame for the enslavement of the diaspora population in the Americas—a very classic example of blaming the victim. However, this is not obviously the conclusion upon which any informed reader must rest his or her analysis. (*Culture of Fiction*, 148)

Captain-Hidalgo goes on to suggest that in the figure of Changó the tie between African Americans in the experience of slavery is given an Afrocentric expression that does not need the intervention of Europeans. This, however, "does not assuage European culpability or heighten African blame in the enslavement of the continent's children" (ibid., 149). Captain-Hidalgo goes on to insist that Changó is "a god of a very human nature" (ibid., 150), and that the "redemption" that he and his people strive for is of this world, political.

While I agree with most of Captain-Hidalgo's points, the very (re)invention of a very human god as a symbol for political (not religious) liberation begs the question of why bring up this god at all, since there might be other viable practical and imaginative models of liberation, including secular ones. If an Afrocentric mythical embodiment for collective African suffering is sought, it is perplexing why that mythical embodiment (Changó) would be given a story that includes his *cursing* black people to slavery! The choice is even more surprising when one considers that the curse (in the version that links it to the Middle Passage) is not part of the traditional African myth. It is true that Changó's curse does not "assuage European culpability," but it is also true that the African diaspora might have good reason to withdraw any allegiance or trust in a god or myth that is capable of so neatly accommodating the callousness of European imperialism. Such difficulties are not simply "surface level," and ultimately point to the extreme difficulty of sustaining mythical and historical views of the world in the same narrative.

I will not elaborate here on the fundamental importance of the conjunction of myth and history in Latin American fiction, except to point the reader in the direction of Roberto González Echevarría's now classic *Myth and Archive*. As González Echevarría compellingly explains, Latin American fiction has always been obsessed with investigating the origins of the Americas. This search into the origins of identity confronts Latin American writers with history ("Latin America" as a construction of the imperial interests that shaped it into existence through conquest and colonial domination) and with myth (the very desire to discover a historical figure, event, place or situation that can be placed at the origin of, and therefore give meaning to, Latin American experience and identity). Throughout the twentieth century Latin American novelists (Carpentier, Fuentes, García Márquez, and others) increasingly approached such nostalgia for mythical origins (and the power interests implicitly attached to it) with detached irony: "History," a single narrative with a capital *H*, was unmasked as mythical construct itself, and myths taken for unquestionable truths were revealed as always already part of historical power struggles. García Márquez's *One Hundred Years of Solitude* is perhaps the most consummate ironic deconstruction of that nostalgia for mythical certainties, at the same time that it is the most affectionate apology for the thirst for myth and meaning in the midst of relentless historical violence.

Zapata Olivella's place in that Latin American context is ambiguous. His early novels of social realism attempt to address historical injustices without reference to myth. *En Chimá* already shows a distanced sympathy for a mythical mindframe. His post-*Changó* novels, *El fusilamiento del diablo* and *Hemingway, el cazador de la muerte*, fit better into González Echevarría's model, as they explicitly combine historical and mythical elements while keeping an uncertain undecidability between both worldviews—either by offering a multiplicity of voices and perspectives in *El fusilamiento*, or by keeping mythical elements inside the monologues of a character who may, or may not, be going insane in *Hemingway*. In *Changó*, however, Zapata Olivella tries something few other Latin American writers have attempted in such a *sustained* manner: to subsume history—the history of slavery and the black diaspora in the Americas—under a mythical framework—Changó's curse on his ekobios.[31] There is no attempt to ironize or otherwise deconstruct that mythical frame, although its strained nature can be divined through gestures like the inclusion of a glossary of mostly African/Afro-Latin American terms at the end of the book: there we see the shadow of the anthropologist author showing behind the magical narrative voice. Within the narrative itself, no tensions are acknowledged: Changó curses his people, the curse becomes synonymous with the struggle for freedom, that struggle is nothing less than the historical combats of the black diaspora. The problem, if there is any, arises for the reader who is puzzled, not by Changó as symbol of rebelliousness but by Changó as the origin of the slave trade.[32]

The problem is made more complex by the fact that, as opposed to the gods of Greek mythology, the Yoruba pantheon is not simply a distant myth, but rather remains part of the living religions of many Africans and Afro-descendants. Thus, what we have here is not simply a myth to explain origins or to offer hope in the present but an Afrocentric theodicy that attempts to explain and offer a teleological solution to the oppression of the African diaspora. Zapata Olivella himself points to this possibility in a passage from *Las claves* that elucidates core aspects of *Changó*'s narrative frame. In an examination of the diverse strategies that the slaves, with their traditional sacred worldviews, used to address the dire reality of their enslavement, Zapata Olivella observes:

> Black slaves had plenty of time to reflect on their enslavement, either to accept it or to reject it. What could their reflections have been in the long days and nights of captivity? The answers found by their religious mentalities must have been in harmony with their beliefs:
>
> 1. Slavery could be a punishment for violating the Natural Law of the Ancestors. They had to resign themselves.
> 2. Slavery was the imposition of strangers who were violating the Natural Law of the Ancestors. They had to rebel.
> 3. Slavery was a major evil that was inexplicable and unavoidable. They had to adjust in order to both accept and resist. (100; my translation)

In the essay, Zapata Olivella goes on to describe how resistance dominated the slaves' response to slavery, even when they had to submit in some ways, such as the seeming acceptance of the master's religion. However, it is hard to avoid the conclusion that the narrative of *Changó* favors the solution of point one, presenting slavery as Changó's punishment, even if in the novel that punishment does not result in acceptance, but rather paradoxically pushes slaves toward rebellion. In the novel's Afrocentric religious perspective, there are invisible forces behind history working for the eventual emancipation of the oppressed. Zapata Olivella evidently takes that perspective very seriously.

The problem with theodicy—the justification of a good and all-powerful god in a world of evil—is that it always potentially justifies the injustice that it tries to explain and even eliminate. This problem remains vital to this day, at least to the extent that religious thinking remains an important component of many liberation struggles around the world. As mentioned above, religion has been an essential component of African American radical thinking from visionaries like Nat Turner to contemporary icons like Martin Luther King and Malcolm X. One can also think of the importance of liberation theologies in Latin American struggles for emancipation from the 1960s to the present.[33] And the problem that the theodicy implicit in almost any religious frame brings to struggles against injustice has certainly been brought up by scholars.[34]

In *Why Lord? Suffering and Evil in Black Theology*, Anthony Pinn neatly summarizes the problem of a theodical approach to the specific case of black suffering. Whether the argument goes that God actually causes or allows suffering in order to purify or punish his followers, or that suffering is the result of human free will and that God inspires good actions but does not impose his will on the free will of his followers,

> These arguments are unacceptable because they counteract efforts at liberation by finding something of value in Black suffering. In essence those arguments go against social transformation activity. Redemptive suffering and liberation are diametrically opposed ideas: they suggest ways of being in the world that, in effect, nullify each other. One cannot embrace suffering as redemptive . . . and effectively speak of liberation. The detrimental nature of arguments for redemptive suffering requires constructive work toward a more appropriate response to black suffering. (17–18)

A "more appropriate" response for Pinn would involve what he calls a "black humanism," which, in terms of the problem we are discussing, simply means leaving god(s) out of the equation. With no god, evidently the effort spent in explaining the very existence of evil in unnecessary: one is left only with human history, which is more than enough. It is not my interest here to get into theological arguments as old as religion itself, although it must be mentioned that one of Pinn's merits, in this and other books, is to highlight that there is, and has been, an important tradition of black humanism that is often neglected in discussions of black liberation movements.[35] What is of interest here is that Zapata Olivella has decided to forego that humanistic possibility by relying on a mythical/religious framework that potentially creates as many problems as it tries to solve.[36]

One possible objection to the problem I am posing is Captain-Hidalgo's observation about Changó: the problem of theodicy only comes up if one assumes a Judeo-Christian concept of god, almighty and good. Changó is a god with all the limitations of a human being. But this begs the question: is fidelity to an Afrocentric worldview worth the commitment to such a problematic figure as Zapata Olivella's Changó? Is he not better left behind, or reinvented in such a way that Afro-descendants do not have to carry the weight of their own enslavement? After all, most Afro-descendants in the Americas are not in a position of having to accept this god for better or worse—the proof is the novel itself, which feels free to reinvent him. To assume otherwise would be to fall in the trap of an essentialist view of black identity, one that the adaptability of black slaves in the Americas refutes.[37]

In one segment of the novel, Toussaint Louverture compares Changó's fate, when he was betrayed by his followers, to Toussaint's own fate after the betrayal of his generals. The Haitian general comments from his jail in Jura: "Now I understand, grieving Changó, your fury, your pain when you were thrown out of the Imperial Oyo, separated from the warm company of your subjects. Exile, apparent death more damaging than the abandonment of the orishas" (159). The parallel is interesting and potentially valuable—Changó's followers, like Toussaint at that point in the novel, can find inspiration in the fact that their god was also exiled from his homeland. For centuries, Christians have found similar inspiration in the idea that their god became human and endured suffering just like them. One might also find similarities between Toussaint's actions and mistakes leading to his "betrayal" by his people and Changó's story—one link being authoritarianism. However, it is quite impossible to imagine Toussaint *cursing* his people to slavery, or his people remaining faithful to him if he had done so. At face value, the novel's Changó remains an unsolvable anomaly.

In its commitment to an Afrocentric theodicy, the road not taken by Zapata Olivella's novel is what Pinn calls "strong humanism":

> Strong humanism need not be nihilistic or defeatist, if it sees potential for goodness within humanity. This system requires that humanity aggressively act to bring about meaning in a world defined by the absurdity of oppression. And this action is guided by a concern for the sanctity of life. That is not to say African Americans can end their oppression if only they stop seeing their suffering as redemptive. Furthermore, I am not arguing that genuine human effort will ultimately destroy oppression. To the contrary, I am asserting that redemptive suffering arguments set up false expectations and thereby eclipse sustainable liberation activity. Nevertheless, even sustained efforts provide only the possibility of total social transformation. (*Why*, 157)

As far as they go, Pinn's words constitute a fair critique of what I consider Zapata Olivella's paradoxical and ultimately problematic attempt to subsume history under the category of myth/religion. The internal contradictions are too acute, and they can hardly be defended as the playful interplay of undecidable perspectives because the text is *too successful* in its attempt to give primacy to its mythical frame. If we take the goal of liberation as seriously as the novel itself proposes, its strategy leaves us in an impasse. Either history is subordinated to myth, or we privilege the historical dimension of the novel and the mythical frame becomes an excessive, unnecessary burden. In the seriousness of its commitment to its Afrocentric religious/mythical frame, the novel disavows the ironic distance that allows for the interplay between history and myth in other political Latin American novels.

However, and contradicting myself, I will attempt a provisional allegorical justification of the novel's mythical dimension in the next section, if only because there is something evidently missing in Pinn's paragraph quoted above. It is clearly true that with god(s) out of the picture the whole problem of theodicy is gone, but it is not necessarily true that religion (whether it explicitly includes theodicy or not) must "eclipse sustainable liberation activity." It is in fact the case that most such activity, particularly among Afrodescendants in the Americas, has been guided by a religious vision. Whether we agree or not with such a religious vision, just that fact gives credence to Zapata Olivella's strategy, and I believe that the key lies, in part, in a couple of paradoxes in Pinn's words: his secular appeal to "the *sanctity* of life" (*Why?*, 157); and the notion that discreet, partial, limited efforts could feed into a vision of "the possibility of *total* social transformation" (*Why?*, 157) (my italics in both quotes). Both phrases introduce such radically lofty aspirations that even a secular frame shows the need of a religious language to express them.

Changó as Horizon of Absolute Freedom

I should state from the outset that my justification of the role of Changó in the novel is an allegorical one, thus a creative misreading. Since *Changó* is a novel that in spite of its framework does not present itself as a sacred text, it is of course perfectly legitimate to approach Changó as a trope, but in doing so I am aware that I am imposing an outside rationalist reading on a figure that is the object of literal devotion on the part of believers in Afro-Caribbean religions. I am justified by the fact that Zapata Olivella seems to be doing something similar: reinventing the myth of Changó that he has come to know and understand as a student and researcher in African/Afro Latin American belief systems. If we knew for a fact that Zapata Olivella was an active practitioner of any Afro-Caribbean religion, we might of course still offer a symbolic reading of Changó in the novel, but we might also be compelled to dig deeper into what the god, *as presented in the novel*, might mean in the context of the author's living faith.

The fundamental question becomes then: what does Changó represent or stand for in the novel? The novel points fairly clearly in one direction: the human thirst for freedom as embodied and led by black struggles for emancipation. As Agne Brown states in the last part of the novel,

> The fact that black people have had to survive so much ignominy, growing more powerful in each re-creation, is irrefutable proof that we are chosen by Changó to fulfill a destiny to free mankind. The Ancestor cult, the link between the living and the dead, will put an end to the myth of individual and selfish gods. (308)

In a similar vein, Malcolm X's spirit announces right after his assassination:

> The days of disunity have passed. Now I live only to gather together the dispersed family of the Muntu. Only in that way will the society predicted by Changó be built, where the living activate the knot that ties them to the dead, where the ekobios of all races can call each other brothers and sisters. (439)

Notice that in both Agne's and Malcolm X's words, Changó pushes humans not only towards emancipation, but towards retying the knot or link to primordial forces. In that context, Changó's "curse" and Changó's imperative of liberation are one and the same: the experience of bondage is the ontological and logical ground for the desire for liberation, they are experienced as one and the same. Moreover, bondage and exile are not only political—they also refer to the "curse" of human alienation (through individualism and selfishness) from the links to ancestors and the spiritual dimension of the world. Thus, the struggle not only involves liberation *from* unfair bondage, but also liberation *into* a higher unity between self and world. All of this includes but is not restricted to black aspirations to emancipation from slavery and oppression.

What Changó represents *in the novel* goes well beyond the desire of one human group to free itself from one particular form of historical bondage. As the ancestors state through the voice of Agne Brown:

> I announce to you the cult of Life and Shadows that inspires the rebelliousness that dwells within us blacks. In the great beyond, only the echo of dreams endures. But—hear me well—life and rebellion do not exist without the presence of the dead. We are the force of all that happened and the powerful source of all that will be. There will be no white armies nor are all the hatreds put together more powerful than this firm will to be and to do. Only by rising up living and dead alike, across all bloodlines, will we fulfill Changó's prophesy. (305)

The concreteness of black experience is not denied, but it is placed in a much larger context, as a vortex between "all that happened" and "all that will be" that includes all bloodlines, all of the living's and the dead's struggles for liberation.[38] That is why a god or divine figure can better express this impulse than any other historical project. Changó represents the desire for liberation as an ontological constituent of human existence and experience: freedom from unjust economic and racial regimes, yes, but also freedom from ignorance, freedom all the limitations that warp human development. Ultimately Changó points to freedom from a sense of disconnection from the totality of the universe that wounds human beings as part of the unique form of self-consciousness that characterizes their particular niche in the evolutionary chain. It is the kind of freedom that Ti Noel fleetingly experiences at the moment of death in *El reino de este mundo*, when, as we saw in chapter 1, his self is recycled into unitive communion with his land and his history.

In his classic *Myth, Literature, and the African World*, Wole Soyinka ascribes a similar function to Yoruba religion in general, focusing like Zapata Olivella on the connection between worlds that is so fundamental in the traditional African worldview:

> And yet the Yoruba does not for that reason fail to distinguish between himself and the deities, between himself and the ancestors, between the unborn and his reality, or discard his awareness of the essential gulf that lies between one area of existence and another. This gulf is what must be constantly diminished by the sacrifices, the rituals, the ceremonies of appeasement to those cosmic powers which lie guardian to the gulf. Spiritually, the primordial disquiet of the Yoruba psyche may be expressed as the existence in collective memory of a primal severance in transitional ether, whose first effective defiance is symbolised in the myth of the gods' descent to earth and the battle with immense chaotic growth that had sealed off reunion with man. For they were coming down, not simply to be acknowledged but to be re-united with

> human essence . . . just as man is grieved by a consciousness of the loss of the eternal essence of his being and must indulge in symbolic transactions to recover his totality of being. (144–45)

That desire to recover the "totality of being" is evidently thwarted by economic, political, social, and cultural oppressions, but it goes beyond them. This realization does not in any way diminish the importance of political struggles for, as the novel suggests, "when an ekobio liberates himself, he brings freedom to his Ancestors who had died in slavery" (337). The struggle is one for total freedom, for universal human (not only political) emancipation, but every instance of political emancipation contributes to that larger liberation.

Clearly, from our allegorical perspective, such absolute freedom cannot be posited as a goal that human beings would ever achieve, but rather as a *horizon of possibilities* that propels human beings forward, with the acute awareness that any victories along the way must be celebrated with the recognition there are always more limitations, injustices, and exclusions to overcome. It is such an understanding that inflects Pinn's words at the end of the previous section: although they advocate gradual, discrete, specific battles and victories, they are informed by the notion of "the possibility of *total* social transformation." That possibility need not be a utopic project that paralyzes us, but rather a horizon that keeps ebbing away as we approach it. That absolute freedom is not a project imposed from above, but an empty signifier that changes its meaning as specific, concrete battles for emancipation are won.

In my description of that total freedom as an ever-receding horizon and as an "empty signifier" I am explicitly drawing on the thought of Argentinean theorist Ernesto Laclau, who has thoroughly reflected on the role of "universals" in particular struggles for emancipation. As Laclau eloquently poses,

> The universal . . . does not have a concrete content of its own (which would close it on itself), but is an always receding horizon resulting from the expansion of an indefinite chain of equivalent demands. The conclusion seems to be that universality is incommensurable with any particularity but cannot, however, exist apart from the particular . . . If only particular actors, or constellations of particular actors can actualize the universal at any moment, in that case, the possibility of making visible the non-closure inherent to a post-dominated society—that is a society that attempts to transcend the very form of domination—depends on making the asymmetry between the universal and the particular permanent. The universal is incommensurable with

the particular, but cannot, however, exist without the latter. (*Emancipation(s)*, 34–35)

Changó is precisely the symbol for that permanent asymmetry. The asymmetry is experienced, as it were, as "a curse," for it spurs relentlessly to action, and it feeds on the dis-ease of the awareness that no specific freedom ever closes the demands of future, broader freedoms.

Yet that lofty notion of the universal transcendence of "the very form of domination" cannot exist without the particular efforts of his ekobios. The novel never loses sight of those particular struggles, and explicitly states the need not to get caught in grandiloquent rhetoric: "In order to be free we must build these guns, ships, factories, books, laboratories. A poem or a speech may make us dream we are powerful: but a hoe can help us plant a tree that feeds us and gives us shelter and heat in order to house and defend our families" (404). However, and equally importantly, none of those achievements can be construed as the final goal of liberation, nor can the content of that goal be defined a priori.

As Laclau also indicates: "This means that the 'good' articulation, the one that will finally suture the link between universal task and concrete historical forces will never be found, and that all partial victory will always take place against the background of an ultimate and unsurpassable impossibility" (*Emancipation(s)*, 63). Changó embodies that ultimate impossibility as a call to action. Although he is a "curse" to the extent that he represents the insurmountable chasm between the universal task of liberation and the historical forces that strive for it, he is also a blessing in his relentless revolt against what we might refer to, following Laclau again, as "the incoherence of establishing universal rights which were restricted to particular sectors of the population" (33). The Haitian Revolution was a clear uprising against precisely that incoherence, as incarnated by "enlightened" revolutionary and postrevolutionary France.

We can also find a parallel to Changó's role in the novel in the thought of Enrique Dussel, who significantly has moved between a *theology* and a *philosophy* of liberation (although without confusing them). Dussel establishes a similar interplay between concrete struggles and universal (but not defined a priori) aspirations. In his *Twenty Theses on Politics*, he proposes a series of "political postulates," which he defines in this way:

A "political postulate" is a logically thinkable (possible) statement that remains *empirically* impossible but nevertheless serves to *orient* action. In every institutional sphere we will demonstrate the existence and usefulness of proposing certain postulates, but we cannot confuse these with the goals of action because they remain *empirically impossible*. Recall the proposed ideal of a "society without classes." This is a postulate: such a society is impossible, but by attempting to overcome the present class relation we discover the possibility for a form of social progress that, at the very least, rejects the domination of the present system (under the form of the bourgeois and working classes) and gives a critical meaning to class domination in the historical present. Formulating the postulate helps us to attempt to dissolve the existing classes, to thereby "approach" the classless society (which like the crossing of asymptotic lines is impossible by definition). (113)

Like Laclau's "always receding horizon," Dussel's "asymptotic lines" match Changó's sifting of transcendent goals out of, and then back into, concrete, historical struggles.[39]

In most of the examples we have seen from the novel, it should be clear that one of the functions of Changó and the text's religious framework is to insure that liberation is never merely defined as freedom *from* any specific oppression, but as freedom *to* more fully participate, first, in a more just and egalitarian society, and second, in a cosmic vision of human beings that includes the legacy of ancestors and the possibilities of future generations. The movement of the novel is not only towards overcoming the past or towards a naive utopianism in the future: it is a movement towards the new that incorporates the old, an impulse of transcendence and inclusion. It is in that regard that Toussaint refers to ancestors as "the compass of the living" (Zapata Olivella, *Changó, The Biggest*, 182).

I referred earlier to the novel's "preferential option for the oppressed black diaspora," and the link to liberation theology's dictum, a "preferential option for the poor," is not casual: the novel's intensely political religious framework resembles that of many liberation theologians.[40] It is not casual that in the section on the United States a character declares, in the best tradition of black liberation theology but also of African American spirituals and gospel: "Jehovah hated slavery so much that he parted the Red Sea so his people could escape" (350).

All the elements that may somehow give meaning and purpose to the figure of Changó come together in the Haitian section of the novel, with its portrayal of the revolution as simultaneously a turning point yet also just that, a single point in the long history of struggles for black liberation. The novel presents the revolution as a central event in the history of the Americas; in the history of the black diaspora; and in the history of an imagined unfolding of universal emancipation. For Haiti was a direct and often ignored agent in the independence of Spanish America, as well as an inspiration in the rebellious spirit of African Americans in the United States. It was also a turning point in the history of the black diaspora, one in which the spirit of maroon slaves throughout the continent was taken to a new level, showing that with the right organization black slaves could challenge any colonial power. The fact that some regimes in the newly independent Haiti were oppressive (and the novel does not shy away from Henri Christophe's oppression) mainly shows precisely the fallible humanity that the colonial regime denied those racialized populations. Haiti also illustrates that the endless interplay of universal goals and specific struggles not only *can* be sustained but in fact *must* be maintained if the fight for liberation is not to become dehumanized or become reductive, and therefore exclusionary. Haiti's history is often a cautionary tale in this regard, an example of roads not to take. Yet it is also true that, in their revolution, the Haitian people were definitely fighting, to quote James's phrase one last time, "in the interest of freedoms wider than [their] own." The thirst for freedom only becomes more intense, and even painful, as concrete victories better reveal the enormity of the tasks still ahead. That is why Changó effect on his ekobios may be described, with strange appropriateness, as a "curse," even if a sacred one.

In the end, it is *Changó*'s great achievement to consistently uphold its "preferential option for the oppressed black diaspora" at the same time that it weaves an epic tapestry of the impulse and struggle toward liberation of vast metaphysical and historical depths. Its only limits those of the imaginations of its specific readers. All of those readers, and not only Afro-descendant ekobios, are interpellated by Changó's angry admonition at the end of the novel: "You are wasting time in achieving your freedom! . . . The hour has arrived for you to understand that, for the living, time is not inexhaustible!" (446). In spite of the novel's mythical framework, the time reference in Changó's final scolding, its urgency, addresses the fleeting nature of human experience. Time is not inexhaustible, although Changó's task for his ekobios may well be.

Conclusion

The Spirit of the Haitian Revolution in the Caribbean

Through its multiples representations, the Haitian Revolution haunts the Caribbean as one of the most compelling, albeit inevitably partial embodiments of the region's history, burdens, aspirations, and possibilities. In that regard, it would not be totally out of place to draw on something like a hauntology, in Derrida's sense of the term, to talk about the revolution. As Derrida argues for Marx's thought and legacy, the Haitian Revolution conjures up what Nick Nesbitt has aptly referred to as the ideal of universal emancipation and its perfect, yet unachievable incarnation. The revolution exists as a necessarily incomplete enactment of an ideal that operates as an always-receding horizon of possibilities (as we saw at the end of the last chapter), always partially betrayed, always successful enough to spur further action.[1]

For some people the Haitian Revolution may also provoke the anxiety and fear that ghosts often elicit. The revolution was frequently manipulated by those who were supposed to uphold its ideals. In addition to being a story of unprecedented success, it is also a cautionary tale, full of unfulfilled promises. Like a specter that is always a creature in-between realms, the revolution and its representations move between what it was and what it was not. It was and is, as we have seen in the previous chapters, many things. And, in addition to what it never was and was never meant to be (the mere massacre of whites its detractors portrayed it as from the beginning, or, to refer to one of the latest racist portrayals, "a pact with the devil," as evangelical preacher Pat Robertson described it after the 2010 earthquake), it was not many things it should and could have been, partly because of its leaders, but also because of its external (colonial) enemies.[2]

As we have seen throughout this book, Caribbean literature has produced great works in its attempt to capture the spirit, or the many spirits, of the revolution. Inevitably and appropriately, each of those textual attempts partially fails to capture the full import of the event, even as it produces a brilliant and even accurate representation of it. Moreover, each representation transforms the revolution by recasting it in a different light, even though the overlaps between those different representations are manifold and significant.

For Carpentier, the revolution works as an embodiment of Latin American autonomy and agency in the face of centuries of imperial European domination. It represents the irruption of "other knowledges" that a long colonial history has tried to push to the margins. From that perspective, the "marvelous real" that the novel extols becomes, in spite of its presentation in the form of cultural feud with European surrealism, an important political gesture against what Mignolo has called the colonial difference. It is not coincidental, then, that *The Kingdom of This World* attempts, even if only with partial success, to focalize events from the perspective of slaves like Ti Noel, rather than focusing on the better known heroic leaders of the revolution.

Such an irruption of marginal voices, perspectives, and agencies is also fundamental for C. L. R. James, who presents the revolution as a persistent reminder of the Caribbean's centrality in the development of modern capitalism, and thus of the importance of Caribbean history for anti-Capitalist struggles. Perhaps paradoxically, what that history also teaches in James's account is that class and economic inequalities are necessary but not sufficient categories to address the oppressive impact of the logic of coloniality. Although James does focus on the exemplary leadership of Toussaint, his text is very much about the dialectical and dialogical relation of masses and leaders, with the former providing the true compass for the actions of the latter. At their best, leaders are translators: they "translate mass feeling into action" (*Black Jacobins*, 121). Ultimately, one may regard that task of translation as also characteristic of committed writers and intellectuals—with James's text providing a prime example in "historicist" mode (to invoke again Paget Henry's terms), and Carpentier's an example of the "poeticist" mode.

Even for an intellectual who takes that translating task seriously the results may be problematic, since the relations and connections between intellectuals and the masses (however one may choose to define those terms) are never simple and transparent. We can see this clearly in Luis Palés Matos's approach to the revolution in Haiti. For Palés Matos it is a reminder of an Afro-Caribbean dimension that has been at the center of Antillean cultural self-affirmation and political rebelliousness, a dimension whose full power the poet both desires and fears for Puerto Rico. However, Palés Matos's reluctance about his subject matter also provides an important caveat about overly simplistic views of the intellectual and the masses. An intellectual does not simply reflect on his/her society; he/she is also a product of that society. Thus, Palés Matos's anxiety about Puerto Rico's links with Haiti (their shared Afro-Caribbean dimensions) are not simply his: they are also Puerto Rico's anxieties about itself, the expression of a society that partially reflects, and partially rebels against, the colonial history out of which it has developed.

Self doubt and anxiety may paradoxically link a writer like Palés Matos to one like Aimé Césaire, who in so many ways is the polar opposite of the Puerto Rican poet. As we have seen, the Haitian Revolution incarnates for Césaire not only the impulse of anticolonial revolt, but also the tensions that the logic of coloniality impose on those struggling against it—their need to affirm their cultural specificity at the same time that they claim the traditions and ideas of the West, which has excluded them, as legitimately theirs too. As I have highlighted, the point that Césaire articulates with such clarity is not the relatively simple one that there need not be any inherent or non-negotiable contradiction or enmity between "the West" and its former colonies—there is, after all, "room for all at the rendez-vous of victory." The point is that the myth of Western modernity has consistently constructed its proclaimed universality at the expense of, and in exclusion of, its colonial others. One of Césaire's most lucid contributions to the examination of that situation is not simply his powerful challenge to it but also his vulnerable display (almost in spite of himself, at times) that the challenge does not always come from self-assurance and fully recovered pride but often from self-doubt, from the uncertainty of conflictive imperatives fueled by the colonial "double bind," and from a partial internalization of the colonial logic, the questioning of which must constantly be recommenced.

The tragic ubiquity of that colonial logic, which structures relations, institutions, and subjectivities in the modern/colonial world system, is one of the main concerns that Derek Walcott emphasizes in his Haitian plays. Although his critique of a view of history that privileges "heroes" and battles may be regarded by some critics as insufficiently celebratory of Caribbean resistance to imperial designs, one may also acknowledge it as an important warning that any "rearticulation and appropriation of global designs by and from the perspective of local histories" (Mignolo, *Local Histories*, 39) must include a critical and honest examination of how the local often responds (politically, through local elites; but also ontologically, in the very way it is defined and articulated, in its inclusions and exclusions) to colonial imperatives. That is precisely the caution advanced by Quijano's concept of the coloniality of power, one that Mignolo's concept of "border thinking" addresses by eschewing the naive idealization of the local in isolation from larger contexts, however defined. In Césaire's words: "one must also liberate the liberator" (*Nègre je suis*, 63). Departing from that cautious Caribbean self-assessment, Walcott's approach to the revolution poses questions that ultimately underlie all of the works examined in this study—questions about justice, forgiveness, and fairness that may never find fully satisfactory answers, but which require our ever renewed attention.

The tension/imbrication of local histories and global designs also plays a prominent role in Edouard Glissant's account of the revolution, which highlights the multiple and arduous decisions—roads to take and not to take—opened up by the development of any successful anti-colonial struggle, particularly if it results in a new "postcolonial" nation. In Glissant's play, Toussaint and Macaïa confront each other as each proposes a different way of navigating the colonial logic of globalized capitalism (with roots in the global hegemony of the modern/colonial order put in place by European imperial expansion), which is able to exploit "new" or "emerging" nations almost as effectively as the old colonial order. His representation poses difficult questions regarding how to avoid—or whether it is possible to avoid—globalization's constraints in a world that becomes increasingly caught in its web. Thus, it is not surprising that Glissant's concerns eventually led him to his repeated efforts to develop new metaphors in an attempt reconceptualize the links between the global and the local—"tout-monde," "chaos-monde," "opacité/rélation"—whether one deems them fully effective or not.

Ultimately, one of the Haitian Revolution's gifts to a rearticulation of the global is its ideal of universal emancipation, posed from the perspective of slaves whose concrete situation gave them a keen perspective of European empires who paid lip service to a universalist rhetoric while holding on to their illegitimate privileges through violent exploitation. It is that particular type of "border thinking" that Manuel Zapata Olivella emphasizes in his novel, which always points in the direction of human solidarity beyond exclusions of any kind, while retaining a practical emphasis on what I have termed a "preferential option for the oppressed black diaspora." Zapata

Olivella sees the revolution as the embodiment of a long tradition of Pan-African resistance—political, cultural, and spiritual. It is, however, a perspective that consistently insists on the fact that, as C. L. R. James stated in the phrase quoted in the previous chapter, "the African bruises and breaks himself against his bars in the interests of freedoms wider than his own" (qtd. in Nielsen, *C. L. R. James*, 81).

The overlaps between these writers are multiple and fruitful, just as the divergences are real and significant. One may highlight a category like cultural identity, in which case Carpentier, with his notion of the marvelous real; Palés Matos, with his interest in Afro-Caribbean aesthetics; and Zapata Olivella, with his emphasis on the spiritual and religious dimensions of Afro-diasporic resistance could be productively grouped together. But Zapata Olivella also offers a long catalogue of violent anticolonial struggles in which race is always in dialogue with other categories like class, a focus that could place him next to James, with his Marxist perspective, and Césaire, with his universalist anticolonial discourse. Walcott and Glissant could be grouped together in terms of their concern about the postrevolutionary paths opened to the Caribbean, and the risk of replicating global colonial patterns in local settings. However, as I will highlight below, James is clearly interested in Walcott's exploration of the role of reconciliation in politics. Carpentier's Ti Noel may offer perspectives that neither Toussaint nor Macaïa have fully considered in Glissant's play. After all, both the general and the maroon leader have more in common with Césaire's heroes, in spite of Glissant's differences with Césaire, than they do with Ti Noel or Walcott's Pompey. Similarly, in spite of James's and Césaire's well-deserved status as fiery anticolonial champions, Césaire's recurrent "Caribbean existential anguish" may have more in common with Walcott's melancholic assessment of the region than with James's staunch revolutionary optimism (although, if we agree with David Scott's reading of James, we might have to incorporate a tragic sensibility to his understanding of the Caribbean). Needless to say, if each of these authors and works only manages to capture and articulate limited aspects of the revolution's full importance, my own emphasis in the chapters of this book only manages to capture a fraction of the manifold dimensions of each of the texts and writers. The revolution's spirit is as complex as Caribbean history, and its partial incarnations invoke histories whose fractures have not been resolved, and futures whose promises never cease to haunt those who aspire to liberation.

Here, as we invoke Caribbean history, we must go beyond Derrida's view of the spectral and haunting, useful and suggestive as it is. Derrida's "hauntology" invokes (among many other things) the irreducible tension between presence and absence that deconstructs Marx's desired "ontology" of a fully incarnated, fully present communism (*Specters*, 128–30). Reading Marx against Marx, Derrida privileges a dimension in Marx's writing that invokes the ghosts of previous and future incomplete and partial European revolutions, among other ghosts, in order to suggest that Marx's fully present revolution can only be purged of those ghosts through an act of erasure that Derrida wants to undo—ontology is always haunted by hauntology (ibid., 202). However, a dimension that Derrida does not highlight is the fact that in its colonial history, the West has long violently articulated an exterior, marginal sphere of partial nonbeing that paradoxically serves as ontological support (and exploited labor, and source of natural resources) for the realm of presumed full being.

I am referring here to what in the introduction I labeled as synechdocal onto-colonialism, and to what Maldonado Torres has defined (following initial formulations by Mignolo and by Wynter) as "the coloniality of being."[3] Coloniality (the logic of modern colonialism) operates (as Césaire suggests) as an ontology, in which the colonized (most of the non-European peoples of the globe from the first moment initiated by Spain and Portugal in 1492, then continued by other Western European powers since the 17th century) are not only defined as quantitatively inferior (less sophisticated arms, for example) but also qualitatively inferior ("almost the same but not white," as Bhabha aptly describes it [*Location*, 89]). As we saw in the introduction and throughout the book, this essentialist logic also governs the "myth of modernity" (as Dussel calls it), since even when the colonial difference is presented as merely a temporal gap (the colonized are primitive, the West is modern), it is a gap that can never be breached. In spite of their differences, all of the accounts of the Haitian Revolution that we have examined attempt to address that colonial double bind.

To put it in Derrida's terms (or rather, metaphors)—while the deconstructionist philosopher performs the necessary task of reminding the self-complacent "living" that the fullness of their being is always already haunted by ghosts never fully there yet never fully absent (so that ontology is always already hauntology), the question we are asking here is, what is the perspective of some of those so-called ghosts or specters, how do they look on the so-called living? The answer from the colonial perspective is that the ghosts do not regard themselves as relative absences that "haunt" the living—they regard "the living" as unfairly enjoying a surplus of being that they have *stolen* from the so-called specters. That theft is constitutive of the "being" of the modern/colonial world, which has been contrived through the workings of the "coloniality of being," as examined by Maldonado-Torres. The Haitian Revolution is an exemplary attempt on the part of those whose being was materially, culturally and spiritually reduced to almost total nothingness (never quite total nothingness—they must always be presented as somehow redeemable in order to justify the "white man's burden") to regain the fullness of their humanity; not a naive ontological fullness that a deconstructionist could easily reveal as always "haunted," but rather the basic, always already precarious being that all *human beings* share.[4]

Fanon eloquently states the point we are making in *A Dying Colonialism*:

> The colonized person, who in this respect is like the men in underdeveloped countries or the disinherited in all parts of the world, perceives life not as a flowering or a development of an essential productiveness, but as a permanent struggle against an omnipresent death. This ever-menacing death is experienced as endemic famine, unemployment, a high death rate, an inferiority complex and the absence of any hope for the future. All this gnawing at the existence of the colonized tends to make of life something resembling an incomplete death. (128)

Fanon's allusion to a life that somehow resembles "an incomplete death" provides an adequate "hauntology" of colonial ontology—the partial but persistent nonbeing of those who have become the objects of the coloniality of power and the coloniality of being. His words also capture the material dimension of that colonial logic (famine, unemployment, etc.) and its effects on colonized subjectivities (inferiority complex, absence of hope). Of course, those effects and conditions are never absolute, and as Zapata Olivella insists throughout *Changó el gran putas* (and Fanon himself exemplifies), the history of colonial oppression is nothing if not the history of the persistent resistance of the oppressed. In that history, the Haitian Revolution plays an important role.

Here I should highlight again that, although issues of gender politics have not been the central focus of this book, they constitute an important dimension of coloniality, as stated in the introduction and at several points throughout the chapters. The problem of gender deserves to be highlighted because it can easily become invisible, as both oppressors and liberators, however defined, ignore its questions and challenges. Thus we may speak, as I suggested in the introduction, about a "coloniality of gender" or the "modern/colonial gender system," to use María Lugones's terms. As we have seen, not only is the logic of coloniality male-centered and almost exclusively heteronormative in in the way it organizes the ontology of what counts as fully human institutionally and existentially but it is also the case that resistance and rebellion, mostly organized around categories like race, class, or nation, often simply ignore the colonial construction of gender. At worst, even liberation movements become complicit with the coloniality of gender, preserving gender inequalities and exclusions as the one dimension of colonial logic that remains naturalized after, and in the midst of, liberation movements. Such is the case of Yette the prostitute in Walcott's plays, and therein we may appreciate the importance of strong women characters like Agne Brown in Zapata Olivella's novel. This is one area in which it may be particularly pertinent to think about "liberating the liberator," as suggested by Césaire, who nonetheless remained anchored in a mostly masculinist discourse throughout his literary career.

As I hope has been clear in the individual chapters of this book, I regard these writers engagement with the coloniality of power, knowledge, and being as an overarching concern that does not erase their individual approaches. On the other hand, while I find the concepts developed by thinkers like Dussel, Quijano, Mignolo, and Maldonado-Torres particularly useful in the description of the problems I have been exploring, we have also seen those problems emerge from the writers themselves, even if, logically, in their own language. We saw, for example, how Césaire refers to the colonial system in Saint Domingue as "more than a hierarchy, an ontology" (*Toussaint*, 33)—an insight into a logic of coloniality that includes but goes beyond formal colonialism.

Similarly, C. L. R. James states in his 1963 appendix to *The Black Jacobins*,

> The people of the West Indies were born in the seventeenth century, in a Westernized productive and social system. Members of different African tribes were carefully split up to lessen conspiracy, and they were therefore compelled to master the European languages, highly complex products of centuries of civilization. From the start there had been a gap, constantly growing, between the rudimentary conditions of the life of the slave and the language he used. There was therefore in West Indian society an inherent antagonism between the consciousness of the black masses and the reality of their lives, inherent in that it was constantly produced and reproduced not by agitators but by the very conditions of the society itself. (407)

While it may not be the language that James, as a Marxist, would use, it is possible to link the "gap" that he describes as inherent to the contrast between the slaves' language and their conditions life to what Mignolo refers to as the "colonial difference," and the "double bind" it creates for the colonized. The "language" that the slaves learn is the language of European modernity that is about to produce the upheavals of the American and French revolutions, all in the name the Rights of Man. The slaves' conditions, and their slavery itself, are a result of the colonial underside of that modernity, and as such the gap between those two realities is unbridgeable, even as they remain intricately linked in the history of Western global hegemony. The issue here is not, as I have insisted throughout the book, to pose some essentialist link between Western modernity and coloniality in the abstract. The issue is how the two were in fact linked throughout the history of European imperial expansion, sometimes perhaps in tension, but just as often in relative harmony, as in "the myth of modernity" that justifies colonial domination as the white man's burden.

The purpose of James' words is to highlight that the ideals of Western enlightenment paradoxically helped galvanize the slaves' consciousness of the injustice of their situation, and their struggle for truly universal emancipation, as Nick Nesbitt has suggested. That notion need not be denied. But the writers studied in this book, including certain moments in James himself, show that that process should not be simplistically construed the slaves' gradually being able to heel to the very modernity that constructed them as inherently inferior to begin with. One might expand James's view by thinking of the "inherent antagonism between the consciousness of the black masses and the reality of their lives" in terms what Enrique Dussel calls "transmodernity." Dussel's transmodern project implies the irruption of other voices excluded by the modern project, creating a "tranversal intercultural dialogue" ("Transmodernity," 41) that "does not presuppose the illusion of a non-existent symmetry between cultures" (ibid., 43), since the asymmetry that is constitutive of the modern/colonial world is precisely what is being addressed. That transmodern project may also be linked to the critique of, and confrontation with, a monolithic Eurocentric reading of history, from the perspective of what Mignolo has called a "pluritopic hermeneutics" (*The Darker Side of Renaissance; Local Histories*). The Haitian Revolution itself cannot be thought of as an example of transmodernity (which ultimately remains, as Ramón Grosfoguel aptly describes it, "an utopian decolonial project" ["Decolonizing," 26]) but as one of many emancipation movements that *points* toward that possibility. The revolting slaves did not simply enact the prescription for freedom provided for them by their enlightened colonizers. They redefined freedom and its possibilities from a position that was not only *other* but also *excluded*.

To conclude, I quote James one last time, again from the 1963 appendix in which, in the wake of anticolonial independence movements, he reflected on his own project in *The Black Jacobins*. There, near the very end of the book, he describes West Indians, the people of the Caribbean, as

> a people in the middle of our disturbed century, concerned with the discovery of themselves, determined to discover themselves, but without hatred or malice against the foreigner, even the bitter imperialist past. To be welcome into the comity of nations a new nation must bring something new. Otherwise it is a mere administrative convenience or necessity. The West Indians have brought something new. (417)

James then proceeds to quote a few lines from a poem by Derek Walcott, "Ruins of a Great House," which builds up to the realization, "All in compassion ends" (James, *Black Jacobins*, 418). However, when we look at Walcott's full poem, we realize that the stanza in which the poet reaches that conclusion starts with the wrathful lines "Ablaze with rage I thought, / some slave is rotting in this manorial lake" (Walcott, *Collected*, 20). James does not quote the opening lines of the stanza, but one might argue that everything that has come before in his own book in a way stands for them.

James's emphasis on the novelty of the Caribbean contribution to the community of nations again points toward the transmodern project. It implies the irruption of perspectives and subjectivities that were not simply absent, but actively marginalized by the modern/colonial world system. That transmodern project ultimately calls for "a decolonial temporal and spatial horizon that involves the critical appropriation of elements of Western modernity along with the opening to multiple conceptions of knowledge and of the critical voices in them. It also involves the recognition and the effort to do away with the hierarchical relations in which these knowledges find themselves locally and globally" (Maldonado-Torres, "Decoloniality," 5). The Haitian Revolution represents one of those moments in history when the possibility of such a project became visible, emerging violently against the violence of the coloniality of power/being/knowledge. All the writers that we have examined in these pages bear witness to the painful emergence of those aspirations to freedom against the brutal resistance of colonialism and the logic of coloniality.

And yet, it is fitting that James finishes his book, and we finish ours, with a repudiation of "hatred or malice against the foreigner, even the imperialist past," and an invocation of Walcott's appeal to compassion. James was not a writer given to the lyrical embellishment of the stark realities of colonialism and the dire costs of liberation struggles. However, "malice against the foreigner," whether we take the foreigner literally or merely as a symbol of Otherness itself, is characteristic of the logic of coloniality. Any true liberation project that does not want to merely invert an unjust power structure must come to terms with that malice in order to overcome it. As James's words suggest, the Haitian Revolution represents many of the loftier ideals, organizational potential, and daring possibilities of a group of people, the Saint Domingue slaves, who at the bottom of abjection dared not only dream about freedom from their own shackles, but also about universal emancipation. That commitment to justice within a much broader horizon of inclusion invoked by Walcott's appeal to compassion is most strongly conveyed by these Caribbean writers' representations of the Haitian Revolution. In their works, the revolution's failures and successes call upon us in the present, in the Caribbean and beyond, to reflect on the past in order to imagine a better future. In that regard all of their works constitute, as Edouard Glissant suggests, prophetic visions of the past.

Notes

Introduction

1. Laurent Dubois's *Avengers of the New World* remains one of the most accessible recent accounts of the events in Haiti. For the revolution's impact on the Caribbean and beyond, see Dubois, *A Colony;* Geggus, *Haitian Revolutionary;* Geggus, ed., *The Impact;* Brown, *Toussaint's Clause;* and Matthewson, *A Proslavery.*

2. It is important to add to the summary of the revolution that throughout the eighteenth century Saint Domingue had become, in spite of its size, one of the richest colonies in the world—thus the French interest in preserving the colony at all costs. The enormous production of the colony was predicated on the huge number of slaves that were brought to it, and the extreme physical cruelty with which they were treated. For examples of the cruel treatment of the Saint Domingue slaves, I refer the reader to the first chapter of James's *Black Jacobins.*

3. For the Trotsky transcripts see James, *At the Rendezvous of Victory;* and James, *C. L. R. James on the "Negro Question."*

4. The years 1958–1962 marked the creation of the weak West Indies Federation among British colonies in the Caribbean. The federation was short-lived, but it preceded the independence of several of its members, including Jamaica and James's native Trinidad in 1962. James, however, often changed his emphasis but not his priorities: in the map of the "postcolonial" Caribbean of the early 1960s that he traces in his "Appendix," he signals out *socialist* Cuba as the island that has moved the closest to his ideals.

5. For different perspectives on the disputes about "natural serfdom" of Native Americans (best exemplified by the debate between Bartolomé de Las Casas and Juan Ginés de Sepúlveda in Valladolid [1550–1551]), see Padgen, *The Fall of Natural Man;* Rabasa, *Inventing America;* Losada, *Fray Bartolomé;* and Mignolo, *The Idea.*

6. Walter Mignolo echoes Césaire when he succinctly states in *The Idea of Latin America:* "Colonization of being is nothing else than producing the idea that certain people do not belong to history—that they are non-beings. Thus, lurking beneath the European story of discovery are the histories, experiences, and silenced conceptual narratives of those who were disqualified as human beings, as historical actors, and as capable of thinking and understanding" (4).

7. Mignolo's notion of the "modern/colonial world system" is itself an expansion and revision of the concept of the "modern world system," developed by Immanuel Wallerstein in order to describe the development and expansion of the modern capitalist globalized world. To Wallerstein's ideas Mignolo adds the crucial element of coloniality/colonialism. See Mignolo, *Local Histories*.

8. Césaire's use of the terms "being" and "nothingness" should not be identified with Sartre's use of them. For Sartre, "nothingness" represents a constitutive aspect of consciousness, its incompleteness, which constantly attempts to fulfill itself and achieve full "being" (without ever achieving it, for consciousness is by definition a lack of full being, an awareness of otherness or non being). Césaire politicizes and historicizes Sartre's terms, reconfiguring that abstract phenomenology of non being as the colonial condition of those who have been expropriated from their being and condemned to seek in vain a fullness (a privilege of the colonizer) that always seems close at hand yet remains perpetually out of reach. For lucid elucidations of the relations of Black and Africana thought and the existentialist tradition, see Gordon, *Fanon;* and Gordon, *Existentia*.

9. For Bernasconi's original article, see his essay "African Philosophy's Challenge to Continental Philosophy" in *Postcolonial African Philosophy: A Critical Reader.*

10. It is important to point out that this process may occur in spite of the "best intentions" of European intellectuals to assist in colonial emancipation. The classic example of that situation is Jean Paul Sartre's take on Aimé Césaire's "négritude," which he praises and supports just as he explains it, dialectically, as a *negative* or antithesis moment whose first moment is white European culture. Although necessary, that negative moment must be transcended and incorporated to a higher synthesis. See "Black Orpheus" in *What is Literature?* Equally well known is Frantz Fanon's response to Sartre's "assistance": "At the very moment when I was trying to grasp my own being, Sartre, who remained The Other, gave me a name and thus shattered my last illusion. While I was saying to him: 'My negritude is neither a tower nor a cathedral, it thrusts into the red flesh of the sun, it thrusts into the burning flesh of the sky, it hollows through the dense dismay of its own pillar of patience . . .' [lines from Césaire's poetry], while I was shouting that, in the paroxysm of my being and my fury, he was reminding me that my blackness was only a minor term. In all truth, in all truth I tell you, my shoulders slipped out of the framework of the world, my feet could not feel the touch of the ground. Without a Negro past, without a Negro future, it was impossible for me to live my Negrohood. Not yet white, no longer wholly black, I was damned" (*Black Skin*, 137–38). As Fanon's words dramatically convey, even in Sartre's "defense" the black man remains trapped in the colonial "double bind."

11. For an analysis of the anxiety that the lack of such a stable, unified self produces on the colonizer, Homi Bhabha's insights on mimicry and colonial discourse remain quite useful. Albert Memmi's classic reflections in *Portrait* also eloquently address the issue of the colonizer's anxiety.

12. See Quijano, "Coloniality of Power"; and Quijano, "Coloniality and Modernity."

13. In a short 1936 preface to his 1934 play *Toussaint Louverture* (later rewritten with the title *The Black Jacobins*), C. L. R. James stated: "The French Revolution was the starting point of a cruel struggle between whites and mulattoes. The mulattoes could own land and slaves, but were denied political rights and social equality. It was only after seeing their masters torture and murder each other for two years that the slaves began their own revolution" (*Toussaint*, 45). While that may not have been his intention, James's words give the impression that there was little resistance on the slaves' part before the French Revolution. As we will see in chapter 3, the

structure of Aimé Césaire's *Toussaint Louverture* can give the same impression. Significantly, by 1938 James opens his historical essay *The Black Jacobins* giving due credit to maroon slaves and figures like Mackandal, and highlighting: "one does not need education or encouragement to cherish a dream of freedom" (18). His 1967 rewrite of his play also begins by emphasizing the centrality of the masses of slaves.

14. The issue here is one of emphasis rather than of taking an either/or position. It is clearly undeniable that the events and ideals of the French Revolution had an enormous impact on the Haitian Revolution, and on figures like Toussaint Louverture. The very title of C. L. R. James's classic *The Black Jacobins* points to that connection. The question is whether enough has been said and researched about how the slaves themselves might have conceptualized their struggle for liberation before, and in addition to, the ideas of the French Enlightenment. For a pioneer work attempting to look at the Haitian Revolution "from below," see Fick, *The Making of Haiti*.

15. In *"Rebelles* with a Cause" Phillippe Girard makes an important contribution to the documentation of the role of women in the Haitian Revolution. Dubois also makes significant points in *Haiti;* see also Dubois and Garrigus, *Slave Revolution*. Garraway's *The Libertine Colony* greatly enhances our understanding of sexual dynamics in the slave cultures of the French Caribbean, which constituted an immediate context for the role of women during the revolution. On the same topic, see also Garrigus, *Before Haiti*.

16. See also Suárez Navaz y Hernández Castillo, eds.; and Lugones "Toward a Decolonial." See also Elina Vuola's critical reading of Dussel's approaches to sexuality, "Thinking *Otherwise:* Dussel, Liberation Theology and Feminism," in Martín Alkoff and Mendieta, eds., and Dussel's response in the epilogue of the same volume. For a different and highly creative and nuanced combination of decolonial and feminist/gender concerns, see Sandoval's influential *Methodology of the Oppressed*. For a thorough overview of the ideas of Dussel, Quijano, Mignolo, and Maldonado-Torres, followed by some critiques of their positions and formulations, see Restrepo y Rojas, *Inflexión decolonial*.

17. Several essays in Munro and Walcott-Hackshaw *Reinterpreting* address the impact of the revolution on Haitian writers and intellectuals.

18. Even my limited corpus in this book—literary works from the twentieth-century Caribbean—focuses on works by several authors who have had a significant impact and lasting influence on the culture of the region, leaving out other lesser known works on the subject. Works that do not form part of my study include the long poem *Las metamorfosis de Makandal* (1998), by the Dominican Manuel Rueda, and *La tragedia del rey Christophe* (1963) (found in *Teatro*), by the Colombian playwright Enrique Buenaventura. I have not included either the Puerto Rican Edgardo Rodríguez Juliá's early novels, which I consider to be closely related to the Haitian Revolution; for those, see Figueroa, "In Search."

19. As I indicate in the chapter on Césaire, the examination of how claims to "universalism/ universality" have historically played a fundamental role in the articulation of the global web of the coloniality of power is different from abstract philosophical speculations on the possibility and desirability of actually discovering/articulating such universal values. In any case, and at the very least, the critique of how the claim to universality has actually been used historically should make us healthily suspicious of the motives, sources and goals of any such attempt, and cautiously skeptical about any claim of having actually *achieved* such universality.

20. Whether the duties of a committed writer, dutifully engaged with history, politics and society, are gladly accepted by all these writers is a different question altogether. For an exami-

nation of how those political commitments can actually provoke inner turmoil and resistance on the part of some Caribbean writers, see Figueroa, *Not at Home.*

21. In his study on Toussaint and Césaire, *Free and French in the Caribbean: Toussaint Louverture, Aimé Césaire, and Narratives of Loyal Opposition,* Walsh also highlights the continued pertinence of White's ideas in the study of Caribbean historiography.

Chapter 1

1. All quotations from Carpentier's novel come from Harriet de Onís's translation, followed by page number in parentheses.

2. For a very lucid and thorough examination of Carpentier's "real maravilloso," and how it is similar yet also different from the better known term "magical realism," see González Echevarría 107–29.

3. Gerard Aching provides a compelling account of how Carpentier and James, in spite of their different approaches, use execution scenes (Mackandal's in Carpentier, a young slave's in James) to vividly covey not only the resilience and persistence of the revolting slaves, but also the colonizers' perplexity when faced by their victims' challenge to the legitimacy of colonial domination.

4. Probably the best-known approach to the novel's structure is that of González Echevarría, which remains fascinating in spite of its excessive reliance on numerical calculations. For other approaches see Volek; and Richard Young.

5. Carpentier's own comments regarding the inclusion of Pauline in the novel refer simply to his surprise at encountering Pauline's palace during his visit to the old Cap-Francais (now Cap-Haitian). He regards the palace as a sign the coexistence of the past and the present, a "synchronism" that for him again points to the Spanish American "marvelous real" (*Tientos,* 107). For more details regarding his sources and use of the Pauline episode, see Speratti-Piñero.

6. C. L. R. James also includes an ironic aside on Pauline in his account of Leclerc's expedition, emphasizing, like Carpentier, the cynical sense of self-entitlement of European colonizers: "At the last moment Bonaparte changed the command, putting his brother-in-law, Leclerc, at the head, a sign of the importance he attached to the venture. Pauline, Leclerc's wife, and their son went with the expedition. She carried musicians, artists, and all the paraphernalia of a court. Slavery would be re-established, civilization restarted, and a good time would be had by all" (*Black Jacobins,* 275).

7. Emir Rodríguez Monegal and Giovanni Pontiero are among the critics who have pointed out, without attempting to explain, Toussaint's absence from the novel. Lizabeth Paravisini-Gebert ("The Haitian Revolution") also points out Toussaint's absence, but her useful analysis focuses on the novel's dismissive treatment of Dessalines, which amounts to a symbolic, if not literal, absence of the actual achiever of Haitian independence.

8. One may even argue that Toussaint Louverture is not mentioned at all. In chapter 7 of the first part of the novel, Carpentier refers in passing to a character called "Toussaint, el ebanista" ["Toussaint, the cabinet maker"], who is carving religious figures for Lenormand de Mezy's wife. This could certainly be a reference to Louverture, as in the first two parts Carpentier does mention in passing other revolutionary heroes like Christophe, referring to their occupations before the revolution. However, the allusion remains mysterious, for the historical Toussaint was a coachman for the Breda family. The name Toussaint is not mentioned again in the novel.

9. For a detailed analysis of Carpentier's declared and undeclared sources for his novel, see Speratti-Piñero, *Pasos hallados en El reino de este mundo*.

10. The topic of Carpentier's influences brings up the interesting question of whether Carpentier was acquainted with James's book. So far I have not encountered any explicit indication that Carpentier had read *The Black Jacobins* before writing his novel, and there are no obvious loans from James's book (as there are from other works) in *El reino de este mundo*. However, one can speculate that it is very likely that Carpentier knew it, and that James's study may be one of those "many" works that dealt with the figure of Toussaint, and that supposedly persuaded Carpentier to stir his novel in a different direction.

11. James had in fact addressed the events of *The Black Jacobins* in a play produced in 1936 with the title *Toussaint L'Ouverture*. James revised the play in 1967, and retitled it *The Black Jacobins*. The original version was published in 2013; the 1967 version may be found in Hill; and in *C. L. R. James Reader*.

12. Kara Rabbitt emphasizes how James explicitly recurs to the structures of classical tragedy in his "emplotment" of the events in the revolution, and how Toussaint's "tragic flaw" is clearly articulated on the basis of important literary tragic heroes ("C. L. R. James's Figuring"). For an examination of the political implications of this "tragic" emplotment, see Scott, *Conscripts*. As Scott aptly observes, the first six paragraphs of chapter 13, in which James spells out his views on the poetics of tragedy and the genre's pertinence to Toussaint's dilemma toward the end of his life, were added to text in 1963's second edition. To Rabbitt's and Scott's observations one might add the possible influence on James of Césaire's portrayal of Toussaint in his *Toussaint Louverture*. There Césaire clearly presents his hypothesis that Toussaint voluntarily removes himself from the political scene in order to preserve the unity among the Saint Domingue masses, an act that responds to Toussaint's "tragic sense of life" (*Toussaint Louverture*, 310; my translation). As James clearly indicates in his bibliography (*Black Jacobins*, 389), in 1963 he was well acquainted with Césaire's book (which in turn was greatly influenced by the first edition of James's book).

13. James's thesis on the connections between slavery and the development of European capitalism was later developed, with special emphasis on England, in Eric Williams's *Capitalism and Slavery*. The thesis remains controversial; for a more recent assessment and critique see Cateau and Carrington, eds., *Capitalism and Slavery*.

14. For a lucid assessment of the Haitian Revolution as the attempt to enact radical (Spinozean) enlightened ideals of universal emancipation, see Nesbitt, *Universal Emancipation*.

15. Multiple aspects of James's diagnosis of the Russian Revolution and the historical meaning of Stalinism can be found throughout his works. For some of his most consistent analyses, see his *World Revolution* and *State Capitalism*.

16. For comics, and movies, see James, *American Civilization;* for cricket see James, *Beyond a Boundary*.

17. For an analysis of James's relations with religion and African traditional beliefs in the context of the Caribbean's "historicist" and "poeticist" philosophical traditions, see Henry, *Caliban's Reason*, particularly chapter 2.

18. James's literary penchant is displayed in an episode when rebellious maroon slaves, which should have been sympathetic to Toussaint's efforts, in fact fight against him, resenting among other things Toussaint's strict prohibition of Vodou (*Black Jacobins*, 309). The maroons warn the French about a forthcoming attack by Dessalines; the French commander is humorously described by James as "uncertain as to what this demoniacal black general would do next" (ibid.).

19. For the importance of Spengler in Carpentier's outlook, and the late career Marxist recasting of his early works see González Echevarría, *Alejo Carpentier*.

20. Paul B. Miller has already made the point of the James/Toussaint similarity by aptly pointing out that, in his constant celebration of the uniqueness of Toussaint as a heroic leader, James also (like Toussaint) moves away from the masses that presumably legitimize Toussaint's leadership ("Enlightened Hesitations", 1075). Naturally, for James what makes Toussaint such a remarkable leader is precisely his deeper grasp of French "enlightened" ideas.

21. Fick makes a compelling case in her book for a view of the Haitian Revolution from "below," that is, from the perspective of the uneducated slave masses, among whom the enlightened ideals of the French Revolution were of secondary importance (*The Making of Haiti*). Nesbitt has criticized some significant omissions on Fick's part, in his own case for the fundamental importance of those ideals in the development of the revolution (*Universal*, 62).

22. There is no doubt that Toussaint opposed and forbid Vodou, and that his role in that religion has not been significant. One possible source of doubt, however, is his assumed surname, "L'Ouverture" (which Toussaint in his later years wrote "Louverture"). "L'ouverture," in French, means "the opening," and it refers, presumably, to Toussaint as he who opens the way to freedom for all the slaves, or Toussaint as he who bravely opens the way among enemy soldiers for his men. However, there is a possibility that Toussaint was aware of his surname's connections to Legba, the powerful Loa who is always invoked first in Vodou rituals, as he opens the way to the other Loas. Madison Smartt Bell uses this connection in his novel on Toussaint, *Master of the Crossroads* ("Master of the crossroads" being a title of the Loa Legba).

23. Evidently scientific knowledge can offer compelling practical evidence for the validity of its claims. Sousa Santos is simply arguing that there are other knowledges that may complement scientific knowledge, not take its place. He also points out that the view of scientific knowledge as a monolithic line of seamless development is itself false: Thomas Kuhn already laid out the problematic character of that simplistic view of scientific progress. Also, at any given moment there may be several conflicting positions or paradigms within the scientific community, and the dominance of one position sometimes responds to political, not strictly "scientific," interests (for an interesting examination of this reality in the case of Physics, see Smolin, *Trouble with Physics*). Finally, there is the well-known reality that science itself cannot offer reliable ground for the ethical application of its discoveries. If we move from "hard" science to other "knowledges," from politics to ethics to ecology, etc., the fact that they are not strictly governed by the scientific method has not stopped the West from dismissing other views as primitive or barbaric. Even on the issue of religion the West has traditionally assumed that its Judeo-Christian tradition somehow purveys self-evident truths that are superior to the religious views of conquered peoples.

Sousa Santos has explored these issues in many of his writings. In addition to *Another Knowledge, Another Production* and *Democratizing Democracy*, which are easily available in English, I have found *Conocer desde el Sur* a particularly useful summary of his concerns. See also Grosfoguel's excellent overview, "La descolonización del conocimiento."

24. "Nature" and "the natural world" are, of course, very slippery concepts. For an excellent overview of their difficulties, see Buell, *Future of Environmental Criticism*.

25. See Farmer, *Haiti After;* Diamond, *Collapse;* and Shawn Miller, *An Environmental History*.

26. George B. Handley has made a compelling argument for how in spite of the "twentieth century neo-colonial and masculine conquest . . . of 'virgin' nature" rhetoric (126) in *Los pasos*

perdidos, Carpentier's baroque aesthetic approach (which includes his ideas on "lo real maravilloso") in fact undermines may of his own anthropocentric assumptions.

27. James's approach to colonialism and Marxism reveals what Sylvia Wynter calls his "pluri-conceptual framework," in which "multiple modes of domination arising from such factors as gender, color, race, class, and education are non-dogmatically integrated" ("Beyond the Categories" 63).

Chapter 2

1. For González's intellectual trajectory, see Irizarry, *José Luis González*. For the controversies around *El país de cuatro pisos,* see Gerald Guiness's introduction to his translation, *The Four-Storeyed Country*.

2. For an extensive overview of Puerto Rican literature from its origins, see Rivera de Alvarez, *Literatura puertorriqueña*.

3. In his text González presents Albizu as the ideological representative of a nineteenth-century, dominant, land-owning class that saw its privileges threatened by the new powerful U.S. economic interests. For González, "the ever-growing weakness of the creole ruling class rendered it incapable of countering American imperialism with a plan of its own for the historical development of Puerto Rico and in fact finally led it to abandon the liberalism that characterized it in the last century, for the conservatism that has so far characterized it in this. The idealization—or rather, the misrepresentation—of the historical past has always been one of the typical traits of the ideology of this ruling class. Pedro Albizu Campos was without a doubt the most coherent and consistent spokesman for that conservative ideology (*Puerto Rico,* 7). For further analysis of the rhetoric of Albizuist nationalism and its nostalgia for the past, see Sotomayor, *Hilo de Aracne,* 179.

4. For a lucid examination of Pedreira's ideological assumptions, see Flores, *Insularismo,* or its English version, "The Insular Vision," included in Flores, *Divided Borders*.

5. For a thorough analysis of Pedreira's historical context, see Flores, *Insularismo,* or its English version, "The Insular Vision," included in Flores, *Divided Borders*. For lucid observations on the persistent marginalization of blackness (both black authors and black subjects) in Puerto Rican literature and culture, see Santos Febres, *Sobre piel y papel*.

6. Throughout this chapter, quotes in English from Palés Matos's poetry will be my translations, followed by the poem title in the case of long quotes, and by the page number of the original Spanish in parentheses. My source is *La poesía de Luis Palés Matos,* Mercedes López-Baralt's magisterial critical edition of Palés Matos's collected poems. There are two useful translations of Palés's poems: Julio Marzán's 2000 *Selected Poems/Poesía selecta,* which includes many poems from *Tuntún* and other selections from Palés's poetry; and Jean Steeves-Franco's 2010 translation of the complete *Tuntún*.

7. For an overview of diverse critical responses to Palés Matos, see Marzán, *The Numinous Site;* and López Baralt, *El barco*. See also Rivera Casellas ("Cuerpo y raza") who places Palés Matos in a wider context of representations of blackness in Puerto Rican literature. For the important connections between Palés Matos and Pedreira, see Ríos Avila, *La raza cómica;* and Rodríguez Vecchini, "Palés y Pedreira." For a lucid examination of Palés Matos's ambivalent relation to Puerto Rican black culture in the context of *negrismo,* see Roy-Féquierè, *Women*.

8. The critic Jean Claude Bajeux, one of the first to place Palés Matos in a Pan-Caribbean

context, enthusiastically reads Palés Matos's emphasis on musicality, sonorities and rhythm as politically liberating.

9. For a more thorough examination of Palés Matos's ironic aloofness, or distance, from the poetic universe he constructs, see Figueroa, *Not at Home*.

10. For a lucid assessment of how Palés Matos and Guillén can, and cannot, be compared, see González Pérez, "Ballad of Two Poets."

11. For Palés Matos's links to *modernismo*, see López Baralt, *El barco*. In "La biblioteca negra," Rodríguez Vecchini developed a compelling reading of *Tuntún* as a "rewriting" in Afro-Caribbean key of Rubén Darío's *modernista* classic *Cantos de vida y esperanza*.

12. Tomás Blanco perceptively suggests that one reason that many of Palés Matos's generational peers reacted negatively to his "black poems" and their international success may have been "the fear that abroad they might consider us a black people—that is to say, a clearly unjustified shyness in the face of certain illogical racial prejudices" (*Sobre Palés Matos*, 34; my translation).

13. On the significance of Llorens Torres, see Díaz Quiñones, *El almuerzo*.

14. In the next paragraph, Palés Matos offers interesting concrete examples of his arguments: "The Haitian deformed the foreign language into *patois*. He translated Catholic symbolism into equivalents within the Vodou cult. This basic cult from the native land, brought by the grandparents and kept in spite of official prohibitions, was practiced in a thousand altars that light up their candles in the jungle. In that manner, the Haitian soul, using the expressive resources of an exotic culture, through subtle but very certain pathways, achieves its essential objectives and is fulfilled with a clearly delineated fullness" (*Obras*, 240; my translation).

15. Ruben Ríos writes: "*Tuntún* is, above all, a hysterical assembly that pulverizes the docile utopia of identity, laying bare its fictitious construction, its performative gesture, its 'made up and concocted' core" (*La raza*, 158; my translation).

16. An interesting example of Palés Matos's ambivalence, one that regards the syncretism that he otherwise celebrates in so many instances, involves the definition of the word *Ecué* that he includes in the glossary ("vocabulario") that he added to the second edition to his book. The definition that he provides is: "god of black Cuban sorcerers. It corresponds (?) to the Christ of white people" (*Tuntún*, 220). The question mark—in Spanish the parenthesis is "(¿?)"—is Palés Matos's. It clearly indicates disbelief, confusion, irony or mockery, as if the identification of Ecué with Christ were going a step too far for the poet. Thus Palés Matos incorporates Afro-Caribbean syncretism in his poetry, yet subtly but clearly marks his distance from it.

17. Palés Matos's ambivalent relation to his poetic material is further revealed in the often-problematic literary and ethnographic sources for the articulation of his "African" images; see Rodríguez Vecchini, "La biblioteca negra"; and López Baralt, "La biblioteca negra" (López Baralt's text was inspired by Rodríguez Vecchini's). Although both Rodríguez Vecchini and López Baralt acknowledge the Eurocentric and often blatantly racist character of Palés Matos's sources, they emphasize his "ironic" appropriation of them (López Baralt, for example, simply states that "Lagarto verde" "rejects the colonized mind-frame, which attempts to imitate the invader to the point of ridicule" [16; my translation]). Such a limited (which does not mean totally mistaken) reading ignores Palés Matos's own Eurocentric representation of the Count of Lemonade's "authentic" character, itself a product of the logic of coloniality. My own reading does not deny Palés Matos's ironic and satirical performance, but rather suggests that there is an agonistic anxiety in Palés Matos's recurrent distance from the black world his poems "represent."

18. While the biographical detail that Palés Matos himself was a white poet is an important part of the problem I am discussing, I do not think it is enough to explain it. On the one hand, Palés Matos's race does not stop him from writing those parts of *Tuntún* where he quite effectively takes up the defense and celebration of an Afro-Caribbean identity before Euro-American interests. On the other hand, Palés Matos clearly saw himself as part of an *Antillean* culture and society (see note 19)—and the *Tuntún* quite clearly presents Africa as an integral part of that culture. While as a white poet Palés Matos is in a position of social privilege, as an Antillean poet he knows himself (anxiously) to be part, not outside, of that spectrum of Afro-Caribbean culture.

19. In an interview Palés Matos stated: "I have never talked about a black, a white, or a mulatto poetry. I have only talked about an Antillean poetry that may express our reality as a people, in the cultural sense of that word . . ." (*Obras*, 237; my translation).

20. As one example, we may look at the "glossary" that Palés Matos included in the second edition of *Tuntún*. In it he includes a word like *dingo*, which he defines as "a wolf-dog from Australia. It is used in the poem "Candombe" in a totemic sense" (*Tuntún*, 219: my translation). Why, one may ask, would the poet use an *Australian* animal as a totem in an *African* poem? The answer is quite simple: the word has a nice "African-sounding" sonority to it, regardless of its lack of "authenticity." It is hard not to read several of the entries in Palés Matos's glossary as further attempts of the poet to distance himself from his Afro-Caribbean material.

21. In a 1932 interview Palés Matos stated: "I have always been 'independentista' [in favor of Puerto Rico's independence], but understand me well, a tragic, dramatic 'independentista,' one of those who naively believe in independence at any moment, in any circumstances, and at any price. I cannot imagine a more practical solution to the great spiritual problem with which our people are engaged" (*Obras*, 302; my translation).

22. For more recent assessments on the socioeconomic conditions of Caribbean societies, see Knight and Martínez-Vergne, *Contemporary Caribbean Cultures*; Ramos, *Desencuentro*; and Palmer, *Caribbean Economy*.

23. For an analysis of the anxiety that the lack of such a stable, unified self produces on the colonizer, see Bhabha, *Location*.

Chapter 3

1. For an overview of the tensions and possible contradictions in Césaire's political career, see Armet, "Aimé Césaire."

2. Although Césaire had retired from active politics (he was mayor of Fort-de-France until 2001), he remained engaged with current events until his death in 2008. For example, he supported Ségolène Royal in her 2007 campaign for France's presidency.

3. In *Friends and Enemies* (chapter 3), Chris Bongie provides an insightful analysis of a late manifestation of France's linguistic universalism in his discussion of Régis Debray's *Haïti et la France* (2004) (the book version of an official government report written by Debray on the relations between Haiti and France). Even in his support of Haiti, Debray cannot stop himself from referring to it as a *Francophone* country. He acknowledges the importance of the Creole language (spoken by the great majority of Haitians) but goes on to state that "Creole cannot provide access to the realm of international relations, to the data of universal knowledge, nor to the culture of the legally constituted state" (qtd. in Bongie, *Friends*, 163). French universalism (or

more precisely, the Frenchness of universalism) remains alive and well in the twenty-first century; it still regards itself not as a sum of particularisms but as a realm beyond them, to which such particularisms (like the Creole language) do not have access.

4. For a concise overview of the contemporary currency of "Western Universalism," see Wallerstein, *European Universalism*. For the colonial logic of the universal claims of Western Modernity, see Mignolo, *Dark Side of Western Modernity*.

5. For a concise overview of this period of Césaire's political life, see Toumson and Henry-Valmore, *Aimé Césaire: Le nègre inconsolé*.

6. In addition to *La tragédie du roi Christophe*, Césaire's two other plays from the sixties, *Une saison au Congo* (1966) and *Une tempête* (1969), also respond directly (albeit allegorically, in the case of *Une tempête*) to the political events and the decolonial impulse of that period. *Une saison* deals with the tragic fate of Patrice Lumumba.

7. "On voit grandement errer à son sujet. Certains de ses admirateurs français disent, satisfaits: 'C'est un produit de notre culture.' D'autres, les réactionnaires: 'méfiez-vous de lui, il a été formé par Prague et par Moscou.' La vérité me paraît tout autre. Il n'est que de regarder son style: abandon à soi et contrôle de soi, véhémence et sagesse, particularisme et humanisme, il a créé en politique le style Africain mais c'est l'Afrique, son passé millénaire qui lui ont enseigné tout cela" (Césaire, "Preface," 6).

8. In a paradox characteristic of Césaire's political career, Touré was Guinea's first president after the French colony voted in 1958 for immediate independence from the metropolis (whereas Césaire had opted earlier for the "overseas department" status for Martinique). *Ferrements* includes a poem titled "Salut à la Guinée" ("Hail to Guinea") that celebrates Guinea's love of freedom.

9. Garraway also highlights the possible connections between Césaire's approach and Laclau's formulations ("What is Mine," 77). See also Figueroa's *Not at Home* and "Between Louverture."

10. For nineteenth-century homages to Toussaint see, for example, William Wordsworth's well-known poem "To Toussaint Louverture," from 1803, as well as J. R. Beard's *The Life of Toussaint L'Ouverture* (1853) and Wendell Phillips's lecture "Toussaint L'Ouverture" (1861).

11. Although it is extremely unlikely that Césaire had any knowledge of *The Black Jacobins* (1938) before publishing his *Cahier* in 1939, James's influence is noticeable throughout Césaire's *Toussaint Louverture*, particularly with regards to the argument that the colonies played a seminal role in the production and accumulation of capital in Europe, which paradoxically led to events like the French Revolution, in which the French bourgeoisie challenged the Old Regime, without realizing that their arguments and guiding principles would be appropriated by Haiti's "black Jacobins" in their struggle for *their own* liberation. We can also detect James's influence in Césaire's comments on how Louverture lost touch with the masses at the critical stage of his struggle, a mistake that contributed to his downfall. I have not been able to locate any explicit references to James in Césaire's works that would give us his assessment of the great Trinidadian's thought or works; he does quote James a couple of times in *Toussaint Louverture* (234; 251). James briefly reviews Césaire's *Toussaint Louverture* in the bibliography of the second edition of *The Black Jacobins;* he is appreciative but finds that "it lacks the fire and constant illumination which distinguish most of the other work of Césaire" (388).

12. For a close literary analysis of the role of Haiti in the poem throughout its different versions, see Pestre de Almeida, *Aimé Césaire: Un saison en Haïti*.

13. For an overview of some of the political and cultural repercussions of the Haitian Revolution in the Caribbean, see Popkin, *Facing Racial Revolution*; Geggus, ed., *Impact*; and Fischer, *Modernity Disavowed*.

14. The original French reads: "il est place pour tous au rendez-vous de la conquête" (*Cahier*, 29). One translation of the phrase renders it as "the rendezvous of victory," which is the form Said was fond of, and which gives its title to one anthology of C. L. R. James's writings (*At the Rendezvous of Victory*). While that translation captures some aspects of Césaire's celebratory declaration of inclusiveness, it lacks the ambiguity of the original "conquest," which remains provocative in a colonial context.

15. The Nigerian writer Wole Soyinka famously riposted that a black man does not need to proclaim his negritude any more than a tiger has to proclaim its "tigritude" (see *Burden*, 141). Césaire himself criticizes the essentializing of negritude in an interview with the Haitian poet René Depestre, insisting that his conception of negritude isn't biological but cultural and historical (Depestre, *Bonjour*, 144). It has frequently been noted that Léopold Senghor's view of negritude does tend to rely on more essentialist notions, and it is mainly (but not exclusively) to him that critics have often responded (see Loomba, *Colonialism/Postcolonialism*; and Young, *Postcolonialism*). In *Voicing Memory*, Nesbitt provides useful details on the relation and actual points of contact between Césaire and Senghor, at least in the initial stages of their careers. See also Kesteloot, *Black Writers*; and Arnold, *Modernism*.

16. For a more thorough examination of the tensions that I discuss in the *Cahier*, see my discussion of the poem in Figueroa, *Not at Home*.

17. Originally written in 1963, the play was revised for a new edition in 1970. The English translation is from 1969, and overall it does a good job of capturing the original edition's main thrust, although it does not do justice to the intensity of Césaire's poetry. I will quote from the 1969 English translation unless otherwise indicated; occasionally I will direct the reader to the original French when a passage from the definitive French edition does not appear in the translation, or I may offer my own translation.

18. In the original French, see pages 20, 40, 84, and 145–46, among others in which Christophe emphasizes the specificity of his black identity. As just one example, in an argument with Pétion in the first scene Christophe highlights the historical tension between blacks and free people of color when he states, "I'm not mulatto, I don't sift my words" (12).

19. At certain points in the play Christophe invokes not only Africa but also African and Vodou gods. By contrast, as with other heroes of the revolution, the historical Christophe's relation to Vodou remains somewhat ambiguous; what is clear in the historical record is that, like Toussaint before him, Christophe persecuted the practice of Vodou and insisted on Roman Catholicism as the official religion of his kingdom. See Dayan, *Haiti*.

20. In his *Aimé Césaire* Raphael Confiant criticizes Césaire for his seeming obsession with masculine heroics. An interesting response to Césaire's traditional rhetoric can be found in Daniel Maximin's novel, *L'isolé soleil*. *Et les chiens se taisaient* was originally published in *Les Armes miraculeuses* (1946); see Césaire *Oeuvres*. It can be found in English in *Lyric and Dramatic Poetry*. For the understudied role of women in the negritude movement, see Sharpley-Whiting, *Negritude Women*.

21. In this chapter, I am respecting Césaire's use of the term "mulatto," which names one of the main sections of his book. In the other chapters, I also preserve the word when it is used by the writers (for example, in Palés Matos's poetry). However, historians have gradually moved

away from a simplistic use of that term, in favor of a more nuanced view of Saint Domingue's social structure, in which, rather than speaking of blacks and mulattoes, it is more accurate to speak about enslaved people and free people of color (many who were mulatto, but some of whom were former black slaves who might even have acquired slaves themselves). One may also distinguish between the wealthier white sugar plantation owners, "les grand blancs," and lower class whites, "les petits blancs." For a description of these complex categories, see Garrigus, *Before Haiti*; and Stewart R. King, *Blue Coat*.

22. For overviews of the justifications of slavery both in France and beyond, and Enlightenment's philosophers' ability, or lack thereof, to effectively address the injustices of the slave system, see Sala-Molins, *Le code noir* and *Dark Side;* Miller, *The French Atlantic Triangle;* Nesbitt, *Universal Emacipation;* Ghachem, *The Old Regime;* and Davis, *Inhuman Bondage*. See also Blackburn's important trilogy of books, *The Making; The Overthrow;* and *The American Crucible*. For an overview of the presence and impact of the Enlightenment in modern Caribbean literature, see Miller, *Elusive Origins*. For the broader issue of the way in which racism and slavery have also found philosophical justifications, see Buck-Morss, *Hegel;* and Patteron, *Slavery*.

23. Buck-Morss's text remains fundamental for any reflection on the relation between Hegel and the Haitian Revolution. In *Voicing Memory*, Nesbitt offers an important alternative approach, which highlights Césaire's productive use of Hegel.

24. For the affective and existential dimension of coloniality, and Fanon's groundbreaking role in its analysis, see Gordon, *Fanon;* Gordon, *Existentia;* and Oliver, *Colonization*.

25. The notion of a French commonwealth, which corresponds to Césaire's long dream of more local autonomy for the Overseas Departments without severing the links with France, seems oxymoronic in the context of France's highly centralized political system (in spite of the creation in 1958 of a French Community). Césaire certainly writes his essay in a moment when his discontent with Martinique's departmental status has reached a high point. For a general overview of Césaire's tensions with France's central government, see Toumson and Henry-Valmore, *Aimé Césaire*. Walsh (*Free and French*) offers an extended and insightful examination of the issues and problems that Toussaint and Césaire share, which Césaire indeed understands as shared problems arising from France's colonial framework even in departmentalization. Hurley ("Is He, Am I, a Hero") offers a compelling reading of Césaire's essay on Toussaint as a self-referential text, in which the poet uses the figure of the Haitian general in order to explore his own political dilemmas.

26. For a reading that focuses on the commonalities of both works (their attempt to challenge a Western hegemonic reading of history), see Madureira, *Cannibal Modernities*.

27. In *Voicing Memory* (chapter 4), Nesbitt offers a compelling reading of how Césaire incorporates Hegelian elements in the *Tragedy*. I certainly agree with Nesbitt that Césaire, like other French and Francophone intellectuals of his generation, felt considerable enthusiasm for Hegel. My emphasis here is that that enthusiasm, as his enthusiasm for other aspects of the European Enlightenment, coexisted with considerable anxiety. As Nesbitt acknowledges, Césaire not only "cannibalized" Hegel but also went out of his way to insist on his commitment to a purely Afrocentric approach—"though Césaire's many Franco-European influences are readily apparent, his politically engaged speeches and interviews often downplayed those influences in favor of the African and African-American cultures celebrated by negritude" (*Voicing*, 122). It is in that self-doubting gesture (which I agree is quite insufficient to "hide" Césaire's European formation and erudition) that I locate Césaire's double bind as a colonial subject; it is visible

throughout most of his poetry and plays. As far as the effectiveness of drawing on Hegel at all to begin with, it goes without saying that the Left and the Right have successfully appropriated the German philosopher. Inasmuch as Hegel's dialectical approach imposes a predetermined goal (in terms of contents, rather than in exclusively heuristic terms) to history, it can be argued that excessive reliance on Hegel by a decolonial thinker like Césaire is problematic indeed. It was that dialectical teleology, when applied by Sartre, that Fanon found so dismaying in *Black Skin* (137–38), even if of course one can also read Hegel into Fanon (after all, as Foucault suggested, one can be Hegelian even in one's attempts to escape Hegel [Nesbitt, *Voicing*, 119]). If the dialectic begins with Europe as its initial "positive" moment, it is likely to remain Eurocentric, no matter how much "otherness" it incorporates. Something like what Mignolo calls a "pluritopic hermeneutics," taking as its point of departure the interaction of multiple literal and metaphorical locations, would be necessary (*Darker Side of Renaissance; Local Histories*). As Buck-Morss convincingly argues, it is precisely the concreteness of the Haitian Revolution that gets erased or silenced in Hegel's appropriation of it in his development of the abstract Master-Slave dialectic. Incidentally, that is also why E. Glissant's insistence on *unpredictability*, as an essential aspect of his vision of liberation, is so important (*Introduction*, 19; *Philosophie*, 67). In the *Tragedy* Christophe states in Glissantian fashion: "The human material needs recasting. How are we going to do it? I don't know. We'll start on a small scale. In our little workshop" (37). However, one can argue that Christophe's Afrocentrism in the play ignores precisely that "I don't know;" it remains immersed in a colonial logic that imposes a Eurocentric narrative, even if that logic disguises itself as the emancipating thrust of a Hegelian dialectic.

28. Edouard Glissant, in works like *Poétique de la relation* and *Traité du Tout-Monde* among others, had a tendency to present tensions similar to those in Césaire's works—now transformed into notions such as "opacité," "poétique de la rélation," "chaos-monde," "tout-monde," and others—as somehow more easily reconciled in the contemporary multicultural, postmodern world. As the critic Celia Britton commented of Glissant in 1999: "he increasingly writes as though the values of Relation, chaos, and diversity have in fact already prevailed" (*Edouard Glissant*, 9).

29. In many regards Césaire is, like the other authors examined in this book, a "colonial subject," in that he was born and educated in a colonial society to which he must adapt even as his relation to it is mainly one of opposition and critique. One of Fanon's great contributions to decolonial thinking, in writings like "The Lived Experience of the Black Man" ["The Fact of Blackness"] chapter in *Black Skin*, is his explicit and eloquent expression of the tensions and anguish of the colonial subjectivity—in other words, his dramatic presentation of how the colonized subject is not always pure rebellion, but rather a node of contradicting desires, many of them produced and fed to him by the colonial system itself. An acknowledgment of that existential dimension of coloniality is vital in its critique. We can often observe those tensions and contradicting desires in Césaire's writings, albeit frequently in spite of the seeming intentions of the poet.

30. For a very general overview of Haiti's symbolic role in Martinique's intellectual imaginary, see Salien, "Haïti vue de la Martinique."

31. The novels in question are *La renuncia del héroe Balatasar* (1974) and *La noche oscura del niño Avilés* (1984). For a more detailed assessment of those novels' connections to the Haitian Revolution, see Figueroa, "In Search."

32. Walsh (*Free and French in the Caribbean*) offers a very useful overview of Césaire's visit to Haiti and the significance of Haiti in his oeuvre.

Chapter 4

1. For the operas based on Dessalines, see Largey, *Vodou Nation*. For a useful overview of Dessaliness's image throughout the nineteenth century and its use by African American writers, see Twa, "Jean-Jacques Dessalines."

2. It is relatively hard to find reliable information on Dessalines, given his polarizing reputation. Important sources are Thomas Madiou's *Histoire d'Haiti* (1817) and Beaubrun Ardouin's *Etudes sur l'histoire d'Haiti* (1853)—both offer a wealth of details on the revolution and were written not long after the events, but they have been accused of bias in favor of the mulattoes or Haitian elites. The most thorough overview of Dessalines's figure, and probably the most sympathetic presentation, is probably Dupont's *Jean-Jacques Dessalines*.

3. Throughout the chapter, all quotes from all three plays will come from that volume, *The Haitian Trilogy*, and will be followed by page number in parenthesis.

4. For an overview of the racial hierarchy in the Saint Domingue colony, see Dubois *Avengers*. As we have seen, in *Toussaint Louverture*, Césaire also vividly portrays a racist social structure that lends its shape to the very structure of his book. As indicated in the notes of chapter 3, contemporary historians prefer the categories of enslaved people and free people of color to the somewhat reductive terms "blacks" and "mulattoes," although the latter have a long history in Haitian history and historiography.

5. In her important *Beyond the Slave Narrative: Politics, Sex and Narrative in the Haitian Revolution*, Deborah Jenson examines official documents, proclamations, and other little studied texts produced by Dessalines. The result is a tremendously complex figure with many links to later developments in anticolonial thought. Jenson highlights Dessalines' emphasis on black agency and the need for self-liberation by any means possible (in which she finds some connections to Malcolm X's rhetoric); the Pan-American discourse of freedom and cooperative sovereignty that dominates his attempts to establish commercial relations with the United States; and, in the same vein, Dessalines' attempt to export the revolution's emancipating impulse to neighboring colonies like Trinidad and Venezuela.

6. For a useful overview of the role of history in Walcott's works, which always connected to the dimensions of place and myth, see Part I of Burnett's *Derek Walcott*.

7. "I knew, from childhood, that I wanted to become a poet, and like any colonial child I was taught English literature as my natural inheritance. Forget the snow and the daffodils. They were real, more real than the heat and the oleander, perhaps, because they lived on the page, in imagination, and therefore in memory" (*What the Twilight*, 62)

8. Earlier in the play Christophe declares more explicitly: "You fools; I do not tie the shoelaces of history; I am the history of which you speak" (28).

9. In the autobiographical poem *Another Life* (1973), Walcott writes of himself and of his painter friend "Gregorias" (Dunstan St. Omer) as young artists:

> . . . drunkenly, or secretly, we swore,
> Disciples of that astigmatic saint,
> That we would never leave the island
> Until we had put down, in paint, in words,
> As palmists learn the network of a hand,
> All of its sunken, leaf-choked ravines,
> Every neglected, self-pitying inlet

Muttering in brackish dialect, the ropes of mangroves
From which old soldier crabs slipped
Surrendering to slush,
Each ochre track seeking some hilltop and
Losing itself in an unfinished phrase . . .
   (Walcott, *Collected*, 194)

10. A similar critique of a Caribbean rhetoric of *male* heroism informs Guadeloupean novelist Daniel Maximin's *L'isolé soleil* [*Lone Sun*] (1981), where the mass suicide of Louis Delgrés's men against Napoleon's forces in 1802 is contrasted to the less celebrated persistence of *women* who survive in order to patiently, and without the pyrotechnics, attempt to build a better future. For an interesting take on the role of the rhetoric of heroism in the very different case of Puerto Rico, see Sotomayor, "La imaginería nacionalista" (*Hilo de Aracne*). Of great interest also is José Martí's ambiguous relation to that rhetoric of heroism, given his iconic status in the Caribbean; see "El reposo de los héroes" in Ramos.

11. We may establish a connection between Toussaint's attitude toward France's "civilized" ideals and Césaire's words, examined in chapter 3, about France not colonizing "in the name" of the Declaration of the Rights of Man, only to begrudgingly acknowledge immediately that maybe those principles did play a role in France's self-appointed "civilizing" role (*Nègre je suis*, 69–70). Thus we see the ubiquity of the colonized subject's double bind with regards to the modern/colonial world system.

12. For a concise overview of the ways the image of Toussaint has been construed by friends and enemies, see the afterword of Madison Smartt Bell's *Toussaint Louverture*. For a view of the revolution that tries to go beyond the almost exclusive emphasis on heroic leaders like Toussaint, see Fick, *The Making of Haiti*; and Fouchard, *The Haitian Maroons*.

13. Both Thieme (*Derek Walcott*, 147) and King (*Derek Walcott and West Indian*, 326) suggest that Yette, divided between her love for the earth and her desire for the city, is a more complex character than Pompey, the simple pleasant totally committed to the land. I agree with that assessment, and Yette's complexity may make her a better representative of the complex pulls (ranging from subsistence farming to insertion into international markets) that have dominated Haiti's history. The play, however, oversimplifies that complexity by racializing it—Yette claims "The white part of me is the town / the black part of me is the country" (36). The reduction of those tensions to racial stereotypes detracts from their presentation in the play.

14. In Walcott's most "epic" work, *Omeros*, one of the main protagonists, the Fisherman Achille, also receives an "education" that gently pushes him away from grand heroic and tragic models of emancipation. Attempting to escape his limited and limiting surroundings, Achille travels in a dream back to the Africa of his ancestors. There, part of his lesson will be the acceptance of his history and legacy: not the passive acceptance that justifies or is indifferent to the injustices of the past, but the ability to fully embrace and inhabit his creolized reality with its many resources and possibilities, in order to better address the injustices of the present. After that initiatory dream, Achille's accepted field of action will be his local, seemingly unglamorous everyday surroundings.

15. To the discussion of the problems that Yette faces within the plot of the play, we might add at another level an analysis of the role Walcott gives her in the play, particularly her association with the Haitian earth itself. Although Yette resists working the soil at first, Pompey gradually educates her about the importance of working the land—a land that she herself sym-

bolically embodies, since we are told that "her skin the same shade as the ground" (334). The feminization of the land (and the fatherland), and moreover the explicit presentation of women as representatives of the land and nature, often respond to problematic gendered categories that ultimately restrict the possibilities of women (more often than not, women of color) as actual human beings. We see a similar problem in the character of Helen in Walcott's *Omeros;* for that case, see Figueroa, *Not at Home.*

16. For the history of Black Power, see Joseph, *Waiting;* Joseph, ed., *The Black Power Movement;* and Ogbar, *Black Power.* For Walcott's personal ambivalence about the Black Power movement and its effects in the Caribbean (particularly Trinidad, where there were violent demonstrations in 1973 after Stokely Carmichael was banned from the island), see King, *Derek Walcott.*

17. All of these issues find complex expression in Walcott's most famous play, *Dream on Monkey Mountain* (1970). The play has been regarded as Walcott's response to the surge of Black Power movements, but even in that case it remains an ambivalent and complicated response. In the play, Makak decapitates the "white goddess" in his attempt to recover his black pride, but it was the white goddess who sent him on his quest to begin with. At the end of the play, Makak's peace with his situation and his identity could be regarded as a renunciation of the violent actions that dominate the previous sections of the play, or as an achievement that that violence, for better or worse, actually made possible.

18. For an overview of the role of racial discourses in the formation of Latin American, see Hyatt and Nettleford, eds., *Race*; and Mignolo, *The Idea.* For an accessible broader overview of the historical development and deployment of racial categories, see Rattansi.

19. Walcott writes in "What the Twilight Says": "One kind of writer, generally the entertainer, says, 'I will write in the language of the people however gross or incomprehensible'" another says: "Nobody else go'understand this, you hear, so le' me write English"; while the third is dedicated to purifying the language of the tribe, and it is he who is jumped on by both sides for pretentiousness or playing white. He is the mulatto of style. The traitor. The assimilator" (*What the Twilight,* 8–9). Walcott is, naturally, the third kind of writer, and his justified resentment against those who jumped on him from both sides is only matched by his rhetorical unfairness, which condescendingly reduces all attempts to write in "the language of the people" as the work of mere "entertainers." Evidently, the accusation does not even do justice to his own use of vernacular Creole in his poetry. On the other hand, Anton in *The Haitian Earth* captures Walcott's tensions as a poet with the imperative for political commitment in the age of Black Power when he complains "Perhaps I should not be a writer but a soldier" (306).

20. Toussaint did have a close relation to his master, Bayon de Libertat, manager of the Bréda plantation. He was already a free black by the time the revolution started in 1791. As for Toussaint's feelings for his former master, the records suggest that they were indeed affectionate; in one of his writings, reflecting on how Bayon granted him his freedom, Toussaint refers to his former master as "one of those men who think more of their duties to fulfill toward oppressed humanity than the product of work of an unfortunate being" (Smartt Bell, *Toussaint,* 70). Thus, Walcott's fictional encounter between Toussaint and Calixte Bréda may be excessive in its pathos, but not totally inaccurate in its portrayal of Toussaint's initial position between two worlds. For an excellent overview of Toussaint's situation before he joined the revolution, see Smartt Bell, *Toussaint.*

21. In "Monotonies of History" Chris Bongie attempts to link the figure of the mulatto Vastey in *The Haitian Trilogy* to Walcott's own conflicts as a mulatto intellectual. The essay

makes many important points about Vastey, although it tends to oversimplify the plays' criticisms of Dessalines and Christophe as mainly examples of the "Mulatto Legend" reading of Haitian history, which serves the self-legitimating purposes of the mulatto elite. At the same time, Anton's important presence is relegated to a footnote.

22. For Walcott's religious preoccupations, see D'Aguiar, "In God We Trust."

23. Aside from the need to make the distinction between love and forgiveness, Deacon Dale's conception of love is significantly different from Derrida's in his belief that "the man who whips you cuts his own flesh," that is to say, in his mystical assertion that in spite of their violence against each other, humans are spiritually one. The logical conclusion is that in hurting the other I hurt myself (and vice versa). Derrida is more Levinasian in his approach: forgiveness, as he understands it, would be compromised by the belief that in loving the other I love myself. The radical alterity of the other must be preserved.

24. For a useful overview of the moral dilemmas posed by Truth Commissions, see Hayner, *Unspeakable Truths*.

25. For the U.S. occupation of Haiti, see Renda, *Taking Haiti*; and Schmidt, *United States*. For an insightful assessment of the 2010 earthquake's connections to Haiti's political and economic situation, see Farmer, *Haiti After*.

26. C. L. R. James praises a similar description of the events in France on the part of Saint Domingue slaves: "And meanwhile, what of the slaves? They had heard of the revolution and had construed it in their own image: the white slaves in France had risen, and killed their masters, and were now enjoying the fruits of the earth. It was greatly inaccurate in fact, but they had caught the spirit of the thing" (*Black Jacobins*, 81).

Chapter 5

1. Unless otherwise indicated, all translations from the play are from the 2005 edition of the 1978 version translated by J. Michael Dash and Glissant himself. There is an older translation of this version of the play, made by Juris Silenieks in 1981. The longer 1961 version of the play was performed on the French radio in 1971. The shorter 1978 version was streamlined for stage performances, and has indeed been performed several times. Overall the "version scénique" retains the substance of the original longer play, mainly shortening long speeches and dialogues, and eliminating a subplot concerning General Charles Belair. It is not my objective here to compare these two versions, except to indicate that in the longer version Toussaint comes across as slightly more assertive (he has more lines). Although I will focus on the latter version throughout this chapter, when necessary I will quote passages from the 1961 version that did not make it to the 1978 version; in those cases, the translations are mine.

To further complicate matters, the Dash/Glissant translation eliminates some very significant lines and scenes from 1978 version of the play. When quoting lines from the 1978 version that *do not* appear in the Dash/Glissant translation I will use Silenieks's translation, and I will use the translator's name in the parenthetical reference.

2. James himself wrote a play on the revolution, titled *Toussaint Louverture*, in 1936 (Paul Robeson played the title character in the staging of that version). In 1967 James rewrote the play, retitling it *The Black Jacobins*. In James's play, the contrast between Moyse and Toussaint plays a central role. The 1967 version is included in Hill; the original version was published in 2013.

3. Césaire presents his hypothesis on Toussaint's self-sacrifice in chapter 15 of the third section of his *Toussaint Louverture,* titled precisely "Le sacrifice" ("The Sacrifice").

4. It could be argued that Césaire does acknowledge the dilemma that Glissant confronts if one contrasts his *Toussaint Louverture,* with its admiration for Toussaint's careful planning for a postcolonial future, to his *Tragedie du roi Christophe,* with its begrudged admiration for Christophe's megalomaniac, but grandiosely tragic, attempt ennoble the black race through his own self-aggrandizement. Christophe remains, nonetheless, a problematic figure, since it is not possible for the author to totally overcome the horrors of the historical Christophe. Additionally, Christophe did share Toussaint's economic concerns about the international market. The contrast between Ariel and Caliban in *Une tempête* may be closer to the tensions in Glissant's play.

5. Certain critics refer to the movement as the "Front Antillo-Guyanais pour l'Indépendence" (for example, Jones, "We Were Going," 249), a name that Glissant himself has used in an interview (Couffon, *Visite à Edouard Glissant,* 50). The ambiguity is significant, as it suggests Glissant's ambivalent position with regards to nationalist politics from early in his career. The Front itself was ambiguous in its proposal of a status for the French Antilles, although it took a clear stand for Antillean self-determination, against assimilationalist departmentalization as it had been established after World War II, and in favor of establishing stronger links with the rest of the Caribbean region. For a lucid examination of the main text produced by the Front, *Les Antilles et la Guyane à l'heure de la décolonization,* see Nesbitt, *Caribbean Critique.*

6. As David Macey indicates, in the appropriation of Fanon by postcolonial studies, Fanon's work has not always been adequately placed in its Caribbean context. See also Mardorossian, "From Fanon to Glissant."

7. Macaïa (presented in the list of characters as a "rebel leader") is based on the historical Congo leader Macaya, who led a band of slaves that always operated on the margins of Toussaint's army. In fact he was briefly taken prisoner by Toussaint in 1795, and actively resisted Toussaint's attempts to impose the plantation system on the former slaves. Interestingly, at least in the early years of the revolution, the historical Macaya insisted on his fidelity to his African (Congolese) royalist political views, declaring himself a "subject of the king of Congo." Macaya also appears briefly as a character in Victor Hugo's *Bug Jargal* (1826). In his play, Glissant omits all of those details and portrays the character as the anarchistic, libertarian opponent to Toussaint. For the historical Macaya, see Thornton, "I am the Subject"; and the appropriate sections in Fick, *The Making of Haiti.*

8. At the same time, it is important not to identify Macaïa's "anarchistic" forest time with some mythical, circular or "premodern" conception of time. Macaïa's forest is the maroon territory in the mountains, his time is not the supposedly progressive march "forward" of modernity/coloniality, but the oppositional time of the colonial difference, which aspires to what one might call, following Dussel, a transmodern vision. Slaves were always already part of modernity, as its underside. Thus, Macaïa's argument is not abstract, about different conceptions of time, but political, about coloniality disguised as "progress," which is the time unit of "modernity."

9. For overviews of roads taken and not taken in Haiti's history, see Dubois, *The Aftershocks*; Fatton, *Haiti's Predatory Republic*; and Farmer, *The Uses.*

10. For Quijano, "One of the fundamental axes of this model of power is the social classification of the world's population around the idea of race, a mental construction that expresses the basic experience of colonial domination and pervades the more important dimensions of global power, including its specific rationality: Eurocentrism. The racial axis has a colonial origin and

character, but it has proven to be more durable and stable than the colonialism in whose matrix it was established" ("Coloniality of Power," 533).

11. In the 1961 longer version of the play, Toussaint states: "Danton, Robespierre, Santhonax, Saint-Just, they are all gone! The Revolution is lost in France; we will defend it here" (111; my translation). This acknowledgment of the French Revolution's most radical actors, and the need to bring that movement to its logical radical consequences, certainly make Toussaint exemplary of the "black Jacobins" that James refers to, even if it does not necessarily reveal a full acknowledgment of the *transmodern* dimension of the Haitian Revolution. In this case, as in others, Toussaint comes across as a more complex figure in Glissant's older version of his play.

12. For some reason the soldier's significant remark and Toussaint's dismissive response ("those who die are eating the earth") are not included in Dash's and Glissant's translation, but they do appear in Silenieks's version.

13. See Couffon, *Visite à Edouard Glissant,* 33–35 and 53–59.

14. Evidently the *figurative* use of the concept of slavery in European revolutionary rhetoric was not unusual, with the *Marsellaise* itself objecting a return to "l'antique esclavage." Among some thinkers the paradoxical rise of the United States as a slave-holding bastion of liberty did not go unnoticed either. See Buck-Morss, *Hegel*; Davis, *The Problem;* and Blackburn, *The American.*

15. As Michel-Rolph Trouillot poignantly points out, "The Haitian Revolution . . . entered history with the peculiar characteristic of being unthinkable even as it happened" (*Silencing the Past,* 73). Of course, that "unthinkability," which is the unthinkability of black slave agency and full humanity in the minds of even "enlightened" Europeans, is itself a sign of the coloniality of power. Buck-Morss's book on Hegel and Haiti offers a compelling overview of the impact of the Haitian Revolution on European thinkers beyond the German philosopher.

16. In describing the revolting slaves as "transmodern" with regards to the ideals of European Enlightenment I do not mean to say that all of them *consciously* shared one abstract, alternative universalist project. Evidently, the revolting slaves came with all kinds of individual and group perspectives and designs, united by the immediate desire to emancipate themselves from slavery. The point here is that in this they were not different from any other human collectivity coming together in revolutionary action (not all the people who rally around a cause do so for the same reason). Buck-Morss aptly illuminates this point in "Universal History," the second essay of *Hegel, Haiti, and Universal History.*

17. Quite surprisingly, the Dash/Glissant translation of the play eliminates the powerful, though humiliating for Toussaint, scene of the removal of his uniform and insignias. To complicate matters further, and limiting ourselves to the original French, in the 1961 version of the play Toussaint retains a lucidity that is eliminated from the 1978 version; he shows this when he states: "We are free today because we are the strongest. The consul retains slavery in Martinique and Bourbon. Thus, we will become slaves when he becomes the strongest" (112; my translation). The significant changes from the 1961 to the 1978 French versions, and then from the 1978 French version to the Dash/Glissant translation suggest a keen indecisiveness, on Glissant's part, as to how he wants to depict Toussaint as a historical figure but also, equally important, as a Caribbean symbol.

Walsh offers an extremely valuable examination of the implications of the historical Toussaint's ambivalent relation to France and Napoleon, as expressed in Toussaint's "texts," which range from letters, to his 1801 Constitution, to the "mémoire" he wrote in prison (*Free and French in the Caribbean*).

18. In a lyrical passage of 2007's *Une nouvelle région du monde*, Glissant links the prison in the Jura mountains to other symbolic spaces of black imprisonment, such as Gorée (in today's Senegal), from where many slaves were shipped to the New World; Dubuc Castle in Martinique, which received some of those slaves; and Robben Island, where Nelson Mandela was imprisoned. With regards to Toussaint, Glissant writes: "The Joux Fort close to Pontarlier where Toussaint Louveture was thrown and where he died of hunger and cold; I always imagine it like a boat that sails across the Jura mountains as its bow beats the swelling waves of the black forests" (*Une nouvelle*, 151; my translation). All of those prisons are "places of both imprisonment and liberation" (ibid.; my translation). An important dimension that *Une nouvelle* brings into the picture, as it links Toussaint to other geographies and time periods, is what Glissant calls, throughout *Mémoires des esclavages* (2007), the need for "transversal histories" of slaveries, slave trades, and liberation struggles, through which the transnational character of slavery and racism, and the resistances against them, can be explored.

19. Glissant's relation to Creole was always ambiguous, to say the least. Although *Monsieur Toussaint*'s prologue refers to the Creole segments as expressing "the pure pleasure of writing at last a language *as one hears it*" (14; Glissant's emphasis), he has severe pages in *Le discours antillais* on Creole as linguistic expression of colonial alienation. In his own work Glissant uses a form of creolized French, and he was critical of the "Creolité" movement as potentially essentialist, whereas he preferred the term "creolization," which pointed to a more fluid, never final aesthetic (Glissant, *L'imaginaire*, 30–31). One might conclude from his comments that Glissant is mainly trying to avoid a certain kind of exoticism that he seems to associate with writing in Creole. His theoretical distinction between *langue* and *langage* in *Le discours* may be in part a way to justify his choice: even while writing in French (*langue*), his outlook, style and attitude (his *langage*) are Caribbean. For a good overview of Glissant's linguistic strategies, see Britton, *Edouard Glissant*.

20. Regardless of how one ultimately judges Glissant's late works, it is hard to disagree with Bongie when he states that "an increasing number of academic readers of Glissant, have, in line with Hallward, understandably registered a certain unease, and even distress, when it comes to his later writings" (*Friends*, 339). Although Britton has consistently argued for the persistent political currency of Glissant's ideas, one can detect echoes of that "unease" when she points out in 1999—that is, before the publication of Hallward's book—that in his 1990s works Glissant "increasingly writes as if the values of Relation, chaos, and diversity have in fact already prevailed" (*Edouard Glissant*, 9). At the very least, then, one could accuse Glissant of unskillfully failing to translate the connection between his ideas and reality into effective writing. Many of the core arguments for or against Glissant revolve around deciding whether in his late works he simply moved toward different, more abstract concerns (which might make him irrelevant or not, depending on whether one finds those concerns useful in the articulation of one's *concrete* battles), or whether he is actually (and problematically and perhaps self-servingly) arguing that engagement in concrete battles of any kind has become a trivial pursuit in our globalized world, and that any battle that does not address primordially global concerns is in fact complicit with the forces of neoliberal globalization. While I lean toward the first alternative, proponents of both positions have found supporting quotations from Glissant's many writings.

21. Glissant equals the "new region of the world" (one his last images for global interrelatedness) to the tout-monde: "It is never true that we are naive in this region, it is not a refuge of dreams or a phantom of hope. Just as well, in it we do not stumble anymore. It is not a chosen land. It does not belong to anyone. *As you already know, without knowing anything yet,* we ac-

claim it and call it Whole-World [Tout-Monde]" (*Une nouvelle*, 76; my translation; Glissant's italics).

22. In his two insightful chapters on Glissant in *Caribbean Critique*, Nesbitt sides with Hallward and Bongie on the criticism of the seemingly apolitical character of late Glissant's theoretical writings. However, Nesbitt also points out that in spite of its more critical focus on the need for a nationalist anticolonial project, *Le discours antillais* already displayed what Nesbitt terms "utopian . . . aesthetic musings thrown out to give a vague veneer of political investment devoid of any sense of what might be involved in constructing the 'collectivity' he [Glissant] invokes" (242). Additionally, as Nesbitt clearly elucidates, both *Le discours antillais* and Glissant's first novel *Le Lezarde* are marked by a clear pessimism and skepticism about the possibility of an anticolonial project of the kind Fanon, for example, had articulated. Even during that period celebrated by some critics as his most "political" Glissant remained stuck in "l'impuissance à sortir de l'impasse" (*Discours*, 13; quoted in the context of the present discussion in Nesbitt, *Caribbean*, 241). As I have tried to demonstrate in this chapter, *Monsieur Toussaint* is also an eloquent example of Glissant's impasse.

23. Boaventura de Sousa Santos's concern with "other (non-Occidentalist) knowledges" (which also imply other imaginaries) offers good examples of areas in which some of Glissant's ideas against the "totalitarian drive of the single root" might be applicable. See, among several of his texts, *Another Knowledge Is Possible*.

24. The question still remains of how the "insights" of Glissant's deconstruction of the logic of coloniality translate into concrete political action. This question is further complicated by the fact that Glissant acknowledges that historical imperialism, in its colonial joining of distant regions of the globe, played an important, albeit paradoxical role in the development of the "totalité-monde" (another term for the "tout-monde") that he praises (see, for example, *Introduction*, 88). Bongie makes this point most cogently in his critique of Glissant's notion of "mondialité" (akin to "tout-monde"), which the Martinican author attempts to distinguish from "mondialisation" (linked to neoliberal globalization) in *La cohée* (Bongie, *Friends*, 334–38). Reading somewhat against the grain of Glissant's rather excessive optimism, I would suggest that the question of practical usefulness remains unanswered because those poetic musings (productive and provocative as they might be) are not *solutions,* but rather extensions of the *impasse* (between Toussaint and Macäia) already present in *Monsieur Toussaint*—attempts to make that impasse *productive* by making it a necessary point of departure rather than a dead-end conclusion. One might argue it is an impasse that any serious post/colonial writer must address, without oversimplifying it, even at the risk of remaining indefinitely perplexed by its conflicting pulls. That perplexity need not entail inaction, and it does not seem to have paralyzed Glissant's engagement with concrete causes (regardless of one's assessment of his political activities).

25. A phrase that Monsieur Libertat the colonist repeats against Toussaint several times in the play is "you cannot change what exists" (*Monsieur Toussaint*, 33; 34; 35; 40; my translation). The use of the word "exists" naturalizes as an ontological given the colonial social order of slavery. Not surprisingly, Toussaint states when talking about liberty and equality, "I work to make them exist" (*Monsieur Toussaint*, 33; my translation). The Dash/Glissant version translates most of those instances (except the first one) as "you will not change the way thing are," a phrasing that softens the ontological essentialism of the original.

26. Glissant's concept of "unpredictability," in conjunction with "tout-monde" and its derivatives, could enter into an interesting dialogue with Hardt's and Negri's "multitude."

27. I am contrasting *Monsieur Toussaint* to Glissant's theoretical works in terms of the impasse with regard to possibilities of action in a post(neo)colonial context. The same questions and preoccupations appear in his novels, beginning with *La Lézarde* (1959) in which the Lézarde river of Martinique, moving from the mountains (associated with maroon slaves) to the coast (associated with captive slaves), already symbolically links many of the positions that I have discussed. While discussing the novels would be too lengthy for the purposes of this book, I would still maintain that, although the novels are certainly more complex in their presentation of Glissant's concerns, his one play still presents the impasse that I am concerned with more concisely and dramatically than any of them. The novels themselves became increasingly abstract and theoretical throughout Glissant's career, to the point that the theoretical volume *Traité du Tout-Monde* has a section presumably written by Mathieu Béluse, a character from *Tout-Monde* who is one of many recurring characters in Glissant's fiction ever since his first novel. For the treatment of the maroon slave in Glissant's novels, see Rochmann, *L'esclave*.

Chapter 6

1. All quotes from the novel in this chapter come from Jonathan Tittler's excellent translation. However, there are very few instances when I have felt Tittler's translation misses an important nuance of the original; in those cases I have modified the translation, and I have clearly indicated it.

2. In 1986 Zapata Olivella published *El fusilamiento del diablo* and in 1993 *Hemingway, el cazador de la muerte*, both of them more formally experimental than his early realistic novels, although without reaching the extreme complexity or sustained lyricism of *Changó*. The most thorough study of Zapata Olivella's works as a whole can be found in Tillis.

3. William Luis, editor of the prestigious *Afro-Hispanic Review*, opens a number of the journal dedicated to Zapata Olivella with this statement: "Manuel Zapata Olivella is one of the greatest writers of Afro-Latin American descent and has earned a permanent place among the best writers in Latin America. His *Changó, el gran putas* (1983) contains all the characteristics of the finest novels of the Boom and post-Boom periods, which gave Spanish American literature instant world recognition, and Zapata Olivella's novel should be required reading for any serious specialist of literature. Unfortunately, this is not the case. We still live in an era in which many scholars of Latin American literature cannot look beyond the writer's African heritage" (5).

4. Some of Zapata Olivella's texts on Afro-Colombian folklore have been compiled in *Manuel Zapata Olivella, por los senderos de sus ancestros*. See also *El hombre colombiano*. Zapata Olivella also traveled with his sister, the dancer Delia Zapata Olivella, in tours that were meant to display Afro-Colombian music in the country and internationally. See his autobiography, *¡Levántate mulato!* For an overview of Zapata Olivella's research as an anthropologist and how it ties in with his work as a novelist, see the biography by José Luis Díaz Granados, published in the website dedicated to Zapata Olivella, manuelzapataolivella.org.

5. For a useful and concise overview of Afro-Colombian history, see the first two chapters of Prescott's *Without Hatreds or Fears*. For a broader perspective on Afro-Latin America see Andrews.

6. In *The Colombian Novel* Raymond Williams expertly situates Zapata Olivella in the context of Colombian fiction. Marvin A. Lewis's important *Treading the Ebony Path* situates the novelist in the more specific context of Afro-Colombian literature.

7. For an overview of some of the most important explorations of the Middle Passage in the Hispanic world, see DeCosta-Willis, "Meditations on History." See also Jackson, "The Black Novel."

8. For a detailed exposition of the novel's structure, see Aguiar. For an appreciation of the degree to which Zapata Olivella truly intended his novel to be a black *epic* (an approach that invites a comparison to Derek Walcott's *Omeros*), see Cuervo Hewitt, "Luís de Camoens."

9. In several of his essays Zapata Olivella refers to works by Jahn and by Tempels, which seem to have influenced his understanding of "Muntu." Those works are certainly not unproblematic, particularly Tempels's. See Coetzee and Roux, eds., *African Philosophy Reader*, chapter 2.

10. For an examination of how language is used in the novel to develop an Afrocentric perspective, see Zoggyie, "*Lengua e identidad.*"

11. I use the notion of "Afrocentrism," with regards to Zapata Olivella, in a very general way to describe his attempt to provide an African (or Afro-descendant) perspective on events (such as slavery, colonialism, and the very value of African culture) in which the dominant perspective has been Eurocentric. Zapata Olivella's assumption is that, in spite of important differences between black groups and individuals, there were shared experiences that can often politically unify the aspirations of Afro-descendants. The term "Afrocentrism" is *not* supposed to indicate an essential or biological unity of all Africans, or the ethnocentric idea that Africans should ignore values and concepts that are not "authentically" African. See Ossa, "*Changó el gran putas* Afrocentric Discourse." For a critique of ethnocentric Afrocentrism (which, paradoxically, often relies on colonial European concepts of what is "African"), see Mudimbe, *Invention of Africa*; and Appiah, *In My Father's House*. It must be mentioned that Zapata Olivella's concept of Africa often draws upon questionable sources like Tempels and Jahn, but his views are always mediated by his direct experience of the survival of African customs in his native Colombia.

12. The living are aware of not only their ancestors but also themselves as ancestors of future generations. For the importance of the link to ancestors, in addition to the works of Tempels and Jahn on which Zapata Olivella relied directly, see Henry, *Caliban's Reason*; Coetzee and Roux, eds., *African Philosophy Reader*; and Houtondji, *African Philosophy*.

13. Although gender is not explicitly thematized as an important locus of oppression/resistance in Zapata Olivella's work, there are strong female characters in his fiction (particularly the black matriarch "La Cotena" in *Chambacú* and Agne Brown in *Changó*) that open the door to a productive exploration of that category.

14. Lucía Ortiz aptly describes the collective struggles of Afro-Colombians that *Chambacú* portrays; see her "*Chambacú.*"

15. For broader historical perspectives on slavery, see Meltzer, *Slavery*; and Patterson, *Slavery and Social Death*. For an overview of the modern/colonial African slave trade, see Davis, *Inhuman*; and Blackburn, *The American*.

16. For different perspectives on the role of enlightened ideals in the Haitian Revolution, besides those of James in *Black Jacobins* and Césaire in *Toussaint Louverture*, see Fick, *The Making of Haiti*; and Nesbitt, *Universal*.

17. Zapata Olivella summarizes many of his observations on the importance of the category of "race" in the Latin American context in his autobiography, *¡Levántate mulato!* For a thorough overview, see Dhouti Martínez, "Rewriting the Other." See also Janis, "Negritude."

18. For a cogent critique of multiculturalism as commonly celebrated in the Unites States, see San Juan Jr., *Racism*.

19. For black literature and humanism in Latin America, see Jackson, *Black Literature*.
20. On the topic of race and Marxist revolution, see also James's fascinating conversations with Trotsky, collected in *At the Rendezvous*.
21. See Verna, *Petión y Bolívar*; Lasso, "Haití"; and Gómez, "La Revolución."
22. For several examples, see Bolívar, *Liberator*.
23. For recent attempts to look at Bolívar without falling into the hero worship paradigm, see Lynch, *Simón Bolívar*; and Langley, *Simón Bolívar: Venezuelan Rebel*.
24. Santiago Castro-Gómez has examined Karl Marx's writings on Bolívar, in which the German philosopher directly addresses Bolívar's treatment of Padilla, an important episode in Zapata Olivella's novel. For Marx, the fact that Bolívar executed Padilla but did not exert violence against his main political opponent, the creole Santander, was indicative of Latin America's absence of modernity. In such a pre-modern, colonial society, "bloodlines and ethnic privilege still constituted the fundamental criteria for honor and distinction" (Castro-Gómez, "(Post)coloniality," 263). Marx subscribed to the notion that "colonialism was nothing more than the past of modernity" (ibid.). As Castro-Gómez clarifies, colonialism/coloniality are in fact an intrinsic part of the project of modernity, and ethnic/racial hierarchies are inherent to the articulation of Eurocentric modern/colonial hegemony. "Coloniality is not the past of modernity; it is simply its other face" (ibid., 283).
25. For the regional and hemispheric impact of the Haitian Revolution, see Geggus, *Impact*; and Gaspar and Geggus, eds., *Turbulent Time*; and also Genovese, *From Rebellion*.
26. In his interview in Harris, Zapata Olivella briefly addresses the diversity of the treatments of the religious theme in his fiction.
27. Ifa is a traditional divination system in Yoruba religion; its answers to diverse questions and situations encompass a rich array of Yoruba oral tradition—poetry, proverbs and stories—that also embodies aspects of the Yoruba worldview. Orunla is the orisha who rules the oracle. See Bascom's books. For Ifa as practiced in Cuban Santeria, see Murphy, *Santeria*.
28. See Cros Sandoval, *Worldview*; and Pinn, *Varieties*.
29. Awole's legend appears in several sources, among which see Abimbola, *Ifá Will Mend*; Feraudy Espino, *Yoruba*; Smith, *Kingdoms*; and Atmore and Stacey, *Black Kingdoms*. There is always the possibility that Zapata Olivella found a version of Changó's story that does include his curse, since his exile from his kingdom is certainly part of his myth. I have not been able to find such a version of his story, although he always appears as an impulsive, passionate, wrathful, and therefore fearsome orisha.
30. In his interview with Krakusin, Zapata Olivella indicates that although Changó is a very important figure, he is not necessarily the best one to emblematize the African diaspora as a whole. He considers that Yemayá, goddess of the sea and mother of the other orishas, would be the most appropriate figure. He goes on to state that Changó is sometimes privileged out of chauvinism ("machismo"), and that even women often give priority to the warrior god with his life-giving phallus. Then he states that he made sure that Yemayá was acknowledged in the novel, which includes a long poem to her (Krakusin, "Conversación," 20). It is hard to figure out what to make of Zapata Olivella's words, for they in fact constitute a possible criticism against his novel: if Yemaya was the better symbol, why construct the novel around Changó?
31. Close to Zapata Olivella would be Miguel Ángel Asturias in texts like *Mulata de tal* (1963). Again, in highlighting the singularity of *Changó*, I am not referring to writing *about* myth, or from a dual perspective that alternates between mythical and rational worldviews, but

rather to the sustained *attempt* to create a mythical framework and focalization for the events portrayed in the novel, even the historical ones.

32. One possible way of understanding Changó's role in the novel would be to link him to the slave trade in Africa before (or independently of) the Europeans, and also to role of some African tribes and groups as middlemen in the European slave trade. There are allusions in the novel to Muslim slave trade in sub-Saharan Africa. Thus, Changó's curse might point to the agency and involvement of Africans in their own history, for both good and evil as in any human group, as opposed to the dominant view of Africans as mere objects of European designs. If that is the intent of the novel, it is certainly not developed in any significant way. For slavery in Africa see Lovejoy, *Transformations*; and Miers and Kopitoff, eds., *Slavery in Africa*. The topic of the place of slavery among Africans in the context of the Atlantic slave trade remains controversial, and it is certainly problematic to contrast it to the modern/colonial, globalized trade organized by European empires. See Manning, *Slavery*; Thornton, *Africa and Africans*; and Davis, *Inhuman Bondage*.

33. Ian Smart calls *Changó* "liberation literature," in an explicit analogy to liberation theology (15). In his suggestive reading, Changó becomes a "trickster" figure who works for the liberation of his ekobios. For a critique of Smart's use of the category "trickster," see Ossa, "There is Nothing."

34. For a recent attempt to address theodical concerns from the Liberation Theology perspective, see Sobrino, *Where Is God?*

35. See Pinn's *Varieties* and *African American Humanist Principles*.

36. For an overview of "the problem of evil" from antiquity, see Larrimore, *Problem of Evil*. See also Rowe, *God and the Problem*.

37. Timothy J. Cox also notices the problem that I am describing, and he reads Changó's actions, from the perspective of the Middle Passage, as a warning that any attempt to recover a pure, original Africa "will lead to a heritage of internal, "national" strifes, not to a pure or idyllic order between the natural and the supernatural worlds" (92). Ultimately, Changó's actions are explained by his excessive vitality, which makes him an all-too-human source of both creativity and war, for ultimately "it is humankind's own life-force Nature that multiplies its sorrows" (ibid.). It is that vitality, with both positive and negative consequences, that the African diaspora has remained faithful to, and which Zapata Olivella celebrates in Cox's reading. Cox concludes by stating that if his reading is not a satisfactory answer to the question of *why* the evils of the Middle Passage occurred (thus bringing up explicitly the question of theodicy), then "the modern mind had better look beyond *the spirit* and instead search for *a reason*, because all the spirit reveals is its mystery" (ibid., 93). Thus, the novel's mythical frame paradoxically invites us to look beyond it to *history* for answers. While I fundamentally agree with many of Cox's points, my reading in the next section puts the emphasis on why religion and myth, or "the spirit," consistently keep coming up in works like *Changó* in spite of repeated attempts to leave them behind.

38. The phrase "all bloodlines" (in Spanish, "todas las sangres") also alludes to the novel *Todas las sangres*, by the Peruvian José María Arguedas. Not unlike Zapata Olivella for Afro-descendants, Arguedas was a great defender of Indigenous rights and culture in his novels, which also try to combine historical and mythical perspectives. It should be noticed that Arguedas was interested in Liberation Theology, and that one of the movement's main figures, Gustavo Gutierrez, acknowledges the priest character in Arguedas's *Todas las sangres* as a "precursor of liberation theology" (Tamayo, *La teología*, 95).

39. For further links between Zapata Olivella's vision and Dussel's philosophy, see González de Allen, "Enrique Dussel."

40. For an overview of Liberation Theology, see Tamayo, *La teología*. See also the classic expositions by Gutierrez (*Theology of Liberation*) and Ellacurria and Sobrino (*Mysterium Liberationis*). For Liberation Theology in the African American context, see Cone, *Black Theology*.

Conclusion

1. In a well-known passage of *Specters of Marx*, Derrida states about the ideal of democratic participation: "Even beyond the regulating idea in its classic form, the idea, if that is still what it is, of democracy to come, its "idea" as event of a pledged injunction that orders one to summon the very thing that will never present itself in the form of full presence, is the opening of this gap between an infinite promise (always untenable at least for the reason that it calls for the infinite respect of the singularity *and* infinite alterity of the other as much as for the respect of countable, calculable, subjectal equality between anonymous singularities) and the determined, necessary, but also necessarily inadequate forms of what has to be measured against this promise" (*Specters*, 81). The revolution in Haiti occupies a similar "gap" between the "infinite promise" of universal emancipation that it invokes, and the "necessarily inadequate forms" that those aspirations have taken in Haitian history. As I suggest later in the afterword, in Haiti's case that "gap" is complicated by the persistence of a colonial frame—both internal, in the form of local elites, and external, in the form of global colonial interests—that opposes Haiti and what it represents.

2. Pat Robertson's words, which naturally provoked much controversy, can be found on many news Web sites on the Internet; for a succinct version see http://www.cnn.com/2010/US/01/13/haiti.pat.robertson/.

3. See Maldonado-Torres, "On the Coloniality," and also Wynter, "Unsettling."

4. Sylvia Wynter eloquently criticizes "the ongoing imperative of securing the well-being of our present ethnoclass (i.e., Western bourgeois) conception of the human, Man, which overrepresents itself as it were the human itself" ("Unsettling," 260). That "overrepresentation" of one concept of the human to the point of overtaking the human itself is characteristic of that surplus of being that characterizes the coloniality of being/power.

Works Cited

Abimbola, Wande. *Ifá Will Mend Our Broken World: Thoughts on Yoruba Religion and Culture in Africa and the Diaspora.* Roxbury, MA: AIM Books, 1997.

Aching, Gerard. "Beyond Sites of Execution: Haiti and the Historical Imagination in C. L. R. James and Alejo Carpentier." In *Sisyphus and Eldorado: Magical and Other Realisms in Caribbean Literature,* edited by Timothy J. Reiss, 103–25. Trenton, NJ: Africa World Press Inc., 2002.

Aguiar, Mario. "*Changó el gran putas o la tormentosa espiral del Muntu en América.*" *Estudios de literatura colombiana* 14 (2004): 11–30.

Allende, Isabel. *La isla bajo el mar.* New York: Vintage Español, 2010.

Andrews, George Reid. *Afro-Latin America, 1800–2000.* Oxford: Oxford University Press, 2004.

Appiah, Kwame Anthony. *In My Father's House: Africa in Philosophy of Culture.* Oxford: Oxford University Press, 1992.

Armet, Auguste. "Aimé Césaire, homme politique." In *Aimé Césaire: une pensée pour le XXIe siècle,* 185–97. Paris: Centre Césarien d'Études et de Recherches/Présence Africaine, 2003.

Arnold, A. James. *Modernism and Negritude: The Poetry and Poetics of Aimé Césaire.* Cambridge, MA: Harvard University Press, 1982.

Atmore, Anthony, and Gillian Stacey. *Black Kingdoms, Black Peoples: The West African Heritage.* London: Orbis Publishing, 1979.

Baer, William, ed. *Conversations with Derek Walcott.* Jackson: University Press of Mississippi, 1996.

Bajeux, Jean-Claude. *Antilia retrouvée. Claude McKay, Luis Palés Matos, Aimé Césaire, poetes noirs antillais.* Paris: Editions Caribéenes, 1983.

Bascom, William W. *Ifa: Communication Between Gods and Men in Western Africa.* Bloomington: Indiana University Press, 1991.

———. *Sixteen Cowries: Yoruba Divination from Africa to the New World.* Bloomington: Indiana University Press, 1980.

Baugh, Edward. "Of Men and Heroes: Walcott and the Haitian Revolution." *Callaloo* 28.1 (2005): 45–54.

Bell, Madison Smartt. *All Souls' Rising.* New York: Penguin, 1995.
———. *Master of the Crossroads.* New York: Penguin, 2000.
———. *The Stone that the Builder Refused.* New York: Vintage Books, 2004.
———. *Toussaint Louverture: A Biography.* New York: Pantheon Books, 2007.
Bernasconi, Robert. "African Philosophy's Challenge to Continental Philosophy." In *Postcolonial African Philosophy: A Critical Reader,* edited by Emmanuel Chukwudi Eze, 183–96. Oxford: Blackwell, 1992.
Bhabha, Homi K. *The Location of Culture.* London: Routledge, 1994.
Blackburn, Robin. *The American Crucible: Slavery, Emancipation, and Human Rights.* London: Verso, 2011.
———. *The Making of New World Slavery: From the Baroque to the Modern, 1492–1800.* London: Verso, 2010.
———. *The Overthrow of Colonial Slavery: 1776–1848.* London: Verso, 2011.
Blanco, Tomás. *El prejuicio racial en Puerto Rico.* Edited by Arcadio Díaz Quiñones. Río Piedras, PR: Ediciones Huracán, 1985.
———. *Sobre Palés Matos.* San Juan, PR: Biblioteca de autores puertorriqueños, 1950.
Bolívar, Simón. *The Liberator: Writings of Simón Bolívar.* Edited by David Bushnell. Translated by Frederick H. Fornoff. Oxford: Oxford University Press, 2003.
Bongie, Chris. *Friends and Enemies: The Scribal Politics of Post/Colonial Literature.* Liverpool: Liverpool University Press, 2008.
———. *Islands and Exiles: The Creole Identities of Post/Colonial Literature.* Stanford, CA: Stanford University Press, 1998.
———. "'Monotonies of History': Baron de Vastey and the Mulatto Legend of Derek Walcott's *The Haitian Trilogy.*" *Yale French Studies* 107 (2005): 70–107.
Bosch, Juan. *De Cristobal Colón a Fidel Castro: el Caribe, frontera imperial.* 3rd ed. Santo Domingo, República Dominicana: Editora Alfa y Omega, 1981.
Braithwaite, Kamau. *The Arrivants: A New World Trilogy.* Oxford: Oxford University Press, 1973.
Braziel, Jana Evans. "Re-membering Defilée: Dédée Bazile as Revolutionay Lieu de Mémoire." *Small Axe* 9.2 (September 2005): 57–85.
Breslin, Paul. *Nobody's Nation: Reading Derek Walcott.* Chicago: University of Chicago Press, 2001.
Britton, Celia M. *Edouard Glissant and Post Colonial Theory.* Charlottesville and London: University Press of Virginia, 1999.
———. "Globalization and Political Action in the Work of Edouard Glissant." *Small Axe* 30 (November 2009): 1–11.
Brown, Gordon S. *Toussaint's Clause: The Founding Fathers and the Haitian Revolution.* Jackson: University of Mississippi Press, 2005.
Buck-Morss, Susan. *Hegel, Haiti, and Universal History.* Pittsburgh, PA: University of Pittsburgh Press, 2009.
Buell, Lawrence. *The Future of Environmental Criticism.* Malden, MA: Blackwell Publishing, 2005.
Buenaventura, Enrique. *Teatro.* Bogotá: Ediciones Tercer Mundo, 1963.

Burnett, Paula. *Derek Walcott: Politics and Poetics.* Gainesville: University of Florida Press, 2000.

Cabrera, Lydia. *Páginas sueltas.* Miami, FL: Ediciones Universal, 1994.

Captain-Hidalgo, Yvonne. "Conversación con el Dr. Manuel Zapata Olivella." *Afro-Hispanic Review* 4.1 (1985): 26–32.

———. *The Culture of Fiction in the Works of Manuel Zapata Olivella.* Columbia: University of Missouri Press, 1993.

Carpentier, Alejo. *El arpa y la sombra.* México, D. F.: Siglo XXI Editores, 1979.

———. *Entrevistas.* Edited by Virgilio López Lemus. La Habana: Letras Cubanas, 1985.

———. *The Kingdom of This World.* Translated by Harriet de Onís. New York: Farrar, Straus & Giroux, 1957.

———. *El reino de este mundo.* San Juan: Editorial de la Universidad de Puerto Rico, 1994.

———. *Tientos y diferencias.* Montevideo: Editorial Arca, 1967.

Castro-Gómez, Santiago. "(Post)coloniality for Dummies: Latin American Perspectives on Modernity, Coloniality, and the Geopolitics of Knowledge." In *Coloniality at Large: Latin America and the Postcolonial Debate,* edited by Mabel Moraña, Enrique Dussel, and Carlos A. Jáuregui, 259–85. Durham, NC: Duke University Press, 2008.

Cateau, Heather, and S. H. H. Carrington, eds. *Capitalism and Slavery Fifty Years Later: Eric Eustace Williams—A Reassessment of the Man and His Ideas.* New York: Peter Lang, 2000.

Césaire, Aime. *Cahier d'un retour au pays natal.* Edited by Abiola Irele. Ibadan: New Horn Press Limited, 1994.

———. *Discourse on Colonialism.* Translated by Joan Pinkham. New York: Monthly Review Press, 2000.

———. "Letter to Maurice Thorez." Translated by Chike Jeffers. *Social Text* 28.2 (2010): 145–52.

———. *Lyric and Dramatic Poetry, 1946–82.* Translated by Clayton Eshleman and Annette Smith. Charlottesville: University of Virginia Press, 1990.

———. *Nègre je suis, nègre je resterai: entretiens ave Francoise Vergès.* Paris: Albin Michel, 2005.

———. *Notebook of a Return to the Native Land.* Translated by Clayton Eshleman and Annette Smith. Middletown, CT: Wesleyan University Press, 2001.

———. *Oeuvres complètes.* 3 volumes. Edited by Jean Paul Césaire. Fort de France, Martinique: Editions Désormeaux, 1976.

———. "Preface." *Expérience guinéene et unité africaine.* By Sekou Touré. 5–7. Paris: Présence Africaine, 1962.

———. *Une tempête.* Paris: Editions de Seuil, 1980.

———. *Toussaint Louverture: La révolution française et le problème colonial.* Paris: Présence Africaine, 1981.

———. *La tragédie du roi Christophe.* Paris: Présence Africaine, 1970.

———. *The Tragedy of King Christophe.* Translated Ralph Manheim. New York: Grove Press, 1969.

Coetzee, P. H., and A. P. J. Roux, eds. *The African Philosophy Reader.* 2nd ed. New York: Routledge, 2002.

Cone, James. *A Black Theology of Liberation.* Maryknoll, NY: Orbis Books, 2010.

Confiant, Raphael. *Aimé Césaire: une traversée paradoxale du siècle.* Paris: Stock, 1989.

Corzani, Jack. *La Littérature des Antilles-Guyane françaises.* Fort-de-France: Desormeaux, 1978.

Couffon, Claude. *Visite à Edouard Glissant.* Paris: Editions Caracteres, 2001.

Cox, Timothy J. *Postmodern Tales of Slavery in the Americas: From Alejo Carpentier to Charles Johnson.* New York: Garland, 2001.

Cros Sandoval, Mercedes. *Worldview, the Orishas, and Santería: Africa to Cuba and Beyond.* Gainesville: University of Florida Press, 2006.

Cuervo Hewitt, Julia. "Luís de Camoens en el reino de Calibán: *Las Lusíadas* en *Changó, el gran Putas* de Manuel Zapata Olivella." *Afro-Hispanic Review* 22.1 (2003): 13–23.

D'Aguiar, Fred. "'In God We Trust'": Derek Walcott and God." *Callaloo* 28.1 (2005): 216–223.

Dash, J. Michael. "The Theater of the Haitian Revolution / The Haitian Revolution as Theater." *Small Axe* 9.18 (2005): 16–23.

Davis, David Brion. *Inhuman Bondage: The Rise and Fall of Slavery in the New World.* Oxford: Oxford University Press, 2006.

———. *The Problem of Slavery in the Age of Revolution, 1770–1823.* Ithaca, NY: Cornell University Press, 1999.

Dayan, Joan. *Haiti, History, and the Gods.* Berkeley: University of California Press, 1995.

DeCosta-Willis, Miriam. "Meditations on History: The Middle Passage in the Afro-Hispanic Literary Imagination." *Afro-Hispanic Review* 22.1 (2003): 3–12.

Depestre, René. *Bonjour et adieu à la négritude.* Montréal: Leméac, 1974.

Derrida, Jacques. *On Cosmopolitanism and Forgiveness.* New York: Routledge, 2001.

———. *Specters of Marx: The State of the Debt, The Work of Mourning & the New International.* Translated by Peggy Kamuff. New York: Routledge, 1994.

Dhouti Martínez, Khamla. "Rewriting the Other: Manuel Zapata Olivella's *¡Levántate mulato!*" *Letras Hispanas* 4.2 (2007): 129–37.

Diamond, Jared. *Collapse: How Societies Choose to Fail or Succeed.* New York: Penguin, 2005.

Díaz-Granados, José Luis. *Manuel Zapata Olivella, su vida y su obra.* Universidad Nacional del Colombia. http://www.humanas.unal.edu.co/colantropos/documentos/manuel_zapata.pdf (accessed 8 August 2014).

Díaz-Quiñones, Arcadio. *El almuerzo en la hierba. (Llorens Torres, Palés Matos, René Marqués).* Río Piedras: Huracán, 1982.

Diego Padró, José de. *Luis Palés Matos y su trasmundo poético.* Río Piedras: Ediciones Puerto, 1973.

Dubois, Laurent. *Avengers of the New World: The Story of the Haitian Revolution.* Cambridge, MA: Harvard University Press, 2004.

———. *A Colony of Citizens: Revolution and Slave Emancipation in the French Caribbean, 1787–1804.* Chapel Hill: University of North Carolina Press, 2004.

———. *Haiti: The Aftershocks of History.* New York: Metropolitan Books, 2012.

Dubois, Laurent, and John D. Garrigus. *Slave Revolution in the Caribbean, 1789–1804: A Brief History with Documents.* New York: Bedford/St. Martin's, 2006.

Dupont, Berthony. *Jean-Jacques Dessalines, itinéraire d'un révolutionnaire.* Paris: L'Harmattan, 2006.

Dussel, Enrique. "Europe, Modernity, and Eurocentrism." *Neplanta: Views from South* 1.3 (2000): 465–78.

———. *The Invention of the Americas: Eclipse of "the Other" and the Myth of Modernity*. New York: Continuum, 1995.

———. "Transmodernity and Interculturality: An Interpretation from the Perspective of Philosophy of Liberation." *TransModernity: Journal of Peripheral Cultural Production of the Luso-Hispanic World*. 1.3 (2012): 28–59.

———. *Twenty Theses on Politics*. Durham, NC: Duke University Press, 2008.

———. *The Underside of Modernity*. Atlantic Highlands, NJ: Humanities Press, 1996.

Ellacurria, Ignacio, and Jon Sobrino. *Mysterium Liberationis: Fundamental Concepts of Liberation Theology*. Maryknoll, NY: Orbis Books, 1993.

Fanon, Frantz. *Black Skin, White Masks*. Translated by Charles Lam Markmann. New York: Grove Press, 1967.

———. *A Dying Colonialism*. Translated by Haakon Chevalier. New York: Grove Press, 1965.

———. *Peau noire, masques blancs*. Paris: Éditions du Seuil, 1995.

———. *The Wretched of the Earth*. Translated by Constance Farrington. New York: Grove Press Inc., 1968.

Farmer, Paul. *Haiti After the Earthquake*. New York: Public Affairs, 2011.

———. *The Uses of Haiti*. 3rd ed. Monroe, ME: Common Courage Press, 2006.

Fatton Jr., Robert. *Haiti's Predatory Republic: The Unending Transition to Democracy*. Boulder, CO: Lynne Rienner, 2002.

Feraudy Espino, Heriberto. *Yoruba: un acercamiento a nuestras raíce*. La Habana: Editora Política, 1993.

Fick, Carolyn E. *The Making of Haiti: The Saint Domingue Revolution from Below*. Knoxville: University of Tennessee Press, 1990.

Figueroa, Víctor. "Between Louverture and Christophe: Aimé Césaire on the Haitian Revolution." *The French Review* 82.5 (2009): 1006–1021.

———. "In Search of the Absent Revolution: Edgardo Rodríguez Juliá's Novels of Invented History." In *Redefining Latin American Historical Fiction: The Impact of Feminism and Postcolonialism*, edited by Helene Weldt-Basson, 65–92. New York: Palgrave Macmillan, 2013.

———. *Not at Home in One's Home: Caribbean Self-Fashioning in the Poetry of Luis Palés Matos, Aimé Césaire, and Derek Walcott*. Teaneck, NJ: Fairleigh Dickinson University Press, 2009.

Fischer, Sybille. "Bolívar in Haiti: Republicanism in the Revolutionary Atlantic." In *Haiti in the Americas*, edited by Carla Calargé, Raphael Dalleo, Luis Duno-Gottberg, and Clevis Headley, 25–53. Jackson: University of Mississippi Press, 2013.

———. *Modernity Disavowed: Haiti and the Cultures of Slavery in the Age of Revolution*. Durham, NC: Duke University Press, 2004.

Flores, Juan. *Divided Borders: Essays on Puerto Rican Culture*. Houston, TX: Arte Público Press, 1992.

———. *Insularismo e ideología burguesa*. México, D. F.: Fondo de cultura económica, 1980.

Forsdick, Charles. "Late Glissant: History, 'World Literature' and the Persistence of the Political." *Small Axe* 33 (November 2010): 121–34.

Fouchard, Jean. *The Haitian Maroons: Liberty or Death*. Translated by A. Faulkner Watts. Preface by C. L. R. James. New York: Edward W. Blyden Press, 1981.

Freyre, Gilberto. *The Masters and the Slaves*. 2nd ed. Translated by Samuel Putnam. Berkeley: University of California Press, 1987.

Garraway, Doris. *The Libertine Colony: Creolization in the Early French Caribbean*. Durham, NC: Duke University Press, 2005.

———. "'What Is Mine': Césairean Negritude Between the Particular and the Universal" *Research in African Literatures* 41.1 (2010): 71–86.

Garrigus, John D. *Before Haiti: Race and Citizenship in French Saint Domingue*. New York: Palgrave, 2006.

Gaspar, David Barry, and David Geggus, eds. *A Turbulent Time: The French Revolution and the Greater Caribbean*. Bloomington: Indiana University Press, 1997.

Geggus, David Patrick. *Haitian Revolutionary Studies*. Bloomington: Indiana University Press, 2002.

Geggus, David P., ed. *The Impact of the Haitian Revolution in the Atlantic World*. Chapel Hill: University of South Carolina Press, 2001.

Gelpí, Juan G. *Literatura y paternalismo en Puerto Rico*. Río Piedras: Editorial de la Universidad de Puerto Rico, 1993.

Genovese, Eugene. *From Rebellion to Revolution: Afro-American Slave Revolts in the Making of the Modern World*. Baton Rouge: Louisiana State University Press, 1979.

Ghachem, Malick W. *The Old Regime and the Haitian Revolution*. Cambridge: Cambridge University Press, 2012.

Girard, Phillippe. "*Rebelles* with a Cause: Women in the Haitian War of Independence, 1802–04." *Gender and History* 21.1 (April 2009): 60–85.

Glissant, Edouard. *Le discours antillais*. Paris: Folio, 1997.

———. *L'imaginaire des langues. Entretiens ave Lise Gauvin (1991–2009)*. Paris: Gallimard, 2010.

———. *Introduction à une poétique du divers*. Paris: Gallimard, 1996.

———. *Mémoires des esclavages*. Paris: Gallimard/La Documentation française, 2007.

———. *Monsieur Toussaint: A Play*. Translated by J. Michael Dash and Edouard Glissant. Boulder, CO: Lynne Riener, 2005.

———. *Monsieur Toussaint: Théatre*. Paris: Éditions du Seuil, 1961.

———. *Monsieur Toussaint: version scénique*. Paris: Gallimard, 1998.

———. *Une nouvelle région du monde*. Paris: Gallimard, 2006.

———. *Philosophie de la relation*. Paris: Gallimard, 2009.

———. *Poetics of Relation*. Translated by Betsy Wing. Ann Arbor: University of Michigan Press, 1997.

———. *Poétique de la relation*. Paris: Gallimard, 1990.

———. *Traité du Tout-Monde*. Paris: Galllimard, 1997.

Gómez, Alejandro. "La Revolución Haitiana y la Tierra Firme hispana." *Nuevo Mundo Mundos Nuevos* 17 February 2006. http://nuevomundo.revues.org/211 (accessed 21 March 2012).

González, José Luis. *El país de cuatro pisos*. Río Piedras: Huracán, 1980.

———. *Puerto Rico: The Four-Storeyed Country*. Translated by Gerald Guinness. Princeton, NJ: Markus Wiener Publishing, Inc., 1993.

González de Allen, Gertrude. "Enrique Dussel and Manuel Zapata Olivella: An Exploration of De-colonial, Diasporic, and Trans-modern Selves and the Politics of Recognition." Center for Global Studies and the Humanities at Duke University. *Worlds and Knowledges Otherwise: A Web Dossier* 1.3 (2006). http://www.jhfc.duke.edu/wko/dossiers/1.3/GGonzalezdeAllen.pdf (accessed 31 March 2012).

González Echevarría, Roberto. *Alejo Carpentier: The Pilgrim at Home.* Ithaca, NY: Cornell University Press, 1977.

González Pérez, Aníbal. "Ballad of Two Poets: Nicolás Guillén and Luis Palés Matos." *Callaloo* 31 (Spring 1987): 285–301.

Gordon, Lewis R. *Existentia Africana: Understanding Africana Existential Thought.* New York: Routledge, 2000.

———. *Fanon and the Crisis of European Man: An Essay on Philosophy and the Human Sciences.* New York: Routledge, 1995.

Grimshaw, Anna. "Introduction." In *The C. L. R. James Reader,* edited by Anna Grimshaw, 1–22. London: Blackwell, 1992.

Grosofguel, Ramón. "Decolonizing Post-Colonial Studies and Paradigms of Political-Economy: Transmodernity, Decolonial Thinking, and Global Coloniality." *TransModernity: Journal of Peripheral Cultural Production of the Luso-Hispanic World* 1.1 (2011): 1–37.

———. "La descolonización del conocimiento. Diálogo crítico entre Frantz Fanon y Boaventura de Sousa Santos." In *Formas-Otras: Saber, Nombrar, Narrar, Hacer. IV Training Seminar de Jóvenes Investigadores en Dinámicas Interculturales,* 97–108. Barcelona: Centro de estudios y documentación internacionales de Barcelona, 2011.

Guinness, Gerald. *Here and Elsewhere: Essays on Caribbean Literature.* Río Piedras: Editorial de la Universidad de Puerto Rico, 1993.

Gutierrez, Gustavo. *A Theology of Liberation: History, Politics, and Salvation.* Maryknoll, NY: Orbis Books, 1973.

Hall, Stuart. "Cultural identity and Diaspora." In *Colonial Discourse and Postcolonial Theory: A Reader,* edited by Patrick Williams and Laura Chrisman, 392-403. New York: Columbia University Press, 1994.

Hallward, Paul. *Absolutely Postcolonial: Writing between the Singular and the Specific.* Manchester: Manchester University Press, 2001.

Hamner, Robert D., ed. *Critical Perspectives on Derek Walcott.* Boulder, CO: Lynne Rienner Publishers, 1997.

Handley, George B. "The Postcolonial Ecology of the New World Baroque: Alejo Carpentier's *The Lost Steps.*" In *Postcolonial Ecologies: Literatures of the Environment,* edited by Elizabeth DeLoughrey and George B. Handley, 117–35. Oxford: Oxford University Press.

Hardt, Michael, and Antonio Negri. *Multitude.* New York: Penguin, 2005.

Harris, Mardella. "Entrevista con Manuel Zapata Olivella." *Afro-Hispanic Review* 10.3 (1991): 59–61.

Hayner, Priscilla. 2nd ed. *Unspeakable Truths: Transitional Justice and the Challenge of Truth Commissions.* New York: Routledge, 2010.

Henry, Paget. *Caliban's Reason.* New York and London: Routledge, 2000.

Hill, Erroll. . . . *a time and a season . . . : Eight Caribbean Plays.* St. Augustine, Trinidad: School of Continuing Studies, 1976.

Hobsbawn, Eric. *The Age of Revolution: 1789–1848*. New York: Vintage, 1996.

Hountondji, Paulin J. *African Philosophy: Myth and Reality*. 2nd ed. Bloomington: Indiana University Press, 1996.

Hurley, E. Anthony. "Is He, Am I, a Hero: Self-Referentiality and the Colonial Legacy in Aimé Césaire's *Toussaint Louverture*." In *Tree of Liberty: Cultural Legacies of the Haitian Revolution in the Atlantic World*, edited by Doris L. Garraway, 113–33. Charlottesville: U of Virginia P, 2008.

Hyatt, Vera Lawrence, and Rex Nettleford, Eds. *Race, Discourse, and the Origin of the Americas: A New World View*. Washington, D. C.: Smithsonian Institution Press, 1995.

Irizarry, Guillermo B. *José Luis González: el intelectual nómada*. San Juan, Puerto Rico: Ediciones Callejón, 2006.

Jackson, Richard L. *Black Literature and Humanism in Latin America*. Athens, Georgia: U of Georgia P, 1988.

———. "The Black Novel in America Today." *Chasqui* 16.2–3 (1987): 27–36.

Jahn, Janheinz. *Muntu: African Culture and the Western World*. Trans. by Marjorie Green. New York: Grove Press, 1994.

James, C. L. R. *American Civilization*. Oxford: Blackwell, 1993.

———. *At the Rendezvous of Victory: Selected Writings*. London: Allison and Busby, 1984.

———. *The Black Jacobins*. 2nd. ed. New York: Random, 1989.

———. *Beyond a Boundary*. Durham: Duke UP, 1993.

———. *C. L. R. James on the "Negro Question."* Jackson: UP of Mississippi, 1996.

———. *The C. L. R. James Reader*. Ed. Anna Grimshaw. Oxford, UK: Blackwell, 1992.

———. *State Capitalism and World Revolution*. Chicago: Charles H. Kerr Publishing Company, 1986.

———. *Toussaint Louverture*. Durham, NC: Duke UP, 2013.

———. *World Revolution 1917–1936: The Rise and Fall of the Communist International*. Atlantic Highlands, NJ: Humanity Press, 1993.

———. *You Don't Play with Revolution: The Montreal Lectures of C. L. R. James*. Oakland, CA: AK Press, 2009.

Janis, Michael. "Negritude, Mestizaje, Africana Philosophy: Zapata Olivella and Multiculturalist Pan-Africanism." *Presence Africaine: Revue Culturelle du Monde Noir/Cultural Review of the Black World* 171.1 (2005): 69–79.

Jenson, Deborah. *Beyond the Slave Narrative: Politics, Sex, and Manuscripts in the Haitian Revolution*. Liverpool: Liverpool University Press, 2011.

Johnson, Lemuel A. *The Devil, the Gargoyle, and the Buffoon: The Negro as Metaphor in Western Literature*. Port Washington, NY and London: Kennikat Press, 1969.

Jones, Bridget. "We Were Going to Found a Nation . . .": Dramatic Representations of Haitian History in Three Martinican Writers." In *The Colonial Caribbean in Transition: Essays on Postemancipation Social and Cultural History*, edited by Bridget Brereton and Kevin A. Yalvington, 247–60. Gainesville: University Press of Florida, 1999.

Joseph, Peniel E., ed. *The Black Power Movement: Rethinking the Civil Rights-Black Power Era*. New York: Routledge, 2006.

Joseph, Peniel E. *Waiting 'Til the Midnight Hour: A Narrative History of Black Power in America*. New York: Owl Books, 2006.

Kaisary, Philip. *The Haitian Revolution in the Literary Imagination: Radical Horizons, Conservative Constraints.* Charlottesville: University of Virginia Press, 2014.

Kesteloot, Lilyan. *Black Writers in French: A Literary History of Negritude.* Cambridge, MA: Harvard University Press, 1991.

King, Bruce. *Derek Walcott: A Caribbean Life.* Oxford: Oxford University Press, 2000.

———. *Derek Walcott and West Indian Drama.* Oxford: Oxford University Press, 1995.

King, Stewart R. *Blue Coat or Powdered Wig: Free People of Color in Pre-Revolutionary Saint Domingue.* Athens: University of Georgia Press, 2001.

Knight, Franklyn W., and Teresita Martínez-Vergne. *Contemporary Caribbean Cultures and Societies in a Global Context.* Chapel Hill: University of North Carolina Press, 2005.

Krakusin, Margarita. "Conversación informal con Manuel Zapata Olivella." *Afro-Hispanic Review* 20.1 (2001): 15–28.

Kuhn, Thomas. *The Structure of Scientific Revolutions.* Chicago: University of Chicago Press, 2012.

Laclau, Ernesto. *Emancipation(s).* London: Verso, 1996.

Langley, Lester D. *Simón Bolívar: Venezuelan Rebel, American Revolutionary.* Lanham, Maryland: Rowman & Littlefield, 2009.

Largey, Michael D. *Vodou Nation: Haitian Art, Music, and Cultural Nationalism.* Chicago: University of Chicago Press, 2006.

Larrimore, Mark. *The Problem of Evil: A Reader.* Malden, MA: Blackwell, 2001.

Lasso, Marixa. "Haití como símbolo republicano popular en el Caribe colombiano, provincia de Cartagena (1811–1828)." *Historia Caribe* 3.8 (2003): 5–18.

Leopold, Aldo. *Sand County Almanac.* Oxford: Oxford University Press, 1949.

Lewis, Marvin A. *Treading the Ebony Path: Ideology and Violence in Contemporary Afro-Colombian Fiction.* Columbia: University of Missouri Press, 1987.

Loomba, Ania. *Colonialism/Postcolonialism.* 2nd ed. New York: Routledge, 2005.

López-Baralt, Mercedes. *El barco en la botella.* San Juan: Editorial Plaza Mayor, 1997.

———. "La biblioteca negra de Palés: hacia una parodia de la etnografía." *Umbral.* Universidad de Puerto Rico, Río Piedras. http://umbral.uprrp.edu/?q=La_Biblioteca_Negra_de_Pal%C3%A9s (accessed 11 Dec. 2012).

Losada, Angel. *Fray Bartolomé de Las Casas a la luz de la moderna crítica histórica.* Madrid: Editorial Tecnos, 1970.

Louis, Patrice. *Conversation avec Aimé Césaire.* Paris: Arléa, 2007.

Lovejoy, Paul. *Transformations in Slavery: A History of Slavery in Africa.* Cambridge: Cambridge University Press, 1983.

Lugones, María. "Heterosexualism and the Colonial/Modern Gender System." *Hypatia* 22.1 (Winter 2007): 186–209.

———. "Toward a Decolonial Feminism." *Hypatia* 25.4 (Fall 2010): 742–59.

Luis, William. "Editor's Note." *Afro-Hispanic Review* 25.1 (2006): 5–7.

Lynch, John. *Simón Bolívar: A Life.* New Haven, CT: Yale University Press, 2007.

Macey, David. *Frantz Fanon: A Biography.* London: Verso, 2012.

Madureira, Luis. *Cannibal Modernities: Postcoloniality and the Avant-garde in Caribbean and Brazilian Literature.* Charlottesville: University of Virginia Press, 2005.

Maldonado-Torres, Nelson. "Decoloniality at Large: Towards a Trans-Americas and Global Transmodern Paradigm. (Introduction to Second Special Issue of 'Thinking through the Decolonial Turn.')" *Transmodernity: Journal of Peripheral Cultural Production of the Luso-Hispanic World.* 1.3 (Spring 2012): 1–10. Web.

———. "On the Coloniality of Being." *Cultural Studies* 21.2–3 (March/May 2007): 240–270.

Manning, Patrick. *Slavery and African Life: Occidental, Oriental, and African Slave Trades.* Cambridge: Cambridge University Press, 1990.

Mardorossian, Carine. "From Fanon to Glissant: A Martinican Genealogy." *Small Axe* 30 (November 2009): 12–24.

Márquez Rodríguez, Alexis. *Lo barroco y lo real maravilloso en las obras de Alejo Carpentier.* 2nd ed. México, D. F.: Siglo XXI, 1984.

Martí, José. *Selected Writings.* Translated by Esther Allen. New York: Penguin, 2002.

Martín Alcoff, Linda, and Eduardo Mendieta. *Thinking from the Underside of Modernity: Enrique Dussel's Philosophy of Liberation.* Lanham, MD: Rowman & Littlefield, 2000.

Marzán, Julio. *The Numinous Site: The Poetry of Luis Palés Matos.* Madison, WI: Farleigh Dickinson University Press, 1995.

Mathewson, Tim. *A Proslavery Foreign Policy: Haitian-American Relations during the Early Republic.* Westport, CT: Praeger, 2003.

Maximin, Daniel. *L'isolé soleil.* Paris: Editions du Seuil, 1987.

Meltzer, Milton. *Slavery: A World History.* Cambridge, MA: Da Capo Press, 1993.

Memmi, Albert. *Portrait du colonisé, precedé du portrait du colonisateur.* Paris: Gallimard, 2002.

Ménil, René. *Antilles déjà jadis, précédé de Tracées.* Paris: Jean Michel Place, 1999.

Miers, Suzanne, and Igor Kopitoff, eds. *Slavery in Africa: Historical and anthropological Perspectives.* Madison: University of Wisconsin Press, 1979.

Mignolo, Walter. *The Darker Side of Renaissance.* 2nd ed. Ann Arbor: University of Michigan Press, 2003.

———. *The Darker Side of Western Modernity.* Durham, NC: Duke University Press, 2011.

———. "The Geopolitics of Knowledge and the Colonial Difference." In *Coloniality at Large: Latin America and the Postcolonial Debate,* edited by Mabel Moraña, Enrique Dussel, and Carlos A. Jáuregui, 225–58. Durham, NC: Duke University Press, 2008.

———. *The Idea of Latin America.* Malden, MA: Blackwell, 2005.

———. *Local Histories / Global Designs: Coloniality, Subaltern Knowledges, and Border Thinking.* Princeton, NJ: Princeton University Press, 2000.

———. "Philosophy and the Colonial Difference." In *Latin American Philosophy: Currents, Issues, Debates,* edited by Eduardo Mendieta, 80–86. Bloomington: Indiana University Press, 2003.

Miller, Christopher L. *The French Atlantic Triangle: Literature and the Culture of the Slave Trade.* Durham, NC: Duke University Press, 2008.

Miller, Paul B. *Elusive Origins: The Enlightenment in the Modern Caribbean Historical Imagination.* Charlottesville: University of Virginia Press, 2010.

———. "Enlightened Hesitations: Black Masses and Tragic Heroes in C. L. R. James's *The Black Jacobins.*" *MLN* 116.5 (2001): 1069–1090.

Miller, Shawn William. *An Environmental History of Latin America*. Cambridge: Cambridge University Press, 2007.

Mocega-González, Esther P. *La narrativa de Alejo Carpentier*. New York: Eliseo Torres & Sons, 1975.

Moraña, Mabel, Enrique Dussel, and Carlo A. Jáuregui, eds. *Coloniality at Large: Latin American and the Postcolonial Debate*. Durham, NC: Duke University Press, 2008.

Mudimbe, V. Y. *The Invention of Africa: Gnosis, Philosophy, and the Order of Knowledge*. Bloomington: Indiana University Press, 1988.

Munro, Martin, and Elizabeth Walcott-Hackwshaw. *Reinterpreting the Haitian Revolution and its Cultural Aftershocks*. Mona/Kingston: University of West Indies Press, 2006.

Murphy, Joseph. *Santeria: African Spirits in America*. Boston: Beacon Press, 1988.

Naipaul, V. S. *The Mimic Men*. London: Penguin, 1969.

Nesbitt, Nick. *Caribbean Critique: Antillean Critical Theory from Toussaint to Glissant*. Liverpool: Liverpool University Press, 2013.

———. *Universal Emancipation: The Haitian Revolution and the Radical Enlightenment*. Charlottesville: University of Virginia Press, 2008.

———. *Voicing Memory: History and Subjectivity in French Caribbean Literature*. Charlottesville: University of Virginia Press, 2003.

Nielsen, Aldon Lynn. *C. L. R. James: A Critical Introduction*. Jackson: University of Mississippi Press, 1997.

Ogbar, Jeffrey O. G. *Black Power: Radical Politics and African American Identity*. Baltimore, MD: Johns Hopkins University Press, 2004.

Oliver, Kelly. *The Colonization of Psychic Space*. Minneapolis: University of Minnesota Press, 2004.

Onís, Federico de. *Luis Palés Matos: vida y obra, bibliografía, antología*. San Juan, PR: Ediciones Ateneo Puertorriqueño, 1960.

Ortiz, Lucía. "*Chambacú, corral de negros* de Manuel Zapata Olivella, un capítulo en la lucha por la libertad." In *"Chambacú, la historia la escribes tú": Ensayos sobre cultura afrocolombiana*, edited by Lucía Ortiz, 155–70. Madrid and Frankfurt: Iberoamericana; Vervuert, 2007.

———. *La novela colombiana hacia finales del siglo veinte: una nueva aproximación*. New York: Peter Lang, 1997.

Ossa, Luisa. "*Changó el gran putas*: Afrocentric Discourse." *Monographic Review/Revista monográfica* 15 (1999): 248–61.

———."There's Nothing Underhanded About Liberation: A Reevaluation of the Trickster Figure." *Afro-Hispanic Review* 17.2 (1998): 46–51.

Padgen, Anthony. *The Fall of Natural Man: The American Indian and the Origins of Comparative Ethnology*. Cambridge: Cambridge University Press, 1982.

Palés Matos, Luis. *Obras: Tomo II. Prosa*. Río Piedras: Editorial de la Universidad de Puerto Rico, 1984.

———. *La poesía de Luis Palés Matos*. Edited by Mercedes López Baralt. Río Piedras: Editorial de la Universidad de Puerto Rico, 1995.

———. *Selected Poems/Poesía selecta*. Translated by Julio Marzán. Houston: Arte Público Press, 2000.

———. *Tom-Toms of Kinky Hair and All Black Things*. Translated by Jean Steeves-Franco. Río Piedras: Editorial de la Universidad de Puerto Rico, 2010.

———. *Tuntún de pasa y grifería*. Río Piedras: Editorial de la Universidad de Puerto Rico, 1993.

Palmer, Ransford W. *The Caribbean Economy in the Age of Globalization*. New York: Palgrave, 2009.

Paravisini-Gebert, Lizabeth. "The Haitian Revolution in Interstices and Shadows: A Re-reading of Alejo Carpentier's *The Kingdom of this World*." *Research in African Literatures*. 35.2 (2004) 114–127.

———. "'He of the Trees': Nature, Environment, and Creole Religiosities in Caribbean Literature." In *Caribbean Literature and the Environment: Between Nature and Culture*, edited by Elizabeth M. DeLoughrey, Renée K. Gosson, and George B. Handley, 182–96. Charlottesville: University of Virginia Press, 2005.

Patteron, Orlando. *Slavery and Social Death: A Comparative Study*. Cambridge, MA: Harvard University Press, 1985.

Pedreira, Antonio. *Insularismo*. Río Piedras, PR: Edil, 1973.

Pestre de Almeida, Lilian. *Aimé Césaire: Une saison en Haïti*. Montréal: Mémoire d'encrier: 2010.

Pinn, Anthony. *African American Humanist Principles: Living and Thinking Like the Children of Nimrod*. New York: Palgrave, 2004.

———. *Varieties of African American Religious Experience*. Minneapolis, MN: Fortress Press, 1998.

———. *Why, Lord? Suffering and Evil in Black Theology*. London: Continuum, 1999.

Pontiero, Giovanni. "The Human Comedy in *El reino de este mundo*." *Journal of Inter-American Studies*. 12 (1970): 528–538.

Popkin, Jeremy D. *Facing Racial Revolution: Eyewitness Accounts of the Haitian Insurrection*. Chicago: University of Chicago Press, 2007.

Prescott, Lawrence. "A Conversation with Nicolás Guillén." *Callaloo* 10.2 (1987): 352–354.

———. *Without Hatreds or Fears: Jorge Artel and the Struggle for Black Literary Expression in Colombia*. Detroit, MI: Wayne State University Press, 2000.

Prieto, Eric. "Edouard Glissant, *Littérature-monde*, and *Tout-monde*." *Small Axe* 33 (November 2010): 111–20.

Quijano, Aníbal. "Coloniality and Modernity/Rationality." *Cultural Studies* 21.2–3 (2007): 168-178.

———. "Coloniality of Power, Eurocentrism, and Latin America" *Neplanta* 1.3 (2000): 533–580.

———. "Coloniality of Power, Eurocentrism, and Social Classification." In *Coloniality at Large: Latin America and the Postcolonial Debate*, edited by Mabel Moraña, Enrique Dussel, and Carlos Jáuregui, 181–224. Durham, NC: Duke University Press, 2008.

Rabasa, José. *Inventing America: Spanish Historiography and the Formation of Eurocentrism*. Norman: University of Oklahoma Press, 1993.

Rabbitt, Kara. "C. L. R. James's Figuring of Toussaint-Louverture: *The Black Jacobins* and the Literary Hero." In *C. L. R. James: His Intellectual Legacies*, edited by Selwyn R. Cudjoe and William E. Cain, 118–35. Amherst: University of Massachusetts Press, 1995.

Ramos, Julio. *Desencuentros de la modernidad en América Latina. Literatura y política en el siglo XIX*. Santiago, Chile/San Juan, PR: Editorial Cuarto Propio / Ediciones Callejón, 2003.

Ramos, Aarón Gamaliel, and Angel Israel Rivera. *Islands at the Crossroads: Politics in the Non-Independent Caribbean*. Boulder, CO: Lynne Rienner Publishers, 2001.

Rattansi, Ali. *Racism: A Very Short Introduction*. Oxford: Oxford University Press, 2007.

Renda, Mary A. *Taking Haiti: Military Occupation and the Culture of U.S. Imperialism, 1915-1940*. Chapel Hill: University of North Carolina Press, 2001.

Restrepo, Eduardo, y Axel Rojas. *Inflexión decolonial: fuentes, conceptos y cuestionamientos*. Popayán, Colombia: Editorial Universidad del Cauca, 2010.

Ríos Avila, Rubén. *La raza cómica: del sujeto en Puerto Rico*. San Juan: Callejón, 2002.

Rivera Casellas, Zaira O. "Cuerpo y raza: el ciclo de la identidad negra en la literatura puertorriqueña." *Revista Iberoamericana*. 65.188–189 (1999): 633–647.

Rivera de Alvarez, Josefina. *Literatura puertorriqueña: su proceso en el tiempo*. Madrid: Partenón, 1983.

Rochmann, Marie-Christine. *L'esclave fugitif dans la littérature antillaise*. Paris: Éditions Karthala, 2000.

Rodríguez Juliá, Edgardo. *Caribeños*. San Juan, PR: Instituto de Cultura Puertorriqueña, 2002.

Rodríguez Monegal, Emil. "*Lo real y lo maravilloso en* El reino de este mundo." In *Asedios a Carpentier*, edited by Klaus Muller-Bergh. Santiago de Chile: Editorial Universitaria, 1972.

Rodríguez Vecchini, Hugo. "La biblioteca negra de Palés." *Nómada: Creación, Teoría, Crítica* 2 (Oct 1995): 49–59.

———. "Palés y Pedreira: la rumba y el rumbo de la historia." *La torre* VII, 27–28 (1993): 595–627.

Rowe, William L., ed. *God and the Problem of Evil*. Malden, MA: Blackwell, 2001.

Roy Féquierè, Magali. *Women, Creole Identity, and Intellectual Life in Early Twentieth-Century Puerto Rico*. Philadelphia, PA: Temple University Press, 2004.

Rueda, Manuel. *Las metamorfosis de Makandal*. Santo Domingo: Banco Central de la República Dominicana, 1998.

Said, Edward. *Culture and Imperialism*. New York: Vintage, 1993.

———. *Power, Politics, and Culture: Interviews with Edward Said*. New York: Vintage, 2001.

Sala-Molins, Louis. *Le code noir, ou le calvaire de Canaan*. Paris: Presses Universitaires de France, 1987.

———. *Dark Side of Light: Slavery and the French Enlightenment*. Minneapolis: University of Minnesota Press, 2006.

Salien, Jean-Marie. "Haïti vue de la Martinique." *The French Review* 77.6 (May 2004): 1166–1180.

Sandoval, Chela. *Methodology of the Oppressed*. Minneapolis: University of Minnesota Press, 2000.

San Juan Jr., E. *Racism and Cultural Studies: Critiques of Multiculturalist Ideology and the Politics of Difference*. Durham, NC: Duke University Press, 2002.

Santos Febres, Mayra. *Sobre piel y papel*. San Juan, PR: Ediciones Callejón, 2005.

Sartre, Jean Paul. "Black Orpheus." Translated by John MacCombie. *What is Literature and Other Essays*. Introduction by Steven Ungar. Cambridge, MA: Harvard University Press, 1988.

Schmidt, Hans R. *The United States Occupation of Haiti, 1915–1934*. New Brunswick, NJ: Rutgers University Press, 1995.

Schor, Naomi. "The Crisis of French Universalism." *Yale French Studies*. 100(2001): 43–64.

Scott, David. *Conscripts of Modernity: The Tragedy of Colonial Enlightenment*. Durham, NC: Duke University Press, 2004.

Sharpley-Whiting, T. Denean. *Negritude Women.* Minneapolis: University of Minnesota Press, 2002.

Shaw, Donald L. *Alejo Carpentier.* Boston, MA: Twayne, 1985.

Silenieks, Juris, trans. *Monsieur Toussaint: A Play.* By Edouard Glissant. Washington, D.C.: Three Continents Press, 1981.

Smart, Ian I. "*Changó el gran putas* as liberation literature." *CLA Journal* 35.1 (1991): 15–30.

Smith, Robert S. *Kingdoms of the Yoruba.* 3rd ed. Madison: University of Wisconsin Press, 1988.

Smolin, Lee. *The Trouble with Physics: The Rise of String Theory, the Fall of a Science, and What Comes Next.* New York: Mariner Books, 2006.

Sobrino, Jon. *Where Is God?: Earthquake, Terrorism, Barbarity, and Hope.* Maryknoll, NY: Orbis Books, 2004.

Sotomayor, Aurea María. *Hilo de Aracne: Literatura puertorriqeuña hoy.* Río Piedras: Editorial de la Universidad de Puerto Rico, 1995.

Sousa Santos, Boaventura de. *Another Knowledge Is Possible: Beyond Northern Epistemologies.* London: Verso, 2008.

———. *Another Production is Possible: Beyond the Capitalist Canon.* London: Verso, 2007.

———. *Conocer desde el sur: Para una cultura política emancipatoria.* Lima: Programa de estudio sobre democracia y transformación global, 2006.

———. *Democratizing Democracy: Beyond the Liberal Democratic Canon.* London: Verso, 2007.

Soyinka, Wole. *The Burden of Memory, The Muse of Forgiveness.* New York: Oxford University Press, 1999.

Speratti-Piñero, Emma Susana. *Pasos hallados en El reino de este mundo.* México: Colegio de México, 1981.

Stone, Judy. *Theatre. Studies in West Indian Literature.* London: Macmillian, 1994.

Suárez-Navaz, Liliana, y Rosalva Aída Hernández Castillo, ds. *Descolonizando el feminismo: teorías y prácticas desde los márgenes.* Valencia: Ediciones Cátedra, Universidad de Valencia, 2008.

Tamayo, Juan José. *La teología de la liberación en el nuevo escenario político y religioso.* Valencia: Tirant Lo Blanch, 2009.

Tempels, Placide. *Bantu Philosophy.* Orlando, FL: HBC Publishing, 2010.

Thieme, John. *Derek Walcott.* Manchester: Manchester University Press, 1999.

Thornton, John. *Africa and Africans in the Making of the Atlantic World, 1400–1800.* 2nd ed. Cambridge: Cambridge University Press, 1998.

Thornton, John K. "'I am the Subject of the King of Congo': African Political Ideology and the Haitian Revolution." *Journal of World History.* 4.2 (1993): 181–214.

Tillis, Antonio D. *Manuel Zapata Olivella and the "Darkening" of Latin American Literature.* Columbia: University of Missouri Press, 2005.

Tittler, Jonathan. "Catching the Spirit: *Changó, el gran Putas* in English Translation."*Afro-Hispanic Review* 21.1/2 (2002): 107–12.

Toumson, Roger, and Simonne Henry-Valmore. *Aimé Césaire: Le nègre inconsolé.* Châtauneuf-le-Rouge: Vents d'ailleurs, 2002.

Trouillot, Michel-Rolph. *Silencing the Past: Power and the Production of History.* Boston, MA: Beacon Press, 1995.

Twa, Lindsay J. "Jean-Jacques Dessalines: Demon, Demigod, and Everything in Between." In *Romantic Circles: A Referred Scholarly Website Devoted to the Study of Romantic-Period Literature and Culture.* http://www.rc.umd.edu/praxis/circulations/HTML/praxis.2011.twa.html (accessed 26 May 2014).

Verna, Paul. *Petión y Bolívar: cuarenta años (1790–1830) de relaciones haitianovenezolanas y su aporte a la emancipación de Hispanoamérica.* Caracas: Oficina Central de Información, 1969.

Volek, Emil. "Análisis e interpretación de *El reino de este mundo*, de Alejo Carpentier." In *Homenaje a Alejo Carpentier: variaciones interpretativas en torno a su obra*, edited by Helmy F. Giacoman, 145–78. New York: Las Americas, 1970.

Walcott, Derek. *The Arkansas Testament.* New York: Farrar, Straus & Giroux, 1987.

———. *Collected Poems, 1948–1984.* New York: Farrar, Straus & Giroux, 1986.

———. *Dream on Monkey Mountain and Other Plays.* New York: Farrar, Straus & Giroux, 1970.

———. *The Haitian Trilogy.* New York: Farrar, Straus & Giroux, 2002.

———. *Omeros.* New York: The Noonday Press/Farrar, Straus & Giroux, 1990.

———. *What the Twilight Says.* New York: Farrar, Straus & Giroux, 1998.

Wallerstein, Immanuel. *European Universalism: The Rhetoric of Power.* New York: The New Press, 2006.

———. *The Modern World System.* 4 vols. Berkeley: University of California Press, 2011.

Walsh, John Patrick. *Free and French in the Caribbean: Toussaint Louverture, Aimé Césaire, and Narratives of Loyal Opposition.* Bloomington: Indiana University Press, 2013.

White, Hayden. *Metahistory.* Baltimore, MD: Johns Hopkins University Press, 1975.

———. *Tropics of Discourse.* Baltimore, MD: Johns Hopkins University Press, 1986.

Williams, Eric. *Capitalism and Slavery.* Chapel Hill: University of North Carolina Press, 1994.

Williams, Raymond. *The Colombian Novel, 1844–1987.* Austin: University of Texas Press, 1991.

Wynter, Sylvia. "Beyond the Categories of the Master Conception: The Counterdoctrine of the Jamesian Poiesis." In *C. L. R. James's Caribbean*, edited by Paget Henry and Paul Buhle, 63–91. Durham, NC: Duke University Press, 1992.

———. "Unsettling the Coloniality of Being/Power/Truth/Freedom: Towards the Human, After Man, Its Overrepresentation—An Argument." *The New Centennial Review* 3.3 (Fall 2003): 257–337.

Young, Richard. *Carpentier: El reino de este mundo.* London: Grant & Cutler, 1983.

Young, Robert. *Postcolonialism: An Historical Introduction.* Oxford, UK: Blackwell, 2001.

Zapata Olivella, Manuel. *El árbol brujo de la libertad: Africa en Colombia—orígenes, transculturación, presencia. Ensayo histórico-mítico.* Buenaventura-Valle: Universidad del Pacífico, 2002.

———. *Chambacú, corral de negros.* Medellín: Editorial Bedout, 1967.

———. *Changó, el gran putas.* Bogotá: Rei Andes, 1992.

———. *Changó, The Biggest Badass.* Translated by Jonathan Tittler. Lubbock: Texas Tech University Press, 2010.

———. *Las claves mágicas de América (Raza, Clase y Cultura).* Bogotá: Plaza y Janés, 1989.

———. *En Chimá nace un santo.* Barcelona: Seix Barral, 1964.

———. *El fusilamiento del diablo.* Bogotá: Plaza y Janés, 1986.

———. *Hemingway, el cazador de la muerte.* Bogotá: Arango Editores, 1993.

———. *El hombre colombiano.* Bogotá: Canal-Ramirez-Antares, 1974.

———. *¡Levántate mulato! "Por mi raza hablará el espíritu"* Bogotá: Rei Andes, 1990.

———. *Manuel Zapata Olivella, por los senderos de sus ancestros. Textos escogidos.* Bogotá: Ministerio de Cultura, 2010.

———. *La rebelión de los genes. El mestizaje americano en la sociedad futura.* Bogotá: Altamir Ediciones, 1997.

———. *A Saint Is Born in Chimá.* Trans. Thomas E. Kooreman. Austin: University of Texas Press, 1991.

———. *Tierra mojada.* Madrid: Editorial Bullón, 1964.

Zenón Cruz, Isabelo. *Narciso descubre su trasero.* Humacao: Editorial Furudí, 1975.

Zoggyie, Haakayoo. "Lengua e identidad en *Changó, el gran putas* de Manuel Zapata Olivella." *Estudios de literatura colombiana* 7 (2000): 9–19.

Index

Aching, Gerard, 252n3
Africa, 5, 25, 43, 45, 46, 57, 61, 62, 95, 97, 98, 101, 102, 104, 105, 106, 108, 117–18, 123, 137, 147–48, 151, 152, 153–56, 162, 175, 180–81, 184–86, 204, 205, 207, 209, 211, 213, 220, 225, 226, 241, 244, 258n7, 260n27, 263n14, 266n7, 270n3, 271n15, 273n32, 273n37; African diaspora, 28, 76, 152, 197–203, 204, 206, 207, 224, 241, 272n30, 273n37; African philosophy, 8, 124, 220, 250n8, 250n9, 271n9, 271n11, 271n12, 273n35; African religions, 28, 33, 36, 38, 46, 48, 50, 105, 174, 197, 198, 200, 202–4, 218–20, 221–25, 227–29, 231, 232, 235, 253n17, 259n19, 272n30; in Puerto Rican culture, 65–67, 77; pan-Africanism, 5, 16, 28, 206, 209, 241; in Luis Palés Matos's work, 25, 74–77, 79–89, 93, 256n17, 257n18, 257n20

Afrocentrism, 27, 28, 29, 84, 102, 105–106, 118, 120, 137, 154, 155, 184–85, 196, 200, 202, 204, 207, 220, 221, 224–25, 227, 229–30, 260n27, 271n10, 271n11

Albizu Campos, Pedro, 65, 255n3
Aleijadinho, 200
Alonso, Manuel, 65
Ardouin, Beaubrun, 176, 262n2
Arguedas, José María, 273n38

Asturias, Miguel Angel, 196, 272n31
Awole, 223, 272n29

Bantu peoples, 46; Bantu spirituality, 197, 198, 220
Baugh, Edward, 138, 142, 165
Benítez Rojo, Antonio, 153
Benkos Biojo, 199, 206, 214
Bernasconi, Roberto, 8, 250n9
Bhabha, Homi, 119, 242, 250n11, 257n23
Black Power, 147, 150, 152, 155, 211, 264n16, 264n17, 264n19
Blackburn, Robin, 16, 260n22, 267n14, 271n15
Blanco, Tomás, 65–66, 76, 77, 256n12
Bolívar, Simón, 200, 206, 207, 212–16, 272n21, 272n22, 272n23, 272n24
Bonaparte, Napoleon, 2, 4, 27, 38, 42–43, 60, 81, 100, 133, 144, 164, 168, 169, 252n6, 263n10, 267n17
Bonaparte, Pauline, 38–41, 252n5, 252n6
Bongie, Chris, 16, 19, 20, 187, 257n3, 264n21, 268n20, 269n22, 269n24
border thinking, 11, 18, 183, 240
Bosch, Juan, 13, 80
Boukman, Dutty, 3, 37–38, 39, 45, 118, 123,

· 291 ·

126, 143, 152, 202, 203, 208, 209, 214, 218
Boyer, Jean Pierre, 47, 56–57, 63, 131, 162
Brathwaite, Kamau, 75
Braziel, Jana Evans, 15
Brelle, Corneille, 138, 149
Britton, Celia, 187, 190, 261n28, 268n19, 268n20
Buck-Morss, Susan, 16, 17, 260n22, 260n23, 261n27, 267n14, 267n15, 267n16
Buell, Lawrence, 55, 254n24
Buenaventura, Enrique, 251n18
Burnett, Paula, 141, 262n6

Cabrera, Lydia, 76
capitalism, 4, 11, 15, 43, 60–62, 89, 113, 157, 174, 238, 240, 253n13, 253n15
Captain-Hidalgo, Yvonne, 223, 224–25, 228
Carpentier, Alejo, 2, 16, 20, 21, 30, 33–34, 62, 73, 137, 196, 226, 252n6, 254n19; *Ecué-Yamba-O*, 77; *Explosion in a Cathedral (El siglo de las luces)*, 40; *The Kingdom of This World (El reino de este mundo)*, 24, 33, 35–41, 44–46, 47–51, 52–59, 60, 63, 84, 127, 152, 203–4, 238, 241, 252n1, 252n2, 252n3, 252n5, 252n8, 253n9, 253n10; *The Lost Steps (Los pasos perdidos)*, 58, 255n26; "La música en Cuba," 41. *See also* marvelous real
Castro, Fidel, 42
Castro Gómez, Santiago, 177, 272n24
Césaire, Aimé, 2, 8, 13, 16, 20, 21, 23, 25, 30, 31, 37, 42, 73, 94–95, 97–99, 118–25, 127, 170–71, 181–82, 210, 239–40, 241, 242, 244, 249n6, 250n8, 250n10, 251n19, 252n21, 257n1, 257n2, 258n5, 258n6, 258n8, 258n9, 259n14, 259n15, 259n20, 259n21, 260n23, 260n25, 260n27, 261n28, 261n29, 261n32, 263n11; *And the Dogs Were Silent (Et les chiens se taisent)*, 107, 169, 259n20; *Ferraments (Ferrements)*, 97; *Letter to Maurice Thorez (Lettre à Maurice Thorez)*, 97–99, 111, 113; *Noria*, 118; *Notebook of a Return to the Native Land (Cahier d'un retour au pays natal)*, 23, 75, 76, 80, 94, 100–103, 115–16, 209, 258n11, 258n12, 259n14, 259n16; *Solar Throat Slashed (Soleil cou coupé)*, 139; *The Tragedy of King Christophe (La tragédie du roi Christophe)*, 25–26, 95–96, 97–98, 103–8, 112–14, 115, 116, 117, 120, 136, 140, 147, 259n17, 266n4; *Toussaint Louverture: the French Revolution and the Colonial Problem (Toussaint Louverture: la révolution française et let problème coloniel)*, 6–7, 25–26, 95–96, 97–98, 109–113, 114–15, 118, 120, 169, 193, 251n13, 253n12, 258n11, 262n4, 266n3, 266n4, 271n16. *See also* negritude
Changó (Yoruba god), 29, 198, 210, 213, 214, 220, 223–26, 227, 228–29, 230–32, 234–36, 272n29, 272n30, 273n32, 273n33, 273n37
Christophe, Henri, 3, 4, 13, 19, 25, 30, 127, 131, 133–34, 175–76, 212, 224, 251n18; in Carpentier's *The Kingdom of This World*, 39; 41, 47, 55–56, 60, 63, 252n8; in Césaire *Tragedy of King Christophe*, 26, 94–95, 98, 100, 103–8, 112–18, 120–21, 124–25, 140, 259n18, 259n19, 261n27, 266n4; in Glissant's *Monsieur Toussaint*, 176, 193; in Palés Matos's poems, 71, 73–74, 78, 82, 85; in Walcott's Haitian plays, 27, 126, 129–30, 134–42, 145–46, 148–152, 154–55, 158–62, 164, 262n8, 265n21; in Zapata Olivella's *Changó*, 202, 236
cognitive justice, 12, 14, 51
colonial difference, 7–10, 13, 31, 60, 76, 92, 99, 110, 119, 125, 167, 176, 201, 209, 210–11, 238, 242, 245, 266n8
coloniality, 7, 8–10, 12–13, 14–15, 18, 19, 20, 24, 25, 26, 27, 28, 31, 34, 49, 51, 60, 61–62, 63, 76, 83, 88, 89, 92, 99, 101, 106, 107–8, 112–13, 115, 119–20, 122, 124–25, 133, 135, 138, 146–47, 165, 167, 176–80, 182, 183, 184, 189–92, 194, 201, 207, 210, 216, 238, 239–40, 242–45, 246, 247, 250n7, 250n12, 251n19, 256n17, 260n24, 261n29, 266n8, 267n10, 267n15, 269n24, 272n24, 274n3, 274n4
Columbus, Christopher, 1, 41, 129, 141

Confiant, Raphaël, 102, 125, 259n20
Corzani, Jack, 170
Cox, Timothy J., 273n37
Creole (as translation of Spanish "criollo"), 80–81, 89, 207, 214, 215–16, 255n3, 272n24
Creole language, 141, 184–85, 257n3, 264n19, 268n19; Creolité, 102, 105, 185, 268n19
Cuba, 2, 18, 38, 41, 48, 55, 59–60, 65, 67, 69, 73, 76, 77, 84, 91, 122, 123, 199, 204, 222, 249n4, 256n16, 272n27

Dash, J. Michael, 49, 265n1, 267n12, 267n17, 269n25
Davis, Angela, 16, 200
Davis, David Brion, 260n22, 267n14, 271n15, 273n32
Dayan, Joan, 15, 50, 127, 131, 134, 259n19
Debray, Régis, 257n3
Declaration of the Rights of Man and of the Citizen, 62, 109, 110, 111, 116–17, 181, 263n11
Depestre, René, 21, 117, 118, 259n15
Derrida, Jacques, 160–63, 237, 241–42, 265n23, 274n1
Dessalines, Jean Jacques, 3, 4, 7, 19, 25, 26, 27, 30, 39, 40, 41, 49, 50–51, 54, 71, 72, 118, 126–34, 135, 137, 138–39, 142–47, 148–49, 150, 151–52, 154, 155, 158, 159, 160–61, 162, 164, 169–71, 175, 176–77, 185, 193, 202, 212, 252n7, 253n18, 262n1, 262n2, 262n5, 265n21
Diego Padró, José de, 66, 67, 81
Douglass, Frederick, 124
Dubois, Laurent M., 16, 172, 173, 183, 249 n1, 251n15, 262n4, 266n9
Dupont, Berthony, 132, 133, 144, 262n2
Dussel, Enrique, 8, 10–12, 13, 14, 15, 18–19, 21, 28, 99, 115, 142, 179–80, 234–35, 242, 244, 245, 251n16, 266n8, 274n39

Easton, William Edgar, 128

Eliot, T. S., 218
enlightenment, 3, 14, 19, 40, 48, 50, 54, 62, 96, 119, 127, 145, 169, 182–83, 207, 245, 251n14, 260n22, 260n27, 267n16
Eurocentrism, 7–9, 14, 18, 27, 28, 33, 34, 49, 52, 61–63, 69, 75, 79, 82–83, 89, 93, 97, 98, 101–3, 106, 130, 137, 149, 152, 153, 171, 177, 180, 185, 186, 189, 207, 216–17, 245, 256n17, 261n27, 266n10, 271n11, 272n24

Fanon, Frantz, 12, 21, 62, 63, 113, 170, 201, 206, 250n8, 250n10, 260n24, 266n6, 269n22; *A Dying Colonialism*, 243; *Black Skin, White Masks*, 9, 12, 62, 102, 106, 125, 147, 150, 167, 213, 261n27, 261n29; *The Wretched of the Earth*, 150
Farmer, Paul, 174–75, 254n25, 265n25, 266n9
Fick, Carolyn, 16, 50, 175, 182, 251n14, 254n21, 263n12, 266n7, 271n16
Fischer, Sibylle, 18–19, 132–33, 216, 259n13
French Revolution, 3, 6, 13, 25, 37, 39, 43–45, 46, 47, 49, 60, 95–96, 100, 109–10, 118, 131, 144, 153, 165, 179, 182–83, 192, 217, 245, 250n13, 251n14, 254n21, 258n11, 267n11
Freyre, Gilberto, 66

García Márquez, Gabriel, 214, 226
Garraway, Doris, 251n15, 258n9
Garvey, Marcus, 200
Geggus, David P., 16, 72, 182, 249n1, 259n13, 272n25
Glissant, Edouard, 2, 20, 21, 30, 127, 135, 200, 241, 247, 261n27, 266n5, 266n6, 268n20, 269n22, 269n23, 269n26; *Caribbean Discourse (Le discours antillais)*, 38, 186, 188, 268n19, 269n22; *L'imaginaire des langues*, 268n19; *Introduction à une poétique du divers*, 190, 192, 194, 261n27, 269n24; *La cohée du Lamentin*, 269n24; *Mémoires des esclavages*, 268n18; *Monsieur Toussaint*, 7, 27–28, 166–95, 203, 207, 240, 241, 265n1, 266n4, 266n7,

267n11, 267n12, 267n17, 268n19, 269n22, 269n24, 269n25, 270n27; *Philosophie de la relation*, 261n27; *Poetics of Relation (Poétique de la relation)*, 28, 157, 186, 189, 190, 261n28; *The Ripening (La Lézarde)*, 269n22, 270n27; *Tout-Monde*, 270n27; *Traité du Tout-Monde*, 189, 261n28, 270n27; *Une nouvelle région du monde*, 268n18, 268n21

globalization, 9, 175, 185, 187–88, 190, 240, 268n20, 269n24

González, José Luis, 64–67, 255n1, 255n3

González Echevarría, Roberto, 225–26, 252n2, 252n4, 254n19

González Pérez, Aníbal, 67, 75, 256n10

Gordon, George William, 129, 141, 160

Gordon, Lewis R., 124, 250n8, 260n24

Grosfoguel, Ramón, 245, 254n23

Guillén, Nicolás, 67–68, 76–77, 256n10

Gutiérrez, Gustavo, 273n38, 274n40

Haiti: 2010 earthquake, 14, 164, 238, 265n25; indemnity payment to France, 56, 162; independence, 4, 13, 16, 22, 23, 26, 38, 39–40, 48, 49, 56, 63, 82, 101, 114, 125, 126, 128, 129, 130, 132–33, 134, 135, 145, 162, 163, 164–65, 170, 171, 174–75, 185, 190, 214, 216, 252n7

Hallward, Peter, 28, 186–88, 268n20, 269n22

Handley, George, 254n26

Henry, Paget, 32–34, 211, 238, 253n17, 271n12

Hobsbawn, Eric, 17, 179

Hughes, Langston, 21, 77, 128, 206

Hugo, Victor, 17, 83, 266n7

humanism, 62, 98, 103, 104, 228–29, 258n7, 272n19

James, C. L. R., 1, 2, 31, 32, 115, 209, 210–11, 214, 236, 241, 249n4; Marxist view of history, 4–5, 24, 60–61, 62, 241, 244, 253n17, 255n27, 272n20. Works: *American Civilization*, 253n16; *At the Rendezvous of Victory*, 249n3, 259n14, 272n20; *Beyond a Boundary*, 42, 253n16; *The Black Jacobins*, 1, 4–5, 19–20, 21, 24, 33–34, 37, 41–46, 47–51, 59–63, 87–88, 100, 109, 114, 117, 126, 127, 132, 136, 140–41, 144–45, 169, 173, 177, 182, 184, 207, 238, 244–47, 249n2, 251n13, 251n14, 252n3, 252n6, 253n10, 253n11, 253n12, 253n13, 253n18, 254n20, 258n11, 265n26; *C. L. R. James on the 'Negro Question,'* 211, 249n3; *Minty Alley*, 42; *State Capitalism*, 253n15; *Toussaint Louverture*, 250n13, 253n11, 265n2, 267n11, 271n16; *World Revolution*, 253n15; *You don't Play with Revolution*, 34, 61, 63

Jefferson, Thomas, 2

Jenson, Deborah, 16, 262n5

Kaisary, Philip, 19, 20, 21, 48, 128

King, Bruce, 141, 263n13, 264n16

King, Martin Luther, 151, 200, 220, 222, 228

Krakusin, Margarita, 207, 221, 222, 272n30

Kuhn, Thomas, 254n23

Laclau, Ernesto, 99, 233–34, 235, 258n9

Las Casas, Bartolomé de, 249n5

Leclerc, Charles, 4, 38–39, 41, 46, 131, 144, 155, 169, 175–76, 193, 212, 252n6

Leopold, Aldo, 57

Levinas, Emmanuel, 12, 161, 265n23

Llorens Torres, Luis, 81, 256n13

López Baralt, Mercedes, 75, 255n6, 255n7, 256n11, 256n17

Lugones, María, 15, 83, 107–8, 146, 243, 251n16

Luis, William, 270n3

Lumumba, Patrice, 95, 258n6

Macaïa: Glissant's character, 27, 168, 172–75, 179, 181–82, 184–85, 186, 188, 191, 193, 194,

240, 241, 266n7, 266n8, 269n14; historical Macaya, 176, 266n7
Macandal. *See* Mackandal
Macaya. *See* Macaïa
Macey, David, 266n6
Mackandal, François, 3, 36–37, 39, 45, 52–54, 57, 64, 71, 72, 84, 85, 88, 118, 126, 152, 168, 171–72, 173, 184, 202, 204, 214, 218, 251n13, 252n3
magical realism, 35, 252n2
Malcolm X, 200, 220, 222, 228, 231, 262n5
Maldonado-Torres, Nelson, 12, 13, 34, 62, 108, 124, 167, 190, 242, 243, 244, 246, 251n16, 274n3
maroon slaves, 2–3, 27, 62, 118, 152, 166, 168, 170, 171, 172, 174, 182–83, 186, 188, 199, 206, 207, 214, 217, 218, 236, 241, 251n13, 253n18, 263n12, 266n8, 270n27
Marqués, René, 65
Martí, José, 59–60, 263n10
Martinique, 44, 54, 69, 84, 120, 261n30, 267n17, 268n18, 270n27; political status, 23, 94–95, 113–15, 121–25, 170–71, 186–87, 258n8, 260n25
marvelous real, 24, 33, 35–37, 38, 41, 47, 48–49, 52, 59, 60, 63, 204, 238, 241, 252n2, 252n5, 255n26
Marxism: Carpentier and, 48, 254n19; Césaire and, 118; Derrida's *Specters of Marx*, 237, 241–42, 274n1; Karl Marx on Bolívar, 272n24; Zapata Olivella and, 211, 221
Marzán, Julio, 255n6
Maximin, Daniel, 259n20, 263n10
Memmi, Albert, 250n11
Menil, René, 102, 125
Mignolo, Walter, 7–10, 11, 12, 13, 15, 18–19, 20, 35, 92, 119, 142, 149, 167, 179, 183, 201, 210, 238, 240, 242, 244, 245, 249n5, 249n6, 250n7, 251n16, 258n4, 261n27, 264n18
Miller, Paul B., 254n20, 260n22
modernity, 18–19, 21, 133, 136, 179–80, 245, 246, 259n13, 272n24; and colonialism, 8, 9, 18–19, 20, 49, 54, 115, 180–81, 245, 250n12, 258n4, 266n8, 272n24; myth of, 7, 10–11, 28, 93, 99, 142, 179–80, 239, 242, 245
Montero, Mayra, 67
Morelos, José María, 200, 206
Moïse. *See* Moyse
Moyse, 3, 143, 169, 172, 175, 176–77, 178–80, 193, 265n2
muntu, 199, 200, 201, 203, 210, 223, 231, 271n9

Naipaul, V. S., 70, 74
negritude, 5, 8, 23, 27, 42, 66, 76, 80, 94, 95, 99–102, 114, 117, 123, 181, 250n10, 259n15, 259n20, 260n27, 271n17
Nesbitt, Nick, 16, 23, 182, 187, 237, 245, 253n14, 254n21, 259n15, 260n22, 260n23, 260n27, 266n5, 269n22, 271n16

Ortiz, Lucía, 271n14

Padilla, José Prudencio, 200, 206, 207, 213–14, 272n24
Palés Matos, Luis, 2, 16, 30, 31, 64, 66–67, 241, 255n7, 256n8, 256n10, 256n11, 257n18, 259n21; *Litoral*, 80; *Obras-Prosa*, 256n14, 257n19, 257n21; *Tuntún de pasa y grifería*, 24–25, 67–93, 239, 255n6, 256n9, 256n11, 256n12, 256n15, 256n16, 256n17, 257n18, 257n20
Paravisini-Gebert, Lisabeth, 53, 252n7
particularism, 96, 98, 102, 104, 108, 115–18, 120, 157, 258n3, 258n7. *See also* universalism; humanism
Pedreira, Antonio, 65–66, 255n4, 255n5, 255n7
Pétion, Alexandre, 4, 126, 129, 131, 134, 151, 206, 212–16, 259n18, 272n21
Piar, Manuel, 206, 207, 213–14
Pinn, Anthony, 228–30, 233, 272n28, 273n35
pluritopic hermenutics, 11, 245, 261n27

Popkin, Jeremy D., 16, 72, 259n13
Prescott, Lawrence E., 68, 270n5
Prieto, Eric, 187, 188
Puerto Rico, 60, 69, 80–81, 84, 121, 263n10; political status, 25, 69, 73, 81, 88–89, 91, 121–23, 171, 255n3, 257n21; racial politics, 25, 64–68, 75–76, 77, 78, 79, 80–81, 86, 87, 88–89, 91, 239, 255n5, 255n7, 256n12

Quijano, Aníbal, 7, 8, 9–10, 12, 13, 15, 34, 61, 83, 146, 177, 210, 240, 244, 250n12, 251n16, 266n10

Rabbitt, Kara, 253n12
race: and coloniality, 7, 9, 12–13, 15, 25, 28, 34, 52, 61, 101, 110, 119, 124, 138, 146–47, 164, 165, 177, 178, 185, 189–90, 201–2, 207, 217, 256n17, 272n24; and class, 5, 22, 29, 34, 61, 122, 146, 163, 164–65, 205, 209–11, 232, 241, 244, 255n27, 266n10, 272n20; racism, 7, 9, 12–13, 16, 21, 22, 24, 27, 34, 52, 62, 63, 82, 83, 98, 101, 104–5, 109, 111, 122, 123–24, 128, 130, 131–33, 138, 139, 145, 146, 148–49, 151, 152–53, 156, 157, 158, 167, 197–98, 201–2, 206, 208, 209, 211, 213, 215, 217, 236, 238, 260n22, 262n4, 263n13, 264n18, 268n18, 271n17, 271n18. *See also* afrocentrism; negritude. *See also under* Puerto Rico
real maravilloso. *See* marvelous real
Rigaud, André, 42, 129, 131, 144, 156, 212
Ríos Ávila, Ruben, 68, 255n7, 256n15
Rodríguez Juliá, Edgardo, 121–24, 251n18
Rodríguez Vecchini, Hugo, 255n7, 256n11, 256n17
Rueda, Manuel, 251n18

Said, Edward, 101, 115–16, 117, 259n14
Sans Souci, 175–76
Santos Febres, Mayra, 67, 68, 255n5

Sartre, Jean Paul, 102, 124, 193, 250n8, 250n10, 261n27
Schor, Naomi, 96, 112
Scott, David, 19–20, 136, 241, 253n12
Shaw, Donald, 39, 41, 48
Smart, Ian, 273n33
Smartt Bell, Madison, 21, 22, 254n22, 263n12, 264n20
Sousa Santos, Boaventura de, 12, 13, 14, 29, 51–52, 157, 254n23, 269n23
Soyinka, Wole, 232, 259n15
Spengler, Oswald, 48, 254n19
Speratti-Piñero, Emma Susana, 41, 252n5, 253n9
Spivak, Gayatri C., 17
Steeves-Franco, Jean, 255n6
synechdoche, 4–6, 59; synechdochal ontocolonialism, 6–8, 13, 242

Tapia y Rivera, Alejandro, 65
theodicy, 196, 220, 227–30, 273n37
Thieme, John, 136, 138, 263n13
Tillis, Antonio, 270n2
Tittler, Jonathan, 224, 270n1
Toussaint Louverture, 3–4, 6, 7, 17, 19, 20, 22, 26, 30, 33, 35, 50, 63, 126, 131–32, 134, 136, 144, 152, 172, 175, 178, 212, 250n13, 251n14, 252n21, 254n22, 258n10, 259n19, 260n25, 263n12, 264n20, 265n2, 266n7, 267n17, 268n18; in Aimé Césaire *Cahier*, 100–101, 103; in Aimé Césaire's *Toussaint Louverture*, 25, 95, 98, 109–13, 114, 118–19, 124, 125, 169, 182, 253n12, 258n11, 262n4, 266n3, 266n4; in Alejo Carpentier's *The Kingdom of this World*, 40–41, 47–48, 49, 54, 252n7, 252n8, 253n10; in C. L. R. James's *The Black Jacobins*, 24, 42–46, 47–48, 49–50, 51, 63, 100, 114, 117, 127, 144–45, 169, 173, 177, 184, 238, 253n11, 253n12, 253n18, 254n20, 258n11; in Derek Walcott's *Drums and Colours*, 129–30, 134, 138, 141, 142, 155–56, 158, 159, 160–61; in Derek Walcott's *The Haitian Earth*,

132, 134, 142, 143–46, 154–55, 156, 158, 163, 164, 263n11, 264n20; in Derek Walcott's *Henri Christophe*, 129, 138; in Edouard Glissant's *Monsieur Toussaint*, 27, 166, 168–95, 240, 241, 265n1, 266n7, 267n11, 267n12, 267n17, 269n24, 269n25; in Manuel Zapata Olivella's *Changó*, 201, 202, 229, 235

Touré, Sekou, 97–98, 258n8

transmodernity, 11, 14, 180, 183, 245–46, 266n8, 267n11, 267n16

Trotsky, Leon, 5, 249n3, 272n20

Trouillot, Michel-Rolph, 17–18, 175–76, 267n15

Tubman, Harriet, 16, 200, 220

Turner, Nat, 200, 220, 228

universalism, 7, 8, 10–11, 12, 17, 23, 25–26, 35, 40, 39, 95–96, 98–99, 101–3, 104, 108, 109–13, 115–20, 132–33, 179, 182–83, 186, 208, 212, 233–37, 239, 240–41, 245, 247, 251n19, 253n14, 257n3, 258n4, 260n22, 267n16, 271n16, 274n1; French universalism, 96–97, 119, 123. *See also* coloniality; modernity; particularism

Vega, Ana Lydia, 67

Vodou, 3, 24, 27, 36, 38, 40, 41, 45–46, 47–51, 52, 53, 58, 60, 63, 69, 71–72, 82, 118, 122, 123, 127, 134, 152, 168, 172, 174, 180, 184, 199, 202, 203–4, 214, 218, 219, 220, 222, 253n18, 254n22, 256n14, 259n19, 262n1

Walcott, Derek, 2, 16, 20, 21, 26–27, 30, 73, 135–36, 139, 150–51, 161–62, 173, 239, 240, 241, 246–47, 262n6, 265n21, 265n22; *Another Life*, 262n9 *The Arkansas Testament*, 37; "The Caribbean: Culture or Mimicry?," 147; *Collected Poetry*, 137, 148; *Dream on Monkey Mountain*, 137, 264n17; *Drums and Colours*, 26, 129–30, 138, 141–42, 155–56, 159, 160–61, 164–65; *The Haitian Earth*, 26, 126–28, 129, 132, 134, 138, 139, 141, 142–47, 150, 151–55, 156–58, 163–64, 165, 244, 263n13, 263n15, 264n19, 264n20, 265n23; *Henri Christophe*, 26, 129, 134, 136, 138, 139–40, 141, 148–49, 150, 151, 262n8; "The Muse of History," 130, 137, 147–48, 154, 156, 159–60, 167, 218, 262n7; *Omeros*, 90–91, 158, 263n14, 264n15, 271n8; "What the Twilight Says," 137–38, 140, 141, 148, 149–50, 264n19

Wallerstein, Immanuel, 250n7, 258n4

Walsh, John Patrick, 252n21, 260n25, 261n32, 267n17

Washington, Booker T., 200

White, Hayden, 17, 20, 29–30, 109

Williams, Eric, 253n13

Williams, Raymond, 270n6

Wordsworth, William, 17, 22, 154, 258n10

Wynter, Sylvia, 12, 242, 255n27, 274n3, 274n4

Young, Richard, 47, 252n4

Zapata Olivella, Manuel, 2, 196–98, 270n3, 270n4, 270n6, 271n8, 271n9, 272n26, 273n28, 274n39; *El árbol brujo de la libertad*, 206, 215, 221–22; *La calle 10*, 196; *Chambacú, corral de negros*, 197, 206, 208, 209, 271n13, 271n14; *Changó el gran putas*, 16, 28–29, 30, 37, 196, 197, 198–236, 240–41, 243, 244, 270n2, 270n3, 271n10, 271n11, 271n12, 271n13, 272n24, 272n29, 272n30, 272n31, 273n37; *Las claves mágicas de América Latina*, 210, 214–15, 216–17, 218–19, 222, 227; *Detrás del rostro*, 196; *El fusilamiento del diablo*, 209, 226, 270n2; *En Chimá nace un santo*, 197, 217–18, 221, 226; *Hemingway, el cazador de la muerte*, 209, 226, 270n2; *He visto la noche*, 206; *¡Levántate mulato!*, 205, 221, 270n4, 271n17; *La rebelión de los genes*, 215; *Tierra mojada*, 196, 209

Zeno Gandía, Manuel, 65

TRANSOCEANIC STUDIES
Ileana Rodríguez, Series Editor

The Transoceanic Studies series rests on the assumption of a one-world system. This system—simultaneously modern and colonial and now postmodern and postcolonial (global)—profoundly restructured the world, displaced the Mediterranean *mare nostrum* as a center of power and knowledge, and constructed dis-centered, transoceanic, waterways that reached across the world. The vast imaginary undergirding this system was Eurocentric in nature and intent. Europe was viewed as the sole culture-producing center. But Eurocentrism, theorized as the "coloniality of power" and "of knowledge," was contested from its inception, generating a rich, enormous, alternate corpus. In disputing Eurocentrism, books in this series will acknowledge above all the contributions coming from other areas of the world, colonial and postcolonial, without which neither the aspirations to universalism put forth by the Enlightenment nor those of globalization promoted by postmodernism will be fulfilled.

Prophetic Visions of the Past: Pan-Caribbean Representations of the Haitian Revolution
VÍCTOR FIGUEROA

Transatlantic Correspondence: Modernity, Epistolarity, and Literature in Spain and Spanish America, 1898–1992
JOSÉ LUIS VENEGAS

Conflict Bodies: The Politics of Rape Representation in the Francophone Imaginary
RÉGINE MICHELLE JEAN-CHARLES

National Consciousness and Literary Cosmopolitics: Postcolonial Literature in a Global Moment
WEIHSIN GUI

Writing AIDS: (Re)Conceptualizing the Individual and Social Body in Spanish American Literature
JODIE PARYS

Learning to Unlearn: Decolonial Reflections from Eurasia and the Americas
MADINA V. TLOSTANOVA AND WALTER D. MIGNOLO

Oriental Shadows: The Presence of the East in Early American Literature
JIM EGAN

www.ingramcontent.com/pod-product-compliance
Lightning Source LLC
Chambersburg PA
CBHW030107010526
44116CB00005B/136